P9-DMY-741

THE CHINESE GENTRY

STUDIES ON THEIR ROLE IN NINETEENTH-CENTURY CHINESE SOCIETY

By CHUNG-LI CHANG/Introduction by Franz Michael

ASHINGTON PAPERBACKS ON RUSSIA AND ASIA WPRA-4 $3.95

THE CHINESE GENTRY

Studies on Their Role in Nineteenth-Century Chinese Society

THIS BOOK is a product of the Modern Chinese History Project carried on by the Far Eastern and Russian Institute of the University of Washington. Members of the group represent various disciplines in the social sciences and humanities. The work of the project is of a cooperative nature with each member assisting the others through critical discussion and the contribution of ideas and material. The responsibility for each study rests with the author.

The Chinese Gentry

Studies on Their Role in Nineteenth-Century Chinese Society

By Chung-li Chang

Introduction by Franz Michael

UNIVERSITY OF WASHINGTON PRESS
Seattle and London

The Chinese Gentry is Number 3 of the Publications on Asia of the Institute for Comparative and Foreign Area Studies, formerly Far Eastern and Russian Institute Publications on Asia.

First printing, 1955
Second printing, 1961
Third printing, 1967
Fourth printing, 1974
First paperback edition, 1967
Second printing, 1970
Third printing, 1974
Library of Congress Catalog Card Number 55–6738
ISBN (cloth) 0–295–73743–3
ISBN (paper) 0–295–97891–0
Printed in the United States of America

Acknowledgment

THESE STUDIES were undertaken by me as a member of the Modern Chinese History Project at the University of Washington. I am therefore deeply indebted to the members of the project who in our cooperative way of working have contributed their thought and material to these studies. Their criticisms and suggestions have constantly been taken into consideration. The chairman of the project, Franz Michael, was largely responsible for the early planning of my research and has worked with me through all its stages. I want to state in gratitude how much of his work and thought has gone into this book. Every member of the project has been of help to me, but I want to thank especially George Taylor, Hellmut Wilhelm, Hsiao Kung-chuan, Vincent Y. C. Shih, Paul Kirchhoff, Stanley Spector, and William Schultz for their criticism and advice. Special thanks are due to Gladys Greenwood for her critical reading of the manuscript and her assistance in the final organization of my material. Much as I owe to these friends and colleagues, I take the final responsibility for the material presented and the views expressed in this book.

CHUNG-LI CHANG

CONTENTS

TABLES

FIGURES

Introduction

THE GENTRY of imperial China were a distinct social group. They had recognized political, economic, and social privileges and powers and led a special mode of life. The gentry stood above the large mass of the commoners and the so-called "mean people." They dominated the social and economic life of Chinese communities and were also the stratum from which the officials came. They were the guardians, the promoters, and representatives of an ethical system based on the tenets of Confucianism which provided the rules of society and of man's relation to man. Educated in this system, they derived from it their knowledge of management of human affairs which was the main qualification for their leading role in Chinese society. During the later dynasties the gentry's position and qualifications became formalized. A system of examinations and degrees controlled by the government determined the membership of the gentry group, which thus came to be more easily recognized and defined. Protected by a ring of formal privileges, which relieved them from physical labor and gave them prestige and a special position in relation to the government, the gentry were all the more free to act in their dominant role.

A study of this group is essential for any analysis of Chinese society in its traditional form as well as in its recent development with all the changes brought about under the impact of the West and of Soviet Communism. Chang Chung-li's studies on the gentry of nineteenth-century China hold, therefore, a central place in the research work on Chinese society under way at the University of Washington. His studies will be of interest not only to students of Chinese history but also to those generally concerned with the understanding of social organization and development.

Many Western accounts have dealt with the Chinese gentry, although no adequate analysis has yet been made. In the nineteenth century, and even earlier, the special character of the Chinese upper group aroused the interest of Western writers. The position of the "literati"—as they were mostly called—was so different from anything known in the West that many writers became interested in describing one or another aspect of their role.

The classical economists and, following them, Karl Marx developed a concept of an Oriental type of society, based on the so-called Asiatic mode of production in which the state controlled an economy based on irrigated agriculture. But they were concerned only with such general concepts.

A first attempt at a systematic description of Chinese society was made at the beginning of the century by E. T. C. Werner, a member of the Spencer school of sociology. In his classification of the Chinese according to the Spencer plan of *Descriptive Sociology*, Werner attempted to group the material available to him according to a typological division. Werner's understanding of the part played by the gentry in both state and society is indicated by his subdivisions under general government. For the Manchu period he classified the scholars (*shih*) as the first and leading social group subdivided into officials and gentry. Werner's classification of Chinese social groups was meant as a case study of a social structure belonging to what his school called the "Oriental stage" in the development of societies. This stage with its rigidity of social status and absence of any "true liberty" was believed to have kept the societies which had allowed themselves to be trapped into it from further social advancement.[1]

This first rather crude and schematic attempt at classification of Chinese society by a sociological school was far outdone by the brilliant sociological studies of Max Weber. In his broad analysis of the interrelationship between ideological and social development, Weber included China as one of his main typological examples. In contrast to the West where, as Weber saw it, Protestant ethics were suited to a society based on individual zeal and thus contributed to the development of capitalism, China's Confucian ideology could not, he thought, contribute to such a development.

China was one of the examples of the bureaucratic state in which Weber had such special interest. For him the tendency of bureaucracy to grow by monopolizing the means of government power was a phenomenon of general development. In his discussion of bureaucratic development as well as in his general theoretical analysis of society, Weber saw the importance of "technical economic factors" in general as well as the specific question of the control of the means of production. But Weber attacked Marxism as an untenable, monocausal theory which could not do justice to the multiplicity of causal

[1] See E. T. C. Werner, *Chinese.* Compiled and abstracted upon the plan organized by Herbert Spencer, No. IX, division III. *Descriptive Sociology; or, Group of Sociological Facts,* classified and arranged by Herbert Spencer (London, 1910), pp. 80–81. Also E. T. C. Werner, "China's Place in Sociology," *The China Review,* XX, No. 5 (1892–3), pp. 305–310.

relations recognizable in social history. For him Marx had overdramatized a "special case," confusing further "economic," "economically determined," and "economically relevant" factors. Weber did not deny the importance of the economic factors, but he saw them in the context of many other factors. He was especially concerned with the political struggle over what he called the "means of administration." Weber was always concerned about the growth of bureaucratic management. In his words, "for the time being, the dictatorship of the official and not that of the worker is on the march."

Bureaucracy, resulting from the increasing demand of a society to satisfy more and more varied wants and for order and protection, could, however, be established only where the society provided an exploitable social stratum to fill the ranks of an expert officialdom. Weber lists five examples of social strata from which the civil service of the rational bureaucratic state could be derived, among them being the clergy, including the Brahmins in India, the Buddhist priests and the Lamas. Another such stratum, listed by Weber in the second place after the clergy, was the "humanistically educated literati." In the West, the training of the Humanist schools was only "a transitory epoch," but in East Asia it had been different. In Weber's words, "The Chinese mandarin is, or rather originally was, what the Humanist of our Renaissance period approximately was: a literator humanistically trained and tested in the language monuments of the remote past. ... This stratum, with its conventions developed and modeled after Chinese Antiquity, has determined the whole destiny of China. ..."

Of this Chinese stratum Weber says, "Confucianism was the status ethic of prebendaries, of men with literary educations who were characterized by a secular rationalism. If one did not belong to this cultural stratum he did not count. The religious (or if one wishes, irreligious) status ethic of this stratum has determined the Chinese way of life far beyond the stratum itself." Weber stressed also the importance of the examination system in initiating "a competitive struggle for prebends and offices among the candidates," a competition he believed to have prevented a joint stand of the gentry against the government. In spite of his scanty Western material, Weber was thus able to gain an extraordinary insight into the structure of Chinese society and state, and into the position of the educated upper stratum, the gentry.[2] It is

[2] The English quotations of Max Weber are taken from *Max Weber: Essays in Sociology*, translated, edited, and with an introduction by H. H. Gerth and C. Wright Mills (New York: Oxford University Press, 1946). See Introduction and pp. 92 f., 212 f., 268, 426. These sections are translated from *Gesammelte Politische Schriften* (München, 1921), pp. 396–450; *Wirtschaft und Gesellschaft*, III, chap. 6, pp. 650–678; "Die Wirtschaftsethik der Weltreligionen" in *Archiv für Sozialforschung*, Vol. 41 and *Gesammelte Aufsätze zur Religionssoziologie* (Tübingen, 1922–3), Vol. I, pp. 237–268 and 395–430. See also Max Weber, *The Religion of China*, translated and edited by Hans Gerth (Glencoe, Ill., 1951).

equally extraordinary that since Weber's time no scholar has attempted any broad social analysis of Far Eastern or, more particularly, Chinese society along similar lines.

Serious attention has been given to the theory of Oriental society, which has been worked out and developed to its present form by Dr. K. A. Wittfogel. This theory stresses the part played by a ruling bureaucracy in the control of waterworks in economies depending on irrigated agriculture. It holds that in such economies the large public works necessary for irrigation, flood control, and canalization gave this ruling bureaucracy power over the large mass of peasant labor.[3] This theory has been of great importance as a hypothesis for the study of Oriental societies and has been of great value to the thinking of our research group in the Modern Chinese History Project. Its strength is that it brings out with great clarity the controlling position of the officials in China, as in other similar societies.

The officials, however, are only part of the story. The social basis for the officialdom was the gentry. The following studies deal with this group in all its complexity, aiming at a new understanding of the Chinese gentry. The facts so carefully gathered by Dr. Chang illuminate the whole position of the gentry in nineteenth-century Chinese society and the gentry's relationship to the state. The gentry is shown as a privileged group which dominated Chinese society. It had most important functions which covered a wide field of social control from ideological leadership to the practical management of political, social, and economic affairs, shading off into the field of administrative functions.

The gentry's relationship to the state was more complex than any simple formula of economic control would indicate. The gentry included the members of the bureaucratic officialdom which represented the state authority. This authority was, however, a rationalization of a broader and different compact of interests than those of the gentry group alone, either material or ideological. On the one hand, the bureaucratic state depended on the gentry for social control and management and to provide its administrative staff. On the other hand, it placed an institutional check on the gentry through state control over admission to membership in this dominant group. This was accomplished by making admission to the gentry dependent on a state-controlled examination system with fixed quotas. This institutional check was paralleled by an

[3] This theory has been bitterly attacked by the Soviet Communists because it runs counter to their theory of unilinear development from slavery through feudalism and capitalism to socialism. Bureaucratism has no place in this dogma and also comes uncomfortably close to a description of the social and political structure established by the Communists in countries where they hold power. In trying to fit such bureaucratic Oriental societies into their dogma, the Soviet Communists have to describe them as feudal, a classification which has been used for political slogans and in pseudoscholarly writings but cannot be taken seriously in academic discussions.

ideological control which forced the members of the gentry into a constant preoccupation with the tenets of the authoritarian aspects of Confucian beliefs. The gentry's relationship to the state was thus of a dual nature, sustaining it and controlled by it.

The gentry's relationship to the officialdom may need, however, some clarification. The educational degree which made one a member of the gentry was a necessary prerequisite for holding an official position. However, only a comparatively small section of the large gentry group actually became officials. During their periods of office tenure they were absent from their home communities. In their official position they represented the government in contrast to all groups of society and were in this capacity not regarded as gentry. But they still remained gentry of their home areas, whether they were at home or were exerting their influence from their distant place of office. The gentry were therefore close to officialdom, and this gave their position a special political importance. Whether functioning as members of a social group or serving as officials of the state, gentry members derived their authority from their educational qualifications as shown in their degrees. Whether in or out of office, the gentry were thus an essential part of the bureaucratic system.

The gentry's control of Chinese society, including its economic aspects, was not dependent on landowning, as will be developed in the following studies. A great number of the gentry can be assumed to have been private landowners, and most of these had their land worked by tenants. However, this fact should not lead one to confuse gentry and landlords. The two groups overlapped but did not coincide. A gentry member was not necessarily a landlord, nor was a landlord necessarily a member of the gentry. A gentry member could be very powerful even if he had no land, while landownership without gentry status gave no such power.

It should also be stressed that the discussion here concerns the gentry of the later imperial time. We have derived our data in the main from the nineteenth century and in part from the whole Ch'ing period. The point has been made that some features of the last decades of this time resulted from a decay of the whole imperial system. But we believe that some of the basic features of our findings on the gentry, taken from two and a half centuries of a long historical development, reflect its earlier forms.[4] Our consideration of the

[4] In his various writings Wolfram Eberhard has given descriptions of the Chinese gentry which, though sometimes contradictory, imply an interpretation of the gentry with which we do not agree. In his *Conquerors and Rulers, Social Forces in Medieval China* (E J. Brill, Leiden, 1952) pp. 122–23, he writes: "Any understanding of the 'gentry' is possible only when one conceives of the 'gentry' as families. Gentry families are usually large, extended families with at least one family center, which is often kept for more than a thousand years. This center of the family usually lies somewhere in the province (the northeastern

nineteenth-century gentry must, however, not be confused by the loose way in which the term has been used during the republic to describe what was in the main a group of landlords when the gentry of the imperial time no longer existed.[5]

We have used the English term "gentry" to translate the Chinese terms *shen-shih* and *shen-chin*[6] which were used during the last centuries of imperial

provinces of China at our period, being the most densely inhabited provinces, and therefore, also the home of the majority of gentry families). Here the family may have, and often has, large property holdings which are rented out to tenants. The family may also have economic interests in activities of temples, such as pawnshops, and in financial or commercial transactions of monasteries. The family may lose its property through mismanagement, bandits, war, etc., but the prestige of the gentry family in its home is so great that any such losses can be restored fairly easily by an energetic member of the family in the same or another generation. Therefore, a process of oscillation . . . undoubtedly occurs but does not change the status of the family in the long run. If such a family stays in its home and takes an active part only in the local administration as city commander, district official or similar posts, we speak of 'local gentry' . . .

"Often, however, the gentry families get interested in the central administration. In such cases, one or several members of the family create a new family seat in the capital of the empire. We find them as officials or officers. But as they are materially comparatively independent (due either to the family possessions at home or to accumulated wealth after official activities), one or several members of such a family may also retire of any social activity and engage in poetry, painting, or other arts. Philosophers usually combine political activity with writing. We can, therefore, say that the gentry consists of landlords, officials, scholars, all within the limits of the family and, seen over a period of time, consisting of more than one generation."

This description is presumably derived from Eberhard's studies of the periods of the T'o-pa Wei and the Five Dynasties. These were periods of political chaos and weak central control, and this may be the reason that Eberhard has overlooked the important role of the imperial government, the difference between appointed officials and gentry, and the vulnerability of the gentry family property holdings so much stressed by him. His definition of gentry remains vague, and even if it were acceptable for the period from which it was developed, it is decidedly inappropriate when applied by Eberhard to later imperial history since Sung times. For this later period Eberhard believes also in the emergence of a new group "which can roughly be called 'middle class.'" According to him, "instead of a number of gentry families of equal standing, we find from now on a much smaller number of very powerful gentry families, plus a quite large number of new families (middle-class families), clients of the large gentry families." The gentry of our sources cannot be divided or characterized in this way.

[5] It is this republican "gentry" which has been the object of several field studies by Fei Hsiao-tung. Fei has, however, also attempted to use his republican studies for an interpretation of the gentry of imperial times. A number of his articles have, since the completion of the writing of the present book, been republished in book form with an introduction by Robert Redfield and six biographies of people of the republican period by Chow Yung-teh under the title of *China's Gentry* (University of Chicago Press, 1953). These selective descriptions of republican times combined with some random thoughts taken from the Chinese classics do not represent a study of the gentry of imperial times despite the claim made in this book and indicated by its title.

[6] The term *shen* has the literal meaning of a girdle or a sash. It came to be used to indicate a holder of a higher academic degree or an official, that is, the wearer of a girdle or a sash. The term was used in the *Lun-yü* (Confucian Analects) X, xiii: "When he was ill and the prince came to visit him, he had his head to the east, made his court robes be spread over him, and drew his girdle across them." (James Legge, *The Chinese Classics,* Vol. I, p. 235; William Edward Soothill, *The Analects of Confucius,* p. 495.) *Lun-yü,* XV, v, says, "Tse-chang asked how a man should conduct himself, so as to be everywhere appreciated. The Master said . . . Tse-chang wrote these counsels on the end of his sash." (Legge, pp. 295–6; Soothill, pp. 723–5.) The other meaning of the term is given in

China to describe the Chinese upper social group. In spite of the frequent vague use made of the term "gentry," we prefer this translation to the Chinese original because "gentry" has already been in use and has more meaning for Western readers. This choice of term requires, however, a warning against colorings of the term "gentry" which do not apply to the Chinese group. In contrast to the English gentry, for instance, membership in the Chinese gentry was not hereditary; entrance had to be gained by each member, and there existed a considerable social mobility for ascending to and descending from this group. The Chinese gentry were also not functionally linked to their land in the way of the English squires, and they were not, in this sense, a "landed gentry." The hard-living, hard-riding style of life of the English gentry was altogether in contrast to the Chinese ideal of the scholarly life.

Another term often applied to the leading Chinese social group is "literati"[7] which has been used because of the emphasis on proved literary qualifications. This term seems to carry, however, a one-sided and exclusive meaning of scholarly life and does not express the general social, economic, and political power of this group. To us the term "gentry" indicates better the totality of

Tz'u-yüan, s. v., where it is stated that the term referred to those who held higher academic degrees or were officials.

For some examples of the frequent use of this term in the nineteenth century, see T'ien Wen-ching, "Ch'in-pan chou-hsien shih-i" ("Imperial Publication on Matters Relating to Magistrates") in *Huan-hai chih-nan wu-chung,* pp. 15, 29, *et passim;* Huang Liu-hung, *Fu-hui ch'üan-shu, chüan* 4, pp. 12 a, 21 a, *et passim.*

The term *shih* indicates a student or a scholar. See for instance *Lun-yü,* IV, ix: "The Master said, 'A scholar, whose mind is set on truth and who is ashamed of bad clothes and bad food is not fit to be discoursed with.' " (Legge, p. 168; Soothill, p. 231.) *Lun-yü,* VIII, vii, reads, "Tseng-tse said, 'The scholar may not be without breadth of mind and vigorous endurance. His burden is heavy and his course is long.' " (Legge, p. 210; Soothill, pp. 391–2.)

For some nineteenth-century examples, see for instance *Ch'in-ting hsüeh-cheng ch'üan-shu* (hereafter abbreviated *Hsüeh-cheng*), 7/3 a, where an imperial edict states "*Shih* are at the head of the 'four people' and are the respected ones of the area. All commoners have respected and honored them because they read the sages' books and have been admitted to the government schools and because their words and actions can all be models to the villagers . . .", *et passim.*

The term *chin* literally means the collar of a robe. During the last dynasties it was used in the same way as *shih* to distinguish the literati. See for instance *Hsüeh-cheng,* 7/13 a, an edict stating that some *shih* have relied on their blue *chin* (collar) to refuse payment of taxes. *Ibid,* 7/19 a, another edict uses *chin* instead of *shih* to designate the same group. Cf. *Tz'u-yüan, wei* p. 58, *shen* p. 165.

The terms were frequently combined as *shen-shih* or *shen-chin* to distinguish the educated upper group as a whole. See for instance Huang Liu-hung, *op. cit.,* 4/9 a–b; T'ien Wen-ching, *op. cit.,* p. 29; *Ta-Ch'ing lü-li hui-chi pien-lan,* 8/40 b.

Officials were sometimes known as *shih-ta-fu.* For the relationship of the terms *shih-ta-fu* and *shen-chin,* see *Tz'u-hai, wei* p. 71, which states that *shen-chin* were *shih-ta-fu* living in their native places. *Tz'u-yüan* also defines *shih-ta-fu* as men in office.

[7] For the use of "literati" by Western writers to describe the Chinese educated group, see for instance Chester Holcombe, *The Real Chinaman,* pp. 225–233; Robert K. Douglas, *Society in China,* pp. 116 ff. See especially Max Weber, *The Religion of China,* chap. v on "The Literati," pp. 107–141. Weber, who recognizes the importance of the connection between education and political power in China, uses the term "literati" to describe the whole Chinese privileged upper group.

the ideological, political, social, and economic position of dominance which this group held.

The study of the gentry of the nineteenth century is also complicated by the fact that the last dynasty, the Ch'ing, was not Chinese but Manchu. The Manchus had come into China with their own people organized in military formation, the so-called banners. They had reserved for themselves a special position in China and held about half the high official posts. But, aside from holding some provincial positions, they remained on the whole in the capital and in the more or less isolated garrisons in a few key strategic locations. They did not affect Chinese social life as a whole. They did not live in the Chinese communities and were, therefore, not gentry, even though some of them held grades, degrees, ranks, or titles. Therefore, they are not dealt with in these studies.

Each of the studies in the present volume takes a different approach and deals with a different set of problems. The first study, entitled "An Inquiry into the Constitution and Character of the Gentry of Nineteenth-Century China," endeavors to describe and define the Chinese gentry. The gentry is seen as a social group with a well-defined institutional basis. Its membership was determined by a state-controlled, formal system of admission with an elaborate hierarchy of ranks and titles. Its privileges were legally provided and socially accepted. In this study, the gentry's social functions, its place in society, and its relationship to the government are examined and evaluated.

The second study, "A Numerical Analysis of the Gentry of Nineteenth-Century China," presents figures on the size of the gentry as a whole as well as on the comparative size of the different groups within the gentry. Such estimates are helpful in evaluating the gentry's position in society, the gentry's relationship to the government, and the government's control over the gentry. The middle of the nineteenth century brought to China the Taiping Rebellion (1850–1864) and the impact of the West starting with the Opium War (1839–1842). The subsequent political and social transformation is reflected in the increase of the total number of gentry and in the change in relative strength of the various gentry strata occurring in the second half of the century.

The third study, "The Examination Life of the Gentry of Nineteenth-Century China, A Critical Analysis of the Ch'ing Examination System," shows that the examination system had remained the basis of the institutional framework of the nineteenth-century Chinese gentry. It was not only the most important gate of entrance to gentry status but also an instrument of government control. The constant preoccupation of the gentry with the never-ending preparation for ever-recurring examinations forced them into an examination life in which their thoughts were channelled into the stream of official ideology. It is significant that it was the scholarly ability of the gentry which the government saw as essential, which it both encouraged and controlled, and shaped in an official mold through the examination system. The decline of the examination system during the nineteenth century was an indication of the deterioration of the social structure of imperial China.

The fourth study is entitled "A Quantitative Analysis of Biographies of Nineteenth-Century Chinese Gentry." Over five thousand biographies of gentry from all provinces have been examined, and the information contained in them has been tabulated according to certain categories. One set of tables shows participation in the various gentry functions. Another analyzes the family background of gentry members and investigates the changing proportions between those who came from gentry families and those who did not. A third set of tables presents data on the economic situation of gentry members. Of especial interest is the large number of gentry who are listed as having large amounts of cash the source of which remains unexplained. The fourth section thus supplements the preceding three studies but also raises new questions.

No claim is made that these four studies provide an exhaustive description of all the aspects and problems of the gentry, but together they are meant to draw the main outlines of the gentry's position in the society of nineteenth-century China. A special study of gentry income in the nineteenth century is now ready for publication.

The institution of the gentry perished with the imperial Chinese state, but the trends of the past persisted in the social transformations that took place. The tradition of an intellectual status group dominating society limited the possibility of a democratic revolution and facilitated the success of Communist bureaucracy which differs from the tradition mainly in its lack of the humanist values of the past. But whether in its old or new form, the Chinese development indicates, as Max Weber said, that "once it is fully established, bureaucracy is among those social structures which are hardest to destroy."

Franz Michael

Seattle
December, 1953

THE CHINESE GENTRY

Studies on Their Role in Nineteenth-Century Chinese Society

PART ONE

An Inquiry into the Constitution And Character of the Gentry Of Nineteenth-Century China

DESCRIPTION OF THE MAIN GROUPS OF THE GENTRY ACCORDING TO THEIR TITLES AND DEGREES

THE POSITION of *shen-shih* or gentry was gained through the acquisition of a title, grade, degree, or official rank which automatically made the holder a member of the *shen-shih* group. The titles, grades, and degrees were meant to indicate the holders' educational standing. Official rank was generally conferred only upon people who had such proof of their educational standing.

The educational grades and degrees were obtained by passing the government examinations, which was the formal way of proving educational qualification. Those who became gentry through examination may therefore be called the "regular" group.

Educational titles could, however, be purchased. While those who bought such titles were usually literate and had some education, they were not required to give any proof of educational qualifications. Such members of the gentry may be called the "irregular" group.

A Western writer of the nineteenth century described both groups of the gentry in the following manner: "*Shin-sze* are people who have obtained some literary degree, which however can be bought with money, as well as obtained by reading books, although all profess to be *tuh-shoo jin*, 'book-reading men.'"[1] The high value set on education and the respect accorded to members of the "regular" gentry were expressed in the words of a high court official: "What makes the *chü-jen* and *fu-sheng* (gentry members through examination) so valuable to the world is the way they raise themselves to their position through poems and books."[2] In their educational standard and

[1] *The Chinese Repository*, I, No. 11, p. 461.

[2] Ch'en Ch'ing-yung, *Chou-ching-t'ang chi*, supplementary *chüan* A/1 a.

social position these gentry members who had achieved their position through examination were superior to those who had purchased their titles. This distinction was stressed by the "regulars" to protect their vested interest in their hard-won positions against the competition of the "irregular" group.[3] There are indications that the central government used this rivalry as one means of controlling the gentry and balanced one group against the other so as to keep them both in hand.[4]

Of these two groups, the "regulars" were, then, those who had passed the government examination. The educational grade that qualified for gentry status was the grade of *sheng-yüan* which was gained by passing a series of examinations. The term *sheng-yüan* is best rendered as "government student." It described government students of the district and prefectural schools.[5] *Sheng* literally means students and *yüan* means a definite number.[6] The whole term referred to a definite number of students admitted through examinations to each district or prefectural school. These *sheng-yüan* could strive for advancement through participation in higher examinations for the degree of *chü-jen*, graduate of the provincial examinations,[7] and the degree of *chin-shih*, graduate of the metropolitan examinations.[8] Some of the *sheng-*

[3] Hsü Ta-ling, *Ch'ing-tai chüan-na chih-tu*, pp. 140–41.

[4] See *infra*, II, on government policy regarding sale of offices and titles.

[5] These schools were not similar to modern educational institutions. The students went only to attend examinations. They remained students for life unless granted higher degrees or titles. For detail see *infra*, III. The translation of *sheng-yüan* as "government students" has not been generally used. *Sheng-yüan* have been more often referred to as licentiates or bachelors of arts, which this writer considers inappropriate since *sheng-yüan* were students and not graduates. Hsieh Pao-chao, *The Government of China (1644–1911)*, pp. 145–6 has almost the same opinion. He writes: "... an admission in the district or prefectural colleges, in fact merely an act of qualifying for provincial examinations, is frequently misnamed a first degree. ... The difficulty of qualifying in these colleges gave importance to the students who qualified, and the especial privileges they enjoyed elevated them above the struggling commoners. In spite of these features, a scholarship remained a scholarship, not a degree *per se*."

[6] Ku Yen-wu, *Jih-chih-lu*, 17/1 a, states that the word *yüan* means a definite number. Ku quoted from the *T'ang-shu* that in T'ang there was for the first time the National College which enrolled 72 *yüan* of *sheng* from sons, brothers, and grandsons of third-rank officials or above, 140 in the Imperial College from heirs of fifth-rank officials or above, 130 in the colleges of four specialized subjects for heirs of seventh-rank officials or above, three levels of prefectural colleges, varying from 60 to 50 to 40 *yüan* of *sheng*, and also three levels of district colleges varying from 40 to 30 to 20 *yüan* of *sheng*. This is the origin of the term *sheng-yüan*. Cf. *Tz'u-yüan*, *s. v.*

[7] Literally *chü-jen* means "recommended men." According to *Tz'u-hai*, *s. v.*, and Ku Yen-wu, *op. cit.*, 16/3 b–4 a, the term first appears in the annal of Chang Ti in *Hou-Han-shu*, the biography of Hsien-yu Shih-yung in *Pei-Ch'i-shu* and the annal of Kao Tsung in *Chiu-T'ang-shu*. It referred to men recommended to the court from various prefectures for the selection of officials. If they were selected, they were no longer called *chü-jen*. If they failed, they had to be recommended again and did not retain the address of *chü-jen*. In the Ming and Ch'ing dynasties, however, it became a degree permanently held by those who succeeded in the provincial examinations. The term *chü-jen* also appeared in the examination section of the *Hsin-T'ang-shu*. See translation by Robert des Rotours, *Le Traité des Examens*, p. 248.

[8] *Chin-shih* literally means "presented scholars," i.e., scholars presented to receive emolument. It was first established as one type of examination in Sui. In Ming and

yüan who had not succeeded in the higher examinations but whose higher scholastic standing was recognized were granted the academic title of *kung-sheng,* "imperial student."[9] The *chin-shih*, *chü-jen*, and *kung-sheng* had risen above the *sheng-yüan.* Together with the many who had remained *sheng-yüan*, they formed this most important section of the gentry qualified through academic rating, the group we have called the "regulars."

From the holders of the higher academic degrees, the *chin-shih*, *chü-jen*, and *kung-sheng*, government officials were selected. Indeed, the gaining of such degrees was the regular way to officialdom. The higher officials came almost exclusively through this regular route, as can be seen in official lists.[10] As officials these men entered government service and carried out functions for the government, but at the same time they remained gentry of their home areas, and their official rank increased their prestige as gentry.

The other way of becoming a member of the gentry was through the purchase of an academic title. This title was that of *chien-sheng*, student of the Imperial College.[11] The great number of *chien-sheng*, with very few exceptions, did not actually move to the capital to study in the Imperial College. For them the title was important because it admitted them to gentry status and privileges and was an opening for further advancement and official positions. Also, the title of *kung-sheng*, mentioned in the first group, was sometimes attained not through examination but through purchase.

This "irregular" way of attaining gentry status could also lead to official rank and position. Those who purchased academic titles could then purchase official rank or position. Indeed, the academic title and the official rank or position were often purchased together.[12] The "irregular" route led only to the lower offices,[13] but such official rank, even though "irregularly" obtained, raised the holder's position as a member of the gentry.

Ch'ing times it became the degree held by those who had succeeded in the metropolitan and palace examinations. See *T'zu-hai, s. v.*; Ku Yen-wu, *op. cit.*, 16/5 a–b.

[9] *Kung-sheng* is translated as "imperial students" since they were selected from district or prefectural colleges for presentation at the capital, theoretically to study in the Imperial College.

[10] See *Ta-Ch'ing chin-shen ch'üan-shu*, 1881, or other years.

[11] *Chien-sheng* literally means the students of the *kuo-hsüeh* or *kuo-tzu-chien*, the Imperial College. On the organization of the *kuo-tzu-chien*, see for instance *Ch'in-ting ta-Ch'ing hui-tien, chüan* 76.

[12] See photostatic copies of actual license plates in Hsü Ta-ling, *op. cit.* Plate III shows the license of *chien-sheng* issued to a commoner in return for payment of 33 taels on Kuang-hsü 28/9/19. Plate IV shows the license of purchased office, assistant *hsien* magistrate, issued to the same person on the same day. In the license he is already referred to as *chien-sheng.*

[13] Civil offices available for purchase were only those of the fifth rank and below in the capital, and of the fourth rank and below in the provinces; military offices available for purchase were of the third rank and below in both the capital and the provinces. For a list of offices that could be purchased, see *Ch'ing-kuo hsin-cheng-fa fen-lun*, 5/318–321.

If one acquired gentry status by purchasing an academic title, one could still become a "regular" gentry member later. The holders of such purchased academic titles could participate in the higher examinations for the *chü-jen* and *chin-shih* degrees. If they passed these examinations, they were then considered "regular" members of the gentry. Some candidates bought the *chien-sheng* title simply to gain speedier admission to the higher examinations.[14]

Among the gentry were also those who had gained their position by acquiring military titles, grades, degrees, or official ranks. There existed in the examination system a special section of military examinations leading to the academic grades and degrees of military *sheng-yüan* (*wu-sheng-yüan*), military *chü-jen* (*wu-chü-jen*), and military *chin-shih* (*wu-chin-shih*). The holders of higher military degrees could become military officers. Men of military education could also buy the academic title of *chien-sheng* and from there move on to military office. The majority of the officers of the Chinese government army, however, rose from the ranks. They had not been gentry first, but the official rank thus obtained gave them gentry status. These military men from the ranks, who were a much smaller and less influential group within the gentry, were an exception to the general rule of educational qualification, since they had gained their gentry status without having first obtained an academic title, grade, or degree.

A CONVENIENT DIVISION OF THE GENTRY INTO TWO STRATA

Each of the ranks, degrees, grades and titles that qualified for general gentry status carried different privileges and degrees of prestige. A detailed description is necessary to show the whole complex picture of gentry power and manifold functions. Overlying the details of this stratification, however, there can be seen a horizontal division of the whole gentry group into an upper and a lower layer.

Within the lower group of such a division will fall the large number of the first examination grade, the *sheng-yüan*, and the buyers of the academic title, the *chien-sheng*, as well as a few other holders of minor titles. The upper layer will be made up of the holders of the higher examination degrees and those who held official titles, whether combined with higher degrees or not.

It has already been pointed out that the staff of the government administration was derived from the gentry. In this regard, the upper gentry had a distinct advantage over the large lower group. Members of the upper gentry

[14] *Kuo-wen chou-pao*, 7/16, p. 1; cf. *infra*, III, note 4.

were officials or those who were qualified for appointment to office, while members of the lower gentry had yet to purchase office or pass higher examinations. In official publications, such as the *Ta-Ch'ing hui-tien shih-li*

TABLE 1

SIMPLIFIED LIST OF GENTRY GROUPINGS

	Regular	Irregular
Upper	Officials *chin-shih* *chü-jen* *kung-sheng* (with several subgroups)	Officials
Lower	*sheng-yüan* (with several subgroups)	*chien-sheng* purchased *kung-sheng*

("Precedents on the Collected Statutes of the Ch'ing Dynasty"), and in local gazetteers, the lower group was discussed under the heading *hsüeh-hsiao*, "schools," while the upper group was discussed under the heading *k'o-chü*, *kung-chü*, or *hsüan-chü*, meaning "selection of officials."

The upper gentry were more privileged than the lower gentry and generally led the lower gentry in performing their functions. While detailed illustrations of gentry privileges and functions as well as statistical studies on activities of upper and lower gentry members will be presented in later sections, a few words will be useful here to justify this two-strata division. In the payment of land tax, for instance, the upper gentry were in an even better position to resist excessive charges, to gain partial or total exemption, or to participate in the sharing of the public revenue.[15] In the organizing of local corps, the upper gentry had a larger control while the lower gentry usually headed smaller units.[16] This distinction was also made within the clans. In ancestral rites in some clans, it was provided that the one highest in official rank should preside, and the meat used at the sacrifice was distributed according to the rank of office previously held and the degree or grade received in examinations.[17] In one clan only the tablets of members who had held ranks as officials and of those who had passed the provincial examinations were admitted free of charge into the ancestral temple upon death. All others had to pay fifty taels in silver for this privilege.[18]

The division between upper and lower gentry actually existed quite formally

[15] Greater exemption was granted to higher officials than to lower officials or those who had not been officials. See *infra*, pp. 37–40.

[16] See *infra*, IV.

[17] Hu Hsien-chin, *The Common Descent Group in China and Its Functions*, p. 126.

[18] *Idem.*

in the marriage, funeral, and sacrificial ceremonies. In the regulations published by the government on the conduct of these ceremonies, the regulations for the gentry differed from those for the commoners. And within the gentry itself, the regulations provided for the upper gentry differed from those provided for the lower gentry group.

In marriage and funeral ceremonies, three sets of regulations were provided under the headings of *p'in-kuan*, literally meaning "officials of various ranks," *shu-shih*, literally meaning "the mass of scholars," and *shu-jen*, literally meaning "the mass of people" (commoners). The first group included officials of the seventh rank and above. Officials of the eighth rank and below as well as holders of the examination grade of *sheng-yüan* and the bought academic title of *chien-sheng* were included in the second group.[19]

In sacrificial ceremonies, regulations were provided under the same three headings. Here it is stated that the *p'in-kuan* group included not only officials of all ranks but also the holders of *chin-shih* and *chü-jen* degrees who resided at their native places and were regarded as equal to seventh-rank officials. Also included were the holders of the academic title of *kung-sheng* who were regarded as equal to eighth-rank officials. The *sheng-yüan*, *chien-sheng*, and *kung-sheng* through purchase were considered as belonging to the second or *shu-shih* group.[20]

The distinction between the upper and lower gentry was also indicated by differences in their garments and hats. For instance, the upper gentry had gold buttons on their hats, while members of the lower gentry had silver ones.[21]

The upper gentry members were naturally more respectfully received by the local magistrates and were in general more privileged and influential than members of the lower gentry. The distinction between upper and lower gentry will be further developed in later sections.

ENTRANCE INTO AND COMPOSITION OF THE LOWER LAYER OF THE GENTRY

The lower gentry were less privileged and powerful than the upper gentry, but they comprised a much larger group. They were represented in many

[19] Wu Yung-kuang, *Wu-hsüeh-lu ch'u-pien*, prefatory remark, p. 8 a–b, also *chüan* 16–19; *Ta-Ch'ing t'ung-li*, 26/esp. 1 a, 6 b; 52/esp. 16 a–b, 19 b, 28 b, 29 a, 30 b.

[20] Wu Yung-kuang, *loc. cit.*; also *Ta-Ch'ing t'ung-li*, 17/esp. 8 a, 16 b. The original order of members of the second group was *kung-sheng* through purchase, *chien-sheng*, and *sheng-yüan*, an order of legal position. According to their social positions, they would appear in the order of *sheng-yüan*, *kung-sheng* through purchase, and *chien-sheng*. The order adopted in the text above is based on numerical size and importance within the gentry group.

[21] *Ta-Ch'ing chin-shen ch'üan-shu*, 1/3 a–6 b.

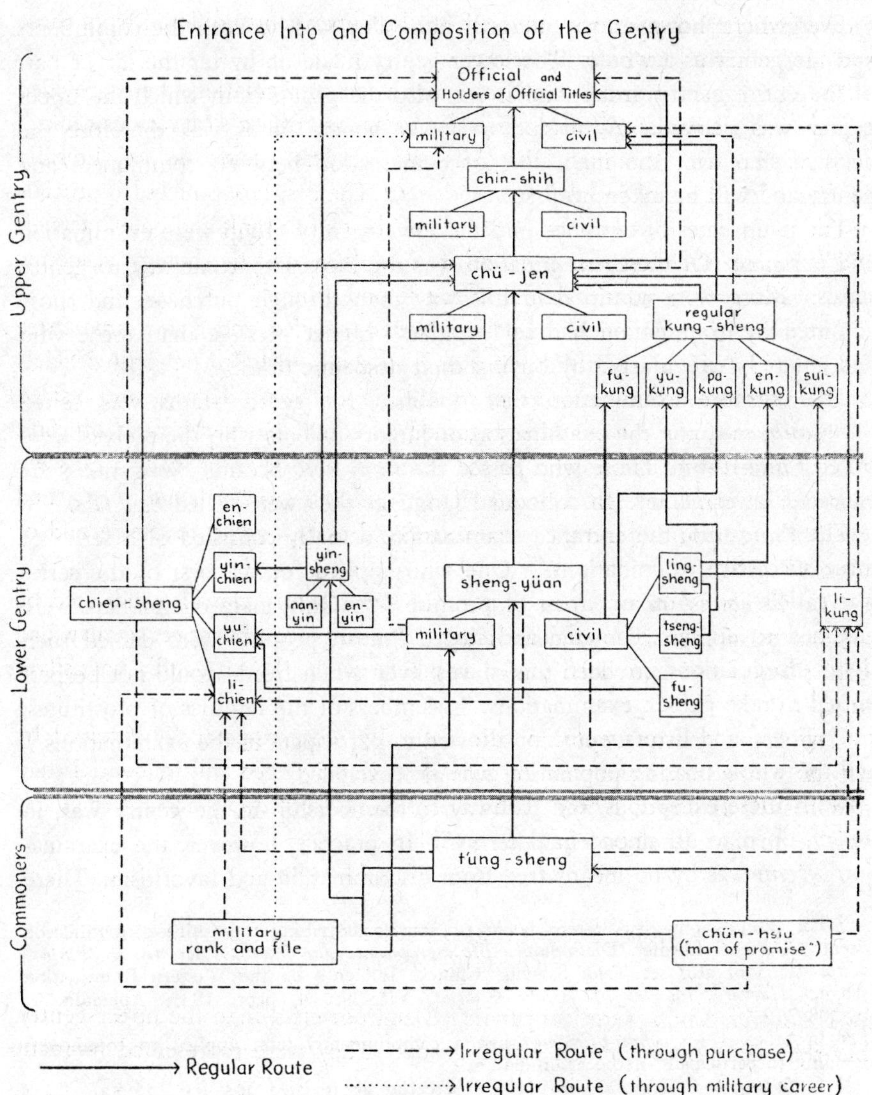
Entrance Into and Composition of the Gentry
Upper Gentry
Lower Gentry
Commoners
Official and Holders of Official Titles
military
civil
chin-shih
military
civil
chü-jen
military
civil
regular kung-sheng
fu-kung
yu-kung
pa-kung
en-kung
sui-kung
en-chien
yin-chien
yu-chien
li-chien
chien-sheng
yin-sheng
nan-yin
en-yin
sheng-yüan
military
civil
ling-sheng
tseng-sheng
fu-sheng
li-kung
t'ung-sheng
military rank and file
chün-hsiu ("man of promise")
Regular Route
Irregular Route (through purchase)
Irregular Route (through military career)

FIGURE 1

more communities and had a free hand in the places where no upper gentry lived, although there were, of course, some smaller communities where there were no gentry at all.

Everywhere, however, the main dividing line was between the commoners and the gentry as a whole. The lower gentry made up by far the larger part of the entire gentry group, and it was also the group from which the upper gentry was derived. Admission to lower gentry status was therefore the decisive step over the main line of demarcation between commoners and gentry and will be taken up first.

The main gates of entrance into the lower gentry group were examination and purchase. Of these, examination was the more important way to gentry status. More were admitted in this way than through purchase, and those admitted by examination had as "regulars" higher prestige than those who had entered "irregularly" by buying their academic titles.

The entrance examination that qualified for gentry status was called *t'ung-shih*, meaning the examination of junior students who themselves were called *t'ung-sheng*. Those who passed the *t'ung-shih* became *sheng-yüan*, the educated lower gentry. In colloquial language they were called *hsiu-ts'ai*.

The *t'ung-shih*, the entrance examination, actually consisted of a series of three successive examinations.[22] One who applied for the first of the series was called *chün-hsiu* or "man of promise."[23] Only male commoners were qualified to apply. The underprivileged "mean people" were denied such rights. Regulations provided that slaves, even when freed, would not be permitted to take part in examinations.[24] Members of the families of prostitutes, entertainers, and lictors were not allowed to participate in the examinations,[25] and the whole boating population was also excluded.[26]

With these exceptions, the pathway to membership in the gentry was, in theory, open to all upon equal terms.[27] In practice, however, the examination system was by no means free from discrimination and favoritism. There

[22] For bibliography of Western books or articles describing the Chinese examination system, see Henri Cordier, *Dictionnaire Bibliographique des Ouvrages Relatifs à l'Empire Chinois*, I, 546; also see Teng Ssu-yü, "Chinese Influence on the Western Examination System," *Harvard Journal of Asiatic Studies*, VII, No. 4, Sept. 1943, Appendix 2, pp. 308–312.

[23] In other words, *chün-hsiu* was just a complimentary term applied to commoners intending to participate in the examinations.

[24] *Ch'in-ting ta-Ch'ing hui-tien shih-li* (hereafter abbreviated *Shih-li*), 155/5 a.

[25] *Ch'ing-shih kao*, 114/1 b.

[26] See "Competitive Examinations in China," *Blackwood's Edinburgh Magazine*, October 1885, Vol. 138, p. 482. The anonymous author states: "Before being allowed to enter his name on the list, each candidate must produce a certificate to prove that he is a free-born subject of the realm, and of a respectable parentage, a limit which arbitrarily excludes not only the whole boating population, but also the children of the police, and all play-actors and slaves."

[27] Those who were observing mourning periods for deceased parents were excluded from these examinations.

were malpractices and corruption; and the fact that the candidates had to secure a guarantee as to their origin and character from gentry members prevented many from participating in the examinations.[28] Nor did all have an equal opportunity to devote themselves to the life of study which the examination system demanded.

The first of the series of three examinations was known as *chou-hsien-shih*, the district examinations. These examinations were held by the *chou* or *hsien* magistrates for candidates from their districts. The successful candidates in the first examination were then known as *t'ung-sheng.* They were qualified to take the *fu* (prefectural) or independent *chou* examinations held by prefects or independent *chou* magistrates. Those who passed then participated in the *yüan* examinations[29] held by the provincial directors-of-studies in the prefectural or independent *chou* cities.[30]

Of these three examinations, the last one was decisive for admission to the *sheng-yüan* group. In the first two of the examinations, the magistrates or prefects could generally let the candidates pass if they wished to be lenient.[31] However, in the *yüan* examinations held by the provincial directors-of-studies, only a certain limited number of students could pass. The central government had established a fixed quota for each such examination. As the number of candidates was always much larger than the quota, only a small percentage—generally about one to two per cent—passed this last hurdle. The decision on admission to the gentry group through examination was therefore in the hands of the provincial directors-of-studies, themselves highly educated men. The magistrates or prefects had only a minor part.[32]

The military *t'ung-shih* also consisted of a series of three examinations. Those who passed these examinations were then admitted to gentry status as *wu-sheng-yüan*, military *sheng-yüan*. Commoners, including soldiers, could participate in the military *t'ung-shih*.

Purchase, the other main gate of entrance into the lower gentry was called *chüan-chien*, meaning the purchase of the academic title of *chien-sheng* by which one nominally became a student of the Imperial College. These

[28] See *infra*, III.

[29] The *yüan* examination was so called because the provincial directors-of-studies had the official designation of *hsüeh-yüan*.

[30] Cf. Chang Chung-ju, *Ch'ing-tai k'o-chü chih-tu*, pp. 3–7.

[31] *Tung-kuan hsien-chih*, 33/10 b; an edict of 1744 ordered magistrates to observe no quota in examinations held by them.

[32] This was pointed out in an edict of 1855, Hsien-feng 5/4/5. The Szechwan provincial director-of-studies, Ho Shao-chi, had questioned the handling of examinations by prefects and *chou* and *hsien* magistrates who had obtained their positions through purchase. The edict states that in such cases the examination papers were always read by assistants and that furthermore the actual admission to *sheng-yüan* status was still in the hands of the provincial directors-of-studies. See *Ch'ing-shih-lu* (hereafter abbreviated *Shih-lu*), Wen-tsung, 164/9 b–12 a.

chien-sheng through purchase were called *li-chien-sheng*, meaning *chien-sheng* (purchased) "in accordance with precedents." The academic title of *kung-sheng*, imperial student, could also be purchased. The purchasers of this title were called *li-kung-sheng*, *kung-sheng* "in accordance with precedents." In exceptional cases, these *li-chien-sheng* and *li-kung-sheng* actually went to the capital to study in the Imperial College,[33] but the great majority did not do so. These latter were lower in social position than the educated *sheng-yüan*.[34]

Commoners could purchase these titles. The "mean people" were excluded from the purchase system as well as from the examination system. Those among the "mean people" who changed their names and, unnoticed, attended examinations or participated in the purchase system were punished besides being deprived of the grade, title, or office thus obtained.[35]

However, these titles were bought not only by commoners but also by *sheng-yüan* who were already gentry members. As *sheng-yüan* they could not step into officialdom. Therefore, *sheng-yüan* who wished to purchase offices first had to buy *chien-sheng* or *kung-sheng* titles. But as *sheng-yüan* they paid less than the commoners for the same title. For instance, according to the regulations of the Board of Revenue, beginning in 1831, *chün-hsiu* who wished to purchase the title of *chien-sheng* had to pay 108 taels in silver. For *sheng-yüan*, the payment varied from 60 to 90 taels.[36]

As has been indicated before, those who wanted to participate in the *t'ung-shih* in order to become *sheng-yüan* had to take their examinations in their native districts and prefectures. In contrast, those who wanted to

[33] The number of students in the Imperial College was limited, varying from 300 to 180 in different periods. Moreover, this number included *chien-sheng* and *kung-sheng* not gained through purchase and in late Ch'ing included also holders of *chü-jen* degrees. See *Shih-li*, 1098/4 b.

[34] Thus in *Ch'ing-kuo hsin-cheng-fa fen-lun*, 3/59, the statement that students of the Imperial College were of higher social status refers to those who actually studied there. The whole section on the special privileges enjoyed by the students of the Imperial College also refers to this limited group.

[35] *Ch'in-ting hu-pu tse-li*, 134/21 b. For actual examples of violation and punishment, see for instance Kuo Sung-tao, *Kuo-shih-lang tsou-su*, 4/42 a–44 a, a memorial dated 1864 reporting on the investigation of T'ang Fu, a former servant of the acting *hsien* magistrate P'an Ming-hsien. T'ang misappropriated land tax money of 2,100 taels. This money was given him for delivery to the provincial treasury, but instead he used it to purchase a sub-prefect position for his son. Then he misappropriated the customs revenue of 2,800 taels for repayment of the land tax money, using the remaining 700 taels to help his son-in-law purchase the office of assistant *hsien* magistrate. After investigation, two other sons were found to have also purchased offices in violation of this regulation. Deprival of their official positions and punishment were requested.

[36] *Shan-sheng ko-fu-chou chüan-chien liang-shu t'iao-li*, p. 1 a; also T'ang Hsiang-lung, "A Statistical Study of the Chüan-chien System in the Tao-kuang Period," *She-hui k'o-hsüeh tsa-chih*, II, 4, December 1931, p. 438; also *Ch'ing-kuo hsin-cheng-fa fen-lun*, 5/359. In some provinces, such as the northwestern province of Shensi, all were required to pay in grain rather than silver. It was even stated that any magistrate who should collect in money would be impeached. See *Shan-sheng ko-fu-chou chüan-chien liang-shu t'iao-li*, p. 1 a–b. In some places payment was made in grass, camels, or horses. See Hsü Ta-ling, *op. cit.*, p. 34.

purchase *chien-sheng* titles could do so either at their native places or at the capital.[37] In special cases, men of some localities were permitted to participate in the purchase of *chien-sheng* titles in districts other than their own.[38]

Examination and purchase were thus the main gates of entrance to gentry status. In addition to these, a few other ways of admission must be mentioned, although the number of gentry admitted through them was relatively very small. One such way of entrance was to become *en-chien-sheng*, *chien-sheng* by virtue of imperial favor. This group was very small. Some were selected from *kuan-hsüeh-sheng*, students of the banner schools and imperial clansmen's school.[39] These, as bannermen, were not real gentry. But some were selected from the small group of *suan-hsüeh-sheng*, students of mathematics, who were probably Chinese.[40]

The title of *en-chien-sheng* was sometimes granted also to descendants of early sages who were originally *feng-ssu-sheng*, students in charge of sacrifices to the sages. Descendants of sages, even mere *chün-hsiu*, who participated in the imperial inspection and lecturing ceremonies held in the Imperial College, were sometimes granted the title of *en-chien-sheng*. This was then a way of entrance to gentry status specially reserved for these descendants.[41]

Another way of entrance into the gentry was the *yin* or inheritance privilege. These gentry members were known as *yin-sheng*, government students through inheritance. They were granted the title in consideration of services rendered to, or suffering undergone on behalf of, the state by one of their progenitors. Regulations provided that such titles could be bestowed for one generation only on one son of the civil and military officials in the capital who were fourth rank or above, civil officials in the provinces who were third rank or above, and military officers in the provinces who were second rank or above.[42] This type of *yin-sheng* was called *en-yin-sheng* or *kuan-yin-*

[37] *Shih-li,* 1098/1 b.

[38] *Shan-sheng ko-fu-chou chüan-chien liang-shu t'iao-li,* pp. 18 b–19 a relates: "In Yü-lin prefecture, Sui-te *chou*, and Yen-an prefecture, which are border regions [of Shensi], the granaries have been empty. Among the local people, very few are well-to-do and enthusiastic in the purchase of *chien-sheng* titles. People of Feng-hsiang, Han-chung, T'ung-chou, etc., who are willing to purchase the titles in Yü-lin, Sui-te, and Yen-an are permitted to do so. The other *chou* and *hsien* magistrates are permitted to collect only from local *sheng-yüan* and *chün-hsiu.* Sons of merchants in Shensi whose native places are in other provinces but who are willing to participate in the purchase of the *chien-sheng* title in Shensi are permitted to do so."

[39] In addition, the bannermen could participate in the *fan-i t'ung-shih,* the translator examination dealing with translation between the Manchu, Mongol, and Chinese languages. The successful candidates of this examination were called *fan-i sheng-yüan.* See *Shih-li, chüan* 365.

[40] *Suan-hsüeh-sheng* were only thirty in number at one time, studying for a period of five years, after which time they would become either *t'ien-wen-sheng* (students of astronomy) or *en-chien-sheng.* See *Shih-li, chüan* 1101–02.

[41] *Ibid.,* 1098/1 b. They were descendants of Confucius, Mencius, Yen-tzu, and Tseng-tzu.

[42] This provision limited the *en-yin-sheng* to a very small number since these ranks were held only by commissioners and above in the provinces and by colonels and above

sheng since the title was granted because of their meritorious official progenitors. Regulations also provided that such titles could be bestowed for one generation on one son of civil or military officials of seventh rank or above who lost their lives at sea or on inland waters while engaged in public service, or who died of illness while holding offices in military camps.[43] This latter type of *yin-sheng* was called *nan-yin-sheng* since the title was granted in consideration of the disastrous death of the official progenitors. If *yin-sheng* were sent to the Imperial College, they were then called *yin-chien-sheng*.

Since the *yin* privilege bypassed the examination and purchase routes to gentry status and lifted the recipient of the title directly into the gentry group, an extensive application of this privilege would be an important factor affecting social mobility. With this in mind, one might attach too much importance to the fact that in Taiping times the *yin* privilege was bestowed upon a wider range of recipients. In a collection of accounts of "loyal" deaths in Chekiang province in the war between the government and the Taipings, there is a preface maintaining that the *yin* privilege was even extended to "loyal" deaths of *chü-jen*, *kung-sheng*, and *sheng-yüan*.[44] A Szechwan local gazetteer gives actual examples of the granting of *yin-chien-sheng* titles to sons of two *kung-sheng* and thirteen *sheng-yüan* martyrs.[45]

However, the exercise of this favor must have been a matter of imperial discretion, and the number of *yin-sheng* actually bestowed was quite small. In the province of Chekiang, mentioned above, in the district of Yü-yao, only five were known to have become *en-yin-sheng* during the whole Ch'ing dynasty, and only three were known to have become *nan-yin-sheng*.[46] Thus, the *yin* privilege, though it must be mentioned as one way of entrance to gentry status, was of very minor importance during the nineteenth century.

In discussions of the gentry, the position of the elders or *ch'i-lao* is often

in the military. In "Public Office in the Liao Dynasty and the Chinese Examination System," *Harvard Journal of Asiatic Studies,* X, No. 1, June 1947, pp. 25 ff., K. A. Wittfogel showed the large proportion of officials who benefited from the *yin* privilege in Liao and other dynasties. See also K. A. Wittfogel and Feng Chia-sheng, *History of Chinese Society: Liao (907–1125),* pp. 456 ff. In the nineteenth century, however, the proportion seems to have been very small.

[43] *Shih-li,* 1098/1 b, 4 b.

[44] *Chekiang chung-i-lu, t'ao* 2, *ts'e* 3, p. 1 a. The preface to the table of deceased loyal gentry says, "Scholars study to know how to be loyal and filial. When the world is in turbulence and one's strength is insufficient to kill the rebels, it is improper to be humiliated. How can one tolerate disgrace and be greedy of living?" It also relates that the Emperor had adopted the suggestions of court officials that *chü-jen, kung-sheng,* and *sheng-yüan,* who traditionally were not given death compensation and *yin* privileges, should be granted the special favor of receiving such privileges, just like officials who died in resisting the rebels or committed suicide in preference to humiliation.

[45] *Hsü-chou fu-chih* (Szechwan), 35/21 a ff.

[46] *Yü-yao hsien-chih, chüan* 23. One of the *en-yin-sheng* entered the Imperial College and became an official. Three other *en-yin-sheng* entered officialdom of a low level. One *nan-yin-sheng* also entered the Imperial College. Two other *nan-yin-sheng* became first captains.

misunderstood. This Chinese term referred to venerated old people and not, as is sometimes believed by Western writers, to village leaders who had actual functions of local government. The Chinese elders did not have such functions.[47]

The elders were a very small group. There was no definite age limit, but in general only people at least sixty years or more of age were counted as old enough for this age distinction. Furthermore, not all old people were given the honorific term of "elder." The elders had to be distinguished also by local prestige, ability, wealth, or general leadership in community affairs. They advised or helped to manage relief bureaus,[48] helped in some localities to expound the sixteen maxims of the "Sacred Edict,"[49] rendered assistance in arresting bandits,[50] and so on. The qualification of social prestige and community leadership, as has been already indicated, was also one of the characteristics of the gentry. What was then the relationship between the gentry and the small group of elders?

Some of the gentry who were old enough could also be referred to as elders although their gentry titles were more valuable. Some nongentry elders were also given official ranks. Special edicts were issued to the effect that commoners who were eighty years of age or above were to be granted ninth-rank official garments and hats, those who were ninety or above were to be granted eighth-rank official garments and hats, and those who were one hundred or above were to be granted seventh-rank official garments and hats.[51] According to an edict of the Yung-cheng reign, one old farmer from each district each year was to be recommended to receive the eighth-rank official garments and hats.[52]

[47] Hsiao Kung-chuan of the Far Eastern and Russian Institute, University of Washington, discusses the system of local government in tax collection, police, etc., in "Rural China, Imperial Control in the Nineteenth Century," now in manuscript.

[48] *Mu-ling-shu*, 14/58 a–60 a.

[49] Wu Yung-kuang, *op. cit.*, 3/1 a–b. On the "Sacred Edict," see *infra*, p. 65.

[50] Tseng Kuo-fan, *Tseng Wen-cheng-kung ch'üan-chi*, "Rescripts," 1/1 b, correspondence with the Hsiang-yin magistrate.

[51] *Yen-yüan hsiang-chih,* 4/20 b, 12/1. *Tung-kuan hsien-chih,* 34/25 a–b, records such an edict issued in 1850 upon the ascendance to the throne of the Hsien-feng emperor. This shows that the special favors granted the elders occurred only on occasions of national celebration.

[52] *Lien-chou chih*, 2/16 a–b, where it is not made clear whether or not this favor was granted to one from each district. In Voltaire's *The Age of Louis XIV*, tr. R. Griffith, p. 411, is the statement: "The new emperor Yung-cheng surpassed his father in love for the laws, and of the public good. No emperor encouraged agriculture more. He carried his attention to this sort of arts so far as to raise to the rank of Mandarin of the eighth order, in each province, those husbandmen, who should be judged by the Magistrates the most diligent, the most industrious, and the honestest men: not that such ploughmen were to relinquish a vocation in which they had succeeded to exercise the functions of judicature, which they were ignorant of; they still remained husbandmen, but with the title of Mandarin; they had a right to sit in the presence of the Governor-general of the province, of eating at the same table with him; and their names were written in gold letters in the public hall." *Tung-kuan hsien-chih*, 33/2 b, however, clearly indicates that this edict was

Such bestowal of official rank did not, however, give the elders in question full official or gentry status. For instance, in marriage, funeral, and sacrificial ceremonies, nongentry elders, even though they had hat and garment decorations, still had to follow the commoners' etiquette.[53] This honor was also not meant to admit them to actual official careers or bestow upon them any of the legal official and gentry privileges beyond a place of courtesy in the official etiquette.

On the other hand, all nongentry elders, whether holding honorary ranks or not, were sometimes distinguished from the large mass of commoners and listed together with gentry or in a place just below the gentry. For instance, in the official ceremony of receiving and reading the imperial edict, the civil officials were placed on the east of the platform, the military officers on the west, the gentry next to the civil officials, and next to the military officers the elders and then the soldiers and commoners.[54]

Elderly commoners who were invited as guests of honor to the "district banquet ceremony" were considered as being singled out from the commoners. As pointed out by one writer, one purpose of this banquet was to encourage local inhabitants to be loyal, filial, orderly, and respectable.[55] Aside from the honor as such, the guests of honor received a tablet and money and, in the words of a contemporary, "fame without passing the examinations."[56]

directed at the *chou* and *hsien* magistrates and therefore it meant recommendation of one from each district.

[53] Wu Yung-kuang, *loc. cit.* Also *Ta-Ch'ing t'ung-li, chüan* 17, 26, 52. In *Chekiang chung-i-lu,* the tables of loyal deaths are presented in the following order: bannermen, officials, *lü-ying* (Chinese army officers), militia officers, gentry, and commoners. A survey of the thousands of gentry records shows that they consisted of officials staying at their native places, expectant officials, holders of official titles, *chü-jen, kung-sheng, sheng-yüan,* and *chien-sheng,* but did not include elders.

[54] Wu Yung-kuang, *op. cit.*, 1/7 b.

[55] Wu Yung-kuang, *op. cit.,* 3/3 a–9 b. Wu listed the *hsiang-yin chiu-li,* the district banquet ceremony, as one of the three means of maintaining moral principles. The other two were the expounding of the "Sacred Edict" and the exemplification of the virtuous (including chaste women, loyal officials and people, virtuous and charitable men, old age, big family, etc.). *Chung-hsiu Meng-ch'eng hsieh-chih shu,* 5/7 b, records that such ceremonies were held on the first day of the first month and tenth month of each year. The local educational officials would report beforehand the first and second guests of honor selected from among elderly gentry and the other guests of honor selected from among virtuous elders. The banquet was held in the government school and the expenses were covered by the local government. *Yen-chou fu-chih,* 7/6 a, records that in Yen-chou the first guest of honor was an elderly upper gentry member, the second guest an elderly *sheng-yüan,* and two or three other guests were virtuous elderly commoners. In *Ch'ing-shih-kao,* 89/10 a–11 a, it is said that from the end of the Tao-kuang period on, the funds for the district banquet ceremonies were used to meet military needs and then banquet expenses were appropriated locally. It goes on to say that while other traditions were preserved, the performance of this ceremony lapsed. According to *Hsü-hsiu Sui-chou chih,* 3/69 b, no such ceremonies were held in Sui-chou after 1813.

[56] See P'an P'iao-ts'an's article in *Mu-ling-shu,* 16/13 b–14 a. It says: "The district banquet ceremony is an occasion held to honor the elderly. . . . There are the first and second guests of honor. The first guest sits in equality with the magistrate, and the second guest sits at a position slightly inferior. . . . The expenses of the banquet are met by the public

The nongentry elders were therefore a special group of commoners who were given some of the prestige otherwise limited to the gentry and who even assisted in some of the gentry activities. But they did not share the main gentry privileges nor did they have the gentry access to official careers.

The main groups of the lower gentry, as described above, had inner divisions with varying distinctions and degrees of prestige. Thus, the civil *sheng-yüan*, the main group in the lower layer of the gentry, was divided into three sections varying in the extent of their privileges and influence. Promotion or demotion from one section to the other was determined by special examinations. The *sui* examinations were held once every three years under the supervision of the provincial directors-of-studies. The results of these examinations determined the promotion, demotion, or even dismissal of *sheng-yüan*.[57] The *k'o* examinations were also held once every three years under the supervision of the provincial directors-of-studies. The main purpose of these examinations was to determine which *sheng-yüan* were qualified to participate in the provincial examinations, but the results of these examinations also affected the promotion or demotion of *sheng-yüan* from one section to another.[58] In other words, there was a continuous check on the educated lower gentry; they could be constantly reshuffled in position and were thus held in control by the pressure of constant preparation for examinations.[59]

The newly admitted *sheng-yüan* who had not yet participated in the *sui* or *k'o* examinations, and those who had participated in these examinations but had been graded in the third or fourth rank, were called *fu-sheng*, literally meaning "supplementary *sheng-yüan*." They comprised the lowest section of *sheng-yüan* and also included those demoted from the other sections of *sheng-yüan*.

The students with the best results in the *sui* and *k'o* examinations became *ling-sheng*, meaning "*sheng-yüan* on stipend." There was a definite and

treasury, and it is necessary to invite those whom public opinion favors. Do not believe lightly in slander by under-clerks of those recommended by the gentry. Since one who participates as a guest in this ceremony is honored by receiving a tablet and money, the rich who have not been in office will be haughty in boasting before the farmers and elders of the countryside, and the sly and wicked will also hope to obtain this honor and cover the faults in their life. Those who want to gain fame without passing the examinations will offer bribes in order to influence people. Those who hate others will also take chances to slander the good. . . ." It goes on to say that sometimes ignorant people in the villages who had accumulated some wealth were deliberately recommended. But these people dared not meet the magistrates and would try a hundred ways to get out of the situation. The wicked would then extort money from them as payment for removing their names from the recommendation list.

[57] Cf. Etienne Zi, "Pratique des Examens Littéraires en Chine," *Varieties Sinologiques*, No. 5, Part 1, ch. 7. Literally, *sui* means "annual"; however, these examinations were held triennially.

[58] *Ibid.*, Part 2, ch. 2; also *Ch'ing-kuo hsin-cheng-fa fen-lun*, 3/35–6. The term *k'o* refers to the provincial examinations.

[59] See *infra*, III.

limited number of them in each government school.[60] The amount of stipend varied from locality to locality, normally about four taels per annum per *ling-sheng*.[61] Whenever *ling-sheng* vacancies occurred,[62] they were filled from the other sections of *sheng-yüan* who were graded high in the *sui* and *k'o* examinations.

The second best students in the *sui* and *k'o* examinations became *tseng-sheng*, literally meaning additional *sheng-yüan*.[63] They came from *fu-sheng* who were graded among the second rank and *ling-sheng* who were graded among the fourth rank in the *sui* or *k'o* examinations, which meant a promotion for the *fu-sheng* and a demotion for the *ling-sheng*. The *tseng-sheng* did not receive stipends, but they were given preference in the filling of *ling-sheng* vacancies. There was also a definite and limited number of them in each government school.

Of all the *sheng-yüan*, the *ling-sheng* were the most privileged and powerful. Besides receiving a stipend, they could rise into the upper gentry group by attaining the title of *kung-sheng*. They were vested with the power to guarantee new candidates in local examinations. If they purchased the title of *li-kung-sheng*, they could be appointed assistant *hsien* directors-of-studies, while other *sheng-yüan* or commoners who purchased the title of *li-kung-sheng* did not thereby become eligible for appointment to educational office.[64]

In general, the civil *sheng-yüan* as a group produced through civil examinations occupied the highest position among members of the lower gentry.

Another examination group was the military *sheng-yüan*. In this group there were no subdivisions. While the civil *sheng-yüan* had to attend one *sui* examination and one *k'o* examination in a three-year period, the military *sheng-yüan* had only the *sui* examination to attend. There was no military *k'o* examination. Like the civil *sheng-yüan*, they were not yet qualified for official appointment without passing higher examinations. They were discouraged

[60] *Shih-li*, 370/1 a.

[61] Cf. *Ch'in-ting ta-Ch'ing hui-tien*, 19/2 b–3 a. This amount is, of course, small, but as *ling-sheng*, one's privileges and prestige were greatly enhanced.

[62] Vacancies could occur in the following ways: (*a*) if the *ling-sheng* passed the provincial examinations and became holders of the *chü-jen* degree; (*b*) if they were selected to receive the *kung-sheng* title; (*c*) if they purchased the titles of *kung-sheng* or *chien-sheng* or purchased their way into officialdom; and (*d*) if they were demoted because of poor results in the *sui* or *k'o* examinations.

[63] The terms for these different kinds of *sheng-yüan* followed the pattern of the Ming dynasty. Ku Yen-wu, *op. cit.*, 17/1 a–b, relates that in early Ming, all *sheng-yüan* (a very small number) received a stipend. Later in places that produced more candidates, additional *sheng-yüan* were permitted to enroll without stipend. As the number of additional *sheng-yüan* steadily increased, a definite quota equal in number to that of *sheng-yüan* on stipend was set, and the other *sheng-yüan* were then termed supplementary *sheng-yüan*. Cf. also *Ch'ing-kuo hsin-cheng-fa fen-lun*, 3/36.

[64] *Shih-li*, 74/2 a.

from joining the ranks of the army and were supposed to devote their attention to preparing for the provincial examinations.[65]

The next largest group of lower gentry was the *li-chien-sheng* group through purchase. It has already been pointed out that they had been commoners or in some cases *sheng-yüan* who contributed silver or grain in payment for nominal or actual entry into the Imperial College. Those *chien-sheng* who had been *ling-sheng* were usually referred to as *ling-chien*; those who had been *tseng-sheng* as *tseng-chien*; those who had been *fu-sheng* as *fu-chien*; but the large majority who had been *chün-hsiu*, i.e., commoners, were called plain *chien-sheng*. This clear division among the *li-chien-sheng* themselves will be useful in our later analysis of how many of them came directly from commoners, and how many of them were from the group which already was privileged, namely, the educated *sheng-yüan*.[66]

Besides the *li-chien-sheng*, or *chien-sheng* through purchase, there were three other types of *chien-sheng*. *En-chien-sheng*, as pointed out earlier, had their origin from either of the two routes: (*a*) selected by imperial favor from *kuan-hsüeh-sheng* or *suan-hsüeh-sheng*; (*b*) bestowed by imperial favor on descendants of sages. *Yin-chien-sheng*, as also mentioned earlier, came from *en-yin-sheng* or *nan-yin-sheng*, government students through inheritance.

The last type of *chien-sheng* was the *yu-chien-sheng*, *chien-sheng* by virtue of noteworthy achievements. They were selected from among *fu-sheng* and military *sheng-yüan* of the different schools in the various provinces.[67] They were a very small group. Their selection was decided on by the provincial directors-of-studies. They were then examined jointly by the Board of Rites and the Imperial College before being formally admitted to the Imperial College.[68]

Finally, there was the other group of lower gentry through purchase. This was the *li-kung-sheng*, imperial students through purchase. These "irregular" *kung-sheng* should be clearly distinguished from the "regular" *kung-sheng*. The "regular" *kung-sheng* belong really to the upper gentry. The "irregulars" had a lower social position and lesser privileges and belonged to the lower gentry, although the line at this point becomes less sharp. Only the "regular" *kung-sheng* could be selected to educational offices, or through court ex-

[65] *Ibid.*, 719/4 b.

[66] *Infra*, II.

[67] *Shih-li*, 1098/2 b.

[68] *Ibid.*, 1098/1 a. In early Ch'ing the selection of *yu-chien-sheng* was not regular. In 1670 a definite procedure was established. An edict of that year states, "In Shun-chih 8 [1651] and 11 [1654], provincial directors-of-studies were ordered to select from among the *sheng-yüan* those who were excellent both in literature and conduct to be sent to the Imperial College for study. This example shall be observed. From each prefectural or district school, one good and young *sheng-yüan* should be selected every second, fourth or fifth year." Cf. *Ibid.*, 1098/1 b.

aminations be appointed as magistrates. Both types of *kung-sheng* might actually study in the Imperial College, which meant residence in the college in Peking, after which they could participate in examinations through which they could secure official titles. However, the "irregular" *kung-sheng* had to stay a much longer time in the Imperial College before they were qualified to participate in such examinations.[69] Also, different official titles were conferred on the different types of *kung-sheng.* In this respect also the "irregular" *kung-sheng* were treated less favorably than the "regulars." [70]

The *kung-sheng* title could be purchased not only by the various kinds of *sheng-yüan* but also by *chien-sheng* or even commoners.[71] There were occasional objections to the purchase system as a whole, and specific objections were raised against the purchase of the *kung-sheng* title because it was close to the avenues of higher careers. For instance, one memorial complained that the *kung-sheng* title was a proper route to official position, but with the expansion of the purchase system, both *sheng-yüan* and *chün-hsiu* could purchase the honored title of *kung-sheng.*[72] An edict also acknowledged that with the purchase system, young men who were not adequately trained in the classics could become teachers of elderly students and others who were better trained in the classics.[73] Therefore, safeguards were provided to the effect that among *kung-sheng* through purchase, only those who were originally *ling-sheng* and therefore well acquainted with the classics, were permitted to be appointed to educational offices.

[69] *Ibid.*, 74/3 b. An edict of 1747 stipulated the different kinds of *kung-sheng* that were qualified to take examinations to obtain official titles with a varying minimum period of study in the Imperial College. This minimum period varied from 6 to 24 months. *Li-kung-sheng* who were originally *chün-hsiu* had to stay in the college for 24 months before being qualified for such examinations. Before 1791 such examinations were held triennially, but later the interval became irregular. An edict of that year stated, "Approved. Those *kung-sheng* who have passed the examinations but have not yet been appointed to actual office amount to more than a thousand. It is therefore not necessary to increase the number triennially. Examinations will be held at the time when more official candidates are needed."

[70] *Ibid.*, 1100/4 a. It was provided that certain types of regular *kung-sheng* who were graded in the first rank in the examinations would receive the title of first-class assistant *chou* magistrate, and those graded in the second rank, second-class *chou* magistrate, and those in the third rank, assistant *hsien* magistrate. *Kung-sheng* through purchase who were graded in the first rank would receive only the title of deputy assistant *hsien* magistrate, and those in the second rank, the title of police master.

[71] *Ibid.*, 1098/1 a. *Kung-sheng* who were originally *ling-sheng* were usually called *ling-kung*; those who were originally *tseng-sheng* were called *tseng-kung*; those who were originally *fu-sheng* were called *fu-kung*; and those who were originally *chün-hsiu* were called plain *kung-sheng.* An understanding of these terms will help in the study of the origin of *kung-sheng* through purchase while going over the local gazetteers, the *Ta-Ch'ing chin-shen ch'üan-shu* and other works.

[72] Hsü Wen-yüan, "A Memorial on the Purchase System," *Huang-ch'ao ching-shih-wen-pien*, 17/48 b. This memorial was written in the K'ang-hsi period.

[73] *Shih-li*, 1098/1 a. An edict of 1723.

ENTRANCE INTO AND COMPOSITION OF THE UPPER LAYER OF THE GENTRY

The upper layer of the gentry was much smaller than the lower layer, but it was a group with great prestige and power. As described above, members of the lower gentry could not directly obtain official posts. In contrast to this, the upper gentry were closely linked with officialdom. The upper gentry consisted of those of higher education and officials. However, the latter, as indicated earlier, did not necessarily all come from the educated group, but could be "irregulars" through purchase or military merit. Thus entrance into the upper gentry was made possible mainly through high academic rating but also through official career.

Nevertheless, the principle which set the upper gentry apart from the lower gentry was their higher education, as shown by their degrees. Examination was the "regular" route of advance into the upper gentry. Both "regular" and "irregular" members of the lower gentry could advance into the upper gentry through the "regular" route. The lower gentry, whether they were the educated *sheng-yüan* or the purchased *chien-sheng* and *kung-sheng*, could participate in the *hsiang-shih*, the provincial examinations.[74] Candidates who succeeded in the civil provincial examinations were called *chü-jen* or provincial graduates, and those who succeeded in the military provincial examinations were called *wu-chü-jen* or military provincial graduates. With the acquisition of the *chü-jen* degree, these men attained upper gentry status.

While the dates of the *sheng-yüan* examinations varied from one prefecture to another and were decided by the provincial directors-of-studies, the civil and military provincial examinations were held on definite dates.[75] They were held in all the provincial capitals triennially at the same time. The military examinations immediately followed the civil examinations and both were supervised by examiners directly sent from the court.

Civil *sheng-yüan*, the educated lower gentry, who intended to participate

[74] For some Western sources on the provincial examinations, see F. H. Ewer, "The Triennial Examinations," *The Chinese Recorder*, III, No. 11, April 1871, pp. 330–332, where an examination held in Canton is described and a translation of the examination essay and theme is given; also see Li Chow Chung-cheng, *L'Examen Provincial en Chine (Hiang Che) sous la Dynastie des Ts'ing (de 1644 à 1911)*; also Yu Yuan Chang, *Civil Service Examination System in China, 1644–1905.*

[75] The regular time for the civil provincial examinations was stipulated in early Ch'ing as follows: "The provincial examinations will be held in the years *tzu*, *wu*, *mao* and *yu* . . . [i.e., triennially] in the eighth month . . . and on the 9th, 12th, and 15th days [i.e., a series of three tests to each examination]. The examinees should enter the examination hall the day before and leave the day after these examination dates." See *Ch'in-ting k'o-ch'ang t'iao-li* (hereafter abbreviated *K'o-ch'ang*) 1/1–2. It was also stipulated that the military provincial examinations would be held in the tenth month of the *tzu*, *wu*, *mao* and *yu* years. *Shih-li*, 716/1 a.

in the civil provincial examinations, had to participate first in the *k'o* or preliminary examinations.[76] They had to take these examinations in their native provinces. However, all *kung-sheng* and *chien-sheng* could participate either in examinations held in the capitals of their native provinces or in those held at Shun-t'ien-fu, the metropolitan prefecture.[77]

At Shun-t'ien-fu there was a separate quota for the admission of *chien-sheng* and *kung-sheng* to *chü-jen* degrees. This meant that these *chien-sheng* and *kung-sheng* did not have to compete on equal terms with the *sheng-yüan*. Judging from the different proportion of number of candidates to the quota, those *chien-sheng* and *kung-sheng* participating at Shun-t'ien-fu had a much better chance of success.[78] This certainly was one of the main advantages and purposes in the purchase of *kung-sheng* and *chien-sheng* titles even by *sheng-yüan*.

The military provincial examinations had no preliminary examinations. Both military *sheng-yüan* and *ping-sheng* (military *sheng-yüan* who formerly had been soldiers) were qualified to participate.[79]

Besides these regularly scheduled triennial examinations, there were the *en-k'o*, examinations held irregularly by virtue of imperial favor. The regularly scheduled examinations were sometimes postponed because of the military situation or for other reasons. In special cases, some provincial examinations were postponed so long that by the time the next examination date was due, one examination was held instead of two. This situation was remedied, however, by doubling the quota of successful candidates for that examination.[80]

Occasionally, *chü-jen* degrees were granted to persons who did not participate in the provincial examinations. For instance, on an occasion of imperial inspection at Tientsin, the Emperor granted *chü-jen* degrees to two *kung-sheng* and one *sheng-yüan*.[81] *Chü-jen* thus obtained were called *en-shang chü-jen*, *chü-jen* bestowed by imperial favor. Throughout the nineteenth century, the

[76] Those who were observing mourning periods for deceased parents were excluded. See *K'o-ch'ang*, 5/9 a–b.

[77] *K'o-ch'ang*, 5/5 a–b.

[78] See *infra*, III, note 9.

[79] *Shih-li*, 716/7 b, 17 b.

[80] For instance, in 1851 an edict stated that students in Kwangsi were engaged in organizing and training local corps to defend their localities against the Taipings, and that the civil and military officials were also occupied with military affairs. The *en-k'o* of that year was therefore postponed until the next year, a regular provincial examination year. Only one examination took place in 1852, but the *chü-jen* quota was doubled. See *K'o-ch'ang*, 1/6.

[81] An edict of 1788 stated: "On this occasion of inspection to Tientsin, students from Chihli and other provinces welcomed the procession and presented poems. Therefore they were individually tested. . . . *Kung-sheng* Wang Su, Wang Chi-sun, and *sheng-yüan* Wu Jung shall be awarded the degree of *chü-jen* and be permitted to participate in the metropolitan examinations the same as other *chü-jen*. Those graded in the second rank shall each receive one bolt of silk." See *Hsüeh-cheng*, 2/13–14.

degree was granted now and then to heirs of meritorious officials who were already gentry members of the *sheng-yüan*, *chien-sheng*, *kung-sheng*, or *yin-sheng* groups and sometimes even to those who were commoners.[82] These cases were, however, very few.

According to regulations, to every five *chü-jen* degrees conferred on candidates in provincial examinations, one *fu-pang* title was conferred. *Fu-pang* literally means "successful candidate on a supplementary list." A holder of the *fu-pang* title could not participate in the advanced metropolitan examinations. Thus a *fu-pang* was often called half a *chü-jen*.[83] However, he was already a member of the upper gentry. When selected to an official post, he was an official through the "regular" route. When he participated in the purchase system, he paid less than members of the lower gentry.

En-shang chü-jen and *fu-pang* were also granted to aged participants who repeatedly failed in the provincial examinations. The regulation provided that the regular *kung-sheng* participants who reached the age of eighty and all other types of participants who reached the age of ninety would be granted the *chü-jen* degree. *Sheng-yüan*, *kung-sheng* through purchase, and *chien-sheng* through purchase who participated in the examinations and reached the age of eighty would be granted the *fu-pang* title.[84] Examples can be found of lower gentry who tried to obtain this upper gentry degree by reporting false ages.[85]

82 *K'o-ch'ang*, *chüan* 53 B.

83 "Notes of Ling-hsiao and I-shih," *Kuo-wen chou-pao*, *chüan* 6, No. 33, Aug. 25, 1929. These notes further relate that if one was again granted *fu-pang* in the succeeding provincial examination, one gained nothing except having more classmates. Only in 1726 was permission given that one who obtained *fu-pang* twice could participate in the metropolitan examination. But this practice was immediately discontinued. In "Jan-an pi-chi," *Chung-ho yüeh-k'an* I, 5, May 1, 1940, it is said that in provincial examinations the examiners purposely deleted the names of those who were already *fu-pang* or *pa-kung* from the new *fu-pang* list and filled the vacancy with other unsuccessful candidates. This point is substantiated by the diary of an examiner who wrote on his supervision of examinations in Kwangtung. *Ibid.*, p. 83. However, in *Hsi-Chin yu-hsiang t'ung-jen tzu-shu hui-k'an*, p. 19 b, the "Autobiography of Yu Tung" says that Yu was *fu-pang* three times.

84 *K'o-ch'ang*, 53/2 a–b. *Fu-pang* was considered as a type of regular *kung-sheng*. Thus one who received the *fu-pang* title because of old age would, on the next examination, be granted the *chü-jen* degree. For instance, *Tung-kuan hsien-chih*, 72/9 b, tells the story of Ch'en Han-yüan who participated in the provincial examinations without success until the age of 81, when he was granted the *fu-pang* title. The next provincial examination he attended would have qualified him to receive *chü-jen* by imperial favor, but he died before the examination took place.

85 *K'o-ch'ang*, 53 A/10 a–13 b, 27 a–b, *passim*. An edict of 1879 stated: "If old-aged candidates of the provincial examinations complete their three tests, they will be memorialized [by examiners] for a grant of *fu-pang* or *chü-jen* regardless of the quality of the tests. In former years, there were usually only one to two, or four to five of them in each province. In recent years, the number has doubled. The records of some of them show that they were already 70, 80, or 90 when they were admitted as *sheng-yüan* and it cannot be guaranteed that there was no cheating. . . . Hereafter, in accordance with the regulation that *kung-sheng* and *chien-sheng* through purchase will be granted such favor after ten examinations [about thirty years], *sheng-yüan* will be granted such favor after three examinations [about nine years]. . . ." *Ibid.*, 53 A/35 a–37 b.

But, on the whole, the total number of *chü-jen* degrees and *fu-pang* titles granted in consideration of old age was very small.[86]

Competition in the *chü-jen* examination was keen, as much so as in *sheng-yüan* examinations. The latter examination brought together men of the same district. The *chü-jen* examination, however, brought together men from the various districts of a province. The successful one or two per cent in the *chü-jen* examinations thus reaped great honors for themselves as well as for their respective villages, towns, or cities. Their success in the examinations and resulting membership in the upper gentry put them in a position to bring material benefits to their home communities through their contacts with governors and other high provincial officials as well as with members of the upper gentry of other localities. Indeed, the *chü-jen* degree was a mark of high academic standing. This distinction was a well-guarded one and was at no time allowed to be jeopardized by the selling of this degree.

Occasionally, however, there were circumventions of this rule. For example, Wu Ch'ung-yüeh, a prominent *hong* merchant who was a *sheng-yüan*, was granted a *chü-jen* degree in 1831 because his father had contributed in his name a sum of 33,000 taels for public works.[87] In 1833 other records also show that several sons of *hong* merchants were promoted to *chü-jen* because they helped finance the suppression of the Lien-chou rebels.[88] In the same year several rich men in the neighborhood of Peking gave the government large subscriptions of rice for the starving masses and as a reward were granted peacock feathers and the *chü-jen* degree.[89]

Such granting of *chü-jen* degrees to those who made financial contributions must have aroused the anger of a censor. This censor pointed out that during the drought in Chihli in 1833 a holder of the *fu-pang* title had contributed 12,000 taels and had been granted the *chü-jen* degree. He conceded that this might be acceptable since *fu-pang* was but one step removed from *chü-jen*, but he objected to the fact that others who were not *fu-pang* and had contributed money were also recommended for the *chü-jen* degree by some censors

[86] *Tung-kuan hsien-chih*, 47/40 a–44 a, listed the men who received official ranks, degrees, and titles because of old age, including some *chü-jen* who were granted official ranks, some *fu-pang* who were granted the *chü-jen* degree and some *sheng-yüan* who were granted the *fu-pang* title because of old age. Combining all three, for this district, there were 11 in Ch'ien-lung period (1736–1795), 20 in Chia-ch'ing period (1796–1820), 14 in Tao-kuang period (1821–1850), 5 in Hsien-feng period (1851–1861), 10 in T'ung-chih period (1862–1874) and 11 in Kuang-hsü period (1875–1908). *Shih-lu*, Hsüan-tsung, *t'ao* 82, *ts'e* 1, p. 14 a, edict of Tao-kuang 27/2/17 (1847), however, pointed out that 184 aged candidates of the provincial examinations of all provinces in Tao-kuang 26 (1846) were granted *chü-jen* and *fu-pang*; their number was approximately 10 per cent of the total number of *chü-jen* and *fu-pang* admitted in that year.

[87] *Kuang-chou fu-chih*, 129/25 b; also Hummel, *Eminent Chinese of the Ch'ing Period*, II, p. 867. Wu was known among Westerners as Howqua.

[88] *The Chinese Repository*, II, No. 2, June 1833, p. 96.

[89] *Ibid.*, II, No. 6, Oct. 1833, p. 287.

and the governor of the metropolitan prefecture. According to the records, his arguments won the Emperor's approval.[90]

In the early Hsien-feng period, when funds were badly needed for the fight against the Taipings, some officials discussed the possibility of allowing the purchase of the *chü-jen* degree. Thereupon, a censor vigorously dénounced such proposals.[91] Though *chü-jen* degrees continued to be gained sometimes through wealth and influence,[92] they never became legally obtainable through purchase.

Since the *chü-jen* were higher in social position than the *kung-sheng*, many of the latter participated in civil provincial examinations in order to raise their prestige and improve their chances for an official career. For the *chü-jen* who failed to pass the metropolitan examinations, there were the provisions of *ta-t'iao*, or special selection of civil *chü-jen* to office.[93] Some *chü-jen* thus became *hsien* magistrates and first-class assistant *chou* magistrates, and other *chü-jen* became *chou* or *hsien* directors-of-studies.[94]

[90] *Yunnan t'ung-chih*, 169/49 b, in the biography of Chu Chen, a native of T'ung-hai, Yunnan. This memorial was presented in 1833 while Chu was censor of the Hu-kuang circuit.

[91] *Kiangsi t'ung-chih*, 150/35 b, the biography of P'eng Ch'ing-chung.

[92] For instance, a memorial of 1890 says, "P'ang Yüan-chi, a gentry member of Wu-ch'eng, Chekiang, who is a *ling-kung-sheng* [*kung-sheng* purchased by one who was originally a *ling-sheng*] and an expectant senior secretary [obviously purchased], has contributed 30,000 taels for flood relief. Formerly, when 10,000 taels were contributed, *chü-jen* degrees were duly granted, as in the case of the salt merchants of Liang Huai and *hong* merchants of Kwangtung. Such examples continued to exist after the rise of military campaigns but were later stopped by the censors. However, a contribution of 30,000 taels is different. In addition, this gentry member was originally a *ling-sheng* of high academic standing. He is rich and righteous-minded, enthusiastic in public affairs, and desirous of promotion. Hence it is recommended that he be granted the *chü-jen* degree and be permitted to participate in the metropolitan examination." See Li Hung-chang, *Li Wen-chung-kung ch'üan-chi*, 69/18, a memorial dated Kuang-hsü 16/8/29.

[93] An edict of 1800 on *ta-t'iao* stated: "A special selection to office from *chü-jen* in various provinces has been announced to be held next year after the metropolitan examination. The purpose is to create more opportunities for self-recommendation to office; thus more of those responsible for local administration will be scholars. This will greatly benefit civil administration and people's livelihood. In recent years, only *chü-jen* who had already participated in four metropolitan examinations were qualified for *ta-t'iao*. It is to be feared that the number of such *chü-jen* is too small for a satisfactory selection. If all *chü-jen* are included in the selection, it is also feared that the number will be too large. . . ." The edict concluded by limiting the privilege of *ta-t'iao* to *chü-jen* who had participated in more than three metropolitan examinations. See *K'o-ch'ang*, 52 B/14–15. Sometimes, as in 1737, all *chü-jen* who failed in the metropolitan examination of that year but were good at classics were given the opportunity of being selected as *chou* or *hsien* directors-of-studies in their native provinces. Cf. *Ibid.*, 52 B/20.

[94] *Ibid.*, 52 B/1. See also *ibid.*, 52 B/20–21, an edict of 1754. The compilers of the *K'o-ch'ang t'iao-li* remarked: "After certain metropolitan examinations, edicts will be issued with regard to *ta-t'iao*. The old practice was a six-year interval for the occurrence of *ta-t'iao*. Since Chia-ch'ing 18th year, the Board of Civil Office will request *ta-t'iao* on the occasion of every fourth metropolitan examination. The Board of Rites will then make pamphlets of names [of *chü-jen*], marked clearly with their age and send to the Board of Civil Office. The latter will then request the appointment of imperial commissioners

The military *chü-jen* were less influential and enjoyed less social prestige than their civil counterparts, the civil *chü-jen*, but they belonged to the upper gentry group. Military *chü-jen* who failed in the military metropolitan examinations could still be selected for military offices.[95]

Holders of civil and military *chü-jen* degrees would strive further to pass the metropolitan examinations.[96] If they passed, they became *chin-shih* or metropolitan graduates. They generally held the highest social position and enjoyed the greatest prestige and influence among the privileged gentry members. Holding this degree, they had direct access to officialdom and were normally given immediate official appointment. Such officials were then known as officials through the "regular" route. Being "regulars," they were appointed to important administrative offices. Those among them who were graded high in the civil metropolitan examination were sent to the honored Han-lin Academy, the academy for the highest literary talents, and from there were sent out as provincial directors-of-studies or were appointed to high central or provincial posts.

These important metropolitan examinations were also held triennially.[97] Successful candidates were graded into three ranks.[98] Age and order of their success in the examinations affected their appointments to various offices.[99] In

from among the princes and high officials for this special selection of officials from *chü-jen* of the various provinces and eight banners. Those graded in the first rank will be appointed on probation as *hsien* magistrates. Those graded in the second rank will be appointed to educational offices. . . ."

[95] It was provided that military *chü-jen* who failed in metropolitan examinations could join the troops and after a period of three years be selected as lieutenants (sixth-rank, first-grade officers). If not selected, they might be recommended to become sublieutenants (seventh-rank, first-grade officers). See *Shih-li*, 566/2 a–b.

[96] The following were not qualified: "*Chü-jen* who have not cleared the tax payment; who have been deprived of the degree due to offenses; who are now under discussion for punishment; who are still in they temporary period of denial of the privilege of participating in the metropolitan examinations." See *K'o-ch'ang*, 7/3 a. Military *chü-jen* who had already been selected to office were not permitted to participate in the metropolitan examinations. See *Shih-li*, 717/1 a. Military *chü-jen* who had reached the age of sixty were also not permitted to participate in examinations. Cf. *Ibid.*, 717/2 a.

[97] The civil metropolitan examinations were to be held in the years *ch'ou*, *ch'en*, *wei*, and *hsü* in the capital on the 9th, 12th and 15th days of the 3rd month. See *K'o-ch'ang*, 1/1 a; also *Shih-li*, 330/1 a. The military metropolitan examinations, which included both field and written examinations, were held in the same years from the 5th day to the 15th day of the 9th month. See *Shih-li*, 717/1 a ff.

[98] The metropolitan examinations also consisted of a series of examinations. The *hui-shih*, generally translated as "metropolitan examination," was actually only the first of the series. Those who succeeded in the *hui-shih* were called *kung-shih*, presented scholars. The *tien-shih*, palace examinations, which were held a month and a half later, were decisive for the final ranking among the successful candidates of the *hui-shih*. The successful candidates of the *tien-shih* were then called *chin-shih*. However, it was seldom that *kung-shih* failed to become *chin-shih*. *Kung-shih* was thus merely a transitional address. Cf. *K'o-ch'ang*, 55/1–3; Fu Tseng-hsiang, *Ch'ing-tai tien-shih k'ao-lüeh*, which also appeared in *Kuo-wen chou-pao*, *chüan* 10, Nos. 1, 2, 3; also see Chang Chung-ju, *Ch'ing-tai k'ao-shih chih-tu*, pp. 32 ff.

[99] For instance, *Shih-li*, 72/1 a–b, the edicts of 1723 and 1724, pointed out that those

general, those rated in the first rank among the civil *chin-shih* were appointed as first-class and second-class *han-lin* compilers. The other civil *chin-shih* were appointed as *han-lin* graduates, assistant secretaries of the different boards or of the Grand Secretariat, or as *hsien* magistrates.[100] Those military *chin-shih* rated in the first rank were appointed to the honored positions of first-class and second-class officers of the imperial guards. The other military *chin-shih* were appointed as third-class officers or subalterns of the imperial guards, and second captains or lieutenants in the army.[101] In all examinations, civil and military, the youngest and most brilliant of the successful candidates were thus retained at the capital as an inner core of trusted officials.

Another way of entering the upper gentry was through the selection of "regular" *kung-sheng* from the civil *sheng-yüan* according to academic standing, accomplishments, or seniority. The selection of *kung-sheng* according to academic standing was handled by a special examination supervised by the provincial directors-of-studies. All the three types of civil *sheng-yüan* could participate in this examination.[102] The successful ones were then known as *pa-kung-sheng*, *kung-sheng* by virtue of special selection, and became members of the upper gentry. *Pa-kung-sheng* examinations were held only once in twelve years.[103] On each such occasion only two *sheng-yüan* from each

who were older were appointed as *hsien* magistrates. In *Fukien t'ung-chih*, *li-chuan*, 39/69 b, the biography of Cho Hsiao-fu says that when he participated in the palace examination the topic for discussion was the superfluous number of soldiers. Cho made harsh and acute points. The reader of this paper was afraid that it would annoy the Empress Dowager and put him in the third rank of successful candidates. He would thus have been appointed as a *hsien* magistrate. A censor commented that Cho's paper was good both in calligraphy and composition. He was then raised to the second rank of successful candidates and was appointed as assistant secretary in the Board of Punishment.

100 *Shih-li,* 72/1 a ff.

101 *Ibid.*, 566/1 a ff.

102 Qualifications for participating in the *pa-kung-sheng* examination were made clear in a reply by the Board of Rites to a provincial director-of-studies in 1776 as follows: "Now the regulation is, in the selection of *pa-kung* from among the *sheng-yüan*, it does not matter whether the one selected is originally a *ling-sheng*, *tseng-sheng*, or *fu-sheng*, but it must be one who is excellent in classics and perfect in conduct and one who has been graded in the top rank in the past *sui* examinations. . . . Those new *sheng-yüan* who have not yet participated in *sui* examinations and whose talents and conduct are therefore not yet well known naturally should not be freely permitted to participate in the selection. . . ." See *Hsüeh-cheng*, 50/21.

103 The purpose of *pa-kung* examinations and the final decision on their frequency are seen in an edict of 1742: "The reason for the selection of *pa-kung* in addition to the selection of scholars through provincial and metropolitan examinations is to get the talents not yet being selected through the latter examinations. . . . Through *en-k'o* [special provincial and metropolitan examinations] and through increase of quota, the number of metropolitan and provincial graduates has been steadily increased. . . . By admitting more *pa-kung*, more candidates are created for a limited number of official positions. . . . Now *sheng-yüan* who are good in classics will naturally be selected through the provincial and metropolitan examinations. They will not rely solely on the selection of *pa-kung* to get into officialdom. In former days, *pa-kung* were selected once in several decades or once in twelve years. The recent practice is once in six years. Hereafter, it shall be once in twelve years. . . ." See *Shih-li*, 1098/10 a; *Hsüeh-cheng*, 50/10 b–11 a.

prefectural school and one from each district school were granted the *pa-kung-sheng* title.[104] Thus the *pa-kung-sheng* were a small group, but they could participate in special court examinations and be appointed as seventh-rank court officials or *hsien* magistrates in the provinces.[105]

The selection of *kung-sheng* according to accomplishments was conducted under the joint supervision of the governors-general, governors, and provincial directors-of-studies.[106] Only *ling-sheng* and *tseng-sheng*, the two higher types of *sheng-yüan*, were qualified for the selection. The selected few were then known as *yu-kung-sheng*, *kung-sheng* by virtue of noteworthy accomplishments.[107] Selection of *yu-kung-sheng* occurred once in three years in the provinces, and the men selected could then participate in a court examination which might result in their appointment as *hsien* magistrates or educational officials.[108]

The selection of *kung-sheng* according to seniority was another "regular" route of entrance to the upper gentry. Those selected were known as *sui-kung-sheng*, *kung-sheng* by virtue of seniority. Only *ling-sheng*, the highest type of *sheng-yüan* were qualified for this selection.[109] Normally, one was selected each year from a prefectural school, two were selected every three years from a *chou* school, and one was selected every two years from a *hsien* school.[110]

Additional *kung-sheng* according to seniority were selected whenever there was a national celebration. The *kung-sheng* selected on such occasions were known as *en-kung-sheng*, *kung-sheng* by virtue of imperial favor. For instance, upon the enthronement of the Chia-ch'ing emperor in 1796 an edict was issued stating: "Orders to the prefectural, *chou*, and *hsien* schools of all provinces. Those who are due for selection to *kung-sheng* this year, shall be

[104] Etienne Zi, "Pratique des Examens Littéraires en Chine," *op. cit.*, Part I, chap. 8, p. 86, correctly points out that the *pa-kung-sheng* were selected once in twelve years in the *yu* years. He also says that they were selected from *ling-sheng* and *tseng-sheng* but neglects to mention the possibility of *fu-sheng* being selected as *pa-kung-sheng*.

[105] Chang Chung-ju, *Ch'ing-tai k'ao-shih chih-tu*, pp. 40–41, relates that *pa-kung* were given certificates by provincial directors-of-studies and were to report at the Board of Rites in the 5th month of the year following the *pa-kung* examination year. As a result of a court examination held for them, a small portion of them would be appointed as 7th-rank court officials in the Board or as *hsien* magistrates in various provinces. Another portion of them would be appointed as second-class assistant *chou* magistrates or as educational officials. Those who were not successful in the court examinations could also apply at the Board of Civil Office to be appointed as *hsien* directors-of-studies or second-class assistant *chou* magistrates. But those who were successful in the court examination naturally had the preference in actual appointments.

[106] *Hsüeh-cheng*, 51/26 b–27 a.

[107] Those selected from *ling-sheng* were also known as *yu-ling-sheng* and those selected from *tseng-sheng* were also known as *yu-tseng-sheng*. See Zi, "Pratique des Examens Littéraires en Chine," Part I, chap. 8, p. 89.

[108] Chang Chung-ju, *loc. cit.*

[109] *Hsüeh-cheng*, 51/2–3.

[110] *Ibid.*, 51/1 a.

called the *en-kung-sheng*. Select the next in seniority to be the regular *sui-kung-sheng*."[111] In some cases, *en-kung-sheng* titles were granted to descendants of sages who were already *ling-sheng*.[112]

These *kung-sheng* together with the holders of the *fu-pang* title, also known as *fu-kung-sheng*, made up the so-called five "regular" *kung-sheng*. They had a higher social position and more privileges than the "irregular" *kung-sheng*, *chien-sheng*, and the "regular" *sheng-yüan* of the lower layer of the gentry. They belonged to the upper gentry and could be appointed directly to educational offices or sometimes to administrative offices.[113]

The "irregular" route to the upper layer of the gentry was the acquisition of official positions or ranks through purchase, military merit, or recommendation. The officials who gained their positions through such special appointments are to be distinguished from officials who came from the examination system. Officials who held the degree of *chin-shih* were known as *chia-k'o ch'u-shen*, officials who were products of the highest level of civil service examination. To acquire official positions through the "regular" examination was an ideal goal of the traditional Chinese scholar. The "regular" officials were not only most honored by others, but they themselves formed a special group to safeguard their privileged and powerful position. However, although the "irregular" officials were in a lower social position than the "regular" officials, their privileges and power definitely set them off from the lower gentry group.

Upper gentry as well as lower gentry could gain promotion through the purchase system. It was stipulated that civil offices in the capital could be purchased by incumbent officials, *chü-jen*, *kung-sheng*, and *chien-sheng*. Civil offices in the provinces could also be purchased by these upper and lower gentry members. Military offices in the capital and in the provinces could be purchased by officers, military *chü-jen*, military *sheng-yüan* and *chien-sheng*.[114] In theory, civil *sheng-yüan* and commoners were not allowed to purchase offices. Since the civil *sheng-yüan* were the educated group, they were supposed to work towards higher academic honors and subsequently become "regular" officials. Commoners were not supposed to make a big stride and immediately step into the upper gentry. In practice, however, both *sheng-yüan* and commoners were permitted to purchase the *chien-sheng* or *kung-sheng*

[111] *Ibid.*, 50/4 b–5 a; also, for example, in the years 1799 and 1809.

[112] *Ibid.*, 50/1 b describes the occasion of an imperial inspection of the Imperial College. Among the members of the clans of the sages who arrived at the capital to attend the ceremony, those who were originally *ling-sheng* were granted *en-kung-sheng*.

[113] *Shih-li*, 74/2 a–3 a.

[114] To cite some examples of the amount of payment for certain offices by certain types of gentry members: *kung-sheng* and *chien-sheng* paid 6,912 taels for the office of senior secretary of a Board in the capital, and 11,808 taels for the office of circuit intendant in the provinces. See *Ch'ing-kuo hsin-cheng-fa fen-lun*, 5/321–2.

titles. They could then forthwith purchase offices. Some of them were never really called *chien-sheng* or *kung-sheng* since they purchased official positions by paying at the same time the price for the *chien-sheng* or *kung-sheng* title and the price for the official position. Thus, those who bought offices were sometimes identified in official reports as officials, gentry, merchants or rich.[115]

There was a difference between the purchase of official positions and the purchase of mere official titles. The former might lead to the holding of actual official posts while the latter would not. Official titleholders apparently enjoyed many privileges equal to those of real officials of the same rank, but the latter's connections and influence naturally raised them to a much more powerful position. Purchases of official titles were, however, more numerous than purchases of actual official positions, and considerably less money was paid for a title without office than for the same title with office.[116]

Official positions or official titles could also be acquired through recommendation. This was possible for both gentry and commoners, but the gentry had a much better chance of success. Those who prepared and made the recommendations were gentry and high officials, and these men generally chose other gentry members for such advancement into official positions. There were various types of recommendations. One was the recommendation of *hsiao-lien fang-cheng*, literally meaning "filial, scrupulous, square, and upright," an honorary term bestowed on obscure scholars with perfect conduct. These scholars were supposedly first nominated by gentry, elders, and commoners of their home communities. Their records were screened by local and provincial officials who then formally recommended them to the court. Those recommended to the court were interviewed by the Emperor and appointed as *hsien* magistrates, assistant administrative officials, or educational officials.[117] Recommendations of *hsiao-lien fang-cheng* were infrequent,

[115] For instance, on one occasion, Li Hung-chang reported on the total amount collected in Kiangsu and Chekiang from officials, gentry, merchants, and rich who participated in the purchase system from Kuang-hsü 15/11 (1889) to Kuang-hsü 16/4 (1890). See Li Hung-chang, *Li Wen-chung-kung ch'üan-chi*, 68/28.

[116] Thus only 3,800 taels were paid for the title of senior secretary of a Board by *kung-sheng* or *chien-sheng*, and 5,248 taels for the title of circuit intendant. These sums were about half of what had to be paid for such actual offices. See *Ch'ing-kuo hsin-cheng-fa fen-lun*, 5/358–9. In actual practice in later years, one could pay as little as 50 per cent of these stipulated sums. See Li Hung-chang, *op. cit.*, 68/25.

[117] The procedure in recommending *hsiao-lien fang-cheng* is illustrated by an edict of 1736: "Governors-general and governors are ordered to instruct the local officials to request the gentry, elders, and commoners for nomination of *hsiao-lien fang-cheng*. Then they should be screened by the magistrates, and in the case of *sheng-yüan* also by the educational officials. The results shall be reported to their superiors. The governors-general and governors shall then make further checks and recommend the appropriate persons to the Board of Civil Service. These records shall then be checked by metropolitan officials. . . . The selected ones will then be interviewed by the Emperor and appointed to office." See *Shih-li*, 75/2 a.

and those recommended were often *sheng-yüan*, the educated lower gentry.[118]

Mu-yu, or personal secretaries, who worked with governors-general, governors, and other officials, could also be recommended for appointment to official positions. The personal secretaries to officials were not part of the official administrative organization. They were hired and paid by the officials themselves.[119] As they did not have official positions, they could be either gentry or commoners. But generally the personal secretaries of magistrates were lower gentry members or commoners, while the personal secretaries of high provincial officials were frequently upper gentry.[120] It was the latter group who especially benefited by this provision of recommendation of *mu-yu* to office. Thus, this way of entrance to official posts was possible but unusual for lower gentry members and commoners.

Occasionally *sheng-yüan* were also specially recommended by provincial directors-of-studies for appointment to office in consideration of their superiority in classics and conduct.[121] In the periods of Hsien-feng, T'ung-chih and Kuang-hsü, "to meet the need of the time," there were also recommendations of other talents by high central officials, Manchu generals, governors-general, and governors.[122]

The acquisition of official positions or titles through military merit occurred through the promotion of soldiers to officer positions as well as through the appointment of gentry or commoners to civil or military posts because

[118] E.g., in *K'uei-chou fu-chih*, 27 A/20 a, it is related that in 1821 the various provinces were ordered to publicly recommend *hsiao-lien fang-cheng*. A *kung-sheng* and others, a total of more than ten men, recommended Hsü Pu-ch'ing who was a *tseng-sheng*.

[119] However, it is interesting to note that a personal secretary to a magistrate was employed by him only through the force of his superior. For instance, in *Kiangsi t'ung-chih*, 156/42 b, the biography of Tu Hung-i identified him as an upright magistrate of the Chia-ch'ing period in Szechwan. When the governor-general recommended to him the governor-general's own personal secretary to be his secretary, he refused to accept the offer. Finally he was forced out of office because of his uncompromising attitude. Personal secretaries to a magistrate of a locality were often taken over by the next magistrate of that locality. See Teng Ch'eng-hsiu, *Yü-ping-ko tsou-i*, 4/13 a–b. Teng, who was a censor, memorialized on Kuang-hsü 9/8/29 (1883) regarding the power held by the personal secretaries. He pointed out that in Kwangtung at that time it was quite common for one to be concurrently a personal secretary to both a superior and a subordinate official. One example given was that of a man who was personal secretary to both a *hsien* magistrate and a prefect. The son of this personal secretary was personal secretary to another *hsien* magistrate. This personal secretary actually controlled the affairs of the districts. The personal secretaries of other nearby prefectures and districts were either his relatives or his partisans. The officials were transferred but this personal secretary remained in his semiofficial position. He had accumulated more than a hundred thousand taels and invested heavily in real estate.

[120] For instance, the famous statesmen, Li Hung-chang and Tso Tsung-t'ang, had been personal secretaries in their capacity as upper gentry. Sometimes subordinate officials became personal secretaries to high officials in order to gain influence and better chances of promotion. This practice was, however, curbed by the Emperor. See *Shih-li*, 75/3 b.

[121] *Ibid.*, 75/2 b.

[122] *Ibid.*, 75/5 b.

of military merit. The latter type of appointment was made more and more frequently during the last half of the nineteenth century. A large number of civil and military officials of that time had originally been militia leaders and officers. Gentry and others who participated in the organizing and training of local corps, actually engaged in combat, and gained military merit were recommended to official positions or titles. However, a check of the officer lists of late Ch'ing times reveals that most military officers were still those who originally came from the rank and file.[123] This was another way of entrance into officialdom which automatically led to upper gentry position.

Thus, within the upper gentry there were a number of different groups which had come from the different routes of entrance to gentry status. This most privileged upper gentry was composed of holders of the *kung-sheng* titles, *chü-jen* and *chin-shih* degrees, as well as all the members of officialdom, active or retired, and holders of official titles. There was no special legal provision to mark them off as the "upper gentry"; but their prestige and influence and their standing in society set them apart from the lower gentry.

GENTRY PRIVILEGES

In a handbook for magistrates, a passage on the appropriate treatment of gentry members by magistrates reads as follows:

> In administering the affairs of a district, the high families [*shen*] are not to be disturbed. They should be met in a virtuous manner and received courteously and are not to be repressed with power and prestige. Also the scholars [*shih*] are at the head of the people, and since the laws and discipline of the court cannot be exhaustively explained to the people, and since the scholars are close to the people and can easily gain their confidence, the learned and virtuous scholars are exactly the ones to rely upon in persuading the people to follow the instructions of the officials. Therefore, they should be loved and treated with importance. When they happen to come because of public affairs, if they are sincere and self-respecting, they should be consulted on the problems of whether bandits exist in their villages, what the jobs of the villagers are, whether the customs of their places are praiseworthy. . . .[124]

Another passage on what should be known by a new magistrate also indicates the government's respect for the strength of the gentry. "How many local men are in active service in the government? How many are retired officials? How many are *chü-jen*, *kung-sheng*, *chien-sheng*, and *sheng-yüan*? What is the traditional way of interviewing them? . . ."[125]

[123] See for instance *Ta-Ch'ing chin-shen ch'üan-shu*, 1881.

[124] Wang Feng-sheng, "On Gentry," in *Mu-ling-shu*, 16/26 b. This book is a collection of essays on various aspects of local administration written by magistrates and scholars and compiled to serve as a handbook for magistrates.

[125] P'an P'iao-ts'an's article in *Mu-ling-shu*, 2/2 b; see also p. 39 a, "An Inquiry into the Custom of the Locality" by Ch'en Hung-mou and p. 44 a, "An Investigation of the General Condition of Various Districts" by Ch'eng Han-chang.

A governor's proclamation stated: "The gentry are at the head of the common people; and to them the villagers look up. All you learned gentry and old men among the people will from this time and afterwards make a work of stirring and brushing up your spirits, to become leaders of the people; and to assist and supply that in which I am defective. ..."[126]

The above passages indicate the importance of the gentry in the eyes of the administrators and show that they formed the leading social group to be treated differently from the commoners. The gentry were generally regarded as the social equals of the local officials. While the officials relied heavily upon their assistance in controlling the mass of commoners, they also respected them as potential troublemakers who could lead the people in threatening and endangering the administration. Thus, it was said that "the *shen* were the respected men of the locality and the *shih* the head of the masses." The relationship between the magistrates and the gentry (*shen-shih*) was therefore different from the relationship between the magistrates and the commoners who were so far removed from the power and prestige of the officials that they would not dare to have contact with the magistrates.[127] In contrast to the commoners, the gentry had free access to the officials. When a gentry member called on an official, he was also freed from the special submissive etiquette which the commoner had to observe.

The privileged position of the gentry was also expressed in a very formal way. Special names of address, decorations, hat buttons, and garments distinguished the gentry, like the officials, from the commoners. Special ceremonies and etiquette were designed to underline the dignity of their position. To express honor and respect, the common subjects had to address all officials as *ta-lao-yeh* (Great Excellency), while all gentry without official rank or title, i.e., the *chü-jen*, *kung-sheng*, *sheng-yüan*, and *chien-sheng*, were to be addressed as *lao-yeh* (Excellency).[128] Among themselves, members of the gentry would use their respective titles.

As an outer mark of their position, all gentry and officials wore buttons on their hats. These buttons differed in material and design according to the position of the wearer. For example, an official of the first rank wore on his official hat a gold button with a flower design, with a ruby on the top and a pearl in the middle; the holders of the higher academic degrees and titles, the *chin-shih*, *chü-jen*, and *kung-sheng*, wore buttons of plain gold; and the lower gentry, the *sheng-yüan* and *chien-sheng*, wore buttons of plain silver.[129]

[126] Proclamation of the Governor of Kwangtung, *The Chinese Repository*, I, No. 11, March 1833, pp. 461 ff.

[127] T'ien Wen-ching, "Ch'in-pan chou-hsien shih-i," *Huan-hai chih-nan wu-chung*, pp. 29 a–30 b.

[128] See Ch'en K'ang-ch'i, *Lang-ch'ien chi-wen*, 10/19 b–20 a.

[129] One emperor specially emphasized the usefulness of buttons on hats in indicating

Similar distinctions existed for the garments of the gentry and officials. Officials of the first rank wore a robe which was embroidered with nine pythons, while the academic degree-holders wore black gowns with blue borders.[130] Aside from the special hats and robes designed for the gentry, a number of luxury articles in wearing apparel were reserved for their exclusive use. Sable, fox, and lynx fur, as well as brocades, fancy embroidery, and gold borders for the decoration of saddles and reins, could be used only by the gentry. No commoner, regardless of his wealth, was permitted to wear these luxury materials, not to speak of the official hats and robes. Violators of these rules were to be punished.[131]

Among the other formal privileges of the gentry was the exclusive right to participate in certain ceremonies. For instance, only gentry members could attend official ceremonies held in the Confucian temples.[132] When clans observed ancestral rituals, clan members who were gentry were specially honored as clan leaders. According to the regulations of some of the clans, the functionaries in annual rites had to be gentry members. If the clan gentry let commoners usurp this privilege, the former were regarded as having dishonored their positions and the clan had served its ancestors falsely.[133]

Aside from such ceremonies in which only the gentry participated, a special part was assigned to the gentry in all community festivals and ceremonies. The honors which the regular degree-holders gained through their success in the examinations brought prestige and glory to their provinces and home communities. The candidates for the examination were sent off in a ceremony by local officials and gentry. The successful candidates of the metropolitan

rank and prestige, and stated that the wearing of proper hats with proper buttons was to be strictly observed or punishment would follow. See Chang Shou-yung, *Huang-ch'ao chang-ku hui-pien, nei-pien,* 1/63 a, edict of T'ung-chih 8/7 (1869).

[130] For details on regulations governing wearing apparel see *Ch'ing-shih kao,* 103/14 a–18 b; see also *Ta-Ch'ing chin-shen ch'üan-shu, ts'e* 1, pp. 3 a–6 b; and Chang Shou-yung, *loc. cit.* See also Ch'ü T'ung-tsu, *Chung-kuo fa-lü yü chung-kuo she-hui.*

[131] *Ch'ing-shih kao, loc. cit.*

[132] Ting Jih-ch'ang, *Fu-wu kung-tu,* 11/10 a–11 b.

[133] More information on this point is given in the following passages: "Should the *tsu* [clan] include scholars and officials among its members . . . the one highest in rank should lead it. . . . An official who loses his position and lives at home is ranked with the commoners. . . . If he is dismissed from office but retains his former functions, then he is to conduct the affairs of the ancestral hall according to the rank belonging to these functions." See Hu Hsien-chin, *op. cit.,* pp. 127–8; the last sentence referred to officials who were deprived of their titles and privileges while being allowed to carry on their duties. "On each of these occasions, twenty-two functionaries take part, and all of them must belong to the gentry; they are chosen according to their rank as officials, not according to the degree they obtained in the examinations. . . . According to the old custom, the meat used at the sacrifices has to be distributed to all the families. . . . Any gentry member who attends the ritual receives two to eight times the ration of an ordinary member, the exact amount being set according to the degree he received in the examinations. . . . At the end of the rites, all the gentry in the *tsu* participate in a big feast, which the old men are also allowed to attend. . . ." Cf. *ibid.,* p. 126.

examinations were honored in a feast by the Emperor himself.[134] The successful *chü-jen* were given a formal banquet by the governor or governor-general of their home province.[135] After this, their return home was an occasion of great joy and festivity. Their deeds were made known in family records and tablets and by the erection of honorary arches.

The position of influence and prestige which the gentry enjoyed found its legal expression in the special regulations on punishment and legal procedure which the Ch'ing codes, edicts, and practice provided. If a member of the gentry committed a crime, he could not be humiliated. If his offense was so serious that he had to be punished, he was first deprived of his honored position so that what happened to the man would not reflect upon the group. As a member of the gentry was the social equal of a magistrate and sometimes his superior in rank, a magistrate could not be given the authority to deprive a gentry member of his position and to punish him. Such authority, especially over the lower gentry, generally remained in the hands of the educational officials who combined this judicial function with their control over the gentry through the examination system which they administered.[136] The gentry were thus protected from regular administrative interference and could be judged only by their educational superiors.

They were, however, also specially protected by law against insults from commoners, a protection which gave their social prestige a legal sanction. Thus, if a member of the gentry was insulted or injured, the offender was punished more severely than if he had insulted only a common subject. For instance, it was provided that an underclerk or soldier who insulted a *chü-jen* would, in accordance with the regulation governing subordinates insulting an official of sixth rank or below, receive seventy lashes.[137] If he insulted a commoner, he would receive only ten lashes.[138]

Moreover, commoners were not allowed to involve members of the gentry as witnesses in law suits.[139] When the gentry themselves were involved directly in law suits, they were not required to attend the trials personally

[134] The feast was know as *ch'iung-lin-yen,* the imperial garden feast. The term was used since the first emperor of the Sung dynasty feasted the new metropolitan graduates in his garden, Ch'iung-lin, in K'ai-feng. See *Tz'u-yüan, s.v.*

[135] This feast was called the *lu-ming-yen*, the "stagbleating" banquet. The term was used since T'ang times when during the feast the participants would sing the ode of *lu-ming* from the *Book of Odes.* See *Tz'u-yüan, s.v. The Chinese Repository*, XV, No. 11, Nov. 1846, p. 575, records the occasion of this formal banquet given by the governor-general of Liang-Kwang in honor of *chü-jen* of that year.

[136] Charges against retired officials had to be referred to the Imperial Court. Cf. Chang Fei, *Chang Wen-i-kung tsou-kao,* 1/28 b ff.

[137] *Ta-Ch'ing lü-li hui-chi pien-lan*, 29/2 b.

[138] *Ibid.,* p. 1 a.

[139] This provision was also supposed to prevent gentry members from meddling in lawsuits.

but could send their servants to the yamen. This was the same treatment as that given incumbent officials involved in lawsuits.[140]

A Western account correctly points out that "one inducement to acquire even the lowest degree of literary rank is that it exempts the graduates from the bamboo." [141] It goes on to say that some high provincial officials were much concerned over the anger of some gentry members at the punishment inflicted on them by certain irresponsible magistrates. Actual disturbances occurred when some magistrates illegally punished some *sheng-yüan.* For instance, the governor of Chekiang reported to the Emperor in 1820 that a magistrate had punished one *sheng-yüan* by forty blows on the palm of his hand and had twisted the ear of another in a complaint of extortion of money by a *sheng-yüan*, thus causing all *sheng-yüan* to refuse to take part in examinations. In 1821 in Honan, when one of their number had been subjected illegally to twenty blows by a magistrate, the *sheng-yüan* rose in a body in open court, dashed their buttons on the ground and walked off, leaving the examiner alone.[142]

When members of the gentry committed offenses, the magistrates had to take special procedures to effect any punishment. If a magistrate neglected such procedures and punished the gentry at his free will, he could be impeached. For instance, the procedures for punishment of *sheng-yüan* were mentioned in the following edict:

> As to *sheng-yüan* who have committed minor offenses, prefecture, *chou*, and *hsien* magistrates should consult with educational officials concerning punishment. Those who have committed serious offenses should be reported to the provincial director-of-studies for deprival of the offenders' position as *sheng-yüan* before any punishment is decided. If the local officials punish the *sheng-yüan* at their own will, the provincial directors-of-studies can impeach such officials.[143]

Another edict on the same subject states:

> *Sheng-yüan* are associated with the examination system from which officials are selected. If the officials treat them as common subjects so that they also will be lashed or punished, it is certainly not an expression of paying special regard towards scholars. Hereafter, in case of serious offense, the local officials should first report to the provincial director-of-studies. Only after his position of *sheng-yüan* is removed should the offending *sheng-yüan* be punished as he deserves. In case of light offense, he should be sent to the district director-of-studies for punishment.[144]

[140] See *Ch'ing-kuo hsing-cheng-fa fen-lun*, 3/42. For regulations concerning officials involved in lawsuits, see *Ta-Ch'ing lü-li hui-chi pien-lan*, 30, 102 a, where the note says that this was to save the officials' face.

[141] *The Chinese Repository*, IV, No. 3, July, 1835, p. 120.

[142] *Ibid.*

[143] *Hsüeh-cheng*, 31/2 a.

[144] *Ibid.*, 32/1 a–b. This edict was issued in 1670 and the one above in 1653. However, the situation was the same in the nineteenth century. Any change in practice would have

This regulation was well understood and practiced by local officials. A handbook for personal assistants of magistrates stated that it was necessary for the *hsien* or district magistrates to report to their superiors on *sheng-yüan* and other members of the gentry who committed offenses:

> *Sheng-yüan* who have committed light offenses subject to lashes and deprival of rank should be reported to the provincial director-of-studies and the superior prefectural and *chou* magistrates. If it is a serious offense, they should be reported to all authorities. *Sheng-yüan* on stipend who have committed crimes should also be reported to the financial commissioner who should cancel their stipend. *Kung-sheng* and *chien-sheng* who are subject to deprival of rank should be reported to all authorities as well as to the provincial director-of-studies.[145]

The gentry were thus a privileged group before the law.

They also had very important economic privileges. Special arrangements in tax payment and labor service conscription were provided for them, and stipends and other subsidies were granted for their educational advancement.

The taxes were of two kinds: *i*, official labor service, and *fu*, property tax paid in money or kind.[146] From the first of these the gentry were exempted. Their dignity, their cultural refinement, and their life of study did not permit them to engage in manual labor. The training which qualified them for leadership exempted them from labor. Their property, on the other hand, was not exempted from tax, although the gentry used their influence to reduce their payments. This distinction is shown in the following imperial edict issued in 1736:

been noted by the compilers of the *Ch'in-ting hsüeh-cheng ch'üan-shu*, which was published in the nineteenth century. Moreover, the next quotation is from a book published in the nineteenth century.

[145] Wang Yin-ting, "Important Notes on Treatment of Law Suits," in *Ju-mu hsü-chih wu-chung*, p. 46 a. As to the division of responsibilities among magistrates and educational officials for the control of various groups of gentry, *Hsüeh-cheng*, 30/11 b–12 a, an edict of 1761 stated: "Educational officials control only the civil and military *sheng-yüan*. If *sheng-yüan* commit offenses and are not found out and clearly reported, educational officials will be impeached according to regulations. As to *kung-sheng* and *chien-sheng* who get their position through purchase, when committing minor offenses, they will be punished jointly by magistrates and educational officials. Other matters will not be the concern of educational officials. So educational officials have not the duty to control them. Hereafter, regarding *kung-sheng* and *chien-sheng* through purchase, who have committed offenses such as sheltering stolen goods, who have become involved in law-suits, who are greedy or otherwise unlawful, the magistrates who have not been able to detect and report on them will be impeached but not the educational officials." For example, three *hsien* directors-of-studies were punished for failing to discipline *sheng-yüan* who led in refusing to pay taxes in northern Honan. See *Shih-lu*, Wen-tsung, 182/10 b, edict of Hsien-feng 5/11/7 (1855). Ting Jih-ch'ang, *op. cit.*, 1/6 b, records the request made by a *hsien* magistrate to the governor for the deprival of the title of a military *sheng-yüan* for leading a group and causing a disturbance. Governor Ting then ordered the judicial and financial commissioners to instruct the prefect to investigate the case in more detail. This shows the difficulty in depriving the gentry of their titles.

[146] Compiler's note, *Ch'ing-chao wen-hsien t'ung-k'ao*, 21/5044.

The payment of land taxes for land owned forms the regular revenue of the country. Regardless of whether one is a gentry member (*shih*) or a common subject, all should pay these taxes. As regards all miscellaneous kinds of labor conscription, the gentry should be exempted from them. ... Hereafter, *chü-jen*, *kung-sheng*, *sheng-yüan*, etc., should all be exempted from miscellaneous labor conscription so that they can devote themselves to study. ...[147]

Because of this principle the gentry were exempted from the payment of all personal taxes, namely, the head tax and the actual corvée. The head tax was an attempt in the earlier part of the Ch'ing dynasty to transform labor service into a money tax levied on the adult male and was originally not levied on property.[148] The gentry's exemption from this tax was indicated in the introductory sentence of the imperial document inscribed on the horizontal stone tablets in government schools.[149] It reads: "The court in establishing schools, selecting *sheng-yüan*, exempting them from head tax, granting them salaries, instructing them through educational officials, and in requesting various officials to treat them with courtesy, aims in all this at cultivating talent for use by the court."[150]

In the imperially published *Hsüeh-cheng ch'üan-shu*, the handbook for provincial directors-of-studies, the following edict is recorded: "The provincial directors-of-studies of various provinces should report after careful investigation the names of *sheng-yüan* and those deprived of rank. Also make them known to the different localities concerned so that the exact names are noted and then exemption from head tax can follow."[151]

In an official compilation of the Ch'ing code and cases, the following statement is found: "*Shen-chin* are exempted from their own head tax. If it is discovered by the local officials that they allow their names to be used by their sons, grandsons, or other members of the clan [so as to avoid the payment of head tax], the *sheng-yüan* and *chien-sheng* will be reported for deprival of position, and those with official ranks will be reported for impeachment. ..."[152]

Thus, gentry members were exempted from the payment of head tax, but this privilege was not extended to members of their families. This had not

[147] *Hsüeh-cheng*, 32/2 a–b.

[148] Head tax in Chinese is called *ting-sui* and sometimes *ting-i*. According to *Ta-Ch'ing lü-li hui-chi pien-lan*, 8/4 a, a male at the age of 16 or more was called *ting* and began to serve in labor conscription. Those aged 15 or less were called "young," and those aged 60 or more were called "old" and were exempt from labor conscription together with the disabled. Thus at the age of 16 or more a man was considered an adult and was subject to head tax.

[149] This document contains eight disciplinary regulations proclaimed to the *sheng-yüan* as the principles to which they should adhere. For detail, see *infra*, pp. 198–9.

[150] *Hsüeh-cheng*, 4/1 a; *Shih-lu*, Shih-tsu, 63/3 a; also recorded in many local gazetteers. The document was first issued in 1652.

[151] *Hsüeh-cheng*, 32/1 a.

[152] *Ta-Ch'ing lü-li hui-chi pien-lan*, 8/40 b–41 a.

always been true. At the beginning of the Ch'ing dynasty, exemptions from payment of head tax were more extensive. An edict of 1648 stated:

> For officials in the capital, those of the first grade are exempted from 30 piculs of grain and 30 shares of head tax ... and those of the ninth grade from 6 piculs of grain and 6 shares of head tax. Officials outside of the capital are entitled to an exemption of half this amount. For *chü-jen*, *kung-sheng*, *chien-sheng*, and *sheng-yüan*, 2 piculs of grain and 2 shares of head tax are exempted. ... For officials who are retired with honor, the exemption is seven-tenths of their original exemption; for those who are merely living at home in retirement, the exemption is half of their original. ...[153]

This quotation shows that at the beginning of the dynasty, a member of the gentry was allowed shares of exemption for more than one person so that some members of his family could also enjoy the privilege. In addition, the gentry were allowed exemption from a certain portion of their land taxes up to a specified amount. But in later times, they were exempted only from their own share of head tax and were not legally exempted from any part of the land tax.

The head tax was amalgamated with the land tax following an edict of 1727. It might thus be argued that the gentry's exemption from head tax was nullified by this amalgamation. The records show, however, that this amalgamation was not completely carried through. In some cases, especially in Shansi province, the taxes remained separate even up to the nineteenth century.[154] But even where they were combined, the head tax was recorded as a separate item in local gazetteers.[155] Where the amalgamation was carried out, this traditional exemption remained legally a gentry privilege and became one of the pretexts of gentry members for paying less of the revised land tax.[156]

The head tax itself was comparatively small. More important was the exemption from the labor conscription which had not actually been abolished with the introduction of the head tax. This exemption has already been mentioned. It was again emphasized in a nineteenth-century edict which stated that civil and military *sheng-yüan* should not be allotted governmental and miscellaneous labor services, since they were the best element among the people, and that the country "in cultivating talents should not let them be humiliated." [157] When this conscription was converted into a land tax, the gentry's exemption also covered these converted taxes. These exemptions from

153 *Shih-lu*, Shih-tsu, 37/21 a–b.

154 Cf. Wang Ch'ing-yün, *Hsi-ch'ao chi-cheng*, 3/11 a, 28 a–36 b, *et passim*; *Shih-li*, *chüan* 157.

155 See for instance *Po-pai hsien-chih*, 6/13 ff.

156 See *infra*, p. 43 ff.

157 *Shih-li*, 720/15 a, edict of 1811. See also *Ta-Ch'ing lü-li hui-chi pien-lan*, 8/40 a.

labor service or the converted taxes applied not only to the gentry themselves but also to the members of their families.[158] For instance, the inscription on a tablet erected in the government school in Li-p'ing, Kweichow, stated that all members of a *sheng-yüan's* family were permanently exempted from labor conscription.[159]

From the land tax and other taxes on property, the gentry were not exempted. Even meritorious officials were exempt only from the land tax due on land which had been awarded to them by the court. They had to pay land tax on land they purchased, as would any other person.[160] Any gentry member who tried to evade tax payment by not reporting or reporting falsely on the amount of land he owned would be punished. Here again the regulations on the punishment of gentry are different from the regulations on the punishment of commoners.[161]

Although the gentry were not exempt from the payment of land tax, they were sometimes allowed to delay payment, as stated in the following regulation:

> Among the *kung-sheng*, *chien-sheng* and *sheng-yüan*, the rich should pay half of the land tax before the 5th month and complete the payment in the 10th month. If tax payment is not cleared by that time, two more months will be allowed so that it must be cleared by the end of the year. The poor ones should pay half before the 8th month and complete the payment by the end of the year. If unable to clear it by that time, the moderately poor should clear it before the 2nd month of the next year, and the very poor before the 4th month of the next year. Those whose tax payment is not cleared within the time limit should be reported for deprival of their respective positions, to be regained after clearance. If some are really desperately needy and the amount owed is of a small percentage, after careful investigation they will for the time being not be deprived of their positions and be permitted to clear it at autumn harvest together with the first half of tax payment due for that year.[162]

[158] *Ibid.*, 8/41 a–b. The regulation provided that the gentry should also report the number of persons in the family who were exempted from various labor services.

[159] *Li-p'ing fu-chih*, 5 a/72 a. In some localities, this privilege was extended to "marginal" or would-be gentry, i.e., candidates in the lowest examinations. In *Shansi t'ung-chih*, 135/2 a in the biography of Wu Chia-i, Magistrate of Pu-ning, Kwangtung, it is said that the traditional practice there was to exempt all *ju-hu* (scholar families) from labor conscription. This encouraged participation in the examinations, and the number of *t'ung-sheng* candidates for the *sheng-yüan* title was several thousand.

[160] *Ta-Ch'ing lü-li hui-chi pien-lan*, 9/18 a. The regulations provided that the stewards for the families of meritorious officials should report to local officials the whole amount of land purchased so that land tax could be apportioned. Those who failed to report from 1 *mou* to 3 *mou* would receive 60 lashes, and so on, and the land would be confiscated. The punishment for any common subject who failed to report from 1 *mou* to 5 *mou* of land owned was 40 lashes, and so on. Cf. *ibid.*, 9/1 a. This means that the stewards of meritorious officials were punished even more severely than the common subjects so as to prevent them from relying on their masters' prestige.

[161] *Ibid.*, 9/2 b. It provided that the gentry who failed to report the ownership of one *mou* of land or more were to be deprived of their respective titles, and also punished if the amount was ten *mou* or more.

[162] *Ta-Ch'ing lü-li hui-chi pien-lan*, 11/41 b; see also *Shih-li*, 383/16 a–b, edict of 1736.

These exemptions relieved the gentry from forced labor or the corresponding converted tax which was a substantial part of the tax burden. In practice their advantage was even greater, since their privileged positions enabled them frequently to escape extra charges and to pay less or none of the land tax for which they were supposed to be held responsible.[163]

Some groups of the gentry also received a monthly stipend from the government; among these were the *ling-sheng*, *sheng-yüan* on stipend,[164] and those *chien-sheng* who actually were studying in the Imperial College.[165] *Sheng-yüan* who intended to participate in the provincial examinations were, in many localities, invited to ceremonies sponsored by the local authorities, entertained at banquets, and given travelling expenses in varied amounts according to the customs of the localities.[166] *Chü-jen* who intended to leave for the capital to attend the metropolitan examinations were also given travelling expenses by the provincial government[167] and sometimes by local governments.[168]

Besides such governmental subsidies, *sheng-yüan* who went to the pro-

[163] See following section.

[164] "The Metropolitan Prefecture and the province of Kwangsi gave either money or rice; the province of Kweichow gave both; the rest of the administrative divisions gave money. Kweichow gave annually four *shih* of rice and one-half tael of silver to each student. The highest figure in rice was twelve *shih*, the lowest, Kwangsi, two *shih* per annum. The highest annual money allowance was given by Shantung—9.6 taels per annum; the lowest by Kansu—0.695 taels; the majority gave between two and five. . . ." See Hsieh Pao-chao, *op. cit.*, pp. 148–9, translated from the *Hu-pu tse-li.*

[165] Only a few *chien-sheng* actually were permitted to study in the Imperial College; they were divided into two groups: those permitted to reside in the college and those not permitted to do so. The former received one tael monthly. In the 11th and 12th months they received an additional allowance for coal of 2 *ch'ien* and 5 *fen*. The latter group received 2 *ch'ien* monthly. See *Shih-li*, 1098/13 b.

[166] The ceremony is known as *pin-hsing*, a term borrowed from *Chou-li*, meaning to raise the virtuous and entertain them as guests at banquets. In *Tao-chou chih*, 5/32 b, it is noted that the ceremony would be held in the 6th month and the travelling expenses would be 5 taels for each participant. In *Pa-ling hsien-chih*, 14/12 a–b, the travelling subsidy was stipulated at 2.5 taels. Both places are in Hunan, but the latter is nearer to the provincial capital. For a description of the ceremony, see also *Yen-chou fu-chih*, 7/5 a.

[167] Hsieh Pao-chao, *op. cit.*, p. 161, has translated the regulations as follows: "The provincial government, out of the treasury, paid the travelling expenses of the candidates [of the metropolitan examinations]. Seventeen of the eighteen provinces paid them in silver, varying from one to twenty taels, while Yunnan paid three taels of silver and a horse. . . . Kwangtung and Anhwei, 20 taels, Kiangsi and Hupeh 17, Fukien 15, Hunan 14, Kwangsi 12, Chekiang and Honan 10, Shansi 7, Shensi 6, Kansu 5, Chihli and Szechwan 4, and Shantung 1." Wu Yung-kuang, *op. cit.*, 5/3 b–4 b, records the following: Feng'tien varied from 9 to 10 taels to each participant of the metropolitan examination; Shantung—a total of 589 taels; Shansi—1944 taels; Honan—2560 taels; Chiang-ning—209 taels; Soochow—853 taels; Anhwei—2843 taels; Kiangsi—1648 taels; Fukien—5967 taels; Hupeh—4642 taels; Hunan—2621 taels; Shensi—4198 taels, all to be equally divided among the participants in the metropolitan examination from the respective provinces; Chekiang—10 taels each; Kansu—5 plus; Kwangtung—varied from 18 to 30 taels plus; Kwangsi—12 taels plus; Yunnan and Kweichow—3 taels and supply of horses at relay stations along the post roads.

[168] *Po-pai hsien-chih*, 6/12 b.

vincial capital and *chü-jen* who went to the capital to attend advanced examinations often received subsidies from their own clans[169] or from gentry-sponsored literary associations.[170] Rent collected from land owned by government schools was often assigned as a subsidy to these candidates. In one locality such rent was to be used to supplement the insufficient salaries of the *sheng-yüan* so that they could devote themselves to study.[171] In another locality, a portion of the rent was to be employed for travel subsidies.[172] In still other localities, funds were collected and rent-yielding land was purchased for the purpose of creating a permanent source of funds for these subsidies.[173]

Upon succeeding in the examinations, the new provincial graduates were each granted 20 taels of flag and tablet allowance.[174] For new metropolitan graduates, grants were provided for the construction of an honorary arch, in addition to other pecuniary allowances.[175] Frequently their own clans also provided allowances as congratulatory gifts.[176]

In times of famine, relief to needy *sheng-yüan* was specially handled apart from the general relief of common subjects. Rent collected from land owned by government schools was used, for instance, to subsidize such needy *sheng-yüan*.[177]

169 For instance in Hu Hsien-chin, *op. cit.*, p. 120, the translation of data on the Tseng clan in Hunan says: "Those who take the *hsiang* [provincial] examination are to be given 4,000 cash; those who take the *hui* [metropolitan] examination are to be given 20,000 cash."

170 Pai Ching-wei, *Feng-hsi ts'ao-t'ang chi*, 6/21 b ff. says that the purpose of such a literary association was to give travelling allowances to participants in the metropolitan examinations and to check the qualifications of participants in the local examinations.

171 *Nan-ning fu-chih*, 40/10 b. This article, however, was written before the nineteenth century.

172 *P'an-yü hsien-hsü-chih*, 10/18 b–19 a. *Ibid.*, 11/4 a records that the Ch'en clan contributed land to the *hsien* school, and part of the rent collected was allotted as subsidies to participants in provincial and metropolitan examinations.

173 *Po-pai hsien-chih*, 4/42 a, records that the *hsien* magistrate purchased land yielding rent amounting to 23 piculs which was to be accumulated and used in the year of examination to subsidize candidates in provincial examinations. *Hsiang-shan hsien-chih*, 15/16 a, records that the gentry collected a total of 29,300 taels for the purpose of promoting participation in examinations, and travelling expenses were one of the important items.

174 Wu Yung-kuang, *op. cit.*, 5/3 b–4 b.

175 *Ibid.*, 5/6 a–b. Civil metropolitan graduates of the first rank were given 80 taels; those of second and third ranks, 30 taels; military metropolitan graduates, 18 taels. In addition there were allowances for new apparel.

176 Hu Hsien-chin, *loc. cit.*, says, "Those who succeed in the second [the provincial examination] are to be given 80,000 cash; those who succeed in the last [the metropolitan] examination are to be given 120,000 cash."

177 These last two points are clearly indicated by the following edict: "Rent from land owned by government schools in various provinces is originally intended for the purpose of disbursement to the various *ling-sheng* and other poor *sheng-yüan*. But the amount is limited, and when a famine occurs, the poor *sheng-yüan* who are not able to support themselves often have to face hunger. This is really pitiful. I [the Emperor] think that as they are in the [government] schools, it is not fitting to order the officials to treat them as poor, common subjects receiving relief. Hereafter, in periods of relief

From the examples given above, it is apparent that the gentry of nineteenth-century China had a definite range of privileges which set them apart from the rest of society. Their position was admired and longed for. As Ku Yen-wu's essay on the *sheng-yüan* stated, "Once one became a *sheng-yüan* one was exempted from official labor, free from the oppression of the underclerks, dressed in the scholars' gowns, received by officials courteously, and not subject to the humiliation of being lashed. Thus the reason for persons wishing to become *sheng-yüan* was not necessarily for the honor of the title but for the protection of their persons and their families." [178]

THE GENTRY'S EXPLOITATION OF THEIR PRIVILEGED POSITION

The gentry's position gave them many advantages. Their privileges provided them with special exemptions and special immunities which were legally recognized and socially accepted. In actual practice, however, the gentry, relying upon their position, often extended their power beyond its formal limits.

Their exploitation of their position is evident in the field of taxation as many gentry members were able to evade payment or even to direct some of the revenue into their own pockets. The gentry landowners were supposed to pay the same amount of land tax and grain tribute as the commoner landowners. In practice, uneven payment of taxes was quite common. Gentry members called themselves *shen-hu* or "gentry household," *ju-hu* or "scholar household," *kuan-hu* or "official household," *ch'eng-hu* or "city household," and *ta-hu* or "big household." They called the commoners *min-hu* or "commoner household," *hsiang-hu* or "countryside household" and *hsiao-hu* or "small household." These terms were used for making differentiations in tax payments.

For instance, Ting Jih-ch'ang, governor of Kiangsu, in describing the unequal burden of grain tribute, admitted that in the Chiang-pei area such terms as *shen-hu*, *min-hu*, *ch'eng-hu*, and *hsiang-hu* were used. The *shen-hu* sometimes paid no grain tribute at all or else paid it at a lesser rate of 2,000 to 3,000 cash for each picul of rice to be paid as tax. *Min-hu* had to pay 6,000 to 7,000 or even 15,000 to 16,000 cash for each picul. On the average the government received only 6,800 cash for each picul of rice to be collected

payment, the governors-general, governors, and provincial directors-of-studies should order the educational officials to send the lists of names of the poor *sheng-yüan* and their native places to the local officials for checking and further reports. Then, according to the number of persons concerned, money and rice shall be allotted from the public account to educational officials for equal disbursement. . . ." See *Hsüeh-cheng*, 32/2 b–3 a, edict of 1738.

[178] Ku Yen-wu, "T'ing-ling wen-chi," 1/17 b–18 a, in *T'ing-ling i-shu shih-chung.*

as tax. Ting also pointed out that the *min-hu* in the countryside were treated even worse than the *min-hu* who lived in the city.[179]

On another occasion, similar discrimination was revealed at T'ung-chou, Kiangsu, in the tax collection from *shen-hu* and *hsiang-hu*, respectively.[180] Governor Ting pointed out that one of the reasons for such wide discrepancy of rates was that the correct amount of land taxes was often unknown to taxpayers. Therefore, he ordered that *chou* and *hsien* magistrates should announce publicly the different rates of land taxes to be paid by owners of different grades of land.[181] He emphasized the need for equitable collection and ordered the abolishment of such terms as *ta-hu* and *hsiao-hu.* He maintained that gentry and commoners should be treated equally in tax collection. Any gentry members who relied on their position and refused to pay taxes, or tried to pay less, thus shifting the burden to the *hsiao-hu*, should be reported by the magistrates for punishment.[182] The effectiveness of these orders is difficult to appraise. On one occasion, Ting contended that the terms *ta-hu* and *hsiao-hu* had been abolished and that there was no discrimination in payment. But he admitted that the malpractice of permitting false reports on bad harvests still persisted, leaving loopholes in the tax collection system.[183]

The inequality of tax payment posed such a serious problem in nineteenth-century China that some members of the gentry themselves proposed the principle of tax equalization. A Kiangsu gentry leader, Feng Kuei-fen, in 1853, argued for tax equalization in a series of four articles, each addressed to a different audience. In the first article, addressed to the officials, he appealed to their self-interest, saying that the blame for corruption fell upon them and implying that they received very little profit. He argued that tax equalization would reduce the cost of collection and leave no opportunity for graft among clerks and runners. In the fourth article, addressed to the commoners, he said that they would benefit from his proposal and warned them against believing rumors spread by clerks and runners who would try to block the measure by suggesting illegal ways of avoiding or paying less tax. In his

[179] Ting Jih-ch'ang, *op. cit.*, 22/1 a–2 b. He goes on to say that the local officials pretended to hate such malpractices but actually felt grateful towards the gentry. He says there were comparatively few *shen-hu*, but the local officials could use their existence as an excuse in reporting their inability to collect the full amount of taxes according to quota. See also 23/1 a–4 b. For some more examples of differences in tax payment between *ta-hu* and *hsiao-hu* in several provinces of the Yangtze region, see also Hsia Nan, "Land Tax Problems in Yangtze Provinces Before and After the Taiping Period," *Ch'ing-hua hsüeh-pao*, *chüan* 10, No. 2, April 1935, pp. 414–16.

[180] Ting Jih-ch'ang, *op. cit.*, 20/3 b, says that some T'ung-chou people went directly to the capital and accused local yamen clerks of overtaxation. The governor investigated and found that the *shen-hu* paid only 2,800 cash for each picul of rice to be collected as tax, while the *hsiang-hu* paid as much as 18,000 cash for each picul.

[181] *Ibid.*, 5/3 b–4 b.

[182] *Ibid.*, 21/2 b.

[183] *Ibid.*, 1/9 b.

second and third articles, Feng spoke to an upper and lower level of the gentry respectively. To the upper gentry, Feng pleaded that since all were taxpayers, why should one pay more than the other? He raised the following questions: Can one guarantee that his heir would be gentry and not a commoner? Can one guarantee that his heir would have farms? Can one guarantee that he would have an heir? To the lower gentry, Feng pointed out that the lesser payment by the gentry gave the clerks an excuse for an extra high extortion from the commoners. The profit of this extortion was divided in such a way that the lower gentry scarcely profited; the clerks and runners had the lion's share of one hundred portions, the officials ten portions, the upper gentry two to three portions, while the lower gentry had only one portion or even less. They gained little but received all the blame and were the scapegoats when trouble arose. Feng added that the Kiangsu provincial director-of-studies, upon whom these lower gentry would have to rely, worked with the officials against them. Would it not then be better for the gentry if the tax burden were equalized?[184]

But, in general, the gentry had no such qualms—and perhaps better percentages.

In trying to avoid payment of the land tax or grain tribute, gentry members often purposely delayed payment in the hope that finally they would evade it. To meet these conditions, a number of regulations were set forth to prevent such occurrences. In the land tax records, gentry members' names were to be marked with signs so that they could be punished if they refused to pay taxes.[185] It was also provided that a separate record should be kept for the gentry, which would clearly show the amount to be paid by them and their actual payment.[186] Such measures were first mentioned in prenineteenth-century times and were reiterated in the nineteenth century.[187]

Gentry members who refused or delayed the payment of taxes could be deprived of their positions and could also be given additional punishment. They could resume their positions only after their tax accounts were cleared. Furthermore, the local officials were required to report once each year to their

[184] Feng Kuei-fen, *Hsien-chih-t'ang kao*, 9/23 a–26 a, articles written in 1853. See also *Huang-ch'ao chin-shih-wen hsü-pien*, compiled by Ke Shih-chün, 31/2 a–b.

[185] *Shih-li*, 172/5 b, in an edict of 1728.

[186] *Ibid.*, in an edict of 1730.

[187] An edict of 1658 stated that gentry members who delayed payment of taxes would be punished according to proportion of nonpayment. Local officials who tried to conceal the facts would be impeached. In 1660, it was mentioned that in the report of collection of taxes by the magistrates, the amount not paid by the gentry should be clearly noted. This information would be submitted to the governors-general and governors for decision on punishment. See *ibid.*, 172/4 b. In the nineteenth century it was also required that the *chou* and *hsien* magistrates should report in separate records the amount of tax owed by the gentry and recommend such gentry members for impeachment. See *Ta-ch'ing lü-li hui-chi pien-lan*, 11/11 a–b.

superiors and the Board of Revenue on gentry members who had not paid taxes, so that measures for punishment could be taken.[188] The following is a detailed regulation governing punishment:

> The amount of land taxes and grain tribute to be paid will be counted in ten parts. If less than four parts are not paid, *chü-jen* will be deprived of their titles and *kung-sheng*, *chien-sheng*, and *sheng-yüan* will be deprived of their titles and receive sixty lashes. If the amount owed is less than seven parts, besides deprival of titles, *chü-jen* will receive eighty lashes, *kung-sheng*, *chien-sheng*, and *sheng-yüan* will wear the cangue for two months and receive one hundred lashes. . . . The civil and military metropolitan graduates and those who have official titles and reside at their native places will receive the same punishment as *chü-jen*.[189]

Despite such regulations, records of violation were plentiful in the nineteenth century. When the government became weaker, the gentry's refusal to pay taxes even led to local rebellion. In one locality, for instance, gentry members organized thousands of people in a movement to refuse tax payment. They burned the yamen and looted the city.[190] In another locality, one gentry member collected money privately according to land ownership and forbade the owners to pay tax to the government.[191]

The cases in which the gentry refused to pay part or all of their land tax and grain tribute occurred mainly in south and east China. As the main land tax and grain tribute burden of the country was borne by these areas, gentry members there were more affected by these taxes, and the government was more concerned with the malpractices in taxation occurring there. Northern and western China, however, were heavily burdened with labor conscription, and here too the gentry tried to misuse their power.[192]

188 *Ch'in-ting ta-Ch'ing hui-tien*, 18/3 b.

189 *Ta-Ch'ing lü-li hui-chi pien-lan*, 11/8 a–b. In *Shih-li*, 330/1 b, there is an edict approving a Chekiang provincial director-of-studies' strict measure of not admitting to provincial examinations *sheng-yüan* who had not cleared their tax payment. The edict discusses the past collusion of *sheng-yüan* with yamen runners in nonpayment of taxes and monopolizing tax collection. This edict was issued in 1728, showing that in early periods, forbiddance to participate in higher examinations was already considered as severe punishment, while according to later regulations gentry were automatically excluded from examinations once they were deprived of their titles. Gentry members who were salt merchants were deprived of their titles if they failed to pay the salt tax. In Tso Tsung-t'ang, *Tso Wen-hsiang-kung ch'üan-chi*, 19/84 ff., a memorial dated T'ung-chih 5/10/12 (1866) requested that the degree of provincial graduate be restored to several salt merchants since they had promised to pay their overdue salt tax.

190 *Shantung chün-hsing chi-lüeh*, 22 B/3 b ff. The incident occurred in 1858 at Lo-an. The leaders were a military *chü-jen* and a *sheng-yüan* with stipend.

191 *Ibid.*, 22 B–6 a. One landowner who disobeyed had his house burned. The incident occurred in 1858 at Ch'i-ho. The gentry member involved was a *sheng-yüan* with stipend.

192 Thus, it was said that to gain the people's allegiance, in the north and west the practice of labor conscription should be abolished, and in the south and east the heavy burden of tax should be reduced. See Chin Wen-pang's letter to P'eng on abolishing labor conscription and reducing the heavy tax burden, in *Huang-ch'ao chin-shih-wen hsü-pien*, compiled by Sheng K'ang, 38/31 a–35 a; see also T'u Chih-shen's memorial on equalization of labor conscription in Chihli in *Shih-li*, 172/7 a, and in *Chi-fu t'ung-chih*, 94/3876–3880.

The inequality in allocation of labor conscription and the practices of gentry in helping others avoid labor service were discussed quite frequently during the Ch'ing dynasty. The problem appeared early in an edict on the situation in Shantung. There commoners had allowed their land to be reported by the gentry as belonging to the latter. The commoners thereby escaped labor conscription since the gentry were legally exempted from it.[193] In contrast to taxes, labor conscription levies were not expressed in definite amounts. As pointed out in one memorial to the Emperor, this gave rise to irregularities through the introduction of numerous varieties of conscript labor. The labor conscription levies were generally based upon the amount of land owned. In many cases, people of the same family name would buy an official title for one of their group, and this titleholder arranged exemption from labor conscription for all of the same family name. As a consequence, the area of land upon which labor conscription was based decreased; this resulted in a heavier burden on the rest. Thus, the memorial pointed out, for the hard-working peasants the burden of labor conscription levies was often ten times that of the regular land tax.[194]

Also, as another memorial pointed out, while the people were allowed at times to delay payment of the regular tax and sometimes even to defer payment indefinitely, the money tax in lieu of labor conscription was levied upon them at all times, even in famine years.[195] In addition, many such collections of money in lieu of labor conscription were of unreportable nature, and the clerks, runners, and soldiers collected more funds than needed, while some gentry members also participated in these transactions.[196]

[193] *Shih-li*, 172/5 a, an edict of 1690.

[194] *Chi-fu t'ung-chih*, 94/3876 ff.; there are five memorials in these pages on the uneven distribution of labor service levies. In Wang Ch'ing-yün, *op. cit.*, 1/25 b–28 b, it was pointed out that in 1690 it was already ordered that gentry members should pay labor conscription levies on their land just like the commoners; this order was issued when the Emperor learned of frequent cases of land being falsely reported as belonging to the gentry. In the nineteenth century the situation became worse. Cf. also Pai Ching-wei, *op. cit.*, 1/6 a–9 b, a memorial written in 1880, reporting the reduction of labor conscription levies in Shensi.

[195] See memorial by Yen Chin-ming, proposing the reduction of the heavy labor conscription in Shensi and Shansi, in *Ch'ing-ch'ao hsü wen-hsien t'ung k'ao*, 28/7797; or in *Shih-lu*, Te-tsung, 95/11 a–12 a; or in *Tung-hua hsü-lu*, 28/18 a–19 b, a memorial written in 1880. Another memorial in 1882, by Chang Chih-tung, urging the reduction of labor service levies in north China contains an article written by Kao Yen-ti on the suffering of the people who were drafted to pull official boats that passed their locality; see *Ch'ing-ch'ao hsü wen-hsien t'ung-k'ao*, 28/7799.

[196] *Mu-ling-shu*, 11/54 a–57 a, contains an article on labor conscription by Chang Chieh in which he described what he saw during his more than ten years in office as a magistrate in Chihli. He said: "Every year Chihli had to pay the expenses of bridge and road repairs and other expenses on the occasions of the Emperor's visits to the hunting grounds and to the mausoleums. Some of these expenses were difficult to declare, and the commissioners and intendants shifted these burdens to the *chou* and *hsien* magistrates, who in turn shifted them to the people. All this had started when a high official reported personally to the Emperor that such expenses would not be borne by the people; therefore, since that time

In many localities, the gentry even went so far as to usurp the actual collection of taxes. Some gentry members handled the taxes of landowners of the same surnames, while others went a step further and forbade the commoner landowners to deliver their own tax payments. In the words of Feng Kuei-fen, some gentry not only specialized in delivering taxes for others but also specialized in nondelivery of taxes for others.[197] They pocketed what should have been handed over to the government.

Such practices persisted throughout Ch'ing times despite constant efforts of the government to stop them. As early as 1696 an edict was issued to forbid the use of such terms as *ta-hu* and *hsiao-hu* in the collection of taxes:

> The bad practice of Hunan is that in the *li* and *chia*[198] the households are divided into *ta-hu* and *hsiao-hu*. The *ta-hu* suppress the *hsiao-hu* as they wish, and in the payment of taxes the *ta-hu* collect them and will not let the *hsiao-hu* pay directly, while some will even drive the *hsiao-hu* to serve them. Hereafter, *hsiao-hu* are ordered to move out of the *chia* of the *ta-hu* and establish their own *li* and *chia*. After the records are compiled, *hsiao-hu* should pay taxes by themselves. Any malpractices of controlling tax payment, refusal of tax payment, extortion, or additional imposition of taxes on the people will call for impeachment by the governors-general and governors for punishment.[199]

In 1724 the Emperor again called on the governors-general and governors to punish *sheng-yüan* and *chien-sheng* who were relying on their position to monopolize the tax payments of others—*sheng-yüan* who called themselves *ju-hu* and *chien-sheng* who called themselves *kuan-hu*.[200] And only three years later, a similar edict was issued.[201]

In the nineteenth century such practices must have become even more frequent, judging from the number of edicts discussing the matter. For in-

the actual situation had never been reported. Because such collections could not be reported, commissioners sent men to order the collection verbally and did not order it through official correspondence. The corrupt magistrates would then try to collect twice the assigned amount. But the magistrates were in turn afraid of the gentry and dared not allocate the burden equally according to ownership of land." According to Chang Chieh, in the northern part of Chihli, in some districts the banners had 30 per cent of the burden and the people 70 per cent, while in others the banners did not take part. In the southern part of Chihli, in some districts the gentry had 30 per cent of the burden while the people had 70 per cent, and in other districts the gentry did not take part. He suggested that the burden should be allotted equally according to land ownership and that even if the gentry were treated differently than the people, there should be a limit to the amount of exemption. He also maintained that those who had become *chien-sheng* and officials through purchase were well-to-do and should participate in public affairs rather than be exempted from money tax in lieu of labor conscription. As the situation actually existed, the main labor conscription burden in Chihli was not borne by the magistrates or by rich gentry and big merchants but by the poor people who owned only a few *mou* of land.

197 Feng Kuei-fen, *op. cit.*, 5/36 b, in a letter written in 1853.

198 Tax collection units; see footnote no. 47.

199 *Shih-li*, 172/5 a.

200 *Shih-li*, 172/5 a–b; also see *Shih-lu*, Shih-tsung, 16/21 b–22 a. In the latter, *kuan-hu* is called *huan-hu*.

201 *Shih-li*, 172/19 b.

stance, in 1826 the Emperor discussed the problem of rich and powerful families and those who could exercise some influence by calling themselves *ta-hu* and monopolizing the collection of grain tribute.[202] In 1842 an edict referred especially to the gentry of Ch'ung-yang, Hupeh, and ordered the punishment of those who monopolized tax collection.[203] In both 1846 and 1865 the use of the terms *ta-hu* and *hsiao-hu* were prohibited again in Kiangsu.[204] In both 1864 and 1865 such prohibition of the terms *ta-hu* and *hsiao-hu* occurred in Chekiang.[205] And in 1882 the monopolization of tax collections by *shen-hu* in Anhwei was condemned.[206]

Refusal of tax payment and participation in tax collection were not the only ways in which the gentry could gain economic advantages. There were many other ways in which the gentry could share in the profits of the administration. Some gentry members tried to share in the profits of officials holding offices in the river works and salt administration or presiding over some rich localities where corruption was known to exist. In one edict the Emperor said that he had heard that officials, *chü-jen*, *kung-sheng*, *sheng-yüan*, and *chien-sheng*, and personal secretaries to officials, while passing by the river works project in Chiang-nan, requested and received financial assistance from officials in charge there. He alleged that such practices must have also occurred in the river works in Honan and Shantung and in the salt administration in various provinces and ordered severe punishment for such malpractices in the future.[207]

Such malpractices among the gentry were sometimes furthered through the coöperation of the clerks and runners and sometimes through the coöperation of the officials themselves. In one locality, for instance, the gentry and the clerks collaborated in extorting payments from commoners.[208] In another case involving a controversy between some gentry landowners and peasants, the officials were called unfair in their adjudication of the case.[209]

The collaboration between gentry and officials for their mutual profit was

[202] *Shih-lu*, Hsüan-tsung, 111/16 a–18 b; also see *Ch'ing-ch'ao hsü wen-hsien t'ung-k'ao*, 2/7511.

[203] *Shih-li*, 172/7 a.

[204] In 1846 the discussion was based on Po-chün's memorial; see *Shih-lu*, Hsüan-tsung, 435/9 a–10 a; also *Shih-li*, 207/4 b; and *Ch'ing-ch'ao hsü wen-hsien t'ung-k'ao*, 2/7513–14. For the case of 1865, see *Shih-lu*, Mu-tsung, 146/15 a–17 a.

[205] *Shih-li*, 172/7 b; see also *Shih-lu*, Mu-tsung, 129/15 a–16 a.

[206] *Shih-li*, 172/7 b–8 a.

[207] *Shih-lu*, Hsüan-tsung, 401/5 a–6 b.

[208] Tso Tsung-t'ang, *op. cit.*, 18/24 ff., in a memorial dated T'ung-chih 5/5/18 (1866).

[209] *Ibid.*, 19/68 ff., memorial dated T'ung-chih 5/10/8, reporting results of investigation of a murder case involving a controversy between a gentry landowner and a peasant, and recommending punishment for several officials for unfairness. *Ibid.*, 20/50 ff., a memorial dated T'ung-chih 5/10/16, referring to the same case, reports the unauthorized execution of some persons convicted of burning houses and recommends punishment for the officials responsible.

furthered by frequent visits and the exchange of gifts. Such practices were frowned upon by the imperial government which disapproved of too much intimacy between the gentry and the local officials.[210]

The gentry also were often successful in infringing upon the judicial authority of the government. Regulations indicate that the government tried to stop such practices. One regulation forbade the gentry to possess instruments of punishment or torture,[211] but actual cases show that violations occurred.[212] Some gentry members, relying on their position, visited the yamen frequently and interfered in local administration. They monopolized law suits and were accused of oppressing the village people. Such practices were said to be common and the Emperor repeatedly stressed their prohibition.[213] Governor Ting Jih-ch'ang's directives to *hsien* magistrates on different occasions again indicate the active interference of gentry members in law suits. In one case, the gentry member convicted of interfering in lawsuits was a *sheng-yüan*; [214] in a second case, a *chien-sheng* and a *sheng-yüan*; [215] and in a third case, a holder of the title of *tu-ssu* or "first captain." [216]

There were innumerable other ways in which the gentry could take advantage of their privileged position. To mention but a few more, along the Kwangtung coast beach lands extended by natural causes were claimed by the gentry as private property.[217] Temples were sometimes controlled by gentry who used them as their personal property.[218] On other occasions, land belonging to temples was confiscated through gentry effort, the rent being reserved for gentry benefit.[219] Gambling was often backed by gentry who could obtain fees from gamblers.[220] One report describes a struggle between incumbent officials and local gentry over the collection of fees from gambling clubs.[221]

[210] *Shih-li*, 389/1 a.

[211] Wu Yung-kuang, *op. cit.*, 23/10 b.

[212] Ting Jih-ch'ang, *op. cit.*, 7/7 a.

[213] T'ien Wen-ching, "Ch'in-pan chou-hsien shih-i," in *Huan-hai chih-nan wu-chung*, 383/1 a ff.; *Ch'in-ting ta-Ch'ing hui-tien*, 32/3 b; *Hsüeh-cheng*, 4/2 b–4 b.

[214] Ting Jih-ch'ang, *op. cit.*, 7/7 a.

[215] *Ibid.*, 28/2 b; upon the occasion of the arrival of a magistrate, Ting pointed out that one *chien-sheng* and one *sheng-yüan* of that *hsien* were known always to interfere in law suits and advised him to be careful. *Ibid.*, 30/5 b–6 a; it was directed that the *chien-sheng* be punished.

[216] *Ibid.*, 23/7 b; the offender was deprived of his title. Ting also directed the magistrate concerned to check on another military *chü-jen* who was said to be monopolizing lawsuits.

[217] *Kuang-chou fu-chih*, 5/13 a–b, edict of 1866, quoting the censor's request to measure such lands and increase the revenue of the state.

[218] *Ibid.*, 7/18 b–19 a.

[219] *Ch'eng-hsien chih*, 6/21–26. Rent was reserved to meet expenses of local examinations and to pay traveling subsidies for candidates.

[220] *Chiu-chiang ju-lin-hsiang chih*, 2/41 a–b; the *chü-jen* concerned was also charged with embezzling relief funds and monopolizing lawsuits. The governor-general ordered deprival of title and punishment.

[221] Kuo Sung-tao, *op. cit.*, 5/18 a–b, a case of 1865. It was reported that the acting

The gentry's participation in the management of local affairs also gave them opportunities for economic gains. For example, there were malpractices in the management of the "ever-normal" granaries. The purpose of the granaries was to lend grain in the spring and collect grain in the autumn so that the people would receive help, while the grain stored thus had a yearly turnover and did not decay. However, it was often not the poor but the gentry and local bullies who received the benefit of the loans.[222]

Thus, in actual practice, the dominant position of the gentry group afforded its members many opportunities for economic gains and other advantages which extended far beyond their formal privileges.

GENTRY FUNCTIONS

The gentry as a social group with a leading position and special privileges performed certain social functions. They concerned themselves with the promotion of the welfare and the protection of the interests of their respective home areas. They represented the interests of their areas vis-à-vis the government officials. They undertook many tasks such as welfare activities, arbitration, public works, and at times the organization of local military corps or the collection of taxes. Their cultural leadership encompassed all the values of Confucian society but was also materially expressed in such actions as the preservation of village temples, schools, and examination halls.

These functions of the gentry were not related to the ownership or location of privately owned land. They were related rather to administrative areas. All gentry functioned in the area of their native districts, but some functioned within a still larger administrative unit—their home prefecture or even their home province. A lower gentry member, belonging to the district government school and having close contacts with district educational officials and the district magistrate, could function effectively within his district but seldom beyond it. It was mostly the upper gentry whose influence and activities extended over a broader area. The connections they established as well as the higher prestige they obtained from passing the advanced examinations gave them close contacts with high provincial officials and with other upper gentry of their provinces.

This point is illustrated in the life of Pai Ching-wei, a *chü-jen* of Shensi, who never held office but who was well known as a scholar and was extremely active and influential in the affairs of his province. In his correspondence with the governor and other provincial officials as well as with upper gentry

lieutenant at Hsin-hui, Kwangtung, arrested a military *chü-jen* and his clique, including some military *sheng-yüan* and *chien-sheng*, and falsely accused them of robbery because of a struggle to control the gambling clubs.

members of the province, he discussed many matters related to provincial affairs.[223] His advice and assistance were highly regarded and one governor after another sought his advice.[224] Among other responsibilities, Pai took charge of relief work for two localities,[225] managed defense work in three prefectures,[226] and promoted an organization to grant subsidies to candidates of metropolitan examinations from several districts.[227]

The life of Wang Shih-to, a *chü-jen* of Kiangsu, also illustrates the broader area of upper gentry functions. He corresponded with high provincial officials on a wide variety of subjects related to provincial affairs. He gave advice on military strategy and petitioned on mining activities in two prefectures,[228] and was also the chief compiler of the gazetteer of his prefecture, Chiang-ning.

The correspondence between gentry rank and functional area will be touched upon again in the later detailed discussion of the specific tasks which the gentry performed.

There are also indications that gentry members tended to move to the administrative centers and that rising in gentry status was often associated with moving to a more important town or city. The two upper gentry members just mentioned, who were so active in their provinces, both resided in the provincial capital. The biography of a Shensi gentry member, whose commoner ancestors had resided in a certain village for generations, shows that he moved to the city and became actively engaged in local defense.[229] In another example, a *chü-jen*, a native of another district of Shensi, took up residence in the provincial capital and participated in relief work for the province.[230] An expectant subprefect through the "irregular" route, who was rich and charitable in his village with several hundred households depending on him, moved to his district city. There he collected a large library which he opened to other scholars, thus helping to prepare the way for his son, who became a "regular" gentry member and was active in district affairs.[231]

Many of the tasks carried out by the gentry were of use to the government. They were tasks which might otherwise have been handled by officials. However, the official staff was too small and the funds inadequate to carry

[222] See T'ien Wen-ching, "Ch'in-pan chou-hsien shih-i," in *Huan-hai chih-nan wu-chung*, pp. 13 b–15 b.

[223] Pai Ching-wei, *Feng-hsi ts'ao-t'ang chi*, *chüan* 2 and 3.

[224] *Ibid.*, Pai's biography, p. 1 a–b.

[225] *Ibid.*, 2/15 a–16 a.

[226] *Ibid.*, 6/12 a.

[227] *Ibid.*, 6/21 b.

[228] Wang Shih-to, *Wang Mei-ts'un hsien-sheng chi,* 10/5 b–6 b, 8 a–9 a. Cf. also *Hsü-tsuan Chiang-ning fu-chih*, 15/78 b ff.

[229] Pai Ching-wei, *op. cit.*, 5/17 b–18 a.

[230] *Shensi t'ung-chih kao*, 84/73 b.

[231] *Ibid.*, 88/12 a–b.

out all the necessary tasks, particularly in the field of local government. Moreover, the officials were handicapped by their short terms of office and their unfamiliarity with local conditions. Government regulations limited the time of official service at any one post and provided also that no official should hold office in his home area. These measures, which had the purpose of preventing officials from establishing local connections and power, also had the effect of hampering their efficiency. In the words of an official, "Officials will be transferred, unlike the gentry who stay at the place and are intimately associated with it. The officials are walled off, unlike the gentry who are close to see and hear.[232]

Of the officials the district magistrates were closest to the life of the people at large. The district magistrate was the sole administrator of a district which could have a population of several hundred thousand people. His difficulty in governing so many people was greatly increased by the brevity of his term of office. Table 2 shows the actual periods of tenure of such magistrates in the districts of Lu-i in Honan and Ch'ang-ning in Hunan.[233]

TABLE 2

ACTUAL TERMS IN OFFICE OF DISTRICT MAGISTRATES

Reign	Lu-i, Honan		Ch'ang-ning, Hunan	
	Number of magistrates	Average term	Number of magistrates	Average term
Shun-chih (1644–1661)	7	2.6 yrs.	4	4.5 yrs.
K'ang-hsi (1662–1722)	11	5.5	14	4.3
Yung-cheng (1723–1735)	5	2.6	5	2.6
Ch'ien-lung (1736–1795).......	17	3.5	15	4.0
Chia-ch'ing (1796–1820)	18	1.4	15	1.7
Tao-kuang (1821–1850)	19	1.6	32	1.0
Hsien-feng (1851–1861)	9	1.2	13	.9*
T'ung-chih (1862–1874)	10	1.3	12	1.1
Kuang-hsü †	23	.9	18	1.5

* Including one who came back to the same office three times; thus the actual time in office could be revised to a higher average figure.

† For Lu-i, the Kuang-hsü records covered the years 1875 to 1897; for Ch'ang-ning, 1875 to 1901.

These records show that the terms of office of the district magistrates were quite short during the whole period of the Ch'ing dynasty and that during the nineteenth century these terms shrank abruptly, the average term of the cases examined ranging from 1.7 to as little as .9 years. This made it difficult

[232] *Huang-ch'ao chin-shih-wen hsü-pien*, compiled by *Sheng K'ang*, 82/45 a, in a memorial by Hui-ch'ing.

[233] *Kuang-hsü Lu-i hsien-chih*, 11 *hsia*/1 a–14 a; *Ch'ang-ning hsien-chih*, 2/2 b.

for any local official to know his district and lessened his interest in any project the results of which he could not see during his time in office.

Official action, especially in the districts, was therefore extremely limited, and actions by the gentry often took the place of administrative actions by the government. Such gentry actions may be called "quasi-official" since the gentry were acting in lieu of the government but not as an agency of the government. The gentry remained a social group and acted on a voluntary basis.

The gentry sometimes acted under the command of officials and in assistance to official actions. In other cases the officials initiated actions for the gentry to carry out but left the latter considerable freedom in their execution. In still other cases the gentry initiated actions for which it gained the approval of the officials and sometimes actual official support, financially or otherwise. Often, however, the gentry simply went ahead with activities which the officials silently accepted or reluctantly tolerated. The coöperation between the officials and the gentry varied according to the task to be performed and also according to the situation of the moment. In times of crisis when the officials' ability to handle their duties was weakened and the problems to be settled increased, the sphere of gentry action naturally expanded. In the words of Hu Lin-i, one of the outstanding governors of the Taiping period, "Since the beginning of the insurrections, officials could do nothing successfully on local affairs without the help of the gentry." [234]

The gentry acted as intermediaries between the government officials and the local people. As indicated earlier, they often advised the officials on the conduct of local affairs, and there were some gentry members whose advice and assistance were repeatedly sought by the local officials.[235] But in representing the interests of their areas, the gentry sometimes came into conflict with the officials. For example, in Canton during the time of the Opium War, a row occurred between all the *sheng-yüan* of a school and the prefect, who seems to have been supporting the foreigners. The *sheng-yüan* ridiculed the prefect, called him a traitor, and finally forced him to resign his office. A contemporary account described the incident as follows:

> On the 16th instant, his honor Yu Paoshun, the prefect of Canton, decked with his "new feather," proceeded in the due course of duty to the Great Hall of Examination, where the literary candidates had assembled for their annual exercises. On his entering, some of these high spirited gentry seemed restive, showed symptoms of discontent, and began to ridicule him. For this they were called to order and sharply reprimanded; whereupon the public voice broke forth. The gentry became clamorous, began to hiss, called his honor a traitor, and hurled their inkstones

[234] Hu Lin-i, *Hu Wen-chung-kung ch'üan-chi,* 4/1057.
[235] *Yunnan t'ung-chih*, 158/34 a.

at his head. Unable to withstand such missiles, the old gentleman determined to withdraw; but on leaving the Hall, one of the most daring of the malcontents attempted to break his chair. A row ensued. The Nanhai hsien, who is second in authority to the prefect, then came forward, soothed these excited literati, and begged them to come again next day for examination, when the judicial commissioner would come to the Hall. On the 18th the prefect had resolved to resign his office immediately. This he has done.[236]

As spokesmen for their areas, the gentry sometimes persuaded the government to accept their point of view. For instance, a retired official, a member of the Soochow gentry, with the backing of other upper gentry succeeded in gaining a reduction of taxes for a large section of his province through his writings and through his contact with the governor who supported his stand in memorials to the throne.[237]

During the Taiping Rebellion, when Soochow had been lost to the rebels and Shanghai was in danger, the upper gentry of Shanghai and those who had fled from Soochow persuaded Tseng Kuo-fan to send Li Hung-chang to protect Shanghai and to recapture Soochow.[238]

In other examples, it is clear that even high provincial officials feared the local gentry who had access to the court and could force them out of their official positions. For instance, a Szechwan official said that he was fortunate to be in a province farther away from the capital and less subject to accusations at court by members of the gentry. As he put it, "Heaven is high and the Emperor is far away." But a gentry member retorted, "The Emperor may be far away, but heaven is near."[239]

In some instances, the gentry used their influence with the government to impose their wishes on local officials. In others, it was the gentry's position as local leaders which was their source of strength. For instance, in Kiangsu, when Kao-yu and other districts had been damaged by flood, a *sheng-yüan* of Kao-yu aroused the people of the city to demand relief despite the governor's memorial to the contrary. The people gathered, refused to open their shops for trade, carried statues of the gods about the streets, and disturbed the yamen.[240]

[236] *The Chinese Repository*, X, No. 9, Sept. 1841, pp. 527–8. Cf. also *Ch'üeh-shan hsien-chih*, 24/16 b, where it is stated that "officials and gentry frequently did not maintain a good relation with each other. With a few troublesome gentry arousing the sentiment, the evil consequences were beyond description." Also see *T'ung-ch'uan fu-chih*, 25/9 a.

[237] Feng Kuei-fen, *op. cit.*, 5/33 a–35 a, also 4/6 a ff. This was Feng's celebrated contribution to the resulting reduction in land tax rates for Soochow, Sung-chiang, and T'ai-tsang in Kiangsu.

[238] Cf. Ch'ien Ting-ming's biography collected by the State Historiography Office in *Ch'ien Ming-su-kung tsou-su*, pp. 1 b–2 a.

[239] *T'ung-ch'uan fu-chih*, 25/9 a. Also see *Hsü-chou fu-chih* (Szechwan), 33/65, where officials at court were described as complaining about mass executions occurring at their native places despite the attempt of the governor of that province to block the complaint.

[240] *Hsüeh-cheng*, 7/17 b.

A great deal of the practical management of local affairs was in the hands of the gentry. Numerous examples in local gazetteers show their very frequent activities in such public works as the repairing of roads, the building of bridges, the dredging of rivers, the construction of dikes, and the promotion of irrigation projects. Examples are given below to illustrate the types of activities in which the gentry engaged and also the range of coöperation between the gentry and the officials.

In the Tao-kuang period a *chien-sheng* of Hua-chou in Shensi financed the building of more than 100 *li* of roads through the mountains, spending 10,000 taels on the project.[241] An official titleholder of Ch'en-ch'eng promoted the construction of a stone bridge and repaired more than ten *li* of hilly roads. He financed these projects and set up a fund to provide for their upkeep.[242] In Ch'u-chou, Chekiang, it is recorded that in the Chia-ch'ing period a *sheng-yüan* spent 14,000 taels on bridge building.[243]

A tabulation of information contained in a local gazetteer shows the gentry's activities in the construction and repair of bridges and ferries in Hui-chou prefecture, Kwangtung, during the Ch'ing dynasty: [244]

	Bridges	*Ferries*
Joint effort of officials and gentry	3	1
Officials	10	1
Gentry	34	17
Commoners	18*	4
Unspecified	48	72

* The gazetteer indicates that those listed under commoner sponsorship were mostly wooden bridges and therefore less costly than the many stone bridges credited to officials and gentry. Those listed for officials and gentry were credited to individuals, while those listed for commoners were sometimes joint efforts of villagers or supported by clan funds.

The gentry's part in such activities is also indicated in the following tabulation compiled from a local gazetteer of Jung-hsien, Kwangsi: [245]

	Bridges	*Ferries*
Officials	3	—
Gentry	52	21
Unspecified	32	22

In another example, during a flood in the Kuang-hsü period, a *sheng-yüan* of Sian, Shensi, who was active in local affairs, initiated and solicited funds for dredging a river and directing the water into the Wei River. He also assisted officials in the dredging of the Ming River.[246]

241 *Shensi t'ung-chih kao*, 89/10 b.
242 *Ibid.*, 89/4 b.
243 *Ch'u-chou fu-chih*, 20/9 a.
244 *Hui-chou fu-chih*, *chüan* 5.
245 *Jung-hsien chih*, 8/8 ff.
246 *Shensi t'ung-chih kao*, 84/10 a-b.

A *fu-kung-sheng* of Sung-yang, Chekiang, promoted the building of dikes and contributed the sum of 2,000 taels to the project.[247]

These are examples of the many projects which were handled by individual members of the gentry and which were of great importance in the everyday life of the people. In projects covering a larger area, a number of gentry would pool their resources and abilities to plan and carry through the work. Members of the upper gentry usually took the lead. Often the provincial officials stepped in to direct or to assist in coördinating the work of the various districts concerned. But whether the projects were directed by officials or by gentry, the latter shouldered the main burden of the execution.

For example, in Lu-chou, Anhwei, in 1879 the building of dams was carried out through gentry effort. The work is described in an article by an upper gentry member of this prefecture. In this area three-tenths of the one million *mou* of farmland were in hilly regions while the rest was vulnerable to flood. By building dams and closing them during the forty to fifty days of danger, floods were prevented and navigation was made possible for the merchants during the rest of the year. Thus, the article concluded, the lives and property of the several million people of the prefecture were protected, while several hundred thousand taels of custom and likin revenues were saved. This project was planned and carried through by a number of gentry members with the support of the provincial officials.[248]

Gentry members often financed such projects with their own money or with funds collected from the local inhabitants, as indicated in examples above.[249] At times, however, they promoted and directed the projects but succeeded in turning over the financial burden to the government. For instance, the repairing of a bridge across the Chang River on the post road at Feng-lo, Honan, had been the responsibility of the local inhabitants of three neighboring districts; eventually the gentry succeeded in lifting the local burden of labor conscription and pecuniary contributions, and the repair funds thereafter came from the provincial treasury.[250] In Huai-an, Kiangsu,

[247] *Ch'u-chou fu-chih*, 20/8 a.

[248] *Hsü-hsiu Lu-chou fu-chih*, 13/29–33.

[249] Additional examples: One official titleholder alone contributed to and supervised the repairing of the road passing the north gate of Tientsin in the Tao-kuang period. See *Tientsin fu-chih*, 43/34 a. One military *sheng-yüan* alone contributed to and supervised the construction of three bridges at Ning-hsiang, Hunan in the Hsien-feng period. See *Hunan t'ung-chih*, 180/3607. In the T'ung-chih period, funds were collected from local inhabitants for a floating bridge constructed in Ch'iao-hsien, Anhwei, through the effort of the gentry. See *Hsü-hsiu Lu-chou fu-chih*, 10/11 b. The same method of financing was used in Yin-hsien, Chekiang, when the gentry initiated the dredging of the rivers which were clogged during the fight with the Taipings. See *Yin-hsien chih*, 9/15–16.

[250] *Lin-chang hsien-chih*, 13/44 a–50 a.

the gentry also succeeded in obtaining funds for the construction of several bridges and dams during the Kuang-hsü period.[251]

Many examples can also be given to show the gentry's part in the promotion of irrigation projects. For instance, in Cho-hsien, Chihli, a *sheng-yüan* of the countryside, who took an active part in such matters as bridge and road construction, establishment of shrines and temples, relief work, and charity schools, also promoted an irrigation project for his locality. In the Chia-ch'ing period, he started a canalization project which irrigated more than 3,000 *mou* (about 500 acres). The gazetteer, which was compiled in the Republican period, states that the villagers were still benefiting from this project.[252]

In Ch'ing-yüan, Chihli, a *chü-jen* who was an influential teacher and was also active in welfare activities became interested in irrigation. During a drought in the Kuang-hsü period he wrote an essay on relief measures in which he pointed out the need for an irrigation project. He secured the coöperation of the local people in promoting and carrying through an irrigation project covering several hundred thousand *mou*. He himself advanced the cost of the labor.[253]

In both these examples, the gentry promoting the projects were concerned with the whole locality rather than with their privately owned land. These two examples also illustrate the usual pattern of gentry action in which the upper gentry functioned in a wider area than the lower gentry.

Another example can be seen in Chien-ch'ang, Kiangsi, a region which was described as partly hilly and partly situated along the lake. Fields in the hilly part suffered from drought while those close to the lake suffered from floods. The records show that the local inhabitants—not the officials—had constructed a total of 513 ponds and dams in the hilly region and had built dikes in the lake region to control the water.[254] Although the records do not specify explicitly whether the local inhabitants were led by gentry in the undertaking of these projects, this was undoubtedly the case since only the active participation of the gentry could have made it technically workable and financially possible.

That the gentry were very much concerned with the problems of irrigation

[251] *Huai-an fu-chih*, 3/20 a, which records that in Kuang-hsü 6, through the petition of Huai-an gentry, the director of grain transport allotted a sum of 3700 taels for the construction of dams there. In Kuang-hsü 10, gentry members were appointed to supervise the construction of several bridges and they obtained from the director of grain transport 2000 taels for the purpose.

[252] *Cho-hsien chih*, 6/25 b–26 a.

[253] *Ch'ing-yüan hsien-chih*, 4/67 a–b.

[254] *Chien-ch'ang hsien hsiang-t'u-chih*, 12/1 b–2 b.

and considered themselves responsible for such work can be seen in their writings. One article by a gentry member of Honan discussed the existence of an "historic" dam, which had long since fallen into decay, and argued for its reconstruction. He blamed the gentry because they had not maintained the dam and named them as the logical group to promote the reconstruction work.[255]

A gentry member of Chekiang was so interested in irrigation problems of his own and neighboring areas that he traveled extensively through many localities of Kiangsu and Chekiang and carefully studied the causes of flood and drought. He worked out detailed plans for correcting the situation throughout the entire area, pointing out at which places rivers should be dredged and at which places water should be conserved. His book on *Southeast Irrigation Problems*, in which these plans were set forth, was published during the Hsien-feng period.[256] His plans were taken seriously and were used on several occasions when actual construction was undertaken.[257]

In some gazetteers the officials were credited with the responsibility for large irrigation projects. But where further information is given in attached memorials, reports, or articles, in almost all cases the gentry are described as active participants in the carrying out of these projects. The following examples are taken from Sung-chiang prefecture, Kiangsu, where irrigation was of particular importance.[258] Most of the projects concerned large rivers or lakes and were therefore of importance for transportation and flood control as well as for irrigation.

Period	*General statement in gazetteer*	*Explanation in attached memorials, reports, or articles*
Chia-ch'ing 23 (1818)	The governor sent two special officials with instructions to dredge the Wu-sung River.	The governor's memorial reported the gentry's petitions and indicated that the work was executed by the gentry and financed by the local people.
Tao-kuang 3 (1823)	A *hsien* magistrate dredged the Cha-chiang.	An attached article pointed out that the original request came from gentry members and that the work was financed by local inhabitants.
Tao-kuang 4 (1824)	A *hsien* magistrate dredged the Mao-hu.	An attached letter from a gentry member to the magistrate suggested the need for the work and the method of doing it.

255 *Ling-chang hsien-chih*, 16/26 ff. and article by Lü Yu.

256 *Hu-chou fu-chih*, 76/44 b, referring to Ling Chieh-hsi, a *sheng-yüan*.

257 Cf. *Sung-chiang-fu hsü-chih*, 7/24 a–25 a. This gazetteer also refers to the recording of Ling's work in still another gazetteer, *Wu-chiang hsü-chih*.

258 *Sung-chiang-fu hsü-chih*, 7/1 b ff.

Tao-kuang 7 (1827)	The governor instructed an intendant to dredge the Wu-sung River.	The governor's memorial mentioned the censor's suggestion of branch irrigation projects to be directed by gentry and elders and financed according to the practice that landowners supplied provisions and tenants supplied labor.
Tao-kuang 15 (1835)	Magistrates of two neighboring districts dredged the Pai-lien-chin.	An attached article and the compiler's annotation show the action originated with gentry landowners of the localities concerned, and that the work was carried through by the joint effort of the magistrates and the gentry. The article states that the cost was met partly by the people themselves and partly by an official "contribution."
Tao-kuang 16 (1836)	The governor instructed three *hsien* magistrates to dredge the P'u-wei-t'ang.	The attached memorial divides the credit among the officials, gentry and commoners. A petition from gentry of these localities discusses methods of carrying out the work and suggests the maintenance of a large dam. The petition was approved by the governor.
Tao-kuang 26 (1846)	The prefect constructed a dam.	The prefect's article attached stated that the gentry members of the prefecture had discussed this construction work and had requested the former prefect to take action. The advantages of the project had been presented to him by members of the upper gentry. The project was also supported by a financial commissioner who was a native of the locality and was at home because of a mourning period.
T'ung-chih 3 (1864)	An intendant dredged creeks around and within Shanghai.	The intendant's attached article referred to his consultation with gentry and elders on the planning of the work.
T'ung-chih 5 (1866)	*Hsien* magistrates of Lou-hsien, Shanghai, and Nan-hui dredged rivers.	The magistrates' attached reports give the decisions and suggestions arrived at in the meetings of "gentry-managers." The reports indicate that the gentry managed the work and that the officials acted as coordinators between the gentry of the different districts.
T'ung-chih 8 (1869)	*Hsien* magistrates of Lou-hsien, Shanghai, and Ch'ing-p'u dredged rivers and built dikes.	The explanation reveals that in this case the officials instructed "managers of the various units" of the locality to carry out the work. The work was to be financed according to the practice that the landowners supplied provisions and tenants supplied labor. The technical plans which were followed were drawn up by a local man.
T'ung-chih 9 (1870)	*Hsien* magistrates of Hua-t'ing, Ch'ing-p'u, Ching-shan, and Shanghai dredged ponds and rivers.	A notation states that the magistrates gathered the city and countryside "managers" and decided how the work would be financed.

T'ung-chih 9 (1870)	*Hsien* magistrates of the prefecture dredged rivers and ponds.	In one case the gentry petitioned for the work to be done and the officials acted as supervisors. Attached is an article by Ling Chieh-hsi,[259] a gentry member of a neighboring prefecture, who was an authority on irrigation problems of this and other areas of southeast China. In the article Ling discusses technical problems of the work on a large lake and certain rivers. In another case a joint report of the *hsien* magistrates states that the "managers" are taking care of the work. That these "managers" were gentry is again explicitly stated in this case. In a third case the *hsien* magistrates reported on the gentry's completion of the dredging of the Wu-sung River together with a petition from the gentry. The gentry asked that it should not become an established practice to expect them to carry out similar work on this river in the future, as their localities received little benefit from it.

Another gazetteer describes a series of irrigation projects in Ninghsia. In dealing with construction and repair work during the seventeenth and eighteenth centuries, the gazetteer usually credits the provincial officials with the responsibility for such work.[260] How the projects were actually worked out is not discussed. The annual repair of the projects during the eighteenth century is discussed in an article by an official. He mentions a definite number of gentry as sectional supervisors.[261] In the nineteenth century, however, there is very little mention of comparable work credited to officials. Annual repair work was continued and was managed by the gentry. A detailed description is given of annual meetings of the gentry concerned with the various irrigation projects at which they planned the work and assigned definite responsibilities to various members of their group.[262]

In some localities gentry members were the directors of the important labor service bureaus which provided labor for official travel and government communications. These directors were often expected to advance the required funds and were permitted to collect the money tax paid by the local people in lieu of labor service. In this, as in so many other gentry functions, the opportunity for personal gain was considerable.

In Shensi province one such bureau was traditionally managed by gentry rich enough to advance the expenses. Their practice was that "at the end of the year the accounts were burned to avoid trouble." In this particular

[259] The same gentry expert on irrigation referred to above.
[260] *Shuo-fang tao-chih*, 6/5 a–b.
[261] *Ibid.*, 7/21 b ff.
[262] *Ibid.*, 7/3 b.

case, the director decided, as a reform measure, not to burn the books. This turned out unfortunately for him, as he was later charged with having "unclear accounts" and lost a great deal of money.[263]

Gentry members were also responsible for the construction and management of granaries in many localities.[264] Decisions on granary policies could affect prices of agricultural products and could save the poor in times of need. Although the managers of granaries were generally appointed by the magistrates from among the local gentry, records reveal that these managers were usually recommended to the magistrates by influential gentry members of their localities.[265]

The gentry also had a great share in local welfare matters. Sometimes officials took the initiative. In such cases the gentry were invited into the magistrates' office for consultation and were often appointed as managers of relief bureaus.[266] In other cases, officials merely approved the organization of relief works, public cemeteries, foundling homes and other such undertakings, while the funds and management came from the gentry.[267] In the regulations governing the management of foundling homes in one locality, for instance, it was provided that the managers should be selected from among *kung-sheng*, *chien-sheng*, or *sheng-yüan* on the basis of group recommendation by the local gentry.[268] One governor quoted Su Tung-p'o of the Sung dynasty as saying that clerks and runners in the magistrates' offices could not reach high posts and therefore would seek only wealth. According to this governor, charity organizations were much less subject to corruption when managed by the gentry than when managed by clerks or any other group.[269]

By far the majority of examples in local gazetteers show that the gentry were active in initiating and establishing charity organizations as well as in individual almsgiving. Well-to-do elders and commoners sometimes contrib-

[263] Pai Ching-wei, *op. cit.*, 5/12 a–14 a.

[264] *Kuang-chou fu-chih*, 65/14 a.

[265] Pai Ching-wei, *op. cit.*, 2/23 a–24 a.

[266] See Liu Heng's writings on relief measure regulations in *Mu-ling-shu*, 14/58 a–60 a.

[267] See Pai Ching-wei, *op. cit.*, 7/13 a ff.

[268] See Ch'en Hung-mou's writings on regulations regarding foundling homes in *Mu-ling-shu*, 15/23 ff. At the time of writing, Ch'en was the prefect of Yang-chou, Kiangsu. For a biography of Ch'en, see Hummel, *op. cit.*, pp. 86–87. Cf. also *Nan-ning fu-chih*, 15/15 a.

[269] Ting Jih-ch'ang, *op. cit.*, 18/2 b–3 a, maintained that gentry when embezzling were afraid of criticism while runners cared only for profit and would not be moved by criticism. He estimated that in charity organizations managed by gentry, 70 to 80 per cent of the fund could be of actual use. If managed by clerks and runners, the persons taking care of the accounts would embezzle 20 to 30 per cent, the persons taking care of other affairs in the organizations would embezzle 20 to 30 per cent, while other clerks and runners not directly related to the organizations would share 30 to 40 per cent, leaving not more than 10 to 20 per cent for the actual benefit of the poor.

uted some funds, but records show that the main part of the financial burden was borne by the gentry.[270]

Although gentry members generally had no judicial power in a strict sense, they settled many disputes by acting as arbitrators. Examples of such gentry action are so numerous that one might conclude that more disputes were settled by gentry than ever came before the magistrates. To give a few examples, one *sheng-yüan* was described as so skilful in settling disputes that the villages of his area were seldom involved in lawsuits.[271] Another *sheng-yüan*, who was described as straightforward and righteous, often settled disputes on property divisions among family members of households in his area.[272] A *kung-sheng* was described as so capable in settling disputes that for more than ten years no lawsuits occurred in his village.[273]

The gentry also functioned as guardians of the traditional moral teachings. This was one of the main aspects of their role in Chinese society. In their whole life the gentry expressed the Chinese cultural tradition. This tradition and the gentry's concept of a true Confucian society,[274] whether it deviated from or conformed with the official line of thought, cannot be dealt with here, but examples will be given to show the outward expression of the way in which they fulfilled this cultural function.

The gentry were actively engaged in teaching and illustrating the moral principles. Materially, they contributed heavily to the establishment of private colleges.[275] It was claimed by contemporary and modern writers that it was in these colleges that the highest scholarly work was carried on. The

[270] For example, *Lung-an fu-chih*, 8/32 b–33 b, credits a number of persons with substantial contributions of rice and caskets in 1800 during the combat with rebels. Among these, gentry members comprised the majority. However, sometimes gentry contribution to relief works was made because of government pressure. For instance, Tso Tsung-t'ang, *op. cit.*, 7/6 ff., memorial of T'ung-chih 2/6/10 (1863), requested the throne to instruct the Kiangsu governor to order Yang Fang, a rich gentry member of Chekiang and dismissed circuit intendant of Shanghai, still staying at Shanghai, to contribute 50,000 piculs of rice for relief work in Chekiang. Tso pointed out that Yang had become wealthy through his merchant activity with foreigners. He also requested that Yang be ordered to return to his home province of Chekiang to help in relief work. For Yang's connection with foreigners, see also H. B. Morse, *In the Days of the Taipings*.

[271] *Pao-ting fu-chih*, 63/15 b.

[272] *Hunan t'ung-chih*, 179/4174.

[273] *Tientsin fu-chih*, 44/64 b.

[274] These points are discussed in unpublished manuscripts, "Ideology of the T'ai-p'ing T'ien-kuo," by Vincent Shih, and "Political Ideology in Nineteenth-Century China," by Hellmut Wilhelm, both of the University of Washington.

[275] *The Chinese Repository*, I, No. 2, June 1832, p. 75, relates the contribution of 31,000 taels by gentry of Chin-shan, Kiangsu, for the erection of a new college; a widow made a present of an estate for the grounds of the institution. Cf. also "History of Wei-ching College" in Liu Kuang-fen, *Yen-hsia ts'ao-t'ang i-shu hsü-k'o*, pp. 1 b–2 a, 11 a. This gives the origin, construction, financing, student subsidies, names of instructors, method of studies and discipline, names of students who succeeded in government examinations, and publications. On the nature of *shu-yüan*, or colleges, in the Ch'ing dynasty, see for instance Ch'en Tung-yüan, *Chung-kuo chiao-yü shih*, 26/444–59.

government schools were supervised by the educational officials who were more concerned with discipline and examinations. The presidents of the private colleges were members of the "regular" upper gentry. *Sheng-yüan* who wanted to become serious scholars often sought admission to these institutions.

The gentry also contributed funds and lands, the proceeds of which were employed to subsidize students.[276] They contributed to the repairing of the Confucian temples, the shrines for virtuous people, and so on.[277]

The gentry, as could be expected, generally were ardent supporters of the examination system from which so many of them derived their power and prestige. Thus, we find the gentry actively engaged in the repairing of government schools. At times the repair work was initiated by the magistrates, but supervision of work and contribution of funds came from the gentry.[278] Some gazetteers reported the story of the repair and reconstruction of these schools since the T'ang dynasty. It is interesting to note that during the earlier periods, this work was done mainly by the magistrates. Only later, during the Ch'ing period, did the gentry take the major part of the responsibility.[279]

The construction and repair of examination halls for local examinations was also generally regarded as the responsibility of the gentry.[280] In one locality the candidates had to bring their own desks and chairs until the gentry there finally collected enough funds to install them in an examination hall.[281] The gentry also contributed to the construction of *hui-kuan*, meeting places for their fellow townsmen in other towns or cities. For instance, the father of the leading statesman, Li Hung-chang, contributed to the construction of the Lu-chou *hui-kuan* in the capital which was later enlarged by Li. There the Lu-chou participants in the metropolitan examinations took their temporary lodging.[282] The Ho-fei *shih-kuan* at Nanking, a clubhouse for Ho-fei participants in provincial examinations, was built through the contributions of Liu Ming-ch'uan, Li's protégé from Ho-fei.[283] Other organizations were sponsored by gentry for the purpose of helping new *sheng-yüan* or for sending gifts to local men who had become court officials,[284] in order

[276] *The Chinese Repository, loc. cit.*

[277] *Yin-hsien chih*, 9/15–16.

[278] E.g., *Hsü-hsiu Lu-chou fu-chih,* 17/46 b, 50 a, 71 a; *Nan-ning fu-chih,* 20/20 a; *Kuang-chou fu-chih*, 66/6 a–b.

[279] *Po-pai hsien-chih*, 4/2 b.

[280] *Kuang-chou fu-chih*, 65/2 b, 10 a, 11 a, 11 b; also, for example, *Hsü-hsiu Lu-chou fu-chih*, 17/82 a, 83 a.

[281] *Chung-hsiu Meng-ch'eng hsien-chih-shu*, 5/28 a, 7/25 b.

[282] *Hsü-hsiu Lu-chou fu-chih*, 17/81 b; cf. *Hsiang-shan hsien-chih hsü-pien*, 4/1 b–2 a.

[283] *Hsü-hsiu Lu-chou fu-chih, loc. cit.*

[284] *Hsiang-shan hsien-chih hsü-pien, loc. cit.* They were the *Yin-chin-chü*, a bureau in charge of payment of "respect money" to educational officials for the new civil and military *sheng-yüan*, and the *T'an-chin-chü*, also known as *Lü-fei-chü*, bureau in charge of payment of traveling expenses for court officials from Hsiang-shan.

to maintain connections at court and enhance local power and prestige. In general, all aimed at the continuation of the existing social order and the position of the gentry.

Since early Ch'ing, there was the enforcement of the semimonthly expounding of the sixteen politico-moral maxims of the "Sacred Edict" intended to indoctrinate the masses with the official ideology. In this process of indoctrination, the gentry were requested to give their assistance. This is substantiated by the following passage: "On the first and fifteenth day of a month, *chou* and *hsien* magistrates should lead educational officials and assistant officials to public meeting places, gather the soldiers and the people, and explain to them the Sacred Edict. In the countryside, establish expounding bureaus in big villages following the traditional practice, and select honest, trustworthy and law-abiding gentry to be the heads and speakers."[285]

In the nineteenth century some magistrates still seriously observed this semimonthly ceremony and personally led in the discussion of these maxims.[286] Some magistrates required candidates of examinations to write the maxims from memory.[287] On some occasions, elderly *sheng-yüan* were recommended to take charge of the expounding of the maxims in the countryside.[288] In

[285] T'ien Wen-ching's article in *Huan-hai chih-nan Wu-chung*, p. 8 a–b. The sixteen maxims were issued by the K'ang-hsi emperor in 1670, each in seven characters. They were later amplified with historical examples and illustrations. Still later they were paraphrased in the colloquial style. Cf. Hummel, *op. cit.*, p. 329. A complete translation in English was made by William Milne and published in 1870 in Shanghai. *The Chinese Repository*, I, No. 8, pp. 297–325, Dec. 1832, contains an extract of Milne's translation. In his translation, the sixteen maxims are listed as follows: (1) Pay just regard to filial and fraternal duties, in order to give due importance to the relations of life; (2) Respect kindred in order to display the excellence of harmony; (3) Let concord abound among those who dwell in the same neighborhood in order to prevent litigations; (4) Give the chief place to husbandry and the culture of the mulberry tree, in order to produce adequate supplies of food and raiment; (5) Hold economy in estimation in order to prevent the lavish waste of money; (6) Magnify academical learning, in order to direct the scholar's progress; (7) Degrade strange religions, in order to exalt the orthodox doctrine; (8) Explain the laws, in order to warn the ignorant and obstinate; (9) Illustrate the principles of a polite and yielding carriage, in order to improve manners; (10) Attend to the essential employments, in order to give unvarying determination to the will of the people; (11) Instruct the youth, in order to prevent them from doing evil; (12) Suppress all false-accusing, in order to secure protection to the innocent; (13) Warn those who hide deserters, that they may not be involved in their downfall; (14) Complete the payment of taxes, in order to prevent frequent urging; (15) Unite the *pao* and *chia* in order to extirpate robbery and theft; (16) Settle animosities, that lives may be duly valued.

[286] Lung Ch'i-jui, *Ching-te-t'ang chi, wen-chi*, 4/13 a.

[287] S. W. Williams, *The Middle Kingdom*, p. 548, on a prefectural examination says, "In addition to their knowledge of the classics, the candidates at this trial are often required to write off the text of the *Sheng Yu* or 'Sacred Edict' from memory." Cf. also Chang Chung-ju, *Ch'ing-tai k'o-chü chih-tu*, pp. 3–7.

[288] *Shih-lu*, Hsüan-tsung, 325/13 b, edict of Tao-kuang 19/8/15 (1839); cf. *Lo-ch'uan hsien-chih*, 13/1 b, where it was recorded that *hsiang-yo*, or expounders of the maxims in the villages, should be virtuous *sheng-yüan* over the age of sixty. See also Wu Yung-kuang, *op. cit.*, 3/1 a–2 a.

general, such duties were handled by various kinds of "regular" gentry, those who had obtained their titles through the examination system.[289]

The gentry were also the compilers of the local gazetteers.[290] One editor explained the purpose of such gazetteers as follows: "For a district to have a gazetteer is the same as for a country to have annals. The gazetteer will narrate past events, and the knowledge of past events will enable one to predict the future. ... The superior men in studying it will understand the developments [of worldly affairs], and the common people in obeying the tradition recorded can maintain their work."[291]

Another editor of a local gazetteer stressed the value of recording biographies of loyal, filial, chaste, and virtuous persons.[292] The gentry believed that the compilation of gazetteers would help maintain general morality and their own prestige. Thus the gentry, especially the "regular" upper gentry, were most enthusiastic in such tasks.[293]

During the early part of the nineteenth century, when China was in a relatively peaceful state, the government retained the control of military and police power and of taxation. During the crisis in the middle of the century, however, the gentry rapidly invaded these fields of action.

With the deterioration of the government forces, gentry members became military leaders of their own local and regional military organizations.[294] The government had to tolerate their tremendous increase in power and maneuvered to use them in suppressing the Taipings and other rebels of the time. Referring to almost any local gazetteer that recorded the growth of

[289] *Hsin-ning hsien-chih*, 14/2 a.

[290] Sometimes magistrates initiated the compilation of gazetteers although the gentry did the actual work. In one example the magistrate not only initiated the compilation but also contributed his administrative allowances to meet printing costs. See *Kuei-chou chih*, preface.

[291] See preface by Yang I-ch'ing in *Chiu-chiang fu-chih*, p. 10 a.

[292] *Ibid.*, preface by Shen Pao-ching, p. 3 a.

[293] For example, the compilers of *Shang-yü hsien-chih* were four *chü-jen*, two *kung-sheng*, one *chü-jen* as proofreader-in-chief, and seven *sheng-yüan* as proofreaders. For *Lan-ch'i hsien-chih*, the compilers were two retired officials, two *chü-jen*, and three *kung-sheng*; the proofreaders were two retired officials, one *chü-jen*, and six *kung-sheng*; and the reporters were one expectant official, five *kung-sheng*, thirteen *sheng-yüan*, one military *chü-jen*, and one military *sheng-yüan*. One gazetteer compiled as late as 1937 shows that gazetteer compiling was heavily loaded with gentry influence and ideology. See *Chi-an ho-hsi fang-kuo hsiang-chih*. Compiler Hsiao listed himself as a *chü-jen*. Two editors obtained *sheng-yüan* under the Ch'ing dynasty. Co-editors included a head of the Chamber of Commerce, a *sheng-yüan*, principals of grade schools, and a returned student from Japan. Clan organization there still showed strength. Clan funds formerly used for subsidies to examination candidates were used for those who studied in high schools and universities. The fund was invested in real estate and rent was collected from the shopkeeper leaseholders.

[294] This point is discussed in detail in "Military Organization and Power Structure in Nineteenth-Century China," an unpublished manuscript, by Franz Michael, University of Washington.

local corps organization in the nineteenth century, it will be found that the organizers and leaders were mainly gentry members.

The upper gentry were usually responsible for the organization and financing of local corps, especially the larger units, while the lower gentry members usually operated within a smaller area, and as commanders of the smaller units, they often participated in actual fighting. For instance, an upper gentry member of Yü-yao, Chekiang, an official who had returned to his home, was active in promoting the organization of local corps in his province. It is recorded that in this undertaking he came into conflict with the circuit intendants and the governor.[295] In another instance, a *kung-sheng* of Hsün-chou, Kwangsi, was active in organizing local corps.[296] A military *chü-jen* of Ch'eng-hsien, Chekiang, headed the organization of local corps and was assisted by lower gentry members.[297] The lesser authority of the lower gentry can be seen in numerous examples. Among them is a description in a provincial gazetteer of a *sheng-yüan* of Chihli who led 200 local corps members against the bandits and died in battle.[298] The same gazetteer lists a *chien-sheng* who led local corps members against the Taipings.[299]

In the middle of the nineteenth century, when the military situation was critical, the government realized that its regular troops could not cope with the rebel forces and began to send high court officials home to their native provinces to organize local corps in their gentry capacity. In this way the government apparently sought to encourage and control the development of local corps. For example, Li Hung-chang's father, Li Wen-an, a court official, was sent back to his native province of Anhwei to organize local corps in 1853 when the Taipings had reached that province.[300] At this time Tseng Kuo-fan, then vice-minister of a board, was observing a mourning period in his native province of Hunan. The court instructed him to remain there to organize local corps. His efforts led to the development of the famous Hunan militia which eventually succeeded in suppressing the Taipings.[301]

The government also encouraged retired officials to organize local corps. For instance, Feng Kuei-fen, a retired court official, was staying at his home in Soochow when the Taipings occupied Nanking in 1853. He took an

[295] *Yü-yao hsien-chih*, 23/23–26. The official was a vice-minister of the Board of Works staying at his native place because of his stepmother's illness.

[296] *Hsün-chou fu-chih*, 47/53 b. Because of his merit in organizing local corps, he was later recommended to an educational post.

[297] *Ch'eng-hsien chih*, 16/1–2.

[298] *Chi-fu t'ung-chih*, 242/8437.

[299] *Ibid.*, 239/8344.

[300] Hummel, *op. cit.*, p. 464.

[301] *Ibid.*, p. 751.

active part in organizing local corps to defend his prefecture. For this, he was raised in his official rank.[302]

Provincial and local officials themselves sometimes promoted and supervised local corps; but the actual operation of these organizations remained in the hands of the gentry, while the officials functioned as coordinators between different local corps or between them and the regular army. For instance, in Pa-ling, Hunan, it was recorded that the local corps there was promoted by the prefect and organized through the effort of a prefectural director-of-studies who went around the countryside to settle problems of financing and disputes as to which gentry members should be leaders. It is also stated that he dispersed unauthorized local corps which sheltered rebel sympathizers.[303]

Gentry members were also instrumental in the construction and repair of fortresses or earthwalls for local defense in many localities. In the memorial of Wang Ch'ing-yün, then governor of Shansi, he favored the continuation of gentry-elder responsibility in the repair of fortresses and in helping officials in local defense.[304] In Shensi, gentry members were also the active group in the construction of fortresses during the Moslem Rebellion. While the gentry usually supervised such construction, cases were found of disputes among gentry members and between gentry and officials over the sites of these fortresses.[305] In Canton fortresses had been built in the Chia-ch'ing period under official leadership while the funds were contributed by local gentry and commoners. These fortresses were repaired by gentry members in the Tao-kuang period, and in the Hsien-feng period gentry directed the construction of more fortresses for defense against the Taipings.[306] To give one more example, Hu Lin-i, governor of Hupeh, also favored the building of fortresses through contributions by local gentry and commoners.[307]

Although the gentry were the main contributors and often controlled the financing of local defense efforts, this control was sometimes retained by the government. During the Taiping period "contribution bureaus" were

[302] *Ibid.*, p. 242.

[303] *Pa-ling hsien-chih*, 19/17 a–20 b.

[304] *Fukien t'ung-chih, li-chuan, 39/6 a,* Wang's biography. This memorial was presented in Hsien-feng 6 (1856), 6th month. Wang pointed out that each *hsien* in Shansi used to have ten to a hundred of these fortresses, a phenomenon not found in other provinces. He also said that the Shansi custom provided that each of the fortresses should have a temple for the local deity and that there were always regulations for such a temple. These temples were controlled by gentry elders.

[305] Pai Ching-wei, *op. cit.*, 6/12 a–13 b. The officials and some upper gentry decided that the fortresses should not be built with the village as a unit but with several villages sharing one fortress. In an emergency the inhabitants of these villages would move into one fortress. In this case the local village gentry wanted to build small fortresses of their own while the upper gentry favored one fortress for several villages.

[306] *Kuang-chou fu-chih*, 64/19 a.

[307] *Huang-ch'ao ching-shih-wen-hsü-pien*, compiled by Ke Shih-chün, 81/9 b–10 a.

established by the government for the collection of "contributions" for military use.[308]

The government naturally claimed control of all tax collection including the all important land tax and grain tribute. But during the time of the Taiping Rebellion, the gentry moved into the field of taxation. In some cases the gentry gained control of existing taxes.[309] In addition, the gentry helped in the establishment of a new type of tax, the so-called *likin*, which was a new tax collected from shopkeepers and traveling merchants.[310] This tax became an established economic institution outside the control of the central government. It provided a direct source of revenue for the provincial governments and was important in the rise to power of a new type of local and regional administration. Sometimes the government took officials from their regular posts and sent them back to their native places where, in their gentry capacity, they collected the *likin* for the new provincial forces.[311] The gentry predominated in the collection of the *likin* in the early years of this tax, although in later years the semiofficial *likin* commissioners began to control the collection in many places.[312]

As shown in the cases above, the gentry took an active part in the affairs of their home areas. As local leaders, they had allied themselves with the

308 The "contribution bureaus" did not depend on voluntary contributions but tried to persuade or force contributions. This is shown in the charge against a retired director-general of river works, P'an Hsi-en, for refusing to contribute to the military fund. The charge was made by Chang Fei who was supervising the contribution bureaus in southern Anhwei. See Chang Fei, *Chang Wen-i-kung tsou-kao*, 1/25 b ff. Chang reported that he had collected 700,000 taels in Hui-chou but not much in Ning-kuo. He blamed P'an for taking the lead in refusing to contribute. Chang pointed out that P'an had accumulated several million taels while in office, yet relying on his position, he would not cooperate. He demanded that P'an contribute several hundred thousand taels. Cf. also *ibid.*, 2/37 ff.

309 An upper gentry member of the time wrote an essay discussing tax collection in its connection with local corps. He defended the situation in his district where five local corps leaders collected taxes and paid a lump sum to the magistrates. He praised this situation as an example of "harmony between local corps and magistrates" and contrasted his district to others where local corps monopolized taxes and paid nothing to the magistrates. Wang Ying-fu, "Essays on Local Corps," *Huang-ch'ao chin-shih-wen hsü-pien*, compiled by Sheng K'ang, 81/9–11.

310 See *Ch'ing-kuo hsin-cheng-fa fen-lun*, 5/174–5; Lo Yü-tung, *Chung-kuo likin shih*, esp. p. 19.

311 Kuo Sung-tao, *op. cit.*, 8/23 a–b, referring to a gentry member of Nan-hai, Kwangtung, who was a prefect of Ch'ih-chou, Anhwei. Later because of his merit in *likin* collection, he was recommended for promotion to the position of circuit intendant and was recalled to service again in Anhwei.

312 *Pa-ling hsien-chih*, 55/7 b. *Likin* commissioners were described here as semi-official since they were not appointed by the central government and were not on the roster of officials. A poem was composed by a contemporary regarding the growing power of the *likin* commissioners: "The salary of *likin* personnel in Hunan is high; the commissioners of a sudden begin to rise. Meeting others, they display a proud and aloof attitude; if merely sitting over a [*likin*] pass is like this, what will one expect of officials?"

existing government, itself staffed by gentry. They performed many necessary functions for their areas and acted as intermediaries between the officials and the local people, advising the officials on local affairs and representing the interests of the area to the officials. In normal times the main interests of the government and the gentry coincided, and they coöperated in keeping the wheels of society turning and maintaining the status quo. Sometimes, when their interests diverged, the gentry criticized or even opposed and blocked official actions but without any serious threat to the central government. But in the critical times during and after the Taiping period, as the strength and efficiency of the central government declined, the gentry took over more and more of the government's functions and authority, and reached a position where they could choose whether to support the government or directly challenge its authority. There were the many isolated cases of individual gentry leaders who led local uprisings.[313] There were other gentry leaders with their own organizations who in the confused condition of civil war shifted their allegiance back and forth between the government and the rebels.[314] And there were those who officially fought for the government but took the opportunity to build up great personal power with their own armies and political machines and control of financial resources. Such men as Tseng Kuo-fan and Li Hung-chang rose to power in this way and created a new kind of local and regional administration.

[313] E.g., during the Taiping period, a *sheng-yüan* moved into the mountains, pretending to escape from warfare and to teach. Even official and rich families joined him. Later his group was reported to be rebellious and was suppressed. Cf. *Shantung t'ung-chih*, 117/3352; "Notes by Ling-hsiao and I-shih," pp. 2–3 in *Kuo-wen chou-pao*, *chüan* 6, No. 49, Dec. 15, 1929; *I-ching*, No. 3, April, 1936, pp. 6 ff.; *Shantung chün-hsing chi-lüeh*, *chüan* 21, 22. *Ibid.*, 11 A/2, records the story of a *sheng-yüan* with stipend who pretended to be organizing local corps but actually gathered the villagers of hundreds of villages and himself became the *t'ang-chu*, secret society chieftain.

[314] E.g., Miao P'ei-lin, a *sheng-yüan* who led local forces back and forth between the government and rebels. See *Wen-hsien ts'ung-pien*, No. 22, pp. 1–8.

PART TWO

A Numerical Analysis of the Gentry Of Nineteenth-Century China

This study especially emphasizes the use of figures. It is an attempt to estimate the size of the gentry group in nineteenth-century China and its proportion to the total population, the change in size from the pre-Taiping to the post-Taiping period, and to interpret the significance of the size and change. The principal components of both the upper and lower gentry, as described in Part One, are also estimated. These figures are useful in assessing the importance of the various groups within the gentry, and they also show the proportion of upper to lower gentry.

The estimates of the size of the gentry are based on figures for the two major groups of gentry, the *sheng-yüan* (through examination) and the *chien-sheng* (through purchase). Almost all gentry members entered the gentry group through one of these two routes. The total of *sheng-yüan* was arrived at as follows:

1. Determine how often examinations for admission of *sheng-yüan* were held.

2. Determine the quota of successful candidates in each of these examinations all over the country.

3. Determine the average age at which *sheng-yüan* were admitted and the average age at which they died, thus arriving at the average span of years that these men were gentry.

4. The number of examinations held in this average span of years multiplied by the quota gives the total number of *sheng-yüan* present in the Chinese population in an average year.

For these estimates, information was obtained from the official publications, the *Hsüeh-cheng ch'üan-shu* and the *Ta-Ch'ing hui-tien shih-li*, and was carefully checked against data obtained from local histories and other semi-official and private works.

The figures on *chien-sheng* were derived from archive material[1] and from memorial collections and local histories. These estimates are not so satisfactory as those of *sheng-yüan* since complete records are not available to this writer. For the same reason, the estimate of pre-Taiping *chien-sheng* is more satisfactory than that of post-Taiping *chien-sheng*. However, some local histories record the names of local *chien-sheng* and the proportion of these *chien-sheng* to other types of gentry recorded serves as a check against serious errors in calculation.

Since upper gentry members were derived from lower gentry and have therefore been included in either the *sheng-yüan* or *chien-sheng* groups, figures on them are not used in estimating the total number of gentry. The figures on the components of both the upper and lower gentry are used to show the changing proportions of the various groups within the gentry.

Tables 15 to 32 show the details of the processes through which the estimates were arrived at. The text explains the methods employed and endeavors to evaluate the sources used, assess the reliability of the estimates, and discuss the significance of the various trends revealed. We cannot hope for a high degree of accuracy in using a numerical approach in a historical study, since we have to rely on writers and records of the past, check one source against another, and still allow margin for error. Nevertheless, estimates arrived at in this way can be useful if used with caution and in conjunction with the results of other types of studies.

As these numerical studies were being worked out, some interesting aspects of the relationship between the government and the gentry emerged. It was through its careful control of the examination quota and frequency that the government was able to regulate the number of "regular" gentry and their distribution over the country. The purchase system produced "irregular" gentry to balance the "regular" group. The whole system was so delicately contrived that the central government could manage it with exactness. But the nineteenth century brought great changes. During and after the Taiping period, the quota system got out of hand and the purchase system dissolved into chaos. The control of the government was weakened, and both the size and the nature of the gentry were greatly changed. Some aspects of the significance and causes of these changes are taken up in this study along with the discussion of the changes themselves.

[1] T'ang Hsiang-lung, "A Statistical Study of the *Chüan-chien* System in the Tao-kuang Period," *She-hui k'o-hsüeh tsa-chih*, pp. 432–44. This work is based on over 6,000 monthly reports from provincial authorities to the court.

FREQUENCY AND QUOTAS OF EXAMINATIONS: A MEANS OF GOVERNMENT CONTROL OVER THE SIZE AND DISTRIBUTION OF THE "REGULAR" GENTRY

As has been pointed out in Part One, the government depended upon the assistance of the gentry in local administration. Local officials did not have the staff or the funds to carry out all the tasks of government. Neither did they have a thorough understanding of local problems since they were not natives of the districts they governed. Therefore, wherever there was need of an administrative unit, there, too, was the need of a group of gentry to help handle local affairs. These gentry generally coöperated with the government because it was in their own interests to do so and because they were well indoctrinated in official lines of thought, mainly through the examination system. This privileged and powerful group was necessary and useful in the management of the country. Yet its support was a burden on the people, and its strength was always a possible threat to the power of the central government. For these reasons the Ch'ing rulers carefully regulated the total number of gentry and their distribution over the country.

They were able to exert such control over the "regular" gentry through the examination system. The first step into "regular" gentry status was to pass the first series of examinations and become a *sheng-yüan*. By adjusting the quotas of successful candidates as well as the frequency of such examinations, the government could regulate the number of these gentry in each locality with considerable accuracy. Quota and frequency of examinations were thus closely related. The question of examination frequency will be taken up first.

Frequency of Sheng-yüan Examinations

Of the three examinations leading to the admission of *sheng-yüan*, the last or *yüan* examination was the decisive one.[2] Each *yüan* examination added

[2] In late Ming times, records show that many examinees were washed out before they reached the *yüan* examinations. But in Ch'ing times, the situation had changed. In Chin-chiang, Fukien, in late Ming times, for instance, the number of *t'ung-sheng* approximated 10,000. The number recommended by *hsien* magistrates to prefects was 7,000 to 8,000; the number sent by the prefect to the provincial director-of-studies was 2,000 to 3,000. See *Ch'üan-chou fu-chih*, 20/6 b. The Ch'ing change is recorded in *Heng-chou fu-chih*, 16/23 a–b as follows: "Edict of Ch'ien-lung 9 (1744): Formerly the *chou* and *hsien* magistrates in examining *t'ung-sheng* and sending the successful ones to the provincial director-of-studies for examination followed the practice of observing some quota. Later, because of the increasing number of *t'ung-sheng*, in K'ang-hsi 39 (1700), it was stipulated that there should be no quota limitation. Early this year, the Board of Rites memorialized and requested permission to limit the number to be sent to the provincial director-of-studies in government schools so as to get rid of the unqualified. This I have already approved. However, it occurs to me that *t'ung-sheng* examinees in various

a new group of *sheng-yüan* to the existing group of gentry. A first step toward estimating the total number of gentry is, then, to find out how often these examinations were held. The shifts in government policy on this matter will also be pointed out.

Although no definite dates were set aside for these examinations, ample evidence shows that during the nineteenth century the civil *yüan* examinations were held twice in three years and the military *yüan* examinations were held once in three years. This pattern was fixed in the late seventeenth century.

The early Ch'ing government had wavered between the policy of having civil *yüan* examinations twice in three years and that of having them once in three years. An edict of 1673 stated:

> Since Shun-chih 18th year (1661), through the request of censors, *sui*[3] and *k'o*[4] examinations have been combined into one examination. Now within three years, the number of students admitted to the prefectural schools is only 20, the big schools 15, middle-sized schools 10, and small schools 7 to 8. According to the official reports of the provincial directors-of-studies in the various provinces, *sheng-yüan* in various schools, within this three-year period, who contributed according to practice [to become *chien-sheng*, etc.], or stepped out for other reasons [such as becoming *kung-sheng* or *chü-jen* or because of death], or were deprived of their titles [because of violation of regulations], amounted to 30 or 40 to 100. Three years is a long period. Holding only one examination will not be storing enough talents and will not stimulate diligent supervision. The old practice of two [*yüan*] examinations, one following *sui* and one following *k'o* examinations should be complied with.[5]

A local gazetteer records the change as follows: in 1647 there were two examinations in three years; in 1658, one in three years; and in 1672, again two in three years.[6] It would then appear that from 1645 to 1647 examin-

districts vary in number. If they are limited by some quota, it is to be feared that some will be forced out because of excessive number of qualified *t'ung-sheng*, or some will be taken in, even though unqualified, merely to fill up the quota. Thus, this quota measure will not be always appropriately carried out. Furthermore, the prefects, *chou* and *hsien* magistrates merely send the examinees to the provincial director-of-studies. Their success depends entirely on the provincial director-of-studies and their number has no effect on the number of *sheng-yüan* admitted. The path should be slightly broadened as a means of encouragement."

[3] The *sui-shih*, or *sui-k'ao*, as described in *Ch'ing-kuo hsin-cheng-fa fen-lun*, 3/35 and Zi, "Pratique des Examens Littéraires en Chine," Part I, chap. 7, and "Pratique des Examens Militaires en Chine," Part I, chap. 5, was held once in three years by the provincial directors-of-studies to examine the *sheng-yüan*.

[4] The *k'o-shih*, or *k'o-k'ao*, as described in *Ch'ing-kuo hsin-cheng-fa fen-lun*, 3/35–36 and Zi, "Pratique des Examens Littéraires en Chine," Part I, chap. 7, and "Pratique des Examens Militaires en Chine," Part II, chap. 2, was held once in three years as a preliminary examination for the provincial examination. The *sheng-yüan* who were ranked in the first or second rank or in the first ten of the third rank were qualified to participate in the provincial examination.

[5] *Shih-li*, 389/21 a.

[6] *T'ung-chou chih-li-chou chih*, 5/50 b.

ations were held once in three years, from 1647 to 1658 (or 1661) twice in three years, from 1658 to 1673 (or 1676) once in three years, and from the latter date onward always twice in three years.

These changes indicate that the early Ch'ing government was concerned with the frequency of examinations for admission to *sheng-yüan* status as one of the factors determining the size of the gentry group. However, after 1673 the frequency of *sheng-yüan* examinations became fixed, and this method of manipulating the size of the gentry was no longer used.

The frequency of examinations can best be described in terms of the duties of the provincial directors-of-studies. The term of office of a provincial director-of-studies was three years, during which time he made two tours to the various prefectures and independent *chou*, the first tour for the purpose of supervising the *sui* examination (to determine the promotion, demotion, or dismissal of existing *sheng-yüan*), and the second tour for the purpose of supervising the *k'o* examination (a preliminary examination for the provincial examination).[7] The civil *yüan* examinations of the various prefectures and independent *chou* were held immediately after the *sui* and *k'o* examinations while the provincial directors-of-studies were still in the respective prefectures. There was no *k'o* examination for the military *sheng-yüan*, and the military *yüan* examinations for admitting military *sheng-yüan* occurred only once in three years following the military *sui* examination.

To cite some examples, a memorial by a Manchu general requested that there be granted for two newly developed districts a quota of four civil *sheng-yüan* for the *yüan* examinations following each *sui* and *k'o* examination, and a quota of four military *sheng-yüan* for military *yüan* examinations following each *sui* examination.[8] Examples can also be drawn from the *Ch'in-ting ta-Ch'ing hui-tien shih-li.*[9] For instance, one edict stated, "Hereafter, the *t'ing* in Jehol shall have a quota of four civil *sheng-yüan* in [each *yüan* examination] following the two examinations of *sui* and *k'o*."[10] Another edict concerning military *sheng-yüan* stated, "Approved. Military students in the capital shall, in accordance with the examples of those in the provinces, be examined by the provincial directors-of-studies once in three years."[11] Many similar examples appear in the same source.

Numerous local gazetteer records can be quoted to show that this same

[7] For detailed description, see *Hsüeh-cheng*, *chüan* 15, on "Matters Relating to the Provincial Directors-of-Studies."

[8] "A Memorial Requesting the Establishment of Schools in Hsin-chiang," *Huang-ch'ao chin-shih wen-pien*, 57/50–51, dated 1769, presented by Wen-fu, Manchu general at I-li. The two localities referred to are Ti-hua and Ning-pien.

[9] *Chüan* 367–80.

[10] *Ibid.*, 371/14 a, edict of 1776. This example shows that the civil *yüan* examinations occurred twice in three years.

[11] *Ibid.*, 719/10 a, edict of 1664.

pattern of frequency was maintained in the nineteenth century. In one prefectural school, for instance, it was recorded that for each *sui* and *k'o* examination, there would be 15 new civil *sheng-yüan* and for each *sui* examination (only), there would be 15 new military *sheng-yüan*.[12]

Accounts by some Western writers furnish additional proof. A translation of an account of an examination schedule, announced by one provincial director-of-studies upon his arrival for a *sui* examination, shows that in addition to the *sui* examinations, he supervised *yüan* examinations for admission to both civil and military *sheng-yüan* status.[13] A similar account of an examination schedule announced on an occasion of a *k'o* examination, in listing the examinations to be given, mentions the examination for admission of civil *sheng-yüan* but does not mention an examination for admission of military *sheng-yüan*.[14] Several other Western writers have also given the frequency of the civil *yüan* examinations as twice in three years. Alexander Wylie points out that the provincial directors-of-studies toured the province twice in three years.[15] T. L. Bullock states, "Twice in every three years, an examination is held in every prefecture for students who have passed their preliminary.[16]

During the nineteenth century, then, the civil *yüan* examinations were held twice in three years, and military *yüan* examinations were held once in three years.

[12] *Pa-ling-hsien-chih*, 17/20 b–21 a; cf. also *Hsiang-shan hsien-chih*, 7/41 a; *T'ung-ch'uan fu-chih*, 13/41 b ff.; *Chih-li Lu-chou chih*, 3/19 b; *Chung-hsiu Meng-ch'eng hsien-chih shu*, 5/5 b; *Hsü-hsiu Lu-chou fu-chih*, 17/76 b.

[13] Zi, "Pratique des Examens Littéraires en Chine," I, chap. 5, pp. 58–59. It took this director-of-studies 23 days to complete his supervision of examinations.

[14] *Ibid.*, I, chap. 9, p. 98. This director-of-studies spent only 17 days supervising the examinations. Included in the examinations were those for the selection of *kung-sheng* "by virtue of noteworthy achievements," those for civil *sheng-yüan*, *chien-sheng*, and *kung-sheng* who wished to participate in the provincial examinations, and the civil *yüan* examinations. This shows that on the occasion of *k'o* examinations there were no examinations for military *sheng-yüan* or for admission to military *sheng-yüan* status. Zi also mentions that civil *sheng-yüan* admitted on the occasion of *sui* examinations were known as *sui-ch'ü*, and those admitted on the occasion of *k'o* examinations were known as *k'o-ch'ü*.

[15] Wylie, *Chinese Researches*, pp. 148–50; he also gives examples of examination procedure and the contents of an examination held in K'un-shan for Soochow prefecture.

[16] Bullock, "Competitive Examinations in China," *Nineteenth Century*, Vol. 36, p. 90. "Competitive Examinations in China," *Blackwood's Edinburgh Magazine*, says: "In due course of time, they are expected to pass in two local examinations. Having succeeded in these, their names are then enrolled for a third, namely, the first of the great national examinations. These are held, twice in every three years, at every prefectural city, and the degree conferred is called Sew-tsae [the colloquial term for *sheng-yüan*]." Some Western writers did not see the over-all arrangement of the frequency of examinations. For example, Chester Holcombe, in *The Real Chinese Question*, p. 66, stated that the examinations were held annually. William F. Mayers in *The Chinese Government*, p. 77, writes that, "In every second year, the provincial director-of-studies would complete a tour of his domain, holding examinations at the different prefectural cities." This would lead one to believe that *yüan* examinations were held once in two years. K. S. Latourette in

Quotas of Successful Candidates in Yüan Examinations

Quotas were allocated to administrative units. Each prefecture and district had its government school for *sheng-yüan*, and each school had a specific quota of *sheng-yüan* to be admitted in each examination. The size of these quotas varied according to the importance and size of the administrative unit. The size of each quota was therefore related to the importance of the administrative unit rather than to the number of participants in the examinations. It goes without saying that, as a rule, larger administrative units had larger numbers of participants. But there was no fixed proportion between the quota and the number of participants in examinations, or between the quota and the population of the area. In terms of chances for the individual participants, there were therefore great inequalities among the various administrative units. These inequalities remained, even though small adjustments were occasionally made.

According to the size and importance of the administrative unit, the schools were classified as large, medium, and small. The quota of admission to civil *sheng-yüan* was first mentioned in 1647 as follows: big school, 40, middle-sized school, 30, and small school, 20. In 1658 an edict stated that the big prefectures should have 20, the big *chou* or *hsien* 15, and the small schools 4 or 5 successful candidates in each civil *yüan* examination. In 1670 it was pointed out that in the big prefectures, *chou*, and *hsien*, the old practice should be followed, that middle-sized schools should have quotas of 12, and small schools should have quotas of 8 to 10. Finally in 1724, it was approved that localities with many candidates could request reclassification as follows: from a small school district to a middle-sized one; from a middle-sized one to a large one; and large districts could ask for a quota equal to that of a prefectural school.[17]

From that time on, there was no further official record on the general policy of quota setting. It seems that the wavering between a lenient and a stringent policy on admission to gentry membership finally came to an end. This picture fits very well with our previous findings on frequency of examina-

The Chinese, Their History and Culture, II, p. 38, also states, "In every *hsien* and roughly every two years in each *fu*, under the proper officials, there were conducted the first of the examinations."

[17] *Shih-li*, 370/1 a–b; *Hsüeh-cheng*, 65/1 a–b. The 1724 change seems to fit with records in local gazetteers. In *Nan-ch'ang hsien-chih*, 12/3 a, it is recorded that at first the civil *sheng-yüan* quota was 15, the quota for a big *hsien*. In 1724, the provincial director-of-studies memorialized that big *hsien* should have an increase of 5, raising them to the same quota as a prefectural school; this was approved. *Chang-chou fu-chih*, 7/10 a–b, states that in Ming times each school generally admitted 100 in each *k'o* and *sui* examination. According to *Hsü-wen-hsien t'ung-k'ao*, 50/3245, the Ming dynasty had quotas only for *ling-sheng* and *tseng-sheng*, but none for *fu-sheng*. The excessive number of *sheng-yüan* in Ming times was criticized by Ku Yen-wu in *Jih-chih-lu*.

tions. Thus, in 1647, when there were two examinations in three years, the quota was at its highest, an attempt presumably to absorb more talents for the new dynasty and to attract more scholars to the examination system. But in 1658 there was only one examination in three years, and at the same time the quota was reduced more than fifty per cent, which was in effect more than a fourfold reduction. This seems to indicate that the Manchu rulers at this time felt less need of gentry helpers and more urgent need of controlling the number of the privileged gentry group. However, in K'ang-hsi times, both the frequency and quota of examinations were again revised, this time towards leniency. Apparently the Manchu rulers then felt that they had a tighter hold over their domain and could safely increase the number of gentry.

This formal regulation of quota for government schools persisted into the nineteenth century. It was not always strictly observed, however. While many localities had exactly the stipulated maximum normal quota, many others had quotas exceeding it.[18] Some of these variations from the stipulated quota were special phenomena of certain provinces, while others were special phenomena of the localities themselves. For instance, an edict states that in the provinces of Chiang-nan (Kiangsu and Anhwei) and Chekiang, larger numbers of candidates had participated in the examinations, and therefore quotas were to be raised accordingly.[19] Later, for the same reason, a number of district schools of Chiang-nan province had a further raise in quota, giving them the same quota as the prefectural schools of Chiang-nan,[20] a quota already higher than that in many other provinces. Irregular raises in quota also occurred in some districts of other provinces, often through the request of gentry members.[21] Thus, as shown in Tables 15–16, many localities had exactly the stipulated maximum quota of 20, although some had a quota of 25 or, as in the case of Canton, as many as 40.[22]

The total quota in the pre-Taiping period for the 1741 schools throughout

[18] *Shih-li, chüan* 370–381, or *Hsüeh-cheng, chüan* 66–86, or as abbreviated in Tables 15 and 16.

[19] *Hsüeh-cheng*, 69/5 b; *Shih-li*, 371/6 a; an edict of 1689 states that the small schools should have quotas of 12 (instead of 8 to 10 as in other provinces), the middle-sized schools 16 (instead of 12), the big schools 20 (instead of 15), and the prefectural schools 25 (instead of 20). The date varies, however, from that recorded in *Wu-hsi Chin-kuei hsien-chih*, 6/16 a, where it is said that in 1684 a quota of 15 was set up for Wu-hsi, and that it was in 1699 (instead of 1689) that the quota was raised to 20 together with other big *hsien* of the province.

[20] *Hsüeh-cheng, loc. cit.*, edict of 1724. This date again varies from that recorded in *Wu-hsi Chin-kuei hsien-chih, loc. cit.*, where it is said that the quota was raised to 25 in 1722.

[21] For instance, *Yung-ning chou hsü-chih*, 5/26 a.

[22] See Tables 15 and 16 under the vertical column of "prefectural school" and horizontal column of "Kwangtung."

the country was found to be 25,089 for each *yüan* examination. (See Table 15.) Among the provinces of China proper, by far the highest total, 2,845, was allotted to Chihli, the province in which the capital was located. Kweichow had a total of only 753, the lowest among the provinces. These early nineteenth-century totals generally show only slight increases over early Ch'ing totals, and these increases were largely due to the establishment of new administrative units and new government schools,[23] or to readjustments of the size of administrative units with corresponding changes in the quotas of the schools.[24]

Quotas for Special Groups

The government set up special quotas for certain groups. Although these special quotas had little effect on the total quota for the country, their existence is of significance in other connections.

For instance, there was a special quota for Hakkas.[25] In Canton, for example, a special quota of four was reserved for Hakka candidates before the Taiping period and six after the Taiping period. The separate quota for Hakkas was established late in the Ch'ing dynasty, the first record of it being found in 1787.[26]

A count shows that before the Taiping period, only four schools in Kwangtung had separate quotas for Hakkas with a total of eight admissions.[27] In one school regulations prevented the Hakka *sheng-yüan* from being promoted to *tseng-sheng* or *ling-sheng.*[28] Furthermore, an edict stated that if there were few candidates, the quota did not have to be filled, while if later the number of candidates should greatly increase, the quota should not be exceeded.[29] After the Taiping period, there were eight schools in Kwangtung that had separate quotas for Hakkas with a total of sixteen admissions, an expression of leniency towards the Hakkas who were the cause of considerable local strife in south China. An edict of 1866 says:

[23] E.g., Yung-sui, Hunan, was a new administrative unit in Yung-cheng times, and by Ch'ien-lung 25 (1760) a school was finally established with a quota of 8 admissions for each *yüan* examination. See *Shih-li,* 376/7 a.

[24] E.g., in 1736, Ts'ao-chou, Shantung, was promoted from a *chou* administrative unit to a prefecture, and the quota was adjusted accordingly. See *Shih-li,* 375/3 a.

[25] The Hakkas were a group of Chinese people who had originated in north China and had settled principally in the border region of Kwangtung, Fukien, and Kiangsi. They speak a dialect intermediate between Mandarin and Cantonese. In the nineteenth century they spread westward into areas already occupied by Chinese who had settled there much earlier, and the two groups often came into conflict.

[26] *Shih-li,* 379/3 a. *Hsüeh-cheng,* 81/11 a.

[27] *Hsüeh-cheng,* 81/1 a–6 b.

[28] *Shih-li,* 379/3 a.

[29] *Ibid.*

The natives and Hakkas in Chao-ch'ing [prefecture], Kwangtung, have for many years stirred up troubles, and engaged in fighting, revenge, and killing. Jui-lin[30] and Chiang I-li[31] have now distributed subsidies to the Hakkas and evacuated them to the prefectures of Kao, Lien, Lei, and Ch'iung [in Kwangtung] and the districts of Ho, Jung, and Kuei [in Kwangsi] to be settled down. All newly moved Hakkas should be permitted to be attached to the various districts and to participate in examinations[32] through the establishment of Hakka quotas. It is permitted that one out of every twenty candidates shall be successful[33] in order to show encouragement.[34]

Separate quotas were also set up for other special groups such as the minority groups of Miao and Yao. The problem of Miao and Yao candidates was discussed since early Ch'ing. In Hunan, these candidates were called *hsin-t'ung*,[35] while in Szechwan, Kwangsi, Kweichow, and Yunnan, they were plainly called *miao-t'ung* and *yao-t'ung*. Separate quotas were set up in many tribal localities as early as the Shun-chih period, but tribal people were by no means treated as equals of the Chinese. In K'ang-hsi times, for instance, an edict pointed out that tribal *sheng-yüan* were denied the privilege of participating in higher examinations or of becoming *ling-sheng* or *kung-sheng*, and that the local authorities need not encourage them to participate in the examinations.[36] Even to participate in the *sheng-yüan* examinations, the candidates had to be guaranteed by *ling-sheng* who were Chinese.[37]

By the nineteenth century, however, tribal candidates of many localities, such as those in Szechwan[38] and Kweichow,[39] were directed to participate in examinations together with the Chinese without separate quotas. In Hunan separate quotas were maintained even after the Taiping period. These tribal candidates actually had a better chance of success than the Chinese candidates. In one locality there were about a hundred tribal candidates to a quota of five.[40] According to the imperial edict, five was the maximum quota which

[30] See *Ch'ing-shih kao,* 200/12 b. Jui-lin was then governor-general of Liang-Kwang, serving in that post from 1865 to 1874.

[31] *Ibid.*, 204/13 b. Chiang was then governor of Kwangtung, serving in that post from 1866 to 1867.

[32] It usually took a long time before an immigrant could be considered as a native of a locality and participate in local examinations. *Yung-ning chou hsü-chih,* 5/32 a–b, records that in Yung-ning thirty years were required before an immigrant could be registered as a native. A moderately wealthy immigrant family had to contribute 30 taels and a wealthy one from 30 to 100 taels for the repair of schools before being permitted to take part in local examinations.

[33] This is a 5 per cent chance of success, as compared to the normal 1 to 2 per cent chance.

[34] *Shih-li,* 379/4 a.

[35] *Hsüeh-cheng,* 78/7 a. *Hsin-t'ung* literally means "new candidates."

[36] *Ibid.*, 62/2 a–b.

[37] *Ibid.*, 82/14 a.

[38] *Ibid.*, 80/13 a.

[39] *Ibid.*, 84/9 a.

[40] *Ibid.*, 78/15 b–16 a.

could be set for tribal candidates in any locality,[41] but the ratio of tribal quota to Chinese quota was quite high in some localities. For instance, in one locality in Hunan bordering Kwangsi, the ratio was 5 : 12,[42] and in another locality bordering Kweichow, the ratio was 2 : 4.[43] A count of the whole province of Hunan shows that 27 localities out of the 80 had separate quotas for the tribal candidates in the early nineteenth century.[44] However, the total tribal quota in Hunan was only 74 as compared to 1219, the over-all quota for the province.[45] This picture remained unchanged in the latter part of the nineteenth century.

Separate quotas for the shed-people (*p'eng-min*)[46] of Kiangsi were first provided in Yung-cheng times. Those who had resided in a locality over twenty years and who were paying land taxes and had ancestral tombs in the locality were permitted to participate in local examinations and were allowed one admission out of 50 candidates.[47] But in 1763 an edict stated that because of the decreased number of shed-people candidates, separate quotas for them were no longer necessary.[48] The decrease in candidates may well have been a result of pressure from native inhabitants.[49] Finally, in the nineteenth century, after some wavering in policy, one locality maintained a quota of four for shed-people,[50] which was increased to six when the shed-people contributed to the military fund during the Taiping period.[51]

While the government tried to lessen conflicts between minority groups and the rest of the people by establishing special quotas, this policy may have

[41] *Ibid.,* 84/5 b.

[42] *Ibid.,* 78/2 b, referring to Ning-yüan.

[43] *Ibid.,* 78/4 a, referring to Ch'ien-chou.

[44] *Ibid.,* 78/1 a–6 b.

[45] The figure of 74 was obtained by counting tribal quotas given in *Shih-li,* 376/4 b–6 a. The figure 1219 appears in Table 15.

[46] The term, "shed-people," refers to a certain group of people who occupied hilly lands in localities of Kiangsi, Chekiang, and Fukien. They lived in sheds and made their living by cultivating hemp, smelting iron, making paper, and processing tobacco. Cf. *Ch'ing-ch'ao wen-hsien t'ung-kao,* 19/5027.

[47] *Shih-li,* 373/2 a; *Hsüeh-cheng,* 72/6 b–7 a. They were permitted to become *tseng-sheng, ling-sheng, kung-sheng,* and participate in examinations in the same manner as the native *sheng-yüan.*

[48] *Shih-li,* 373/2 b; *Hsüeh-cheng,* 72/8 b. The edict points out that there used to be several hundred shed-people candidates in some localities, but except for Wan-tsai, which still had 240 candidates, there were only 50 or even as few as 10 candidates in the various localities.

[49] For instance, *Hsüeh-cheng,* 78/19 a–b, an edict of 1803, refers to a lawsuit brought by native candidates of a locality of Hunan at the Office of Gendarmerie at the capital, accusing eighteen families of unlawfully taking examinations in their locality; it was pointed out that since the natives had not succeeded in surpassing the immigrants who had been settled there for a long time, they brought lawsuits one after another.

[50] *Shih-li,* 373/2 b. In 1804 an edict says that there should be separate quotas for shed-people at Wan-tsai; in Chia-ch'ing 10 it was stated that separate quotas were not needed; and in Chia-ch'ing 13, separate quotas were re-established.

[51] *Ibid.,* 373/3 a–b; effected in 1863. The increases in quota granted in consideration of financial contributions are discussed in detail later in this section.

sometimes actually increased the psychological barrier between these special groups and others under the regular quotas. Unsuccessful candidates often resented their failure and were dissatisfied.

Separate quotas also existed since early Ch'ing times for merchants of the salt monopoly[52] in Chihli, Chekiang, Shantung, Shansi, and Kwangtung, the salt producing and distribution centers. In 1858, Szechwan salt merchants were also permitted to have separate quotas as a reward for their huge contribution to the military fund.[53] In this case, separate quotas obviously did not show discrimination against the merchants but were a special favor granted to them in consideration of their financial support. The separate quotas allowed them a much greater chance of success in the examinations.[54]

A count shows that the total merchant *sheng-yüan* quota was 81 before the Taiping period and 110 after the Taiping period. (See Table 17.) Of this total, Chekiang alone had 50 admissions before the Taiping period and gained an additional 10 during the Taiping period by contributing to the military fund. Since ten was the maximum increase in quota permitted through financial contribution, the Chekiang salt merchants had fully exploited the opportunity and displayed their financial strength.[55] •A survey of the origin of these Chekiang merchants reveals that they were from

[52] The official documents refer to these special quotas as "merchant quotas." That the merchant quotas actually concerned only the salt merchants can be clearly seen by reading the many edicts and memorials in *Shih-li, chüan* 348; *K'o-ch'ang, chüan* 21; and *Hsüeh-cheng, chüan* 85; where the terms "salt merchant" and "merchant" registration were used interchangeably. For instance, in Chihli, the merchant school admitted those of *shang-chi*, or merchant registration, and those of *tsao-chi*, or salt-producer registration. Both registrations were repeatedly mentioned together, indicating both were in the salt business at Ch'ang-lu, Chihli. In the provincial examinations, the *sheng-yüan* of both *shang-chi* and *tsao-chi* origin were classified under *lu-tzu-hao.* The word *lu* means salt. Finally, that during the Ch'ing dynasty, *shang-chi* referred to salt merchants and not to all merchants is explained by definition in *Ch'in-ting ta-Ch'ing hui-tien,* 17/1 b, where it says that there were 4 registrations, namely, *min-chi, chün-chi, shang-chi* and *tsao-chi*; *shang-chi* were defined as "sons and brothers of merchants who were permitted to append themselves to the provinces where business was operating." Since merchants existed and businesses operated in all provinces, the last phrase of the definition must refer only to the licensed salt monopolists, the most influential merchants of the time. A check of the location of these merchants showed that their localities were salt centers. To give one more example, an edict of 1778, given in *Hsüeh-cheng* 85/6, states that merchant registration status should be verified by showing the salt merchant's license. However, examples might be found of men not of merchant families participating in examinations under the merchant quota. For instance, Shen Chao-lin (1801–1863), who died as acting governor-general of Shensi-Kansu, was from a scholar family in Hanchow but participated three times in the *shang-chi t'ung-shih.* However, he succeeded on the fourth occasion by participating with the commoner group. See Shen Chao-lin, *Shen Wen-chung-kung chi, nien-pu,* p. 3 a.

[53] *Shih-li,* 381/3 a.

[54] *Ibid.*, 381/1 a. One out of ten would be successful in other provinces, and one out of twenty in Szechwan. For further details on merchant quotas, see *infra*, III, p. 184.

[55] They paid at least 100,000 taels to earn this increase of quota. For regulations on permission to increase quotas in consideration of financial contributions, see later passages.

Hui-chou prefecture, Anhwei, a place from which many merchants came.[56] In the localities where these big salt merchants resided, the merchant quota maintained a high ratio to the regular quota. The Chekiang merchant quota of 50 was divided among the three schools as follows: Hangchow prefectural school, 20; Jen-ho, 15; and Ch'ien-t'ang, 15.[57] The regular quotas of these schools were as follows: Hangchow prefectural school, 25; Jen-ho, 25; and Ch'ien-t'ang, 25,[58] not greatly different from the merchant quotas.

The merchants in Shansi also took full advantage of the opportunity to increase their quota through financial contributions. The original merchant quota of 10, assigned to the An-i school,[59] was doubled. This again indicates the financial strength of the salt merchants as compared with other groups. However, these special quotas for special groups, although interesting and significant, formed only a minor part of the total quota for the country.

Changes in Quota during the Taiping Period

The relative stability of the *sheng-yüan* quota since early Ch'ing times was greatly disturbed during the Taiping period. Regulations were established providing for the contribution of money to the military fund by local people who were, in turn, to be rewarded with increases in the *sheng-yüan* quota of their native places. Such a regulation first appeared in 1853 when there was an urgent need to increase the public revenue in order to meet the ever increasing expenses of war against the Taipings. An edict of that year says:

> At present, in the military camps to the south and north of the Yangtze, relief soldiers for the suppression of the rebels have amounted to more than 200,000. I, the Emperor, have not spared the use of funds in order to exterminate the evil for the people, and the amount already allotted has amounted to more than 27,000,000 taels. At this moment of gathering a great number of soldiers, the need of military funds is even more urgent. It is therefore necessary to depend on the people's effort for aid to military supplies. ... As requested by the Grand Secretary and others, it is ordered that the governors-general and governors of various provinces should persuade and guide [the people in contribution]. Whether the provinces have already participated in contribution or not, when the gentry, merchants, and commoners contribute to the military fund an amount of 100,000 taels in one province, an increase of one in the civil and one in the military *chü-jen* quota in that province [for one provincial examination] will be allowed. If a *t'ing* or *chou* or *hsien* gathers an amount of 2,000 taels, an increase of one in the civil and one in the military *sheng-yüan* quota [for one *yüan* examination] will be allowed. If the number of increases exceeds the number provided in the original quota, then use the excess in the next examination. If the amount of contribution is compara-

[56] *Shih-li*, 381/1 b–2 a.
[57] *Ibid.*, 381/1 a.
[58] *Ibid.*, 372/3 a.
[59] *Ibid.*, 381/1 a.

tively large, so that there still will be excess even after the several following examinations have their maximum increases, it is permitted to point this out and be duly given permanent increases in quota. ... As to the contributors themselves, it is still permitted that whatever rewards they deserve may be requested, and will be granted with favor in addition [to the quota arrangement].[60]

Later in the same year, another edict stated:

As to the contributions in various provinces, when a round number is being accumulated, the respective governors-general and governors should duly memorialize. Besides the rewards granted to the contributors, each *t'ing*, *chou*, or *hsien* that has gathered 2000 taels will have a temporary increase [*chan-kuang hsüeh-o*] of one in their civil and military *sheng-yüan* quota. If the money contributed exceeds the maximum limit of increase [the original quota of the locality], it will be counted in the increase of quota for the following examination. If the amount of money contributed is relatively large, it is permitted to request permanent increases of quota [*yung-kuang hsüeh-o*]. Each *t'ing*, *chou*, or *hsien* that gathers 10,000 taels can enjoy a permanent increase of one civil and one military *sheng-yüan* in its quota, and the maximum [permanent] increases will be ten for any locality. ...[61]

This ingenious measure for raising money had the effect of completely changing the existing quota arrangement. Some localities were able to increase their quotas a great deal, while others were unable to do so. Whether or not the original apportionment of quotas was fair and just is certainly to be questioned, but the change evidently afforded advantages to wealthy regions.

The importance of this change in quota policy was noted by contemporary observers and later writers. One Western account reports the following:

It was proposed to raise the supplies by the sale of literary rank... but the matter seems to have been not at all to the taste of some of the literati of China; and one of the last Peking Gazettes contains a proposal by which the end will be obtained without degrading the literary character. It is proposed that each district shall be called on for a voluntary subscription, and in proportion to that subscription, a larger number of scholars will be admitted from that district. ... At present, after great weeding out of the examined, only a very small number is chosen, and many are left out, who may not be inferior to the successful candidates. Each district according to its liberality will therefore have the means of obtaining more grades for its literary men than formerly, and at the same time there will be no prostitution of character by lessening the standard of examination. We imagine that this measure will, if carried out, be very effective as appealing to a most assailable point in the character of the Chinese—their literary vanity.[62]

[60] *Shih-lu*, Wen-tsung, 89/10 b–13 a, edict of 1853. See also *Shih-li*, 370/1 a. According to Ch'en K'ang-ch'i, *Lang-ch'ien chi-wen*, 6/2 b–3 a, it was Lei I-hsien, who later introduced the *likin* tax, who first proposed this measure in 1852.

[61] *Shih-li*, 720/5 a. Thus if a district gathered a sum of 10,000 taels there could be either a temporary increase of 5 civil and 5 military *sheng-yüan* for the coming examination only or a permanent increase in quota of one civil and one military *sheng-yüan*.

[62] *North China Herald*, April 2, 1853, No. 140, p. 138, column 4, quoted from *Hongkong Register*, March 15, 1853.

Another commented as follows:

As we have seen that only the qualified students could have the privilege of taking the provincial examinations, we can readily infer that the purchased scholarships were to increase the entries of a certain district in their provincial contest, providing a greater possibility to outdo their rival districts in the race for literary honors and government representation.[63]

Others lamented the great ease of admission into government schools as a result of this change and denounced such measures as degrading the schools by using them as instruments for profit.[64] Before the Taiping period there had been temporary increases in quota on such occasions as the ascendance to the throne by a new emperor,[65] or the sixtieth anniversary of Kao-tsung's reign.[66] But the nature, extent, and effects of increases in quotas during the Taiping period through military contribution were completely different. The earlier temporary increases were a special favor from which all localities benefited equally, but the increases during the Taiping period gave a disproportionate advantage to certain localities. This is illustrated by a case which appeared in a memorial by Chang Fei,[67] the data of which are tabulated in Table 3.

Table 3 shows that Hsi-hsien, the place of origin of the Hangchow salt merchants, and later the Shanghai tea merchants, collected as much as 288,485 taels in this short period, while Chin-hsien collected only 2,836 taels. Thus one made full use of the new regulations, while the other scarcely benefited at all. The Chin-hsien case, however, was exceptional. Another memorial pointed out that the locality was able to contribute more money, but the "big" and rich gentry were reluctant to part with their funds.[68] It seems that the promotion of local interests was not always a sufficient motive to induce some to part with their money. In general, however, the wealthy localities far surpassed the poorer ones in quota increases.

Localities could request either permanent or temporary increases, but they naturally preferred permanent ones. The amount of money required to obtain five temporary increases would obtain one permanent increase. Thus,

[63] Hsieh Pao-chao, *op. cit.*, p. 150.

[64] Shen Shou-chih, "Chieh-ch'ao pi-chi," *Jen-wen yüeh-k'an,* April 15, 1936, *chüan* 7, No. 3, pp. 5 and 6, a reprint of personal notes of a man of the Taiping period.

[65] For example, see E. C. Bridgman, "The Emperor Taokwang: his succession to the throne of his father, coronation, with notices of his character and government," *Chinese Repository*, Vol. X, No. 2, Feb. 1841, pp. 87–98; *T'ung-jen fu-chih*, 5/7 ff. The increases were generally 7 for a large school, 5 for a middle-sized school, and 3 for a small school.

[66] *T'ung-jen fu-chih*, 5/7 ff.

[67] Chang Fei, *Chang Wen-i-kung tsou-kao*, 2/37 ff., memorial of Hsien-feng 9/4/24 (1859).

[68] See *ibid.*, 1/25 b ff., memorial of Hsien-feng 8/6/13 (1858) reporting big and rich gentry for refusal to lead in contribution to the military fund.

TABLE 3

REQUESTS FOR INCREASES OF EXAMINATION QUOTAS IN RECOGNITION OF MILITARY FUND CONTRIBUTIONS IN SOUTH ANHWEI

(Hsien-feng 5/5 [1855] to Hsien-feng 9/4 [1859])

Place	Amount contributed (in taels)	Permanent increases in *sheng-yüan* quota	Temporary increases in *sheng-yüan* quota
Hsi-hsien	288,485	10 (for Hsi-hsien) 10 (for Hui-chou prefecture)	44
Hsiu-ning	159,399	10	29
Wu-yüan	53,228	5	1
I-hsien	113,719	10	6
Ch'i-men	31,348	3	
Chi-hsi	55,942	5	2
Chin-hsien	2,836		1
Chin-te	5,572		2
T'ai-p'ing	54,021	5	2
Ch'ing-yang	20,038	2	
Shih-ti	14,378	1	1
Totals	798,966	61	88

Note: In addition, two permanent and two temporary increases in *chü-jen* quota were requested in accordance with the regulations. It was pointed out that the rewards for most of the individual contributors had already been requested.

for example, all the localities of South Anhwei upon gathering a sum of 10,000 taels would request one permanent increase rather than five temporary increases until they reached the limit of ten permanent increases. This will help us later on in computing the amount of permanent and temporary increases in quota.

The contributions so far discussed were for the military funds controlled by the government. In the latter part of the Taiping period, the practice of granting increases of examination quotas in return for financial contributions was even extended to contribution to the *t'uan-lien* (local corps) funds. This was first proposed by a censor in 1858. According to a memorial presented by the governor of Kwangsi in 1865, such contributions were to assist the gentry and people in organizing local corps and suppressing bandits. The accounts were supposedly audited by local officials but did not have to be reported to the Board of Revenue.[69] This shows that the central government had to acknowledge the growth of local corps organizations and the ever increasing political, military, and financial powers of the gentry organizers

[69] *Chen-an fu-chih*, 14/23 b–25 a, a memorial by Governor Chang K'ai-sung, requesting increases in both *sheng-yüan* and *chü-jen* quotas on account of contribution to the local corps fund by 32 localities in Kwangsi amounting to 765,821 taels. The censor referred to is Meng Ch'uan-chin.

while at the same time attempting to preserve some official control over them.[70]

In order to keep the quota system from getting completely out of hand, the government set up the limit of ten permanent increases for each locality. In 1858, a supplementary regulation further stressed that for localities whose quotas were less than ten, the permanent increases, if any, should not exceed the original quotas.[71] However, these limits were sometimes exceeded. For instance, in 1858 the Shanghai school secured a permanent quota increase of ten because of financial contributions.[72] This was as much as they were supposed to have, but in 1865 they were granted four more permanent increases because of the effort made by gentry and commoners in the defense of the city.[73]

After the suppression of the Taipings when the strain on the military budget was somewhat eased, the government discouraged further permanent increases in quota. In 1868 an edict stated:

> The increase of *sheng-yüan* quota in various provinces through contribution in accordance with the old regulations shall be that for each *t'ing*, *chou*, or *hsien* that collects an amount of 4,000 taels, there shall be granted one temporary increase. If the amount is 20,000 taels, there shall be granted one permanent increase. If contributors have already requested their own rewards, or if the collections have been counted towards the increase of *chü-jen* quota, the contributions shall not be permitted to be counted again in the request for the increase of *sheng-yüan* quota.[74]

Thus twice the amount of money was to be contributed to gain each increase of quota, and while formerly one sum could lead to three types of compensation, namely, rewards for the contributors, increase in *chü-jen* quota, and increase in *sheng-yüan quota*, it now led to only one of the three. By 1871 the practice of granting permanent increases in *sheng-yüan* quota finally came to an end. An edict of that year stated: "All contributors in the various provinces will be permitted to request only temporary increases in *sheng-yüan* quota. None will be permitted to request permanent increases in quota. The amount of silver is altered so that any locality which collects

[70] Unpublished monograph by Franz Michael, "Military Organization and Power Structure in Nineteenth-Century China."

[71] *Shih-li*, 370/1 a.

[72] *Ibid.*, 371/8 a.

[73] *Ibid.* From this it appears that on special occasions, permanent increases in quota could occur without actual monetary contributions being made to the government. But it is possible that such increases might still be rewards for contributions. Since this locality had already obtained the maximum amount of increases through contribution, the extra increase was justified on a different basis. In general, however, such cases were rare.

[74] *Shih-li,* 720/5 a; 370/1 a–b.

10,000 taels will be permitted to have one temporary increase in quota of one civil and one military *sheng-yüan*."[75]

However, the damage was done. The wealthy localities had already met their maximum allowance of permanent increases while the others could no longer apply for increases. The increase in quota in the post-Taiping period was mainly due to the practice of giving permanent increases in quota in return for financial contributions, as shown in Table 4.

TABLE 4

A SUMMARY TABLE OF CIVIL SHENG-YÜAN QUOTA BEFORE AND AFTER THE TAIPING PERIOD*

Division	Pre-Taiping Quota	Post-Taiping Quota		
		Regular Quota	Permanent Increases (due to contribution)	Total
8 Banners	109	109	33	142
Fengt'ien	71	130	29	159
Chihli	2,845	2,848	40	2,888
Kiangsu	1,402	1,408	360	1,768
Anhwei	1,289	1,289	315	1,604
Chekiang	1,800	1,803	374	2,177
Kiangsi	1,350	1,350	670	2,020
Fukien	1,187	1,208	347	1,555
Honan	1,631	1,633	235	1,868
Shantung	1,830	1,830	123	1,953
Shansi	1,536	1,542	84	1,626
Hupeh	1,087	1,107	427	1,534
Hunan	1,219	1,229	418	1,647
Shensi } Kansu }	1,865	1,133	103	1,236
		882	7	889
Szechwan	1,366	1,374	544	1,918
Kwangtung	1,326	1,339	409	1,748
Kwangsi	1,019	1,027	105	1,132
Yunnan	1,323	1,369	3	1,372
Kweichow	753	766	1	767
Merchant	81	89	21	110
Totals	25,089	25,465	4,648	30,113

* Summarized from Tables 15 and 16.

The column of permanent increases in Table 4 shows that Kiangsi had most fully exploited the opportunity of increasing its *sheng-yüan* quota, the next in line being Szechwan, Hupeh, Hunan, Kwangtung, Chekiang, Kiangsu, and Anhwei, while last of all is Kweichow with a permanent increase of only one for the whole province. This further substantiates the view that the wealth of the various provinces was one of the main factors in the race for

[75] *Ibid.*

increases in *sheng-yüan* quotas, although it was by no means the sole factor involved.

In the provinces where actual battles were fought, and the need for defense was strong and immediate, local contributions to the military effort naturally flowed in. The gentry and commoners, driven by the fear of losing everything, naturally increased their money contributions. Hence, for instance, in Kiangsu, a province where the Taipings were for approximately ten years, fifty-seven out of seventy-eight schools obtained permanent increases in *sheng-yüan* quotas.[76] In Shansi, where the threat of the rebels was much less, only twenty-seven out of the one hundred and twenty-one schools obtained such permanent increases.[77]

On this point of permanent increases in *sheng-yüan* quota, it is also of interest to know who made these contributions. A typical example can be taken from the province of Chihli. In 1854 an edict stated that when the rebels approached Tientsin, the gentry there contributed to the military fund and organized local corps, and that five permanent increases were therefore granted to the prefectural school of Tientsin and three to its *hsien* school. In 1859, because of contributions to the military fund by the gentry and the rich, four permanent increases were granted to the *hsien* school of Tientsin. In 1865, because of contributions to the military fund by gentry and commoners, two permanent increases were granted to Nan-kung. In 1866, because of contributions to the military fund by merchants and commoners, six permanent increases were granted to the *hsien* school of Tientsin. In 1869, one permanent increase was granted to Ta-hsing because the military officers of that locality had contributed to military supplies.[78]

Sometimes officials on active duty in other provinces also made financial contributions for the benefit of their home areas. For example, in 1869 a *hsien* magistrate of Hsiang-yin, Hunan, contributed 10,000 taels and obtained a permanent increase of the *sheng-yüan* quota of his home locality, Lou-hsien, Kiangsu.[79] This occurred immediately after the suppression of the Taipings, but most of the contributions to increase quota were made during the Taiping period.

Hence, through contributions the 1,810 government schools of the post-Taiping period had increased their *sheng-yüan* quotas to a total of 30,113,[80]

[76] Obtained by actual count from data in *Shih-li*, 371/7 b–8 b.

[77] Obtained by count from data in *ibid.*, 375/6 b–7 a.

[78] *Ibid.*, 371/4 b–5 a.

[79] *Sung-chiang-fu hsü-chih*, 17/13.

[80] See Table 16 based on data as of 1886. As pointed out before, the pre-Taiping school figure based on data of 1812 is 1,741. If we take another figure from a year in between, for instance 1825, we find the figure to be 1,788. (*Shih-li*, 1096/5 b.) (This figure is slightly high since it includes also the imperial clan school and others.) Thus, there was a gradual increase despite a fall in population during the period. See Table 32.

the increase being unevenly distributed among the provinces. Chihli still had the highest total, but its lead was greatly cut down because of its relatively small contribution to the military fund. Kweichow and Kansu, which had contributed little, remained at the bottom of the list. In general, the provinces along the coast and the Yangtze had more or less paced each other in the race for more increases in quota, leaving other provinces lagging behind.

In connection with the point of examination quota, the question arises as to how many participated in these local examinations, and what chance a candidate had to become a *sheng-yüan*. This is in effect to ask about the number of *t'ung-sheng*, the students aspiring to become gentry. We will not attempt to go into detail on this question, but to give some idea of it may be useful.

In the Shun-chih period, one writer said that in big *hsien*, there were not less than two thousand candidates while in middle-sized and small *hsien* there were over a thousand.[81] An edict of 1761 pointed out that Mou-chou and other places in Szechwan had a quota of 12 or 8 while participants were relatively few, but that in Tzu-chou and other places in the same province, the number of participants varied from 700 to over 1,000, while the quota was 8, 10, or 12.[82] Obviously, even before the nineteenth century, the number of participants in different localities could vary from a few hundred to over two thousand, so that the candidates' chances of success varied greatly according to the locality.

Increases in quota through contribution could have led either to greater or less equality among the various localities in the ratio of candidates to quota. However, it seems that the trend was toward a little more equality, as it was generally the localities with a large number of candidates which most fully exploited the opportunity of increasing quotas in this way. In Hunan, for instance, Liu-yang usually had 2,000 participants in the civil examination for admission of *sheng-yüan*, as reported in the local gazetteer, while the quota was only 12; but An-hsiang, though it had only slightly over 200 participants, had a quota of 15.[83] This fact was brought to the attention of the court, and an edict of 1852 authorized an addition of 3 to the Liu-yang quota by cutting the An-hsiang quota from 15 to 12.[84] This was only a slight correction of the original unbalance. Under the provision of contribution to the military fund, Liu-yang then acquired the maximum

[81] Hou Fang-yü, "Give Importance to Schools," *Huang-ch'ao ching-shih wen-pien*, 57/11.

[82] *Hsüeh-cheng*, 80/16 b.

[83] *Liu-yang hsien-chih*, 8/17 b.

[84] *Ibid.* Cf. also *Shih-li*, 376/8 a.

number of increases in quota, namely, ten, while the An-hsiang school did not get even one.[85] Of course, the inequality was still very great.

To give more examples of the number of participants in the examinations, in Nan-yang, Honan, it was reported that since the beginning of the nineteenth century there were almost 2,000 participants competing for a quota of 16 civil and 16 military *sheng-yüan* admissions.[86] Nan-yang had only one permanent increase during the Taiping period.[87] Po-pai, Kwangsi, was recorded to have an examination shed which would hold 1,500 candidates,[88] while the quota there was originally 12,[89] later raised by a permanent increase of 6.[90] Nan-ning prefecture in the same province had an examination shed with 2,260 compartments, 600 of which were added in 1827.[91] Nan-hai and P'an-yü in Kwangtung were each reported to have upward of 2,000 candidates in 1832, while nearby Hsiang-shan was said to have not half so many.[92] However, Hsiang-shan evidently had more candidates later on, for the examination shed built in 1889 would accommodate 2,000 candidates.[93] Hsin-hui, Kwangtung, was also reported to have approximately 2,000 candidates in the civil examinations and 200 in the military examinations in the early part of the nineteenth century.[94] In a prefectural or *fu* examination in Canton in 1833, 25,000 candidates coming from seven districts were reported to have participated.[95] Five thousand to 6,000 candidates were said to have participated in a *yüan* examination supervised by the provincial director-of-studies in Canton in 1835.[96] Another *yüan* examination held in Soochow prefecture, Kiangsu, was attended by some 10,000 candidates.[97]

[85] *Shih-li,* 376/8 b.

[86] *Hsin-hsiu Nan-yang hsien-chih*, 6/4 b–5 a.

[87] *Shih-li,* 374/5 a.

[88] *Po-pai hsien-chih*, 4/37 b. As described, the examination shed consisted of one group of compartments made of stone, and four groups to the left and right made of boards. The wall around was nine feet high.

[89] *Shih-li,* 379/7 a.

[90] *Ibid.*, 379/9 a.

[91] Ch'eng-lin, "On Repair of Nan-ning Prefectural Examination Hall," *Nan-ning fu-chih,* 52/23 a.

[92] S. W. Williams, *The Middle Kingdom*, p. 547. Williams commented that the number of candidates depended upon the population and the literary spirit of the district.

[93] *Hsiang-shan hsien-chih hsü-pien*, 4/1 b.

[94] *Hsüeh-cheng*, 81/15 a.

[95] *The Chinese Repository*, Vol. II, No. 1, May, 1833, p. 47. The candidates of different districts assembled on different days, according to notice previously given by the prefect who presided at the examination.

[96] *Ibid.*, Vol. III, No. 10, Feb. 1835, p. 488. The source merely says, "literary examinations having been in progress in the provincial city," without indicating clearly whether it was a *yüan* or *fu* or *chü-jen* examination which was referred to. As the *chü-jen* examination would be held in the autumn, this possibility is ruled out. The *fu* examination just referred to, which was held in the same place two years earlier, shows many more participants. Therefore, it can be concluded that it is the *yüan* examination which is referred to.

[97] *Wylie, op. cit.*, pp. 148–50.

Some of the examples presented above seem to suggest that although the quota had increased, the number of candidates also had increased. However, this does not seem to have always been the rule. According to a gentry member writing in the late nineteenth century, it had become much easier to become a *sheng-yüan* by that time. The number of candidates in that writer's native place, Wu-hsien, Kiangsu, had been decreasing while the quota had increased. When that writer himself had participated in the examinations in the Tao-kuang period (1821–1850), approximately 1,000 candidates competed for 25 admissions. The writer pointed out that this number of candidates was already lower than that in the late eighteenth or early nineteenth century. He went on to complain that since the Taiping period, people cared too much for ease and luxury and paid less attention to education. Only five or six hundred now participated in the examinations. Finally he stated that with the permanent increases in quota during the Taiping period, it had become much easier to pass the examinations.[98]

This writer did not limit his remarks to the conditions in his own district but was expressing his concern over the general deterioration of good customs and the declining literary spirit of the time. One might speculate that the merchant influence in society was finally exploding, and the people in general no longer regarded the examination route to gentry status as the only good career. Such a change would no doubt greatly affect the social and economic life of the country and undermine the control system of the central government, which was greatly dependent on the indoctrination of the upper social group through the examination system.

From the above examples and other available data, the average number of *t'ung-sheng* in a locality would be estimated at little over 1,000 and certainly not over 1,500.[99] The total number of *t'ung-sheng* would probably amount to close to 2,000,000.

Military Sheng-yüan Quotas

So far our discussion of the quota problem has dealt with the civil *sheng-yüan*. Complete records of the civil *sheng-yüan* quotas of different localities can be found in official documents, but no such records were preserved for

[98] Shen Shou-chih, "Chieh-ch'ao pi-chi," in *Jen-wen yüeh-k'an*, *chüan* 7, No. 3, pp. 5–6.

[99] Wm. A. P. Martin, "On the Competitive Examination System in China," *American Oriental Society Journal*, Proceedings at Boston, May, 1869, p. lv. Martin puts the average at two thousand, but this must be an overestimate based on data on a few coastal localities, especially those of Kwangtung. If his average were correct, the total number of *t'ung-sheng* would be approximately three million. However, in *The Chinese; Their Education, Philosophy and Letters*, pp. 40–53, he estimated that two million candidates were taking examinations at one or another level, of whom only one or two per cent were finally successful. This estimate is too low if he really meant to include all the *sheng-yüan* and *chü-jen* who attended one or another kind of examination. See *infra*, III.

the military *sheng-yüan.* We cannot, therefore, determine the total military *sheng-yüan* quota by actual count but must work from less complete data.

As pointed out before, the official regulations on civil *sheng-yüan* quotas in 1670 were as follows: big prefectures, 20; big *chou* or *hsien*, 15; middle-sized schools, 12; and small schools, 8 to 10. The regulations on military *sheng-yüan* quota in 1671 were as follows: prefectural schools, 20; big *chou* or *hsien* schools, 15; middle-sized schools, 12; and small schools, 7 to 8.[100] From this it would appear that at that time the quotas for civil and military *sheng-yüan* were practically the same.[101]

In the nineteenth century, some localities, such as those of T'ung-ch'uan prefecture, Szechwan, had the same quotas for both civil and military *sheng-yüan.*[102] However, the records of many other localities show a difference between the two quotas almost always in favor of the civil quota.[103] A careful check into the records of some of the local gazetteers reveals that the change occurred mainly in the early Yung-cheng period (1723–1735). In Pa-ling, Hunan, the quota in early Ch'ing times was 15 for both civil and military *sheng-yüan*, but in 1724 the civil quota was increased to 20.[104] In Nan-ch'ang, Kiangsi, the civil and military quotas had both been 15, the quota for a big *hsien*, but in 1724 the provincial director-of-studies, Shen I-chi, memorialized and received approval that big *hsien* should have an increase of 5 in civil quota and no increase in military quota.[105] Hsing-kuo, Hupeh, had an original quota of 15 civil *sheng-yüan* which was increased to 20 in 1726.[106]

The reason for this change was not reported in the records. It may have been the excessive number of civil examination candidates as compared with the military, or it may have been that the court thought there should be an even larger proportion of civil gentry, since it was this group on which the government depended for social control and management in the communities.

Some of the differences between the civil and military *sheng-yüan* quotas originated after the Yung-cheng period. While the permanent increases effected during the Taiping Rebellion were generally the same for both civil and military quotas, there were occasional variations in favor of the civil quota. In Yung-ning, Kweichow, for instance, it was recorded that the original quotas were 8 for both civil and military *sheng-yüan*, but in 1838

100 *Shih-li,* 719/3 a.

101 Data for the same years are not available, but as no change in civil quota was mentioned for K'ang-hsi 10 (1671), these figures are comparable.

102 *T'ung-ch'uan fu-chih,* 13/41 b ff.

103 E.g., the different localities of Huai-an prefecture, Kiangsu (*Huai-an fu-chih,* 21/5 b ff.); of Kuang-chou prefecture, Kwangtung (*Kuang-chou fu-chih,* 72/3 a ff.).

104 *Pa-ling hsien-chih,* 17/20 b–21 a.

105 *Nan-ch'ang hsien-chih,* 12/3 a.

106 *Hsing-kuo chou-chih,* 8/6 a.

when the gentry requested a quota increase because of the increased number of candidates, two increases for civil and one for military *sheng-yüan* quota were effected.[107] In Tao-chou, Hunan, on one occasion, upon the contribution of back pay by Hunan militia from this locality fighting in Kiangsi, only one civil quota increase was effected; thus we find the record of permanent increases there of 6 civil and 5 military in *sheng-yüan* quota.[108]

Although complete records are not available, a number of local gazetteers do give such information on their own localities. Table 18 is a tabulation of the data available for 153 localities spread over eleven provinces (among which there is the complete record for all localities of Kwangsi province).[109] According to these figures, the military *sheng-yüan* quota was approximately 85 per cent of the civil one in the pre-Taiping period. During the Taiping period, practically the same increases were effected in civil and military *sheng-yüan* quotas, thus raising the military *sheng-yüan* quota to 88 per cent of the civil one in the post-Taiping period. On this basis, we arrive at the following estimates of military *sheng-yüan* quota for the whole country: pre-Taiping period, 21,233; post-Taiping period, 26,806. (See Tables 20 and 22.)[110]

THE SIZE OF THE GENTRY BEFORE AND AFTER 1850

Average Span of Years of a Sheng-yüan

To estimate the number of "regular" gentry existing at any one time in the pre-Taiping or post-Taiping periods, the next procedure is to determine the average age at which examination candidates were admitted to *sheng-yüan* status and their average age at death. In other words, we shall try to find out the life expectancy of a *sheng-yüan* at the time he became a member of the gentry.

The age of candidates in an examination held in Canton was reported to

[107] *Yung-ning chou hsü-chih*, 5/26 a.

[108] *Tao-chou chih*, 5/33 a–b.

[109] This random selection of localities might be questioned. Further, the completeness of the Kwangsi data as compared with the incompleteness of data for other provinces might be seen as a weak point. However, the increase of civil *sheng-yüan* quota of big *hsien* in Yung-cheng times was universal, and to have complete data available for a province is an advantage. Thus, for instance, in the table the prefecture of T'ung-ch'uan, Szechwan, is not representative of the whole province since it happened to be a prefecture with no *hsien* schools classified as "big."

[110] These figures are not arrived at by simply using the total pre-Taiping and post-Taiping civil *sheng-yüan* quota figures given above. They are the sums of military *sheng-yüan* quotas worked out province by province. This is necessary because (1) the merchant schools had only civil *sheng-yüan* and no military *sheng-yüan* quotas; (2) "temporary" increases in quota during the Taiping period have not yet been included in the post-Taiping civil *sheng-yüan* quota given above.

be from "the lad of fifteen years to the hoary head of seventy and upwards." [111] In T'ung-chou, Kiangsu, the youngest candidate recorded who succeeded in becoming a *sheng-yüan* was a boy of only eleven.[112] A boy in Shensi supposedly could compose at the age of seven, gaining himself the name of a "divine" lad, and it was claimed that he became a *sheng-yüan* at the age of nine.[113] These are naturally exceptional cases and were therefore specially noted. The average age of becoming a *sheng-yüan* does not seem to have been beyond twenty-five. One gentry member mentions in his autobiography that he obtained the *sheng-yüan* title at the age of twenty-six which he considered as late.[114] Since there are no complete examination records for *sheng-yüan* as there are for holders of higher degrees, we resort to the autobiographies of eighty *sheng-yüan* in Wu-hsi and Chin-kuei in the post-Taiping period, ranging from one who became a *sheng-yüan* in 1871 to some who succeeded in 1905, the last year of the examination system.[115]

TABLE 5

AGE OF ADMISSION TO SHENG-YÜAN STATUS

Age Group	Number	Per cent
16–20*	15	19
21–25	35	44
26–30	23	29
31–35	6	7
36–40	1†	1
Totals	80	100

* The lowest age is 16. Yu T'ung, who claimed in his autobiography to have become a *sheng-yüan* at 14, was found by calculation to have succeeded at 17.
† The age is 39.

From Table 5 we see that the largest number of *sheng-yüan* were admitted between the ages of 21 and 25. The average age of admission of these eighty *sheng-yüan* is approximately 24. This fits quite well with the average age of obtaining *chü-jen* and *chin-shih* degrees which we shall show later to have been approximately 30 and 35 respectively.

111 *The Chinese Repository,* Vol. II, No. 1, May, 1833, p. 47.

112 *T'ung-chou chih-li-chou chih*, 13/85 b, referring to Li Sun-yüan of the Tao-kuang period.

113 *Shensi t'ung-chih kao*, 82/16 b, referring to Chu K'ai of the Taiping period, a native of An-k'ang.

114 *Hsi-Chin yu-hsiang t'ung-jen tzu-shu hui-k'an, ts'e shia*, p. 44, referring to Hu Chieh-ch'ang.

115 *Ibid.* The autobiographies are arranged in the order of these men's year of success in becoming *sheng-yüan.* As each autobiography gives the date of birth, the age of becoming *sheng-yüan* can be computed.

Satisfactory information on the average age of death of *sheng-yüan* is even more difficult to secure. Table 19 is a tabulated study of the age of death of men who had biographies and who were born between 1731 and 1880, arranged in five-year age groups and broken down into three periods of fifty years each. The age of death of these men, almost all of whom were gentry, is relatively advanced. The average age of death declines from 63.6 in the first period (1731–1780) to 61.1 in the second period (1781–1830) and to 57.8 in the third period (1831–1880). It might be argued that these men studied were more or less those having outstanding accomplishments, and that a generalization based on a study of this special group could not be applied to others. However, in local gazetteers where there are records of aged persons, many were listed as over 80 years of age, including both gentry and commoners.[116] The total of aged persons in all provinces was once reported to be as high as one and a half million.[117] The number might have been somewhat exaggerated by the provincial officials in order to please the Emperor, but it does give support to the idea that the average age of death of gentry, as derived from our tabulation, may not be too high a figure.

Checking our rough figure with the results of other studies, it is interesting to see that they coincide closely with each other. In the "Life Table for a Southern Chinese Family from 1365 to 1849," the conclusion reached is that the expectation of life at 20 was 37.7 years for males and 39.7 years for females.[118] Hence, the adults of this family, on the average, lived to about the age of 60, close to our figure. According to Seifert's life tables of Chinese farmers, the expectation of life at zero age is 34.85 for males and 34.63 for females; at 20, it is 40.74 years for males and 40.08 for females.[119] Another field study by Chen Ta, made at Ch'eng-kung, Yunnan, indicates that the average life expectancy in Ch'eng-kung at zero age was 36.0 years

[116] E.g., *T'eng-hsien chih, chüan* 18, (Kwangsi), where hundreds were listed including a considerable number of gentry.

[117] *Ch'ing Shih-tsung Hsien-huang-ti sheng-hsün*, 49/14 a–b, as quoted in an edict of 1726. This figure refers only to commoners over 70. They were to enjoy government beneficence. See *T'ai-ho hsien-chih*, Introductory *chüan*/7 b. However, in *The Chinese Repository*, Vol. IX, No. 5, Sept., 1840, p. 259, old men over 70 enjoying government beneficence in 18 provinces were reported to total less than 400,000.

[118] J. C. Yuan, "Life Table for a Southern Chinese Family from 1365 to 1849," *Human Biology*, May, 1931. Yuan's results have been summarized by Chen Ta, *Population in Modern China*, p. 36. Yuan attempts to construct life tables from genealogical records of the Li family of Chung-shan, Kwangtung. These records refer to 3,748 males and 3,752 females who were born between 1365 and 1849. Life tables have been constructed for them at each quinquennial age from 20 to 75.

[119] H. E. Seifert, "Life Tables for Chinese Farmers," *Milbank Memorial Fund Quarterly*, Vol. XI, No. 4, Oct., 1933; Vol. XII, Nos. 1, 2, 3, Jan., April, July, 1934. This study was based on data on rural population collected through farm surveys made by the University of Nanking between 1929 and 1931, including 2,817 male deaths and 2,682 female deaths in 101 districts spread over 17 provinces.

for both sexes.[120] However, Chen Ta did not give the expectation of life at the age of 20. Working from the data he collected, this writer found that the expectation of life at 20 was close to 35—an average age of death of 55.[121] This figure is the lowest among the various studies, but it is still close to our rough estimate.

Although some of the figures arrived at in the above do not apply to the nineteenth century, nor to what we consider as the gentry group, we should be able to safely assume that the average age of death of gentry members was about 57 or 58. The post-Taiping average was probably somewhat lower as a consequence of war and other disturbances. However, it is doubtful that the difference would be very great, and therefore no attempt is made here to set an arbitrary figure for the difference. We shall assume, then, that an average *sheng-yüan* was admitted to his privileged status at the age of 24 and died at the age of 57, having been a member of the gentry for approximately 33 years.

Estimate of Total Number of Sheng-yüan

As we have seen earlier, there were two civil and one military *yüan* examinations every three years. Hence, including the *yüan* examination in which our imaginary *sheng-yüan* succeeded, during the 33 years that he was a gentry member there would be 22 civil and 11 military *yüan* examinations in each locality. But by the time he was going to see the 22nd civil or 11th military *yüan* examination, we have assumed that he would have died and been offset by a new member from the 22nd civil or 11th military *yüan* examination in his locality. Similarly, another *sheng-yüan* who was admitted in an examination immediately following the one that admitted our imaginary *sheng-yüan* would presumably be offset by a new member of the 23rd civil or 12th military *yüan* examination, and so on. In other words, if the quota is practically a constant, we would then arrive at a constant figure for the *sheng-yüan* total. Therefore, the number of civil *sheng-yüan* at any one time would be 21 times the quota and that of the military *sheng-yüan* would be 10 times the quota. From this basis, the total number of *sheng-yüan* can then be derived.

The total number of *sheng-yüan* thus arrived at includes, of course, those who later became *chien-sheng*, *kung-sheng*, *chü-jen*, *chin-shih*, and officials. There is no need to make deductions for them, since they remained gentry

[120] Chen Ta, *loc. cit.* The field work was done between Feb., 1940, and June, 1944, during which time a total of 4,254 male deaths and 4,136 female deaths in Ch'eng-kung were reported.

[121] Data based on Chen Ta, *op. cit.*, p. 96, Table 22. From his table, we see that about half of the deaths were those of children under the age of 5.

members. The figure should perhaps be slightly discounted to account for those who were deprived of their titles because of offenses; however, this factor has been disregarded here because there is no evidence to show that it would make an appreciable difference.

The number of *sheng-yüan* existing at any one time in the pre-Taiping period can then be computed as follows: 21 times the civil quota of 25,089 equals 526,869 civil *sheng-yüan*; 10 times the military quota of 21,233 equals 212,330 military *sheng-yüan*. This is a total of approximately 740,000 *sheng-yüan*. The number of *sheng-yüan* and their distribution over provinces is shown in Table 20.

In computing the number of *sheng-yüan* in the post-Taiping period, however, we have to consider another factor. In the earlier discussion of quotas, we arrived at post-Taiping quotas by including the important permanent increases but not the temporary increases in quota. Temporary increases through imperial favor on occasions of national celebration occurred throughout the nineteenth century, but they were occasional and can be disregarded. However, temporary increases through contribution to the military fund during and after the Taiping period were an important factor.

For example, in the districts of Ch'ang, Yüan, and Wu, in Soochow prefecture, the number of *sheng-yüan* admitted from 27 examinations during the 40 years before the Taiping period was 1,724 by actual count. The number of *sheng-yüan* admitted from 28 examinations during the 40 years in and after the Taiping period was 2,790, an increase of 1,066 or approximately 60 per cent. (See Table 21.) All these three districts had secured 10 permanent increases of quota—the maximum allowed.[122] However, this accounts for only 840 of the increase. The remaining increase of 226, amounting to one-fifth of the total increase, was mainly due to temporary increases obtained through financial contributions. Hsi-hsien, Anhwei, also had a large number of temporary increases, as noted above in Table 3.

The Soochow example, in which the proportion of temporary increases to permanent increases is more than 20 per cent, is an unusual case. Many districts secured few, if any, temporary increases. As mentioned earlier, a locality could obtain a temporary increase in quota, in the Hsien-feng period, for instance, by collecting 2,000 taels, but it would be to the advantage of the locality to apply for a permanent increase if the amount collected reached 10,000 taels. It is therefore inconceivable that the number of temporary increases would be very high.[123] Obviously, also, the permanent increases

[122] *Shih-li*, 371/7 b.

[123] The regulation provided that the temporary increases in quota for each examination could be as high as the original quota. Shen Shou-chih, *loc. cit.*, seemed to think that

had a cumulative effect, while the temporary increases raised the quota for one examination only. For example, in the 11 localities of southern Anhwei, the approximately 60 permanent increases in quota in 20 civil *yüan* examinations account for the admission of 1,200 *sheng-yüan*, while the temporary increases of 88 account for only 88 *sheng-yüan.* Since complete information is not available, temporary increases have been roughly estimated as 5 per cent of the permanent increases.[124]

The total number of *sheng-yüan* in the post-Taiping period is thus estimated to be approximately 910,000, as shown in Table 22. This is an increase of 23 per cent over the pre-Taiping figure. It is to be noted that Ku Yen-wu,[125] the well-known early Ch'ing scholar, once made a rough estimate of the number of civil *sheng-yüan*, saying, "All together, the country's *sheng-yüan*, with some three hundred to a *hsien*, are not under half a million."[126] Amiot also wrote in 1777 that the (civil) *sheng-yüan* quota was 24,701, and estimated the total number of *sheng-yüan* at 20 times the quota, namely,

such opportunity would be fully utilized by all localities and thus estimated that the total additional (civil and military) *sheng-yüan* alone, admitted after one such examination, would be well over a hundred thousand. Shen, being a gentry member of Wu-hsien, Soochow, based his estimate on his experience in his own locality, which was unusually wealthy. Therefore, his estimate is far too high.

124 Some records might give the impression that temporary increases might be as big a factor as permanent increases. For instance, in Lou-hsien, Kiangsu, we find that in 1860 there was one temporary increase in quota and two permanent increases; in 1863 there were three temporary increases and one permanent increase; and in 1869, one permanent increase. (*Sung-chiang-fu hsü-chih*, 17/13.) However, as we have already shown, unless the temporary increases were kept up steadily, they would still be only a small fraction of the total increases over a period of years.

125 (1613–1682). See Hummel, *op. cit.*, p. 423.

126 Ku Yen-wu, "T'ing-ling wen-chi" in *T'ing-ling i-shu shih-chung*, 1–17 b. Lin Yu-tang, in *My Country and My People*, p. 228, incorrectly translated Ku's statement as, "There must be half a million of these students in the three hundred *hsien*." There were about 1,400 *hsien* at that time, and Ku was not discussing the number of *hsien* but the number of *sheng-yüan* in each *hsien.* Three hundred multiplied by the number of *hsien* results in a figure close to half a million. Hsieh Pao-chao also attempted to reach figures for *sheng-yüan*, and even for *ling-sheng* and *tseng-sheng.* However, his figures are rough and he did not understand the problem. He says, "Every year, approximately 50,000 students were taken into the district colleges by this process. They received a sort of allowance from the provincial government either in money or rice. . . . In addition to these salaried students, about 50,000 additional students (*tseng-sheng*), 80,000 extra students (*fu-sheng*), and 4,650 purchased scholarships were annually given. . . . The total number of students qualified in each of the two tours of the educational commissioners in the whole country was then, roughly estimated, about 286,500 . . . so in every three years, 573,000 students were qualified for the provincial examinations." (*The Government of China*, pp. 148–50.) In the first place, *sheng-yüan* were not admitted in every year. Second, we have shown that the quota of *sheng-yüan* was only 25,339 in the pre-Taiping period and 30,515 in the post-Taiping period. This is only about one-tenth of Hsieh's figure. Hsieh evidently did not devote time to counting and counted only the purchased scholarships. The worst mistake is to say that every year 50,000 became *ling-sheng*, 50,000 became *tseng-sheng*, and 80,000 became *fu-sheng.* Our estimate of the expectation of life after one became a *sheng-yüan* was 33 years. 50,000 multiplied by 33 would be, 1,800,000 *ling-sheng* alone at any one time receiving stipends from the government. The government could not possibly have afforded it. Finally, how he reached the figure of 286,500 is not clear.

494,020.[127] These figures are quite close to our estimate of 526,869 civil *sheng-yüan* in the pre-Taiping period. Our figure should be slightly higher than his, since we estimate for a later period and the *sheng-yüan* quota had been gradually increasing. Thus the *sheng-yüan* total remained little changed for the first two hundred years of the dynasty but made a drastic shift upward in late Ch'ing. A summary of the increases in *sheng-yüan* total in each province is presented in Table 6.

TABLE 6

A SUMMARY TABLE OF SHENG-YÜAN TOTAL IN THE PRE-TAIPING AND POST-TAIPING PERIODS*

	Pre-Taiping *Sheng-yüan* Total	Post-Taiping *Sheng-yüan* Total	Percentage of Increase
8 Banners	3,219	4,325	35
Fengt'ien	2,091	4,832	131
Chihli	83,925	86,182	3
Kiangsu	41,362	53,754	30
Anhwei	38,029	48,756	28
Chekiang	53,100	65,974	24
Kiangsi	39,830	62,197	56
Fukien	35,017	47,380	35
Honan	48,111	56,382	17
Shantung	53,990	58,565	8
Shansi	45,316	48,694	7
Hupeh	32,067	46,997	47
Hunan	35,659	50,329	41
Shensi / Kansu	55,015	63,646	16
Szechwan	40,296	58,762	46
Kwangtung	39,116	53,309	36
Kwangsi	30,059	34,063	13
Yunnan	39,083	40,882	4
Kweichow	22,213	22,817	3
Merchant	1,701	2,751	61
Totals	739,199	910,597	23

* Summarized from Tables 20 and 22.

Fengt'ien had a special readjustment of quotas, but the other quota increases were mainly obtained through financial contributions. In the eighteen provinces of China proper, Chihli still had the highest number of *sheng-yüan* in the post-Taiping period, but it had had little increase over the pre-Taiping figure and was now closely followed by Kiangsi which had had

[127] Jean Joseph Marie Amiot (1718–94). This statement is contained in his correspondence on population of China published in the *Memoires concernant l'histoire, les sciences, les arts, les mœurs, les usages, etc., des Chinois,* No. 6. See Wang Shih-ta, "Estimates on Recent Chinese Population," *She-hui k'o-shüeh tsa-chih*, Vol. I, No. 3, pp. 41–48, esp. p. 43.

an increase of 56 per cent. Shantung, which had been in the second position, now fell to the fifth, with Kiangsi, Chekiang, and Szechwan surpassing it. Hupeh and Hunan were catching up with 47 and 41 per cent increases, respectively.

To get a better picture, one should compare the ratio of total *sheng-yüan* to total population in each province for both the pre-Taiping and post-Taiping periods. This raises the question of population figures. Wang Shih-ta has presented summaries of forty-five estimates by different Western and Chinese writers and organizations, most of which deal with the population during the nineteenth century.[128] Population estimates can also be found in Western sources.[129] The present paper is no place to discuss in detail the relative validity of the different estimates of population. Our aim here is to get the most reliable figures for the period under survey. For this, the official records, used with caution, are still the best source to rely upon. Hence, the population figures used for the pre-Taiping period are those of 1842 based on Popoff's collection from the Board of Revenue.[130] The population figures used for the post-Taiping period are those of 1885 based on Raymond C. Tenney's collection from the Board of Revenue.[131]

Table 7 shows that in the pre-Taiping period Chihli and Shantung had the highest number of *sheng-yüan.* However, percentagewise, in relation to population of the respective provinces, Yunnan is at the top, the number of *sheng-yüan* being 0.63 per cent of the population of the province, and Kweichow is in the second position. On the surface it seems that the Manchu government had adopted a lenient policy in the granting of *sheng-yüan* quotas to border provinces. But, as suggested before, this indicates the government's concern with having an adequate number of gentry to assist in managing and controlling all localities. In the post-Taiping period, Yunnan and Kweichow ranked only seventh and eighth percentagewise among the provinces, since their contributions to the military fund had not matched their substantial increase in population.

The table also shows that in Shansi and Shantung there was little change in the proportion of *sheng-yüan* to the whole population of the province.

[128] Wang Shih-ta, *op. cit.*, Vol. I, No. 3, pp. 32–130 and No. 4, pp. 34–105; Vol. II, No. 1, pp. 51–105; also Wang Shih-ta, "Estimates of Chinese Population Made in the Last Ten Years," *She-hui k'o-hsüeh tsa-chih*, Vol. II, No. 2, June, 1931, pp. 125–223.

[129] *The Chinese Repository*, Vol. I, No. 9, pp. 345–63, and No. 10, pp. 385–97, also presents a collection of figures from several Chinese and English sources. Among others, see also Walter F. Willcox, "A Westerner's Effort to Estimate the Population of China and Its Increases Since 1650," *Journal of the American Statistical Association*, Vol. XXV, No. 171, Sept., 1930, pp. 255–68.

[130] See Wang Shih-ta, *op. cit.*, Vol. II, No. 1, pp. 58, 65.

[131] *Ibid.*, pp. 85, 97, 104 b. It has been doubted that the population of Szechwan in 1885 had increased to as much as 71,000,000. Wang discusses the validity of this and other population figures.

TABLE 7

SHENG-YÜAN TOTAL BY PROVINCE IN PROPORTION TO POPULATION

	Pre-Taiping period			Post-Taiping period		
	Sheng-yüan total	Population (in 1,000's)	Per cent	*Sheng-yüan* total	Population (in 1,000's)	Per cent
8 Banners	3,219			4,325		
Fengt'ien	2,091			4,832		
Chihli	83,925	36,900	.23	86,182	17,900	.46
Kiangsu	41,362	29,600	.14	53,754	21,300	.25
Anhwei	38,029	36,600	.10	48,756	20,600	.24
Chekiang	53,100	30,400	.17	65,974	11,700	.56
Kiangsi	39,830	26,500	.15	62,197	24,500	.27
Fukien	35,017	25,800	.14	47,380	23,500	.20
Honan	48,111	29,100	.17	56,382	22,100	.25
Shantung	53,990	36,200	.15	58,565	36,500	.16
Shansi	45,316	10.300	.44	48,694	10,800	.45
Hupeh	32,067	28,600	.11	46,997	33,600	.14
Hunan	35,659	20,000	.18	50,329	21,000	.24
Shensi } Kansu }	55,015	29,800	.19	63,646	8,700	.73
Szechwan	40,296	22,300	.19	58,762	71,100	.08
Kwangtung	39,116	21,100	.19	53,309	29,700	.18
Kwangsi	30,059	8,100	.37	34,063	5,100	.67
Yunnan	39,083	6,200	.63	40,882	11,700	.35
Kweichow	22,213	4,800	.47	22,817	7,700	.31
Merchant	1,701			2,751		
Totals	739,199	402,300*	.18	910,597	377,500	.24

* This total is very close to the total of 414,686,994 in 1842 given in *Shih-lu*, Hsüan-tsung, 387/32 b.

Both *sheng-yüan* and population figures remained quite stable. On the other hand, most other provinces show drastic changes in their percentages. Thus, for instance, the percentage in Chekiang rose from 0.17 per cent to 0.56 per cent, and in Shensi and Kansu together it rose from 0.19 to 0.73 per cent. The majority of the provinces showed increases and the proportion of total *sheng-yüan* to total population rose from 0.18 to 0.24 per cent, a 30 per cent increase.

Chien-sheng—Gentry through Purchase

Having studied the major group of gentry, the *sheng-yüan*, we now take up the other main group, the *chien-sheng*, most of whom secured their titles through the purchase system. Relatively few obtained this title in other ways.[132] We have distinguished between the actual and nominal studying

[132] For discussion of the various kinds of *chien-sheng*, see *supra*, I, p. 19.

in the Imperial Academy of Learning. The number of *chien-sheng* actually studying in the Academy was very small. Both *chien-sheng* and *kung-sheng* studying there numbered at one time only 300; later the number was reduced to 180, and then increased again to 270.[133]

The title of *en-chien-sheng* (*chien-sheng* by imperial favor) was granted very rarely and only to members of special groups. Therefore, this small group is a negligible factor in estimating the total number of *chien-sheng.* There were also very few *yin-chien-sheng* (*chien-sheng* by inheritance) and *yu-chien-sheng* (*chien-sheng* by virtue of noteworthy achievements). For example, in Sung-chiang prefecture, Kiangsu, which had one prefectural school and seven *hsien* schools, there were during the years 1816 to 1882 only six *en-yin-sheng* and sixty-three *nan-yin-sheng* altogether; [134] and not all *yin-sheng* became *yin-chien-sheng.* In short, *chien-sheng,* proportionally speaking, were almost all *li-chien-sheng*, those who obtained their titles through purchase. This fact was reflected in several edicts. An edict of 1723 stated: "Students of the Imperial Academy come through contributions of funds. Very few can write good essays. ..." [135] Another edict issued in 1685 reads as follows: "The only way to become *chien-sheng* is through contribution of funds. Poor scholars have no means to reach there. ..." [136]

Data on the number of men who purchased *chien-sheng* titles and the amount of money collected from the purchasers during each of the thirty years of the Tao-kuang reign (1821–1850) are available for all provinces

[133] *Shih-li,* 1098/2 a, 8 a, 8 b, 9 b. Ch'en Ch'ing-chih, *Chung-hua chiao-yü shih,* pp. 464–65, wrongly charged that the number was not clearly stipulated in the Ch'ing code. He said only one section under the Imperial Academy in *Ta-Ch'ing hui-tien* has the following: "Those who study in the Academy 156; those who study outside but attend examinations in the Academy 120." Ch'en commented that the total did not exceed 300 and he expressed his suspicion as to this small figure. He estimated that in the 18 provinces there were 184 prefectures, 64 independent *chou,* 16 independent *t'ing,* 150 *chou,* 10 *t'ing,* and 1,301 *hsien.* There was to be one *pa-kung-sheng* selected from each of the *fu, chou,* and *hsien* schools in a twelve-year period. Ch'en reasoned that if the number of localities were divided by 12, and those who were graded in the 1st and 2nd rank and then appointed directly to office were excluded, there would be at least 100 *pa-kung-sheng* in the Academy. He said further that since there was one *sui-kung-sheng* selected from each prefecture each year, two in three years from each *chou,* one in two years from each *hsien,* there would therefore be at least 650 *sui-kung-sheng* in the Academy. However, this is a yearly figure. Ch'en did not account for the total number of *sui-kung-sheng.* Also, he did not show that a man who entered the Academy would stay there for as long three years. (See *Shih-li,* 1098/1 a.) Ch'en also estimated that the *fu-kung, yu-kung, and yu-chien* would number at least 150. He thought there would be about 10 *kung-sheng* and *chien-sheng* from the banners and the metropolitan prefecture, and that the total would be at least 900. He did not explain why the students actually studying at the Academy amounted to less than 300. He did not seem to see the difference between actual and nominal students of the Academy. To become an actual student in the Academy, one had to pass the entrance examination. The actual students of the Academy received stipends and had to be limited in number.

[134] *Sung-chiang-fu hsü-chih,* 23/26–29.

[135] *Shih-li,* 1098/2 a.

[136] *Ibid.*

except Chihli. The figure for Chihli would necessarily be larger than that for any of the other provinces, since men from other provinces were also permitted to purchase the title at the Board of Revenue in the capital. An approximate figure will therefore be allotted to Chihli in our final estimate of the total number of *chien-sheng*, while in the following discussion Chihli will have to be left out in order to preserve the exactness of the other figures.

The Tao-kuang data on *chien-sheng* enable us to make a fairly accurate estimate of the size of the pre-Taiping *chien-sheng* group. In Table 23 the data have been assembled into five-year groups so that the amounts collected and the number of participants in earlier and later periods can be compared. This comparison shows a steady decrease over time. In the last five years of Tao-kuang, the number of participants dwindles to less than half of the number in the first five years of Tao-kuang, decreasing from 79,226 to 33,450. A short study of the amount of collections from purchasers of *chien-sheng* titles shows that from Chia-ch'ing 5th year (1800) to the end of Chia-ch'ing (1820), a period of twenty years, the amount of collections was 40,724,167 taels, not including any collections from Shansi and Chihli,[137] while the total collected in the thirty-year period of Tao-kuang, including Shansi, was only 33,705,646 taels. Thus there was a steady decline in the purchase of *chien-sheng* titles throughout the first half of the nineteenth century.

This downward trend might well have been related to the changing distribution of wealth over different periods. Possibly, the concentration of wealth in fewer hands was constantly going on, so that the financial ability of individuals to participate in the purchase of *chien-sheng*, which required only a little over 100 taels, was constantly decreasing.[138]

There is no doubt about the general decline in the purchase of *chien-sheng* titles during the Tao-kuang period, but the degree of decrease varied greatly among the provinces. The degree of decrease from the first five years to the last five years of Tao-kuang, averaged out for all provinces, was more than 50 per cent. But in the provinces of Yunnan and Kweichow the decreases

[137] T'ang Hsiang-lung, *op. cit.*, p. 538.

[138] It might be argued that sometimes it was not the individual as such who purchased the title. Several family members might pool their money to get the title for one member so as to secure protection for the whole family. Or even further, fellow villagers might help out in such an investment. With such combined efforts, 100 taels probably would not be too difficult to collect. However, such cases could not have been too numerous, or else everyone would have had protection and there would have been no victims of overtaxation or other kinds of exploitation. It was not that just anyone could profit by becoming a *chien-sheng*. It still often depended on the individual. For instance, the Taiping leader, Wei Ch'ang-hui, even though he was financially well able to purchase the *chien-sheng* title, was not accepted by the local gentry because of his low origin. See Chien Yu-wen, *T'ai-p'ing chün Kwangsi shou-i shih*, p. 155. Cf. *Hsün-chou fu-chih*, *chüan* 56; also Lo Erh-kang, *Chung-wang Li Hsiu-ch'eng tzu-chuan yüan-kao ch'ien-cheng*, p. 45.

were negligible, while in Kiangsu the number of participants decreased from more than 10,000 to less than 3,000. Other provinces that had a more than average decrease include Honan, Shensi, Hupeh, Hunan, Shensi, Kansu, Szechwan, and Kwangtung. If the decrease of purchase of *chien-sheng* titles was related to the concentration of wealth, this indicates that concentration of wealth was more prevalent in the provinces along the coast, along the Yangtze, and in the northwest.

In general, these figure do illustrate the relative financial strength of the provinces. The provinces which are known to have been less wealthy certainly had far fewer participants in the purchase of *chien-sheng* titles. The order of the provinces according to number of participants was, however, somewhat modified over time because of the difference in degree of decrease of participation. Thus in early Tao-kuang, Kiangsu and Kwangtung were at the top of the list in the number of participants, with Kiangsi following. However, the degree of decrease is lower in Kiangsi. Hence, looking over the totals of participants during this thirty-year period in the various provinces, we find that Kiangsi leads with the figure of 38,552, while Kwangtung is second with 38,264. Percentagewise, according to population of the provinces, Kwangtung leads and Kiangsi is second.

The number of men who participated in the purchase of *chien-sheng* in all provinces (except Chihli) during the thirty years of the Tao-kuang period is then found to be 315,535. However, these *chien-sheng* figures include some who were already *sheng-yüan* since both *sheng-yüan* and commoners were qualified to participate in the purchase. We must know then if any appreciable number had already reached gentry status by becoming *sheng-yüan*, so that the *chien-sheng* figure can be added to the *sheng-yüan* figure to reach the gentry total without duplicate counting.

Let us first see the amount of money the different kinds of *sheng-yüan* and commoners had to pay to become *chien-sheng.* It is recorded that during the first years of Tao-kuang, the commoners had to pay 108 taels if they participated in the capital and 100 taels if they participated in the provinces. Beginning from Tao-kuang 7 (1827), they paid 120 taels at either place. From 1831 to the end of Tao-kuang (1850), they paid 108 taels at either place. *Fu-sheng*, throughout the whole Tao-kuang period, paid 90 taels, whatever the place of purchase; *tseng-sheng* paid 80 taels, and *ling-sheng* 60 taels.[139]

Provided with this information and turning back again to the data on *chien-sheng* figures, we find that those who participated in the purchase were almost invariably all commoners. For example, in the first five years of

[139] See T'ang Hsiang-lung, *op. cit.*, p. 438; see also *Ch'ing-kuo hsin-cheng-fa fen-lun*, 5/359.

Tao-kuang, we have shown that a commoner paid 100 taels in his home province for the title of *chien-sheng*. During that time, 10,169 men purchased *chien-sheng* titles in Kiangsu, and the amount collected was 1,015,580 taels. If all these men were commoners originally, the amount collected would have been 1,016, 900 taels. The difference of 320 taels could only mean that there were thirty-two *fu-sheng* or sixteen *tseng-sheng* or a combination within these limits among the 10,169 men. Such participation then was negligible. We can therefore assume that *chien-sheng* through purchase were practically all commoners originally.[140] This assumption is supported by the fact that among the officials through purchase we find very few who were originally *fu-chien-sheng*, *tseng-chien-sheng* or *ling-chien-sheng*, but many who were identified as plain *chien-sheng*.[141] Also, in the reports of deaths of officials, gentry, and commoners, we find very few of the other kinds of *chien-sheng* but many plain *chien-sheng*,[142] persons who were originally commoners.

To reach a figure for the total of pre-Taiping *chien-sheng*, we shall first see the average number of years that one was a *chien-sheng*. The average age of death would probably be the same for *chien-sheng* as for *sheng-yüan*. However, it is hard to determine the average age of becoming a *chien-sheng*, since there are no records comparable to those which exist for *sheng-yüan*. The gentry through purchase were not organized into groups like the regular gentry and had no motive for recording the time they purchased their way into gentry status. Therefore, we can only make a rough estimate of the average age of attaining *chien-sheng*. We should expect this age to be a few years later than that for *sheng-yüan*. It seems reasonable to think that the largest group of *chien-sheng* purchasers would buy the title only after having failed to pass examinations to become *sheng-yüan*. They might try the examinations several times since they would naturally prefer to have the honor and prestige of being "regular" gentry. On the other hand, they could not afford to delay too long in achieving the protection and privileges that went with gentry status. For this reason, we have roughly set the age of becoming *chien-sheng* at 27, which is three years later than the *sheng-yüan* age. This would give the *chien-sheng* a life expectancy of 30 years at the time they purchased their titles.

140 This significant relationship between amount of money collected and number of men is not seen by T'ang Hsiang-lung, as he treats the two sets of data in different tables Table 23 shows that in Yunnan and Kweichow exactly all who participated were originally commoners. The figures match up very well for all provinces except Shansi and Kansu, where for some unknown reason the amount collected exceeded what it should have been.

141 E.g., see *Ta-Ch'ing chin-shen ch'üan-shu*, 1881.

142 E.g., see *Hsü-tsuan Yangchow fu-chih* 10/7–14; *Shang-yü hsien-chih*, section on biographies.

A small group purchased *chien-sheng* titles in order to bypass the *sheng-yüan* examinations and speed up their participation in provincial examinations. Such persons were usually officials' sons who were favored with special quotas in the provincial examinations.[143] This small group we should expect to be younger than average. On the other hand, some men whose families had been poor purchased *chien-sheng* only after they had acquired wealth. These men would be older than the average. This group would also be small. Neither this group nor the group of officials' sons was large enough to affect the average *chien-sheng* age very much, but in any case they would to some extent offset each other.

If then we set the *chien-sheng* life expectancy at approximately 30 years, we shall simply take the figure for the total participants in the Tao-kuang reign, which is a 30-year period (see Table 23), and add to it an approximate figure of 40,000 men for Chihli. This gives a total of 355,535 for the pre-Taiping *chien-sheng* figure.

Even if a 10 per cent margin of error is allowed for the estimated life expectancy of *chien-sheng*, the resulting 10 per cent difference in the *chien-sheng* total would not greatly affect the gentry total or the proportion of *chien-sheng* to other groups within the gentry.

For the estimate of post-Taiping *chien-sheng*, there are no solid data available as there are for pre-Taiping *chien-sheng.* We have shown that the purchase of *chien-sheng* titles was constantly declining in the pre-Taiping period and have interpreted it as being related to the declining financial strength of individuals. After the Taiping period, the financial strength of most individuals, except for those who profited as a result of the war, was very likely declining even more. However, there were not fewer *chien-sheng* in the post-Taiping period. On the contrary, the purchase system as a whole, including the purchase of *chien-sheng,* flourished in the late nineteenth century, not in the sense of amount of collection, but in the sense of number of participants. Beginning in the Hsien-feng years (1851–61), the government made successive attempts to maintain the flow of funds from the purchase system through discount measures. A contemporary writer stated that before the Tao-kuang period, the amount paid for some official posts was over 1000 taels in actual silver. After the rise of the Taipings, equivalent posts could be purchased at the capital with silver notes or copper notes worth only about 200 taels in actual silver. In the provinces the price for such offices was only 100 taels. This writer complained that "the number of officials was more than that of the people."[144]

[143] See *infra*, pp. 184–6.

[144] Shen Shou-chih, *loc. cit.* Cf. Yen Ching-ming's memorial in *Ch'ing-ch'ao hsü-wen-hsien t'ung-k'ao*, 93/8532.

According to this description, the drastic measures in permitting discounts reached their peak in the post-Taiping years. This is also shown by some of Li Hung-chang's memorials. In 1887 Li proposed that the currently enforced 20 per cent discount on the nominal purchase price of titles be changed to 40 per cent so as to increase revenue by increasing sales. Li suggested that if *kung-sheng* and *chien-sheng* through purchase wished to enter the provincial examinations or purchase actual offices, they should then pay the 40 per cent originally discounted.[145] In 1890 Li pointed out that *kung-sheng* and *chien-sheng* through purchase were paying only 50 per cent of the stipulated amount; Li suggested it should be further reduced to 40 per cent.[146]

As a point of interest, we should also note the change in method of collection. In the pre-Taiping years, the Board of Revenue had effective control of the licenses. The purchasers in the provinces were first given only a receipt for money paid. Monthly reports were then made by the provincial treasury and sent to the Board together with a copy of the receipt; on this basis the licenses of *chien-sheng* and others were issued. Only the license itself was the evidence of purchase and the proof of privileges accrued to the purchaser.[147] Thus revenue from the purchase system was at that time completely centrally controlled.

Later on, because of the urgent need to meet military expenses, the various provinces requested the Board to issue blank licenses to be used in the provinces to speed up the transactions. Here the central control then gradually gave way to regional autonomy. By 1906 we find a memorial by the Board of Revenue which reads as follows:

> Since the 11th month of Kuang-hsü 28th [1902] up to the present, based on the request of Chihli, Szechwan, Liang-Kwang, Liang-Chiang, Fengt'ien, Shantung, Kansu, and other provinces, the number of blank licenses issued amounts to 436,700. Checking on the number which the various provinces have reported to the Board requesting reward, they have only used up about 100,000 blank licenses. A great amount has not been reported. Those who have requested more blank licenses have therefore been rejected. Although the purchase system cannot be immediately stopped, malpractices should be prevented. Malpractices in relation to blank licenses such as [illegal] discounting and transfers and pretense of loss of license, etc., have been numerous. The Board-issued licenses have been used to fool the purchasers without reporting for them, so that there are those who throughout their lives do not know that their licenses have not been approved [by the Board]. The proceeds of the purchase system have merely satisfied the greedy with no benefit to the public service. . . .[148]

[145] Li Hung-chang, *Li Wen-chung-kung ch'üan-chi*, 60/13–15, memorial of Kuang-hsü 13/ intercalary 4/17.

[146] *Ibid.*, 68/25, memorial of Kuang-hsü 16/7/2.

[147] Cf. *Ch'ing-kuo hsin-cheng-fa fen-lun*, 5/365–66.

[148] *Ibid.*

The above memorial not only indicates the central government's loss of control over such revenue, but also shows the abundance of purchasers. If in four years the number of purchasers known to the Board of Revenue was 100,000, more than half of whom would be those seeking the title of *chien-sheng*,[149] the total number of *chien-sheng* emerging in a thirty-year period would be more than 400,000.

Examples from Anhwei further show the large number of *chien-sheng* in the latter part of the nineteenth century. In a report of money collected from purchasers of offices, official titles, and *kung-sheng* and *chien-sheng* titles from men of Hui-chou and Ning-kuo prefectures, it was pointed out that from Hsien-feng 5/5 (1855) to Hsien-feng 10/8 (1860), 1,326,750 taels and 626,768 strings of cash were collected, a total of approximately 1,600,000 taels. This information was given as background to the detailed section of the report which deals with approximately the last six months of the period mentioned. This was the 11th report on Hui-chou and the first on Ning-kuo. The Hui-chou report showed 29 purchases of actual offices, yielding a total of 23,865 taels; 375 purchases of official and honorific titles, yielding 70,435 taels; 649 purchases of *kung-sheng* and *chien-sheng* titles, yielding 56,684 taels. The Ning-kuo report showed 4 purchases of actual offices, yielding 5,550 taels; 30 purchases of titles, yielding 3,680 taels; 13 purchases of *kung-sheng* and *chien-sheng* titles, yielding 1,648 taels.[150]

Thus in the rich prefecture of Hui-chou, in about six months, more than 600 purchased the titles of *kung-sheng* and *chien-sheng*, and most of these would have purchased the latter. If the proportion of the different types of purchasers to the amount of collection remained the same for the whole five-year period, there would have emerged in that time in Hui-chou alone more than 6,000 *kung-sheng* and *chien-sheng* through purchase,[151] of whom about 5,000 would have been *chien-sheng*. In the whole province of Anhwei,

149 In Hui-chou prefecture, for instance, in the several months reported, 649 purchased *kung-sheng* and *chien-sheng* titles among a total of 1,107 purchasers. At that time 88 taels were required for commoners to purchase *chien-sheng* titles. (Cf. the Kiangsi example later.) 649 multiplied by 88 comes very close to the report on the amount collected from these men. This means that the 649 purchasers were largely commoners buying *chien-sheng* titles, and the few who purchased *kung-sheng* titles requiring a higher payment were offset by the few purchasers of *chien-sheng* titles who were originally *sheng-yüan* and therefore paid less than commoners. That *chien-sheng* through purchase were a much larger group than *kung-sheng* through purchase can also be shown by gazetteer materials to be given in later passages.

150 Chang Fei, *Chang Wen-i-kung tsou-kao*, 8/31 ff.

151 The 11th Hui-chou report shows 56,684 taels received under the category of *kung-sheng* and *chien-sheng*. The other categories yielded 94,514 taels, a ratio of approximately 6 to 10. If the same ratio prevailed for the 1,600,000 total, 600,000 taels came from purchasers of *kung-sheng* and *chien-sheng*, which was about ten times the amount in this 11th report.

however, in any five-year period in Tao-kuang, the total of participants in the purchase of *chien-sheng* never greatly exceeded 3,000.[152] Even though other prefectures in Anhwei might have been much less active than Hui-chou in the purchase system,[153] the total Anhwei figure for post-Taiping *chien-sheng* probably would have been double that of the pre-Taiping figure. It is doubtful that the pace of purchase would have slackened after the five years covered in the Hui-chou report, when the price of academic titles was becoming lower and lower.

The report of the acting governor of Kiangsi gives, however, a different picture for that province. He says that in Kiangsi from Hsien-feng 4/3 (1855) to Hsien-feng 11/11 (1862), in accordance with the regulation of reduced payments, 1,018 purchased *chien-sheng* titles at the provincial treasury, paying a total of 88,704 taels; and in the localities, 1,163 purchased *chien-sheng* titles, paying a total of 102,280 taels.[154] In the 12th month of *Hsien-feng* 11, there was no collection in the localities while the provincial treasury received from 4 purchasers a sum of 352 taels. It is indicative of the declining central control that this sum of 191,336 taels paid by 2,175 *chien-sheng*, even though reported, was retained in the provinces to be used for rehabilitation and rations of soldiers and militiamen.[155]

We have shown that Kiangsi had the largest number of *chien-sheng* in the pre-Taiping period. We have also shown that on the whole the number of post-Taiping *chien-sheng* should be even larger. However, according to this report covering seven and a half years, the number of new *chien-sheng* in Kiangsi was less than half that of the last five-year total in the Tao-kuang period. Even though we assume that part of the collection was not reported, the difference should not be so great.[156] But this certainly does not mean that the financial strength of Kiangsi had declined. It has already been shown that Kiangsi was the province that most fully exploited the permission to expand the *sheng-yüan* quota by making contributions to the military fund. The contributors of Hsien-feng times, while increasing the *sheng-yüan* quota, at the same time received rewards in titles or offices for themselves. If fewer

152 See Table 23.

153 The Ning-kuo prefecture as described has an extremely low figure.

154 These figures show that the purchasers were largely commoners, since the total amount collected comes very close to the number of purchasers multiplied by the amount paid by a commoner which was at that time 88 taels.

155 Li Huan, *Pao-wei-chai lei-kao*, 1/16 a–b, memorial of T'ung-chih 1/1/24 (1862).

156 Chang Fei, *op. cit.,* 2/37 ff., points out that he had collected already 1,100,000 taels while requesting rewards for most of the individual contributors (not yet all) amounting to 895,791 taels. However, Li Huan's memorial indicates that those who purchased *chien-sheng* were all included in his report. It might be, as mentioned in the Kuang-hsü Board of Revenue memorial, that some purchasers were not reported at all, but there is no proof that they would constitute a sizable number. Besides, Li had a good reputation. (See Hummel, p. 458.)

were of the *chien-sheng* bracket, this means there were more of the other categories that required higher payment. From this it can be inferred that in Kiangsi there was an abrupt change towards the concentration of wealth, so that more were able to pay a sizable lump sum and fewer were able to pay a smaller sum.

However, the Kiangsi report quoted above deals with the time when *chien-sheng* payment was only slightly reduced. As the *chien-sheng* title steadily became cheaper, more and more people would have been able to purchase it. It would very likely be an overestimate to take the Anhwei example as a norm and judge that the post-Taiping *chien-sheng* figure should be twice as much as the pre-Taiping one. From all available indications, it seems reasonable to put the increase at 50 per cent. The post-Taiping *chien-sheng* figure, including those who later were promoted to other categories of gentry, would then be approximately 534,000.

Total of Gentry Proper

Since most other categories of gentry had their origin either as *sheng-yüan* through examinations, or as *chien-sheng* through purchase, and since other means of entering the gentry group are relatively negligible factors, we can now arrive at the grand total of gentry by adding the figures for these two decisive groups. This is presented in Table 8.

TABLE 8

TOTAL OF GENTRY PROPER IN PRE-TAIPING AND POST-TAIPING PERIODS

Type of Gentry	Pre-Taiping total	Per cent	Post-Taiping total	Per cent	Rate of Increase (Per cent)
Sheng-yüan	739,199	68	910,597	63	23
Chien-sheng	355,535	32	533,303	37	50
Grand total	1,094,734	100	1,443,900	100	32

Number of Gentry and Their Immediate Dependents

The above totals of approximately 1,100,000 for the pre-Taiping gentry and 1,400,000 for the post-Taiping gentry are figures for the gentry proper. The gentry proper are to be clearly distinguished from the examination aspirants who might be called "marginal gentry"; from the elders whose prestige and functions were in some ways similar to those of the gentry; and from relatives or followers of the gentry who might be called "hangers-on."

Only the gentry and their immediate dependents enjoyed gentry privileges and protection. Non-gentry brothers, adult sons, or other relatives of gentry members, whether they were examination aspirants or not, were not called gentry and did not legally have the privileges of gentry. A brother of a gentry member could be more influential than a brother of a commoner, but he still had to work for his own admission to gentry status to secure gentry privileges and power. Fathers of gentry members might be raised to the status of elders, but they were still not gentry. Therefore, to estimate the total number of persons included within the scope of full gentry protection, we should consider only the gentry and their immediate dependents, which would include their wives, concubines, if any, and their younger children.

Since Chinese families are thought to be large, and the gentry would be especially well able to support many dependents, one might suppose that the Chinese gentry would have had especially large families. It seems, however, that the gentry families were not actually so very big.

One contemporary *chin-shih* record at hand has been employed for the study of this problem. The results are shown in Table 24. The average size of the families of these men was 4.96 or roughly 5 persons. Pending further study, this figure is used here.

This figure corresponds fairly well with estimates of the size of the Chinese family based on figures for the population as a whole. In Feng-hua, Chekiang, the 1908 census shows a record of approximately 70,000 households with a population figure of approximately 270,000, an average of approximately four to a household.[157] Ch'ang-hsing, Chekiang, was reported in 1803 to have approximately 95,000 households with a population of approximately 360,000. This was also an average of four to a household. The census conducted immediately after the Taiping Rebellion shows the ratio to have dwindled to about two to a household.[158] In Ching-chou, Hunan, the census of 1836 as well as the one of 1873 shows a ratio of five to one household.[159]

Some population studies have also dealt with the problem of the size of the family. Willcox finally adopts the idea of five to a household, after lengthy discussion.[160] Rockhill has shown an average of four persons to a household.[161] But Willcox has pointed out that all the returns Rockhill cited as

157 *Feng-hua hsien-chih*, section on population.

158 *Ch'ang-hsing hsien-chih*, 7/13. In 1867 there were only 10,512 households and a population of 21,969. By 1872 there were 35,593 households and a population of 79,588, indicating the amount of migration into this district during and after the war.

159 *Ching-chou hsiang-t'u-chih*, 2/21 b. The 1836 figure is 28,378 households and 128,567 persons. The 1873 figure is 16,382 households and 74,152 persons.

160 Willcox, *loc. cit.*

161 W. W. Rockhill, "An Inquiry into the Population of China," *Report of the Smithsonian Institution for 1904*, pp. 659–676.

indicating a small household seem to have been returns of adults only.[162] Finally, Chen Ta's recent field work in ten regions spread over various parts of China, shows only 4.84 persons to a household.[163]

These estimates indicate that the Chinese family in general was not very large.[164] Our estimate of the nineteenth-century family, arrived at in the *chin-shih* study mentioned above, indicates that the average gentry family was not much larger than the average for the total population.

If we take this figure of five members for the gentry family, the pre-Taiping gentry total including family members would amount to approximately 5,500,000 and the post-Taiping gentry total including family members would amount to approximately 7,200,000.

Distribution of Gentry

This gentry total was somewhat unevenly distributed among the Chinese provinces. It has been stated earlier that the regular gentry quota was related to the local administrative units and did not depend on the size of population. The distribution of *chien-sheng* was not determined by any planned policy measures but developed according to the varying demand for purchase in the provinces. As a result, the proportion of gentry to population varied from province to province.

In the first half of the nineteenth century, the proportion of gentry to population varied from 0.7 per cent in Anhwei to 3.5 per cent in Yunnan. (See Table 32.) Most of the provinces had a percentage of between 1 and 2, except for the border provinces where the population was low but a considerable number of gentry was nevertheless maintained. In the second half of the century, we find a change in the distribution. The percentages in all provinces except Szechwan, Hupeh, Kweichow, Yunnan, and Kwangtung have increased and now vary from 0.6 to 5.0 per cent. Szechwan has the lowest percentage as a result of an abrupt upward shift in population, while Chekiang, Shensi, and Kansu have the highest percentages. The distribution of the gentry over provinces before and after the Taiping period is shown

[162] Willcox, *op. cit.*, p. 259.

[163] *Op. cit.*, p. 22. The ten regional censuses include a total of 3,170,555 persons.

[164] Thus, as pointed out by Chen Ta, *op. cit.*, p. 22, "As the traditional Chinese family is sometimes composed not only of parents and children but also of paternal and maternal relatives, it is occasionally thought in the West that the size of the Chinese family must be quite large. This belief, which was formerly shared by the intelligentsia in China, tends to lose weight now, as reliable factual data become gradually available. In China the high birth rate is usually accompanied by a high death rate, resulting in the rather small number of surviving children in the family. As to the kinsmen and relatives who live with the family, the cases are not so common and their number is not so numerous as formerly believed."

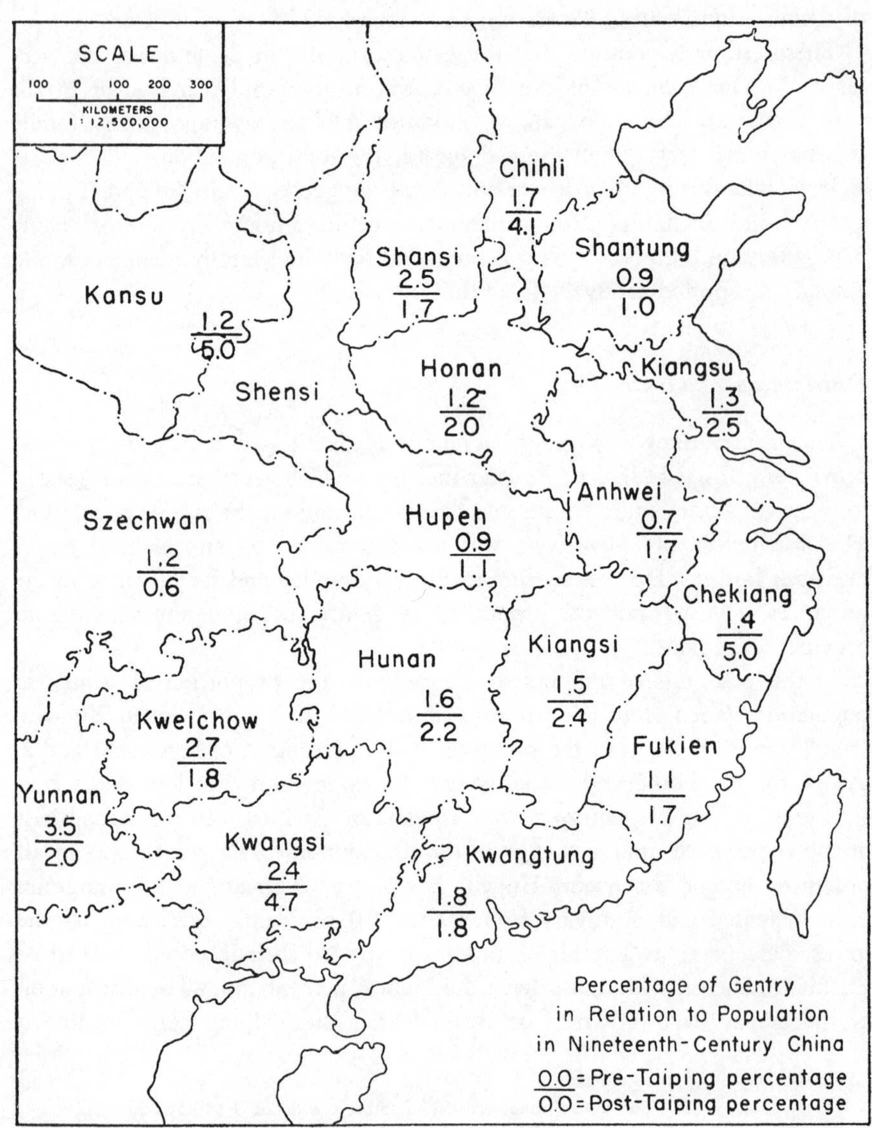
SCALE
100 0 100 200 300
KILOMETERS
1 : 12,500,000
Chihli
1.7
4.1
Shansi
2.5
1.7
Shantung
0.9
1.0
Kansu
1.2
5.0
Honan
1.2
2.0
Shensi
Kiangsu
1.3
2.5
Anhwei
0.7
1.7
Szechwan
1.2
0.6
Hupeh
0.9
1.1
Chekiang
1.4
5.0
Kiangsi
1.5
2.4
Hunan
1.6
2.2
Kweichow
2.7
1.8
Fukien
1.1
1.7
Yunnan
3.5
2.0
Kwangsi
2.4
4.7
Kwangtung
1.8
1.8
Percentage of Gentry
in Relation to Population
in Nineteenth-Century China
0.0 = Pre-Taiping percentage
0.0 = Post-Taiping percentage
CARTOGRAPHIC LABORATORIES, GEOGRAPHY DEPARTMENT, UNIVERSITY OF WASHINGTON

FIGURE 2

in Figure 2. In Kwangtung and Hupeh, there was practically no change in the proportion of gentry to population before and after the Taiping period. In Shensi and Kansu, there was a fourfold increase in the proportion. Chekiang had the next largest increase. In border provinces, which were quite inactive in contribution to the military fund, the proportion of gentry to population had dropped down to the ratio of the other provinces. This change of ratio in all provinces further indicates the weakening of the government's control over the number and distribution of the gentry.

AN ESTIMATE OF THE SIZE OF THE VARIOUS COMPONENTS OF THE GENTRY

Arguments for dividing the gentry into an upper and a lower layer have been presented in Part One. Let us see now how the various components of the two layers appear quantitatively and what the significance of such a distribution may be.

We have shown that of the two main routes of entrance to gentry status, becoming *sheng-yüan* through examination or becoming *chien-sheng* through purchase, more gentry members emerged through the former or "regular" route, although the ratio of *sheng-yüan* to *chien-sheng* declined after the Taiping period.[165] Emperor Shih-tsung (the Yung-cheng reign) once strongly advocated the expansion of the purchase system, not because of the revenue produced, but as a counterbalancing force against the cliques formed among the gentry through examination. In an edict of 1727 he stated:

> Recently I (the Emperor) see that among those who rise through the examination system, not only are many careless and perfunctory, but many are also corrupt and law-breaking. The practice of teacher-student [examiners and successful examinees], and classmate relationships associated with favoritism and appeals to feelings, is seen everywhere and is unbreakable. If the official career should be left completely to those who rise through examinations, they would just firmly join together and work for their private interest against the public interest. This is of great harm to the public welfare and to the livelihood of the people. The purchase system should be appropriately expanded.[166]

Thus, the Yung-cheng emperor considered the purchase system as a means of control, and his use of it is in contrast to the increased sale of academic titles that occurred during and after the Taiping Rebellion when the need for revenue was the government's main concern.

[165] *Supra*, Table 8, p. 111.

[166] Edict of 1727. See *Ch'ing-kuo hsin-cheng-fa fen-lun*, 5/308. For the Yung-cheng emperor's disapproval of clique formation among examination degree-holders, cf. edict of 1729 in *Shih-lu*, Shih-tsung 5/27 b–33 b. He also wrote a treatise on cliques to be expounded to the people together with the Imperial Maxims of the K'ang-hsi emperor on the 1st and 15th day of each month. (*Hsüeh-cheng*, 4/12 b–13 a.)

In considering the upper gentry, it will be of interest to see how the "irregulars" through purchase compared with the "regulars" through examination in reaching upper gentry status and in obtaining official posts.

Upper Gentry

Officials and holders of official titles. The first subdivision of the upper gentry would include the civil and military officials and holders of official titles. Incumbent officials were also gentry of their home areas and are therefore included in our computation. The total number of civil and military officials at the capital and in the provinces has been given as approximately 27,000.[167] Of this number, approximately 20,000 were civil officials,[168] and 7,000 were military officers.[169] Among the civil officials, approximately 2,000 were key regional and local officials[170] and 1,500 were key educational officials.[171] Approximately half of the civil officials were court officials and the other half were officials in the provinces.[172]

For officials through the "regular" route, Latourette has made a very rough estimate that "the holders of degrees in the service of the State probably seldom if ever exceeded ten or fifteen thousand."[173] Official lists show that men through the "regular" route held approximately half the 20,000 civil official posts, that they generally controlled the high court offices and key regional and local offices, and almost exclusively controlled the educational offices.[174] The rest of the civil official posts were held by men through the "irregular" route, mainly through purchase first to *chien-*

[167] See Feng Kuei-fen's discussion of the excessive number of officials in *Ch'ing-ch'ao hsü wen-hsien t'ung-k'ao*, 115/8735, written in 1855. This figure was based upon data in the *Hui-tien* and does not include such offices as *han-lin* compilers, the numbers of which were indefinite.

[168] Cf. Ch'u Fang-ch'ing's discussion on civil service in *Huang-ch'ao chin-shih wen-pien*, 17/6 b. He argued that the number of *chin-shih* was small and that there were enough offices for them and also for the *chü-jen* and *kung-sheng.* He blamed the insufficiency of offices on the excessive admission to office through other routes.

[169] *Ta-Ch'ing chin-shen ch'üan-shu*, 1881, 5/15–16, gives the list as follows: 16 provincial commanders-in-chief; 64 brigade-generals; 120 colonels; 164 lieutenant-colonels; 373 majors, 425 first captains; 869 second captains; 1,912 lieutenants; 3,521 sublieutenants; a total of 7,464.

[170] *Ch'in-ting ta-Ch'ing hui-tien*, 4/4 b–18 a.

[171] *Ibid.*, 6/1 a gives the list as follows: 19 provincial directors-of-studies; 190 *fu* and *t'ing* directors-of-studies; 210 *t'ing* and *chou* directors-of-studies; 1,150 *hsien* directors-of-studies. If the 1,512 assistant directors-of-studies are included, the total number of educational offices was approximately 3,000.

[172] *Ibid.*, *chüan* 4 to 6, shows more than 9,000 regional and local officials.

[173] K. S. Latourette, *The Chinese: Their History and Culture*, II, 48 and 49.

[174] See *Ta-Ch'ing chin-shen-lu* or *Ta-Ch'ing chin-shen ch'üan-shu*, also known as "The Red Book." The Far Eastern and Russian Institute of the University of Washington has selected several years and worked out charts on the types of officials, their origins, etc. This work was initiated by Dr. C. K. Yang, worked out with this writer, and further developed by Dr. Franz Michael.

sheng and then to official posts. Thus, the government's effort to counterbalance officials through the "regular" route was at least partially successful.

However, the picture changed in the post-Taiping period, especially in regard to local offices. The "regulars" were still in the majority but their lead was somewhat cut down. Of the more than 9,000 provincial and local offices listed in 1836, approximately 4,800 were held by "regulars" and 2,400 by those who were originally *chien-sheng*. In 1908, of about the same number of regional and local offices, approximately the same number of 4,800 was held by "regulars," but 3,500 were now of *chien-sheng* origin at the expense of others through the special routes of recommendation, hereditary right, and so forth.[175]

The above figures give some idea of the nature of the bureaucratic setup but do not actually help us in deciding the number of gentry members who were officials, among whom would be included not only incumbent officials but also those waiting for appointment and those who had retired. Some men remained officials all their lives, but some were only occasionally active in the service.[176] It is difficult to get a reasonable estimate of the rate of turnover of officials. The best solution is to see their proportion to other gentry groups (the total number of which has a sound basis) as obtainable from data in local gazetteers.

Table 9 shows that all *chin-shih* or metropolitan graduates generally got into office, that about one-third of *chü-jen* were able to do so, and that also some *kung-sheng* and even *sheng-yüan* occasionally stepped into officialdom. This proportion is about what one would expect. When the pre-Taiping and post-Taiping periods are compared, however, the latter period shows a decreased proportion of *chin-shih* and *chü-jen* appointed to office and an increased proportion of *kung-sheng* (including *kung-sheng* through purchase from the original status of *sheng-yüan)*, and even *sheng-yüan*. Consequently, even though the total of gentry through the "regular" route increased substantially in the post-Taiping period, the percentage of those appointed to office does not drop as much as might be expected. However, the increase in the number of officials without an increase of actual official posts means that there were more expectant officials and also more retired officials because of the higher rate of turnover.[177]

[175] *Ta-Ch'ing chin-shen-lu*, 1836 and 1908.

[176] For instance, Liu Chin-sheng of the Tao-kuang period was an acting *chou* magistrate for a short period. He stepped out for a mourning period upon the death of his father and never re-entered officialdom. (*Ling-chang hsien-chih*, 9/17 a–b.) Ku Yen-wu in "Age in Becoming Officials," in *Huang-ch'ao chin-shih wen-pien*, 17/17 a–b, says that the average age of being in office was from 30 to 60, but he pointed out that one would be in office for less than 30 years because of mourning periods for parents, waiting for appointment, etc.

[177] Cf. *supra*, p. 53, Table 2, where actual terms in office of *hsien* magistrates are

TABLE 9

PROPORTION OF "REGULAR" GENTRY WHO WERE OFFICIALS*

	Chia-shan		Soochow	
	1818–1850	*1851–1883*	*1818–1850*	*1851–1883*
No. of *sheng-yüan* and *kung-sheng*	677	825	1422	2141
No. appointed to office	18	28	20	55
Per cent	2.7	3.4	1.3	2.6
No. of *chü-jen*	34	22	105	147
No. appointed to office........	14	8	45	32
Per cent	41	36	43	22
No. of *chin-shih*	7	4	27	42
No. appointed to office	7	3	26	40
Per cent	100	75	96	95
Total of gentry through "regular" route	718	851	1554	2330
Total appointed to office	39	39	91	127
Per cent	5.4	4.6	5.9	5.4

* *Sources: Chia-shan ju-p'an t'i-ming-lu and Kuo-ch'ao san-i (Soochow fu Ch'ang Yüan Wu san-i) chu-sheng-p'u.* Since our calculations have indicated that a *sheng-yüan* had a life expectancy of thirty-three years when he entered the gentry, a thirty-three year period is taken before and after 1850.

The table also shows that in the nineteenth century almost five per cent of the gentry through the "regular" route were able to step into officialdom. But as Chia-shan and Soochow were well known for producing degree-holders and officials through the "regular" route, we cannot take five per cent as an average for all localities but must also take into consideration the localities which show very low records.[178] If it is assumed that three per cent is the average, there would be approximately 22,000 active and retired civil officials through the "regular" route at any one time in the pre-Taiping period and approximately 27,000 in the post-Taiping period.

The number of officials through purchase and other "irregular" routes was small in some localities but large in others. T'eng-hsien, Kwangsi, had only 83 in the whole Ch'ing dynasty who purchased official titles and offices,

shown to be shorter in later periods. However, some of the magistrates leaving one post were immediately transferred or promoted to some other post; this is different from retirement since no vacancy was created for new officials.

[178] For example, Hsin-ning, Hunan, had only one *chin-shih* during the whole dynasty, and the candidate upon whom this degree was bestowed received it because of old age after he had repeatedly failed in the metropolitan examinations. The civil officials recorded there had their origin mostly through military merit during the Taiping period and there were also some through purchase and recommendation. See *Hsin-ning hsien-chih,* 5/18 a ff.

of whom only 7 purchased actual offices, while 111 in the whole dynasty obtained offices through the "regular" route or through recommendation.[179] Yen-chou, Chekiang, has a record of 148 in the whole dynasty who purchased offices.[180] Many other examples can be given, and most of them show that the number was not very large. (See Table 25.) On the other hand, the Anhwei report given above certainly indicates a more active participation in purchase of offices after the rise of the Taipings.[181] It therefore seems reasonable in computing the number of active and inactive officials through the "irregular" route to apply a ratio based on figures for active officials given above.[182] The ratio of officials through the "regular" route to officials through purchase in a pre-Taiping year was about 2 to 1. The ratio in a post-Taiping year was about 4 to 3. This would give an approximate total of 11,000 active and inactive civil officials through purchase for a time in the pre-Taiping period and 20,000 in the post-Taiping period. Allowing for a small number of officials through other routes, the total number of gentry who were active or inactive civil officials would be approximately 35,000 in the pre-Taiping period and 50,000 in the post-Taiping period.

As indicated above, there were about 7,000 military posts and 20,000 civil ones, a ratio of 1 to 3. Gazetteers, in listing local men as civil officials and military officers, show in general this same ratio.[183] If the rate of turnover was the same for military officers as for civil officials, there would have been 12,000 military officers at a time in the pre-Taiping period and 17,000 in the post-Taiping period.

Civil and military officials differed greatly in their origin. In the civil posts the "regular" gentry were dominant, but this was not true of the military offices. A good number of military *chin-shih* were retained as imperial guards at the court, and some military *chin-shih* and *chü-jen* served as officers in the Board of War.[184] However, in the provinces they comprised a very small part of the total number of officers and did not control the highest military offices there. Table 26 shows the military officers in the

[179] *T'eng-hsien chih, chüan* 13 and 16.

[180] *Yen-chou fu-chih*, 17/26 ff. The origin of the purchasers is as follows: *ling-kung*, 24; *tseng-kung*, 5; *fu-kung*, 18; *li-kung*, 4; *ling-chien*, 1; *fu-chien*, 7; *ling-sheng*, 1; *chien-sheng*, 88.

[181] *Supra*, p. 109.

[182] *Supra*, p. 117. The ratio of 4,800 to 2,400 is 2 to 1, and the ratio of 4,800 to 3,500 is approximately 4 to 3.

[183] See Table 25. Middle and lower bracket military officers were permitted to serve in their own provinces, while civil officeholders were not. Their stay in office probably was longer than that of civil officeholders. However, gazetteer materials show that the number of civil officials through purchase and recommendation, which would be almost half of the total civil officials, was still in most cases much higher than the number of military officers through the "irregular" route.

[184] See *Ta-Ch'ing chin-shen ch'üan-shu*, 1881, Bk. 1, sections on Board of War and Imperial Guards.

year 1881 according to rank and origin. Only one of the provincial commanders-in-chief was a military *chin-shih.* Officers from the rank and file definitely predominated both in numbers and in their occupation of key posts. Out of the more than 7,000 military officers in the provinces, approximately 5,500 came from the rank and file and 10 of them were provincial commanders-in-chief.

The holders of official titles do not seem to have been very numerous before the Taiping period; and in some localities, in the post-Taiping period, they still did not greatly outnumber those who actually held offices.[185] On the other hand, the Anhwei example given above again points to a higher figure.[186] Taking the figures for the gentry who were civil or military officials in the pre-Taiping period (47,000) and in the post-Taiping period (67,000) as a basis for our estimate, we might put the number of holders of civil and military official titles at about 30,000 in the pre-Taiping period and at about 80,000 in the post-Taiping period.

Thus the total of all officials and holders of official titles would then amount to around 80,000 for a pre-Taiping date and 150,000 for a post-Taiping date. Except for the military officers from the rank and file, most of these men rose from the status of either *sheng-yüan* or *chien-sheng.* The advancement of men out of the lower gentry group does not affect the figures already arrived at on the total number of gentry since these estimates were based on the life expectancy of gentry members at the time they became *sheng-yüan* or *chien-sheng.* However, in considering the groups within the gentry, deductions will be made from the *sheng-yüan* and *chien-sheng* figures to account for those who advanced into the upper gentry.

Chin-shih. The *chin-shih*, or graduates of the metropolitan examinations, practically all became officials, and they have therefore already been accounted

[185] *Hsing-kuo chou-chih*, 17/3 ff., records that 176 purchased *chien-sheng* titles and official posts before the nineteenth century, of which 31 were holders of official titles. In the nineteenth century, only those having official posts and titles were recorded; 113 had posts or were on the waiting list and 135 had titles. Cf. also *T'eng-hsien chih*, *chüan* 13 and 16. There it is shown that the most commonly purchased civil official title was that of assistant *chou* magistrate and the most commonly purchased military title was that of lieutenant.

[186] *Supra*, p. 109, where it is noted that a much larger number purchased official titles and honorific titles than actual offices. But this number undoubtedly includes a considerable number of honorific titles, mostly conferred upon deceased parents or grandparents. Honorific titles as recorded in *Kao-chou fu-chih*, *chüan* 30–36, for example, show the following: Mou-ming, 1,061 (one incumbent official alone generates several titles for parents, grandparents, parents-in-law, etc.); T'ien-pai, 468; Hsin-i, 341; Hua-chou, 364; Wu-ch'uan, 518; Shih-ch'eng, 173. *Chih-li Mien-chou chih*, *chüan* 36 and 37, records the following: *shou* or honorific title to the contributor himself in Mien-chou, 6; *feng* or honorific title to the living parents of contributors, 18; *tseng* or honorific title to deceased parents, 34. In Te-yang, all 25 honorific titleholders were listed under *tseng.* In An-hsien, only one obtained an honorific title under *tseng.* In Mien-chu, there were 3 *shou,* 2 *feng*, 20 *tseng.* In Lo-chiang, there were 4 *feng* and 5 *tseng.*

for in that group. However, as the *chin-shih* degree was the highest honor attainable, these men considered themselves a separate and superior group, and it is of interest to see the size of this central group in comparison to the other groups of gentry.

The exact number of civil *chin-shih* can be determined, as the number of *chin-shih* degrees conferred in all the metropolitan examinations held in the Ch'ing dynasty is available. The source used is a work based on tablet inscriptions of names of new *chin-shih*.[187] It is to be noted that the *Ch'in-ting ta-Ch'ing hui-tien shih-li* records the *kung-shih* figures rather than the *chin-shih* figures.[188] The *chin-shih* degree was granted after the palace examinations, while *kung-shih* was merely an intermediary title given to those who were successful in the metropolitan examinations but had not yet participated in the palace examinations. The two sets of figures usually varied very little, although occasionally there was a considerable difference.[189] The number of *chin-shih* and *kung-shih* degrees conferred in the metropolitan examinations during each year of the Ch'ing dynasty is shown in Table 27.[190] To mark off the years for our computation, we first show the average age of successful metropolitan examination candidates in Table 10.

An average *chin-shih* before the Taiping period would therefore be admitted at 36 and would have at that age a life expectancy of approximately 22 years. The number of *chin-shih* admitted in the 12 metropolitan examina-

[187] *Tseng-chiao Ch'ing-ch'ao chin-shih t'i-ming pei-lu.* This study is based mainly on tablet inscriptions of names of new *chin-shih* which also give their order of success and their native places. Other materials such as some local gazetteers and *Hui-shih t'ung-nien ch'ih-lu* are also used.

[188] This point has been clarified to me by Fang Chao-ying through correspondence. It is not correct, therefore, for Hsieh Pao-chao, *op. cit.*, p. 184, to describe his table as *chin-shih* conferred in the metropolitan examinations. His figures based on *Hui-tien shih-li* are actually *kung-shih* figures.

[189] For instance, in 1723 the metropolitan graduate quota was fixed at 180, but then 78 more were admitted from the declined papers. *Shih-li*, 350/2 a. Thus *ibid.*, p. 36, still gives the quota as 180, while Fang's *chin-shih* list has 246 for that year. The remaining small discrepancy might be attributed to persons not participating in the palace examinations because of illness or mourning. For instance, in *Hsiang-fu hsien-chih*, 15/77 a–78 b, in the biography of Feng Tuan-peng, it is related that after passing the metropolitan examination, he received the news of the death of his father. He had to report it and be disqualified from participating in the palace examination.

[190] Looking at Table 27, we can see a definite trend of increase and decrease in quota for the whole dynasty. In the Shun-chih years, some quotas were as high as 450. When Sheng-tsu ascended the throne, he turned to a strict policy in the metropolitan as well as in the *sheng-yüan* quotas. Thus in many metropolitan examinations held in K'ang-hsi years, the quota was only 150 although on a few occasions it was as high as 300. In the first half of the Ch'ien-lung reign, the quota for *chin-shih* turned toward leniency but tightened again in the second half. In one of the late Ch'ien-lung years, only 97 were admitted, the lowest number ever recorded. Then the quota was raised again, and in Chia-ch'ing and Tao-kuang years, it generally fluctuated around 200. This quota was generally maintained in Hsien-feng and the first part of T'ung-chih, but beginning in the second half of T'ung-chih, i.e., after the Taiping Rebellion, and to the end of the dynasty, the quota was generally slightly over 300.

TABLE 10

AGE OF ADMISSION TO CHIN-SHIH*

Age groups	1835		1868		1894	
	No.	Per cent	No.	Per cent	No.	Per cent
16–20	3	1.1	4	1.8	1	0.4
21–25	17	6.1	29	12.8	26	10.6
26–30	45	16.1	48	21.2	54	22.0
31–35	59	21.1	51	22.5	64	26.1
36–40	63	22.6	49	21.6	63	25.8
41–45	44	15.8	33	14.5	29	11.9
46–50	35	12.6	9	3.9	6	2.4
51–55	11	3.9	3	1.3	2	0.8
56–60	2	0.7	1	0.4		
Totals	279	100.0	227	100.0	245	100.0
Average age	Approximately 36		Approximately 34		Approximately 33	

* *Hui-shih t'ung-nien ch'ih-lu*, 1835, 1868, 1894. These materials were first exploited by Dr. C. K. Yang.

tions between 1829 and 1850 was 2,536 (as shown in Table 27). An average *chin-shih* after the Taiping period would be admitted at 34 and would have at that age a life expectancy of approximately 24 years. The number admitted in the 11 metropolitan examinations held between 1852 and 1874 was 2,643 (as shown in Table 27). Thus, at the eve of the rise of the Taipings, there would have been approximately 2,500 *chin-shih*, and by 1875 there would have been approximately 2,600.

An even smaller group, coming from the small group of *chin-shih*, was the *han-lin*, members of the Han-lin Academy, the highest literary institution. These were the men who had ranked highest in the metropolitan examinations. They formed the reservoir from which examiners for provincial examinations and provincial directors-of-studies were appointed. They were in a position to form teacher-student cliques based on examination relationships and so build up their personal political power. It was usually these *han-lin* who held the highest positions in officialdom. This group was therefore extremely important although it included only 650 members at the eve of the Taiping period[191] and about 750 by the year 1875.[192]

It is also of interest to see from what provinces the *chin-shih* came. It was customary for the Board of Rites at the time of the examination to request the Emperor to decide on a quota for each province theoretically

[191] Add the *han-lin* figures in Table 27 for examinations between 1829 and 1850.
[192] Add the *han-lin* figures for examinations between 1852 and 1874.

based on the number of participants. The big provinces (in the sense of large number of examination candidates) usually had a quota of approximately 20; middle-sized provinces had a quota of between 10 and 20; and small provinces had a quota of less than 10. In actual practice, a province's quota usually remained about the same from one examination to the next.[193] An example of the distribution is given in Table 11.

TABLE 11

METROPOLITAN EXAMINATION QUOTA, 1889*

Province	No.	Province	No.	Province	No.
Manchu Bannermen..	8	Shensi	14	Szechwan	14
Mongol Bannermen..	3	Kansu	9	Fukien.............	20
Chinese Bannermen..	6	Kiangsu...........	25	Taiwan	2
Chihli.............	23	Anhwei	17	Kwangtung	16
Fengt'ien..........	3	Chekiang..........	24	Kwangsi	13
Shantung..........	21	Kiangsi	22	Yunnan............	12
Shansi	10	Hupeh	14	Kweichow	11
Honan	17	Hunan	14	Total	318

* *Shih-lu*, Te-tsung, 268/14 b.

Kiangsu and Chekiang had higher quotas, although the difference was not very great. There was no limitation on the order of success, and since the Kiangsu and Chekiang candidates excelled the others, they had a better chance of entering the Han-lin Academy. Studies on the three most successful candidates in each metropolitan examination reveal that more than half of them were Kiangsu and Chekiang men.[194] The three districts

[193] Cf. Shen Shou-chih, "Chieh-ch'ao pi-chi," *Jen-wen yüeh-k'an, chüan* 7, No 3, April 15, 1936, where it is said that in one Tao-kuang year, the Board officials again presented the quota of a previous examination to the Emperor for reference. The Emperor thought that the former quota of 10 for Honan was too large for the number of Honan participants on this occasion and marked the figure 9 there while forgetting to erase the original figure 10. The Board officials knew this was a mistake, but not wanting to offend the Honan candidates, they announced it as 19 which was then an established norm for later examinations.

[194] See Huang Yen-p'ei, "Ch'ing-tai ko-sheng jen-wen t'ung-chi chih i-pan," *Jen-wen yüeh-k'an, chüan* 2, No. 6, August 15, 1931, pp. 1–3. Of the *chuang-yüan*, the first successful candidates, in the 114 metropolitan examinations held in the Ch'ing dynasty, 49 were Kiangsu men and 20 were Chekiang men. Three were bannermen. According to Hummel, Vol. I, 208–209, Ch'ung-ch'i, in 1865, was the first to break the tradition that no bannermen should receive high honors in civil examinations. Huang, pp. 3–4, also gives the families that for generations had *chin-shih* degree-holders in the family. Most of these families were located in Kiangsu and Chekiang. *Ibid*., pp. 8–9, also gives the origin of grand secretaries, governors-general and governors. Except for the bannermen, who held a much higher proportion than the number of Chinese from any province, Kiangsu and Chekiang headed the list. They were closely followed by Shantung, Hunan, and Anhwei, especially in the posts of governor-general and governor. This was certainly a result of the military success of the Hunan and Anhwei gentry leaders.

of Ch'ang, Yüan, and Wu in Kiangsu, which are combined in one district today, alone produced sixteen men who ranked in the highest position in different metropolitan examinations.[195]

On the number of military *chin-shih*, complete information is not available, but some idea can be gained from comparison. In 1655, when the military metropolitan quota was set at 120, the civil one was 450; in 1659, the ratio was 100 to 350; in 1661, the ratio was 300 to 400; in 1664, it was 100 to 150; in 1670, 200 to 300; in 1676, 150 to 195; in 1679, 100 to 150.[196] These early Ch'ing examples mostly show a ratio of 2 to 3. A ratio of roughly 2 to 3 seems to have prevailed also in the nineteenth century.[197] We shall tentatively say, therefore, that there would be approximately 1,500 military *chin-shih* at any time both before and after the Taiping period. The military and civil *chin-shih* together would total about 4,000 in the pre-Taiping period and about 4,100 in the post-Taiping period.

Chü-jen. The next group among the upper gentry was made up of the *chü-jen*, the graduates of the provincial examinations. They came from *kung-sheng*, *chien-sheng*, and *sheng-yüan*, all of whom were qualified to participate in these examinations. Although there is no comprehensive material covering the quotas of all provincial examinations in the nineteenth century, the data available show that they did not vary greatly before and after the Taiping period. In 1834, for instance, the quota was 1,371;[198] in 1851, 1,770;[199] in 1881, 1,254;[200] in 1885, 1,521;[201] and in 1891, 1,529.[202] The norm is said to be 1,439.[203] The distribution among the provinces in 1881 was as follows: Shun-t'ien-fu, 229; Chiang-nan, 114; Kiangsi, 104; Chekiang, 94; Fukien, 85; Hupeh, 51; Hunan, 45; Honan, 71; Shantung, 69; Shansi, 60; Shensi, 61; Szechwan, 60; Kwangtung, 72; Kwangsi, 45; Yunnan, 54; and Kweichow, 40.[204]

195 *Ibid.*, pp. 5–7.

196 For 1655 data, see *Shih-li*, 719/1 b. For others, see *ibid.*, 717/1 a–b.

197 In certain examination years during the war, the quota was drastically reduced. For example, there is recorded in *Shih-lu*, Wen-tsung, 7/31 a, an edict of Hsien-feng 11/10 (1861) setting the quota at only 25, not even providing any for some provinces. The distribution was as follows: Manchu and Mongol bannermen, 3; Chinese bannermen, 2; Fengt'ien, 1; Chihli, 10; Shensi and Kansu, 1; Honan, 1; Shantung, 1; Shansi, 2; Hupeh, 1; Hunan, 1; Szechwan, 1; and Chekiang, 1. Evidently there were few candidates from the southern provinces which were affected by the war. Such decreases in quota were caused by the war and were very likely made up for in the years following by special quota increases.

198 *Chia-wu chih-sheng t'ung-nien ch'üan-lu*, 1834.

199 *Hsin-hai chih-sheng t'ung-nien ch'üan-lu*, 1851.

200 *Ta-Ch'ing chin-shen ch'üan-shu*, 1881, *ts'e* 1, p. 20.

201 E. L. Oxenham, "Ages of Candidates at Chinese Examinations."

202 *Hsin-mao-k'o hsiang-shih shih-pa-sheng t'ung-nien ch'üan-lu*, 1891.

203 *K'o-ch'ang*, 20/1 a–3 a; *Ch'ing-kuo hsin-chang-fa fen-lun*, 3/132–33.

204 *Ta-Ch'ing chin-shen ch'üan-shu*, 1881, *ts'e* 1, p. 20. The Shun-t'ien-fu figure includes quotas set aside for Chihli *sheng-yüan*, for bannermen, and also for *kung-sheng*

These figures show that the *chü-jen* quota was, on the average, a little higher after the Taiping period than before it. This slight increase was mostly due to the provisions for permanent increases in quota through contribution to the military fund discussed earlier. These provisions applied to provincial examinations as well as to the district examinations. In 1853, it was provided that provinces contributing an amount of 100,000 taels would have one temporary increase in both the civil and military *chü-jen* quotas, and that those contributing 300,000 taels would have one permanent increase.[205] In 1868 the regulation was amended so that if the contributors had already been individually rewarded, or if the *sheng-yüan* quota had already been increased because of the contribution, the same amount of money could not be a basis for a further claim for increase of *chü-jen* quota.[206] In 1874 the government stated that there would be no more permanent increases in *chü-jen* quota, and that for a contribution of 300,000 taels one temporary increase would be granted.[207] By this time, Shansi, Kiangsu, Anhwei, Chekiang, Kiangsi, Fukien, Hupeh, Hunan, Kansu, Szechwan, Kwangtung, and Yunnan had each permanently increased their quota by 10.[208]

Thus, the permanent and temporary increases in quota had effected a slight increase in the number of *chü-jen* by the post-Taiping period, but the court seemed reluctant to increase the quota very much. Li Hung-chang tried on different occasions to increase the *chü-jen* quota for Anhwei but did not succeed.[209] On the average, approximately 1,400 obtained the *chü-jen* degree in a provincial examination year before the Taiping period and 1,500 in the post-Taiping period. To estimate the total of *chü-jen*, we must first determine the average age of admission to *chü-jen*. Table 12 summarizes information on the age of admission of two groups of *chü-jen*.

The average age of admission to *chü-jen* in both 1834 and 1851 appears to be between thirty and thirty-one, giving *chü-jen* a life expectancy of approximately twenty-seven years at the time they received the degree. The number of *chü-jen* in the pre-Taiping period would then be approximately 18,000 and in the post-Taiping period approximately 19,000.[210] This number

and *chien-sheng* of other provinces participating in the metropolitan provincial examinations.

205 *K'o-ch'ang*, 24/3 a–6 b.

206 *Ibid.*, p. 8 a–b. Cf. Chang Fei, *Chang Wen-i-kung tsou-kao*, 2/37 ff., memorial of Hsien-feng 9/4/24 (1859), requesting increases in both *sheng-yüan* and *chü-jen* quotas for a certain amount of money collected.

207 *K'o-ch'ang*, 24/8 b–9 a.

208 *Ibid.*, pp. 1 a–2 b.

209 *Hsü-hsiu Lu-chou fu-chih*, 17/76 b ff., records that in 1864, 1866, 1869, and 1871 Li asked for increases in *chü-jen* quota, on three occasions for permanent increases and once for temporary increases, on account of contributions by local men in Anhwei and by Huai-chün commanders.

210 During the 27 years before 1850, 13 provincial examinations were held, 9 being

TABLE 12

AGE OF ADMISSION TO CHÜ-JEN*

Age groups	1834		1851	
	No.	Per cent	No.	Per cent
14–15			4	0.2
16–20	51	3.7	74	4.2
21–25	212	15.5	324	18.3
26–30	365	26.6	426	24.1
31–35	301	22.0	401	22.6
36–40	234	17.1	242	13.7
41–45	112	8.2	163	9.2
46–50	51	3.7	72	4.1
51–55	32	2.3	40	2.2
56–60	8	0.6	14	0.8
61–65	2	0.1	10	0.6
66–70	3	0.2		
Totals	1,371	100.0	1,770	100.0
Average age	Approximately 31		Approximately 31	

* The 1834 figures are collected from *Chia-wu chih-sheng t'ung-nien ch'üan-lu.* The 1851 figures are collected from *Hsin-hai chih-sheng t'ung-nien ch'üan-lu.* These materials were first exploited by Dr. C. K. Yang. Cf. E. L. Oxenham, "Age of Candidates at Chinese Examinations."

includes 2,500 who later became *chin-shih* and approximately 6,000 who rose into officialdom either by purchase or through special selection.[211] If these *chin-shih* and officials are deducted, the number who remained *chü-jen* would be approximately 10,000. This fits quite well with the report that the number of men who mustered triennially for the metropolitan examinations was generally about 8,000,[212] since some allowance must be made for those who did not appear for examinations because of mourning periods and for those who had stopped participating after repeated failures.

The quota of military *chü-jen*, according to an edict of 1687, was to be

regular ones and 4 through imperial favor. (These numbers are the same as those of metropolitan examinations in that period. Cf. Table 27.) The same number of examinations was held from 1852 to 1877. The *chü-jen* totals were then obtained by multiplying the average quota for each examination by the number of examinations.

211 Cf. percentage of *chü-jen* appointed to office in Table 9, *supra*, p. 118.

212 T. L. Bullock, "Competitive Examinations in China," p. 91. In Bard, *Chinese Life in Town and Country*, p. 98, it is said that about 14,000 candidates presented themselves at Peking for every triennial examination, and that not more than 1,500 succeeded in getting their degrees. 14,000 must be an overstatement, and never as many as 1,500 were successful. A very low figure is given in an edict of 1868 which states that, "In recent years the number of participants varies from 4,000 or more to 3,000 or more." (*K'o-ch'ang*, 1/24 b.) This, however, refers to the war years when many candidates, especially in provinces distant from the capital, could not participate in examinations because transportation was disrupted.

in accord with the quota of civil *chü-jen.*[213] However, the nineteenth century record shows the military quota to be somewhat lower than the civil one. The norm was set at 1,011, not including quotas for the eight banners. The distribution among the provinces was as follows: Shun-t'ien-fu, 113; Shantung, 51; Shansi, 54; Honan, 58; Chiang-nan, 99; Kiangsi, 54; Chekiang, 64; Fukien, 70; Hunan, 34; Hupeh, 41; Shensi, 69; Kansu, 58; Szechwan, 61; Kwangtung, 64; Kwangsi, 36; Yunnan, 52; and Kweichow, 33.[214] The military quotas of the majority of the provinces, with a few exceptions such as Shensi and Szechwan, were lower than the civil ones, thus giving a lower total for the country. Since the ratio of military to civil *chü-jen* quota is about 5 to 7, there would be about 13,000 military *chü-jen* in the pre-Taiping period and 13,500 in the post-Taiping period. If deduction is made for those who became military *chin-shih* or went directly into officialdom, there would probably remain about 8,000 military *chü-jen* existing at any one time. The total number of *chü-jen,* both civil and military, would then amount to approximately 18,000. One writer's statement that there were more than 21,000 unemployed *chü-jen* thus does not seem to be too much of an overstatement.[215]

Kung-sheng. The last group of upper gentry, the "regular" *kung-sheng,* will be discussed according to its subdivisions. For *sui-kung-sheng* or *kung-sheng* by virtue of seniority, the annual quota for the whole country before and after the Taiping period was slightly under 1,000, as shown in Table 28. Although no statistical study has been made on the average age of becoming a *kung-sheng,*[216] we can imagine that it would be in the man's late thirties, since *kung-sheng* were selected by virtue of seniority as *ling-sheng* and must have repeatedly failed to pass the provincial examinations. Therefore, it is probably safe to assume that an average *sui-kung-sheng* had a life expectancy of 20 years at the time he received this title. Thus, the total of *sui-kung-sheng* at any one time either before or after the Taiping period would be around 20,000.

The *en-kung-sheng,* or *kung-sheng* through imperial favor, emerged only through special imperial instructions whenever there were national celebrations such as the beginning of a new reign. The record shows that *en-kung-sheng* appeared in 1644, 1653, 1669, 1675, 1698, 1713, 1723, 1735, 1750, 1751, 1761, 1771, 1780, 1785, 1790, 1796, 1799, and 1809.[217]

[213] *Shih-li,* 716/1 b.

[214] *Ch'ing-kuo hsin-cheng-fa fen-lun,* 3/172.

[215] Robert K. Douglas, *Society in China,* p. 116. However, it is not clear whether this figure refers to total *chü-jen* or civil *chü-jen* alone. If the latter is meant, then the figure is much too high.

[216] It can be done by working through such books as *Kwangtung kuei-yu-k'o pa-kung yu-kung ch'ih-lu.*

[217] *Hsüeh-cheng,* 50/1–5.

Thus in the 61 years of the K'ang-hsi reign (1662–1722), there were only 4 *en-kung* years, and in the 60 years of the Ch'ien-lung reign (1736–1795) there were only 7 *en-kung* years. They did not necessarily correspond with years of metropolitan and provincial examinations through imperial favor.[218] In fact, there were on the whole more *en-kung* years than special examination years.

En-kung then appeared in 1819, 1820, 1821, 1825, 1835, 1845, 1850, 1852, 1853, 1855, 1860, 1861, 1865, 1872, 1875, 1879, and 1881.[219] It seems that in the first half of the nineteenth century, the number of *en-kung* years largely kept pace with earlier records, but after the rise of the Taipings, the tempo definitely increased, so that the court gave the impression of showing greater favor to the gentry. With the attainment of this title, the *sheng-yüan* crossed the important dividing line between lower and upper gentry. They were then eligible for appointment to certain offices. They no longer had to participate in examinations for *sheng-yüan*, and they enjoyed higher prestige and more privileges.

From 1831 to 1850 there were three *en-kung* years, while in the twenty years after the rise of the Taipings there were six or practically seven *en-kung* years. The next problem is to determine the quota for *en-kung-sheng* in each of these years. The imperial edicts regarding the granting of the *en-kung* title always say that all schools in the provinces should let the first in order to become *kung-sheng* be called *en-kung*, and the second in order be called *sui-kung*.[220] But this should not mislead us into assuming that the *en-kung* quota was the same as the *sui-kung* quota. Some schools were permitted to produce two *sui-kung* in each year while others were permitted to produce only one in six years. On the average, each school produced approximately one in two years. On the other hand, the edicts quoted above meant that each school, regardless of its size, generally should have one *en-kung* in each of the *en-kung* years. This accounts for the fact that in six of the localities in Sung-chiang prefecture, where they produced one *sui-kung* in four years, there were in the Hsien-feng period fewer *sui-kung* than *en-kung*. (See Table 29.) Multiplying the number of schools by the number of *en-kung* years, we get a pre-Taiping *en-kung* figure of approximately 5,000 and a post-Taiping figure of approximately 12,000. This striking difference between the *en-kung* figures before and after the Taiping period can be seen if we compare the number of different types of *kung-sheng* in different periods as recorded in local gazetteers.[221]

218 Cf. Table 27.

219 *Shih-li*, 384/4 a–b.

220 Also see *Sung-chiang-fu hsü-chih*, 22/19 a.

221 Thus the totals of the different types of *kung-sheng* in several localities, as given

Pa-kung-sheng were selected only once in twelve years. Since early Ch'ing, in *pa-kung* years, two were to be admitted to *pa-kung* from each prefectural school and one from each *chou* or *hsien* school.[222] Often an administrative district was split into two, thus having two schools. At first the two schools usually shared the quota of one *pa-kung*, but when both schools began to have a considerable number of *sheng-yüan*, each was given a separate quota of one *pa-kung*.[223] Nevertheless, the *pa-kung* quota had to be at least as many as the number of schools, which was 1741 in the pre-Taiping period and 1810 in the post-Taiping period.[224]

As all *sheng-yüan*, except for the newly admitted ones who had not yet participated in the *sui* examinations, were qualified to participate in the *pa-kung* examinations, the average age of becoming *pa-kung* would be lower than that of becoming *sui-kung* or *en-kung*, approximately in the early thirties. If the life expectancy of an average *pa-kung* at the time he attained this degree is set at approximately 24 years, we can multiply the quota by 2 to arrive at a total of approximately 3,500 *pa-kung* for the pre-Taiping period and 3,600 for the post-Taiping period. The ratio of these figures to the *sui-kung* and *en-kung* figures fits quite well with the ratio as seen in gazetteer materials. (Cf. Tables 25 and 29.)

The *yu-kung-sheng*, according to regulations, were selected once in three years; five to six were selected from a big province, three to four from a middle-sized province, and one to two from a small province.[225] It was reported, for instance, in 1891 that six *yu-kung* were produced in Kiangsu.[226] In 1863, an edict pointed out that the total of *yu-kung* from all provinces in one selection amounted to only 60 to 70.[227] If we assume that on the average a *yu-kung*, at the time he attained this degree, would have a life expectancy of 24 years, the same as a *pa-kung*, there would be about 500 *yu-kung* at a time either before or after the Taiping period.

in Table 25, do not show as accurate a picture as Table 29 where attention is given to differences in different reign periods. There was also the very small number of *en-kung* granted to descendants of sages. In *Hsüeh-cheng*, 50/1–3, for instance, in 1669, 15 were granted; in 1724, 15 were granted; and in 1738, 31 were granted.

222 *Shih-li*, 384/4 b ff.

223 *Ibid.* Many such changes are recorded there.

224 See Tables 15 and 16. We roughly offset the number of new schools with the number of prefectural schools. A report on the *pa-kung* examination held in 1886 gives the number of *pa-kung* admitted in that year as 451. This figure, if correct for that year is lower than that provided by regulations. (Zi, "Pratique des Examens Littéraires en Chine," p. 86.) Chekiang had 40, Chihli 35, Szechwan and Shantung 33, Kiangsu 32, etc.

225 *Shih-li*, 385/3 b ff.

226 Zi, *op. cit.*, p. 88. According to the announcement of the governor-general and provincial director-of-studies, twelve more were announced on a supplementary list so that when those on the main list passed the provincial examinations, those on the supplementary list could be promoted to fill the vacancies.

227 *Shih-li*, 385/4 b.

The *fu-kung-sheng*, were those who failed to become *chü-jen* in the provincial examinations but did well enough to be placed on the secondary successful list. Their number cannot be determined by figuring their ratio to other types of *kung-sheng* as recorded in local gazetteers. A locality could have very few *fu-kung* for the whole dynasty simply because only a few happened to be on that secondary successful list.[228] However, the number of *fu-kung* has a definite relation to the number of civil *chü-jen* since it was provided that to five *chü-jen* admitted, one would be admitted on the secondary list.. Thus, the *fu-kung* figure would be 3,600 for the pre-Taiping period and 3,800 for the post-Taiping period.

The total of "regular" *kung-sheng* thus is approximately 32,000 for a pre-Taiping time and approximately 40,000 for a post-Taiping time as shown in Table 13.

TABLE 13

TOTALS OF DIFFERENT TYPES OF "REGULAR" KUNG-SHENG IN THE PRE-TAIPING AND POST-TAIPING PERIODS

	Pre-Taiping	Per cent	Post-Taiping	Per cent
Sui-kung-sheng	20,000	61	20,000	50
En-kung-sheng	5,000	15	12,000	30
Pa-kung-sheng	3,500	11	3,600	9
Yu-kung-sheng	500	2	500	2
Fu-kung-sheng	3,600	11	3,800	9
Totals	32,600	100	39,900	100

This *kung-sheng* total is not a net figure. A number of these men would later pass in provincial examinations. An even higher number would step into officialdom, for *kung-sheng* held the majority of the educational offices[229] and were also eligible for other posts. Theoretically, all "regular" *kung-sheng* could be appointed to office, but in actuality they could not have all stepped into officialdom. Undoubtedly those who could afford it took advantage of the purchase system and did not wait their turn to get official positions.

[228] E.g., the district of Tzu-t'ung had only 3 *fu-kung* during the whole dynasty. See Table 25.

[229] Chang Chung-ju, *Ch'ing-tai k'o-chü chih-tu*, p. 5, describes the qualifications of educational officials as follows. Each *fu*, *t'ing*, *chou*, and *hsien* had two educational officials. The head in the *fu* was *fu* director-of-studies, in the *chou*, *chou* director-of-studies, and in the *hsien*, *hsien* director-of-studies. The other was the assistant director-of-studies. *Fu* director-of-studies was the lowest official post to which *chin-shih* were appointed. One might be promoted to this position from *chou* or *hsien* director-of-studies or demoted to it from *chou* or *hsien* magistrate. The posts of *chou* or *hsien* directors-of-studies were filled by *chü-jen* through *ta-t'iao* or special selection or through selection from the five types of *kung-sheng*. Assistant educational officials were also selected from the five *kung-sheng*. *Ling-kung* (*kung-sheng* purchased from the original status of *ling-sheng*) could further purchase to assistant educational offices.

To estimate the proportion of "regular" *kung-sheng* appointed to office, data on two localities have been tabulated in Table 14.

TABLE 14

PROPORTION OF "REGULAR" KUNG-SHENG APPOINTED TO OFFICE*

Period	Ch'u-chou, Chekiang		Per cent	Sui-chou, Honan		Per cent
	No. of *kung-sheng*	No. appointed to office		No. of *kung-sheng*	No. appointed to office	
Shun-chih (1644–1661)	156	76	48	35	16	46
K'ang-hsi (1662–1722)	378	67	18	68	17	25
Yung-cheng (1723–1735)	119	30	25	24	7	29
Ch'ien-lung (1736–1795)	444	65	13	82	26	31
Chia-ch'ing (1796–1820)	243	18	7	57	10	17
Tao-kuang (1821–1850)	332	25	7	29	00	00
Hsien-feng (1851–1861)	144	19	13	16	2	12
T'ung-chih (1862–1874)	116	12	10	9	00	00
Kuang-hsü† (1875)	8		0	20	1	5
	1,940	312	16	340	79	23

* *Ch'u-chou fu-chih*, 17/34 b–67 a; *Hsü-hsiu Sui-chou chih*, 5/39 a–56 b.

† Only covers Kuang-hsü 1st and 2nd years for Ch'u-chou and Kuang-hsü 1st to 17th years for Sui-chou.

Table 14 shows a definite decline in the proportion of "regular" *kung-sheng* appointed to office in the nineteenth century. Many educational offices were still held by *kung-sheng*, but more of such *kung-sheng* seem to have been *kung-sheng* through purchase from the original status of *ling-sheng* who, strictly speaking, would be considered "irregular" *kung-sheng*.[230] This also explains why the percentage of Soochow and Chia-shan *kung-sheng* appointed to office (as shown earlier in Table 9) increases after the rise of the Taipings,

[230] See, for instance, *Ta-Ch'ing chin-shen ch'üan-shu*, 1881, under the names of educational officials. *Hsing-kuo chou-chih*, 15/28 a–29 b, has a special record of purchased *kung-sheng* originally through examination (*cheng-tu li-kung*). There were 57 of them, of whom 27 had official posts, largely educational positions. *Hangchow fu-chih*, 23/46 ff., shows that many *kung-sheng* in Ming times obtained official posts. However, only a few did in Ch'ing times.

since the figures in that table include those who purchased from their original position of *sheng-yüan.* Needless to say, this is the effect of the expansion of the purchase system. In short, the deduction for *kung-sheng* who later became *chü-jen* or officials need not be over 5,000. The net total of "regular" *kung-sheng* would then be 27,000 and 35,000 respectively for the pre-Taiping and post-Taiping periods.

Summary of Upper Gentry Groups. Summing up the different groups of upper gentry, we find in the pre-Taiping period, approximately 80,000 civil and military officials and holders of official titles, 18,000 civil and military *chü-jen*, and 27,000 "regular" *kung-sheng*, a total of 125,000. In the post-Taiping period there were approximately 150,000 civil and military officials and holders of official titles, 19,000 civil and military *chü-jen,* and 35,000 "regular" *kung-sheng*, a total of 204,000. *Kung-sheng* and *chü-jen* listed above were all "regular" gentry. Of the group of officials and titleholders, approximately half were "regular" gentry in the pre-Taiping period, but only a third were "regular" gentry in the post-Taiping period. The rest were mainly gentry through purchase with some also from other routes such as recommendation or military promotion. Thus, about 80,000 of the pre-Taiping upper gentry had originally been *sheng-yüan* and about 40,000 had risen through purchase from *chien-sheng.* In the post-Taiping period, about 100,000 were originally *sheng-yüan* and about another 100,000 were through purchase from *chien-sheng.*

Lower Gentry

Included in the lower gentry, as described in Part One, were the *sheng-yüan, chien-sheng,* and the *li-kung-sheng* or *kung-sheng* through purchase. The *li-kung-sheng* will be taken up first.

Kung-sheng through purchase. The regulations provided that to purchase the title of *kung-sheng, ling-sheng* paid 108 taels; *tseng-sheng* paid 120 taels; and *chien-sheng* and *fu-sheng* paid 144 taels.[231] A commoner could therefore purchase to *kung-sheng* if he first bought a *chien-sheng* title. This raises two problems: first, the total number of *li-kung,* and second, the proportion of those who were originally *sheng-yüan* to those who were originally commoners.

Lacking complete data for the first problem, we proceed again through comparison with other groups of gentry, especially the "regular" *kung-sheng.* The number of *li-kung* varied considerably from one locality to another. In Hsin-t'ien, Hunan, for instance, the number was extremely low—only four

[231] See *Ch'ing-kuo hsin-cheng-fa fen-lun,* 5/359.

during the whole dynasty. The editor of the gazetteer remarks: "There was no special group of *li-kung* in the district and collection from such was extremely low. Although the locality is small, there is certainly no excess of [titleholders]."[232] His statement implies that in small localities the proportion of "irregulars" to "regulars" would usually be higher than the general average, since very few from small localities succeeded in becoming *chü-jen* and *chin-shih*. Many other examples show that though there were more *li-kung* in an average district than there were in Hsin-t'ien, they were generally a much smaller group than the "regular" *kung-sheng*. The data on hand have been tabulated in Table 30, and from this information it would appear that the number of "irregular" *kung-sheng* was about one-third that of the "regular" *kung-sheng*. If this is the ratio, the total of "irregular" *kung-sheng* would be approximately 10,000 in the pre-Taiping period and 13,000 in the post-Taiping period.

On the second problem of the origin of *li-kung*, materials are even more difficult to secure. However, some local gazetteers did clearly distinguish the "irregular" *kung-sheng*, who were originally *ling-sheng*, from other "irregular" *kung-sheng*. Of the 73 "irregular" *kung-sheng* in Tao-chou, Hunan, in the Ch'ing dynasty, 20 were identified as *ling-kung*.[233] Of the 39 "irregular" *kung-sheng* in Jung-hsien, Kwangsi, in the Ch'ing dynasty, 3 were identified as *ling-kung*.[234] The question is then whether the "irregular" *kung-sheng* who were not originally *ling-sheng* were originally *tseng-sheng* and *fu-sheng* or commoners. There is material to show that *tseng-sheng* and *fu-sheng* sometimes made up a high proportion of the purchasers to *kung-sheng*. In Hsin-ning, Hunan, for example, the record shows that while 5 "irregular" *kung-sheng* were originally *ling-sheng*, 3 were originally *tseng-sheng*, and 20 were originally *fu-sheng*.[235]

At any rate, the number of "irregular" *kung-sheng* as a whole was not very large, and the number of "irregular" *kung-sheng* who were originally commoners was even much smaller. Nevertheless, even though they were a relatively small group, we should see how successful they were in penetrating into officialdom. We have already seen the increasing number of local offices obtained by *chien-sheng* in the late nineteenth century. The *li-kung*, as indicated earlier, were gaining in the holding of educational offices. For instance, in Szechwan in 1881, among the *kung-sheng* who held educational offices, almost 60 were *ling-kung*, *tseng-kung*, or *fu-kung*, while about 80 were the five types of "regular" *kung-sheng*, a ratio of 3 to 4.[236]

232 *Yung-chou fu-chih*, 12 B/34 b.
233 *Tao-chou chih*, 8/14 a ff.
234 *Jung-hsien chih*, 17/11 b–13 a.
235 *Hsin-ning hsien-chih*, 5/15 b–16 a.
236 *Ta-Ch'ing chin-shen ch'üan-shu*, 1881, *ts'e* 4, pp. 1 a–19 b.

The plain or commoner-originated *kung-sheng*, though barred by regulation from holding educational offices, held more central government offices than did the "regular" *kung-sheng.* For instance, in 1881, in the Board of War, among the *kung-sheng* who were second-class assistant secretaries, 37 were *li-kung* and 28 were "regular" *kung-sheng*, a ratio of approximately 4 to 3.[237] Although the "regular" *kung-sheng* had a greater opportunity to obtain higher offices, the increase in the number of "irregulars" holding lower offices is significant.

Sheng-yüan. In our earlier discussion of the total number of gentry, we concluded that in the pre-Taiping period, there were about 530,000 persons who entered the gentry as civil *sheng-yüan* and 210,000 who entered as military *sheng-yüan*, a ratio of 2.5 to 1. In the post-Taiping period, there were about 640,000 persons who entered the gentry as civil *sheng-yüan* and 270,000 who entered as military *sheng-yüan*, the proportion of military *sheng-yüan* having declined slightly.

Only about 18,000 of the civil and military *sheng-yüan* were able to advance into the upper gentry as civil *chü-jen* and about 13,000 as military *chü-jen.* The military *sheng-yüan* therefore had a better opportunity of advancement. More than 30,000 of the civil *sheng-yüan* could advance into the upper gentry as "regular" *kung-sheng*, but the total number of civil *sheng-yüan* unable to advance through the "regular" route was still much greater than the number of military *sheng-yüan* similarly situated. Therefore, many more civil *sheng-yüan* than military *sheng-yüan* participated in the purchase system.

We have shown that about 80,000 of the upper gentry in a pre-Taiping time and 100,000 in a post-Taiping time were originally *sheng-yüan.* Approximately one-fourth of them were originally military *sheng-yüan.* Deducting those who rose to upper gentry, making allowance for some who purchased to *li-kung,* the net *sheng-yüan* figures would then be approximately 460,000 civil *sheng-yüan* and 195,000 military *sheng-yüan* at a time in the pre-Taiping period and 550,000 civil *sheng-yüan* and 250,000 military *sheng-yüan* at a time in the post-Taiping period.

The civil *sheng-yüan* were divided into *ling-sheng*, *tseng-sheng,* and *fu-sheng.* The *ling-sheng* had higher prestige than other *sheng-yüan*, held the right to guarantee the character of local examination candidates, and received government stipends and other extra privileges. The exact numbers of *ling-sheng* and *tseng-sheng* can be shown since the records of their quotas are available. The number of *ling-sheng* and *tseng-sheng* in the various schools was first standardized in 1647: there were to be 40 in a prefectural

[237] *Ibid., ts'e* 1, pp. 39 b–45 a.

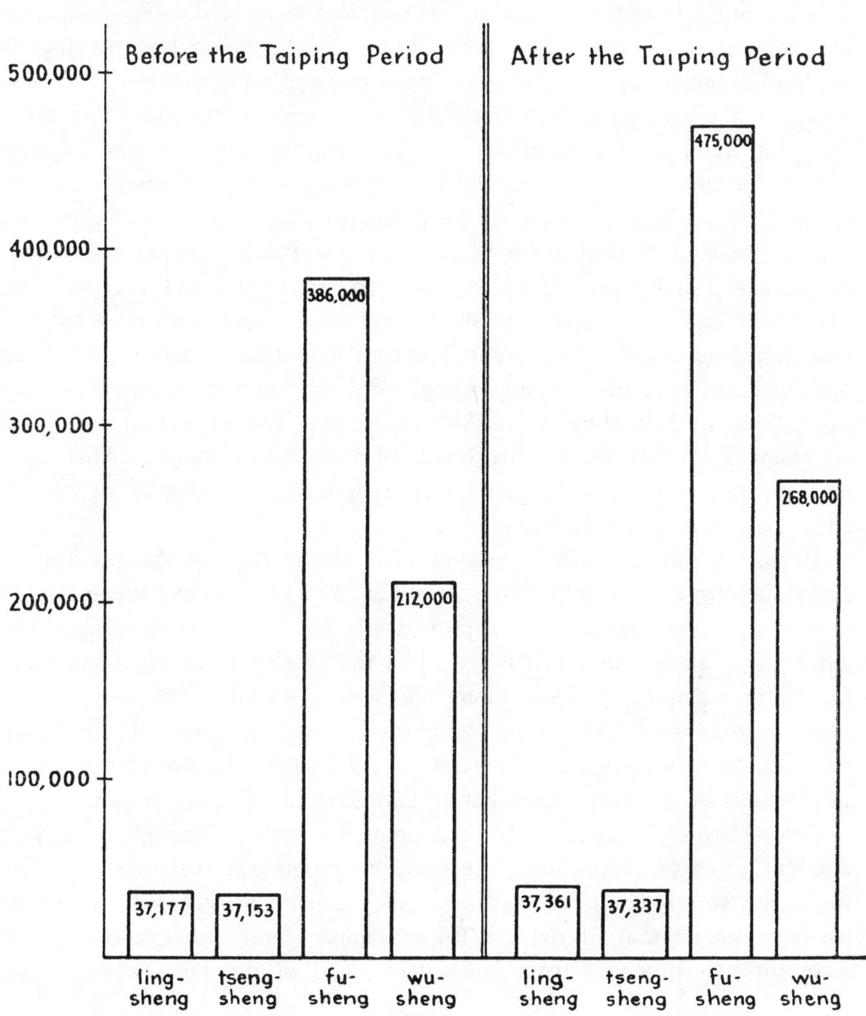
A Comparison of the Size of Various Subdivisions of the Sheng-yüan Before and After the Taiping Period
Before the Taiping Period
After the Taiping Period
500,000
400,000
300,000
200,000
100,000
37,177
37,153
386,000
212,000
37,361
37,337
475,000
268,000
ling-sheng
tseng-sheng
fu-sheng
wu-sheng
ling-sheng
tseng-sheng
fu-sheng
wu-sheng

FIGURE 3

school, 30 in a *chou* school, and 20 in a *hsien* school. Quotas for *tseng-sheng* were to be the same as those for *ling-sheng.*[238] This means that if there were 300 civil *sheng-yüan* in a certain prefectural school, 40 of them would be *ling-sheng*, another 40 would be *tseng-sheng*, and 220 would be *fu-sheng.*

A study of the *ling-sheng* and *tseng-sheng* quotas shows that there was only a negligible change in the number of *ling-sheng* and *tseng-sheng* after the Taiping Rebellion. (See Table 31.) Chihli, which had the highest *sheng-yüan* quota, also had the most *ling-sheng* and *tseng-sheng*—3,568 *ling-sheng* at a pre-Taiping time and 3,580 at a post-Taiping time and about the same number of *tseng-sheng.*[239] Kwangsi, the home of the Taipings, had the lowest quota with only 1,141 *ling-sheng* at a pre-Taiping time and 1,140 at a post-Taiping time. If we compare Kwangsi with Kweichow, the former had 21,399 civil *sheng-yüan* in the pre-Taiping period and 24,003 in the post-Taiping period, while the latter had 15,813 and 16,107. (See Tables 20 and 22.) Thus the number of civil *sheng-yüan* in Kweichow was about one-fourth less than in Kwangsi before the Taiping period and one-third less after the Taiping period. But the number of *ling-sheng* and *tseng-sheng* in Kweichow was 1,506 before the Taiping period and 1,521 afterward, so that Kweichow had one-third more than Kwangsi. This shows how the proportion of *ling-sheng* and *tseng-sheng* to the total number of civil *sheng-yüan* could vary among the provinces.

To summarize the subdivisions of civil *sheng-yüan*, in the pre-Taiping period, among the 460,000 civil *sheng-yüan*, 37,177 were *ling-sheng*, 37,153 were *tseng-sheng*, and the rest, approximately 386,000, were *fu-sheng.* This latter group alone was much bigger than the group of military *sheng-yüan.* In the post-Taiping period, among the 550,000 civil *sheng-yüan*, 37,361 were *ling-sheng*, 37,337 were *tseng-sheng*, and the rest, approximately 475,000, were *fu-sheng.* The chart in Figure 3 shows the size of the various subdivisions of the *sheng-yüan* before and after the Taiping period.

Chien-sheng. It has already been pointed out that although there were different kinds of *chien-sheng*, the purchase group was the only large one, the other groups being so small that they can be disregarded. However, we have shown that of the pre-Taiping upper gentry total, about 40,000 were through purchase from *chien-sheng*, and of the post-Taiping upper

[238] *Hsüeh-cheng*, 65/1 a; also *Shih-li*, 370/1 a. The latter reference, however, incorrectly stated that there would also be 30 *ling-sheng* for the *hsien* schools. Elsewhere in this source and in other sources the figure is given as 20.

[239] According to regulations, a locality was to have the same number of *ling-sheng* and *tseng-sheng.* In practice, however, some localities varied from this standard. E.g., according to *Shih-li*, 379/1 b–2 a, Ho-p'u, Kwangtung, had 20 *ling-sheng* and only 13 *tseng-sheng*; Ch'in-chou, Kwangtung, had 9 *ling-sheng* and 18 *tseng-sheng*. Therefore, the total figures for *ling-sheng* and *tseng-sheng* are different.

gentry total, about 100,000 were through purchase from *chien-sheng*. Deducting these sums from our gross *chien-sheng* figures and also making allowance for *chien-sheng* who purchased to *li-kung*, the net *chien-sheng* figures would be approximately 310,000 for the pre-Taiping period and 430,000 for the post-Taiping period. Thus the *chien-sheng* figures have trailed right behind the *fu-sheng* figures. Of course, many localities varied considerably from the pattern indicated by the general totals.[240]

Proportions of the Various Divisions of Gentry

Now that the principal groups within the gentry have been estimated, we can reconstruct the picture of the gentry total with special attention to the proportion of upper to lower gentry and the proportion of gentry through purchase to gentry through examination. The chart shown in Figure 4 will help to illustrate these problems.

Among the 1,100,000 gentry at a time in the pre-Taiping period, only about 120,000, approximately 11 per cent, belonged to the upper layer. Among this million gentry, only approximately 350,000 or 32 per cent were "irregular" gentry. Among the 1,450,000 gentry at a time in the post-Taiping period, approximately 200,000 belonged to the upper layer, which had now increased from 11 to 14 per cent of the whole gentry group. Among this million and a half gentry members, approximately 530,000 or 36 per cent were now "irregular" gentry. Thus, as the total number of gentry increased, some inner changes were also going on. The proportion of upper gentry to lower gentry was growing, and the proportion of "irregulars" to "regulars," especially among the upper gentry, was also on the increase.

SUMMARY OF FINDINGS

When the Manchus established their government in China, they chose to follow by and large the Ming institutions but sought to provide ample checks on factors that had led to the downfall of earlier dynasties. This policy they applied to the gentry institution. The Manchus took it over *in toto* and used it as an instrument in the difficult task of consolidating their conquest. The early Manchu emperors were much concerned with such

[240] For instance, in gazetteer records of gentry martyrs during the Taiping period, *fu-sheng* and *chien-sheng* usually had the highest figures; in some localities *fu-sheng* had a higher figure than *chien-sheng*, while in others the reverse is true. E.g., *Lan-ch'i hsien-chih*, in 1861, records 67 *fu-sheng* martyrs and 62 *chien-sheng* martyrs. In *Hsü-tsuan Yangchow fu-chih*, 10/7–14, from 1853 to 1858 there were 21 *sheng-yüan* and 20 *chien-sheng* martyrs. From 1861 to 1862, in *Shang-yü hsien-chih*, it is recorded that 23 *fu-sheng* and 36 *chien-sheng* were reported in the first list; 4 *sheng-yüan* and 2 *chien-sheng* in the second list; and 2 *sheng-yüan* and 14 *chien-sheng* in the third list. Other factors may have caused the larger number of deaths among certain groups of gentry, but these data are indicative at least of the large number of *chien-sheng* in some localities.

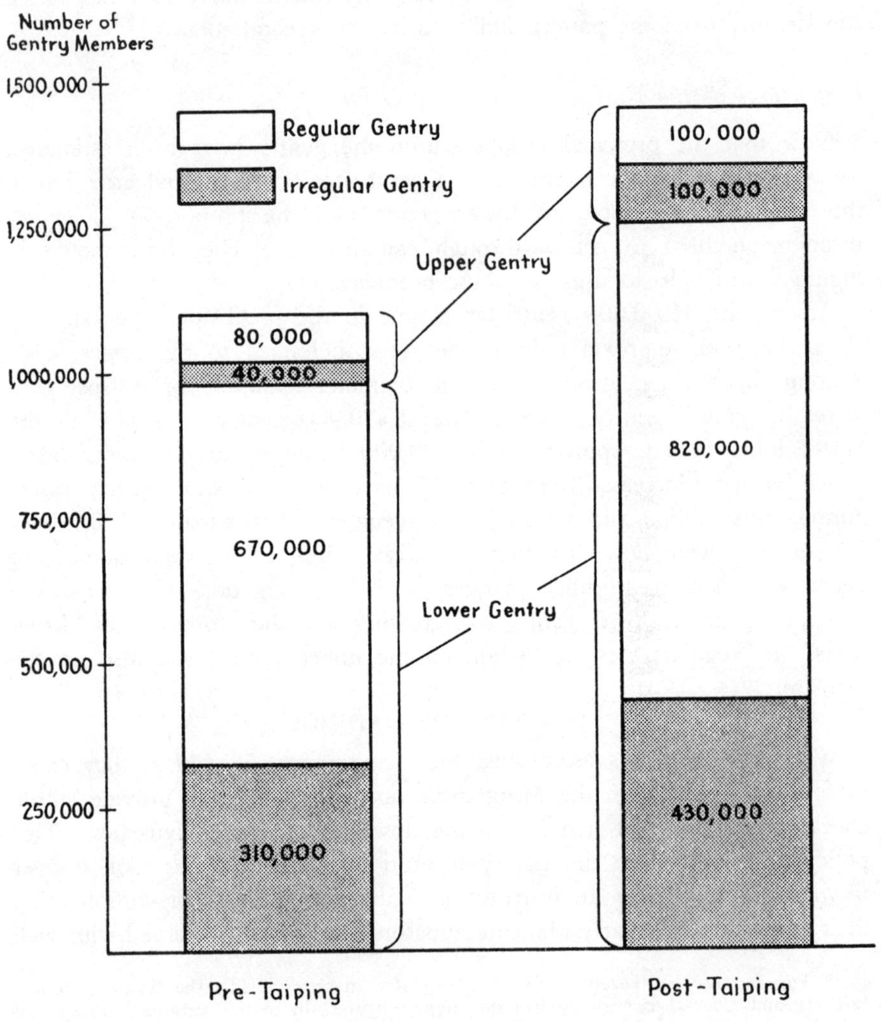
Proportion Between Upper and Lower Gentry and Between "Regular" and "Irregular" Gentry Before and After the Taiping Period
Number of Gentry Members
1,500,000
1,250,000
1,000,000
750,000
500,000
250,000
Regular Gentry
Irregular Gentry
Upper Gentry
Lower Gentry
80,000
40,000
670,000
310,000
100,000
100,000
820,000
430,000
Pre-Taiping
Post-Taiping

FIGURE 4

problems as the frequency of examinations and the size of quotas of admission which determined the size of the group of "regular" gentry. As an additional safeguard, they also continued the purchase system, not so much for the revenue produced as for the creation of a group of "irregular" gentry to balance the "regular" group.

The nineteenth century brought great changes in the gentry. Certain conclusions regarding these changes can be drawn from the numerical analysis presented above.

1. The number of gentry proper in the nineteenth century was a sizable figure. In the first half of the nineteenth century, it already amounted to an impressive total of over a million members. With family members included, the total would amount to approximately five and a half million which was 1.3 per cent of the whole population. This large group of gentry had special privileges and protection for themselves and their immediate family members. Many gentry members exploited their position for further gains. The burden of this privileged group upon the commoners was no doubt a heavy one.

2. Gentry members were distributed all over the country exerting broad influences with their privileges and power. A minimum number was found in any locality, large or small, as the court was interested in maintaining in each administrative unit an appropriate number of gentry.

3. The Ch'ing dynasty used the purchase system at first to create a group of gentry to balance the "regular" gentry. The purchase system was intermittently employed and discontinued until Chia-ch'ing 5 (1800) when it became a going concern and after that time continued to produce "irregular" gentry.[241] Throughout the first half of the nineteenth century there was a steady decline in the purchase of *chien-sheng* titles, the main source of "irregular" gentry. This may perhaps be interpreted as an official policy to keep down the number of "irregulars," or it may possibly have been the result of the increasing concentration of wealth and the declining financial strength of individuals. Nevertheless, the "irregular" gentry remained during this period a sizable group constituting more than 30 per cent of the gentry proper.[242]

241 Cf. Ying-ho and others' memorial of 1822, as quoted by T'ang Hsiang-lung, "A Statistical Study of the Chüan-chien System in the Tao-kuang Reign," p. 437.

242 In *Ch'ing-ch'ao hsü wen-hsien t'ung-k'ao*, 84/8423, the preface to the official selection sections complained about the abundance of "irregulars" and the tendency toward "more officials than people." It argued that with the abundance of officials came abundant malpractices, and to expect them to be martyrs at their posts was like begging hide from the fox. *Ibid.*, 93/8527, section on officials through purchase; the introduction recognizes the significance and number of this group and discusses the addition of this group under the heading of official selection. This category was not a separate section in *Ch'ing-ch'ao wen-hsien t'ung-k'ao*, a similar work of an earlier period.

4. After the rise of the Taipings, the government, in search of new revenue to meet military needs, permitted increases in the "regular" gentry quota of the localities which made contributions to the military fund. The court had formerly kept a careful restraint on the quota system, but it now let the control slip from its hands. The localities themselves were allowed to take the initiative in increasing their quotas. Although the government posted a maximum permissible increase and later, after the suppression of the Taipings, tightened the whole provision for quota increases, the damage had already been done. Wealthier localities had outstripped their rivals in the race for honors and government representation, and the total quota was greatly increased. The number of "regular" gentry had risen from 740,000 in the first half of the century to 910,000 in the last half, an increase of 23 per cent.

5. The rise of the Taipings also caused a great change in the purchase system. The original purpose of creating an offsetting group of gentry was lost. The desperate need for revenue led the government to cut prices in order to increase sales. Now the number of "irregulars" grew rapidly. From the first half of the century to the second half, they increased 50 per cent, and more and more of them moved into official positions with the government. The situation was such that we find "regular" gentry regretting the trouble taken in passing the metropolitan examinations.[243] The first promoters for the revival of the dynasty in the T'ung-chih period opposed the increase of the "irregulars"[244] but did not succeed in reducing their number or power.

6. The total of gentry proper including family members in the late nineteenth century increased to well over seven million as a result of the drastic increases in the numbers of both "regular" and "irregular" gentry. This is an increase of over 34 per cent. The gentry together with the members

[243] Chiang Ch'i-ling, "A Memorial Presenting Twelve Proposals for Revival in Response to Imperial Edict," *Huang-ch'ao ching-shih-wen-hsü-pien*, compiled by Sheng K'ang, 13/30 a. The Taipings seized upon this situation and made vigorous attacks against the Manchus in an effort to win over the gentry. Thus Hung Jen-kan's proclamation on new political administration in *T'ai-p'ing t'ien-kuo shih-liao*, p. 146, says: "In selling offices and titles, do they [the Manchus] pity the effort of studying ten years at a cold window? In exempting [one] tax while collecting other taxes, do they know the hardship of farming?"

[244] Li Shu-ch'ang, "A Memorial of Proposals in Response to Imperial Edict," *Huang-ch'ao ching-shih-wen-hsü-pien*, compiled by Sheng K'ang, 13/56 b, puts Chiang Ch'i-ling, a gentry member and former governor of the metropolitan prefecture, as the first to present proposals for revival of the dynasty. Chiang Ch'i-ling, *op. cit.*, pp. 30 ff., says that not only were there far too many purchased officials but that governors preferred to appoint them, rather than financially poor officials through the "regular" route, to actual posts. This memorial was presented in 1862 after Emperor Mu-tsung ascended the throne and issued orders for straightforward proposals. In *ibid.*, p. 61 a, the editor commented that a great number of proposals by various court and provincial officials and gentry were presented in that year. The ones collected are those which were officially approved.

of their families had increased from 1.2 per cent to 1.9 per cent of the total population. The already heavy burden of the commoners was thereby increased.

7. In the first half of the nineteenth century, only 11 per cent of the gentry were upper gentry. They comprised a small but powerful group, the inner core of the gentry. More than half of these were gentry through the "regular" route. Some localities had very few upper gentry, since they failed to produce scholars who could pass in provincial and metropolitan examinations, while other localities had the honor of many such outstanding men. These men were thoroughly indoctrinated in official ideology and were expected to carry the main load of quasi-official functions in the perpetuation of the dynasty. In the second half of the nineteenth century, the number of upper gentry drastically increased. It amounted to 14 per cent of the increased gentry total. But now the proportion of "regulars" and "irregulars" within the upper gentry had changed. Half of the upper gentry were now gentry through the "irregular" route.

Thus, in the nineteenth century important changes in the gentry occurred. The total number of gentry increased considerably, and with this increase the composition of the gentry changed, too. The "irregular" gentry gained in proportion and made a stronger inroad into the upper layer of the gentry. Even the "regular" gentry no longer regarded the examination system with the same respect as in former times.

These changes indicated the weakening of the government. The gentry outgrew the restraint of government control and became difficult to manage. The lesser regard for the traditional principles of the system undermined the gentry's loyalty to the government.

These changes also affected the gentry's traditional role and standing in society. The changed composition of the gentry affected the quality of gentry leadership. Thus, the change in the size and character of the gentry not only undermined the government but contributed to the disintegration of a society which had been dominated by this group.

TABLE 15

CIVIL SHENG-YÜAN QUOTA BEFORE 1850*

Provinces and Other Quota Divisions	Prefectural Schools				*Chou* Schools				*T'ing* Schools				*Hsien* Schools				Other Schools//				Grand Total	
	No. of Schools	Quota §			No. of Schools	Quota			No. of Schools	Quota			No. of Schools	Quota			No. of Schools	Quota			No. of Schools	Quota
		Highest	Lowest	Total		Highest	Lowest	Total		Highest	Lowest	Total		Highest	Lowest	Total		Highest	Lowest	Total		
8 Banners	.	.	.	.	.	.	.	.	.	.	.	.	.	.	.	.	4	60	8	109	4	109
Fengt'ien	3	13	4	26	4	5	4	19	.	.	.	.	7	7	2	26	.	.	.	.	14	71
Chihli	11	25	6	232	22	26	15	449	.	.	.	.	122	26	10	2110	4	18	10	54	159	2845
Kiangsu	8	25	20	183	6	25	13	121	.	.	.	.	62	25	10	1084	2	10	4	14	78	1402
Anhwei	8	25	20	190	9	25	12	177	.	.	.	.	50	25	8	894	2	16	12	28	69	1289
Chekiang	11	25	25	275	1	.	.	25	1	.	.	8	76	25	12	1492	.	.	.	.	89	1800
Kiangsi	13	20	20	260	2	22	12	34	2	8	8	16	74	20	8	1040	.	.	.	.	91	1350
Fukien †	10	30	20	210	2	18	18	36	.	.	.	.	62	20	4	941	.	.	.	.	74	1187
Honan	9	20	17	173	10	22	15	162	1	.	.	8	97	23	8	1280	1	.	.	8	118	1631
Shantung	10	20	18	196	11	20	15	202	.	.	.	.	96	20	8	1382	3	20	15	50	120	1830
Shansi	9	17	15	151	16	20	8	232	.	.	.	.	87	20	8	1113	4	12	8	40	116	1536
Hupeh	10	20	8	183	8	20	12	119	.	.	.	.	61	20	5	785	.	.	.	.	79	1087
Hunan	9	25	14	162	7	20	15	125	3	8	6	20	61	20	8	912	.	.	.	.	80	1219
Shensi, Kansu	15	20	3	143	24	20	4	309	5	9	4	32	118	25	6	1373	1	.	.	8	163	1865
Szechwan	12	20	8	185	19	15	8	207	9	12	2	54	110	12	5	904	2	8	8	16	152	1366
Kwangtung	9	40	12	225	11	32	8	162	.	.	.	.	80	22	10	939	.	.	.	.	100	1326
Kwangsi	11	20	10	202	18	20	4	241	1	.	.	2	50	20	4	574	.	.	.	.	80	1019
Yunnan	14	20	10	237	31	20	12	493	3	20	20	60	34	20	3	505	3	12	8	28	85	1323
Kweichow	12	23	17	217	14	15	4	170	4	10	4	23	34	20	4	343	.	.	.	.	64	753
Merchant ‡	.	.	.	.	.	.	.	.	.	.	.	.	.	.	.	.	6	.	.	81	6	81
Totals	184	.	.	3450	215	.	.	3283	29	.	.	223	1281	.	.	17697	32	.	.	436	1741	25089

* Source: *Ch'in-ting hsüeh-cheng ch'üan-shu, chüan* 66–86. Although the book was published in 1812, the figures are generally representative of the pre-Taiping period, since there was no substantial change up to the Taiping period.

† The prefecture of Taiwan (Formosa) is included.

‡ See Table 17.

§ Quotas of schools having highest and lowest quotas are given in columns headed "highest" and "lowest." The totals were arrived at by actual count.

// Including *hsiang, ch'i, wei, sha ssu-shih szu* and *ching* schools.

TABLE 16

CIVIL SHENG-YÜAN QUOTA AFTER 1850*

Provinces and Other Quota Divisions	Prefectural Schools				*Chou* Schools				*T'ing* Schools				*Hsien* Schools				Other Schools //				Total Regular Quota	Permanent Increases in Quota			Grand Total	
	No. of Schools	Quota §			No. of Schools	Quota			No. of Schools	Quota			No. of Schools	Quota			No. of Schools	Quota								
		Highest	Lowest	Total		Highest	Lowest	Total		Highest	Lowest	Total		Highest	Lowest	Total		Highest	Lowest	Total		Highest	Lowest	Total	No. of Schools	Quota
8 Banners	.	.	.	.	.	.	.	.	.	.	.	.	.	.	.	.	4	60	8	109	109	.	.	33	4	142
Fengt'ien	5	9	3	26	6	6	2	27	11	5	2	33	16	7	2	44	.	.	.	.	130	7	1	29	38	159
Chihli	11	25	6	235	22	26	15	449	.	.	.	.	121	26	10	2092	5	18	10	72	2848	13	1	40	159	2888
Kiangsu	8	25	20	183	6	25	15	121	.	.	.	.	62	25	10	1090	2	10	4	14	1408	14	1	360	78	1768
Anhwei	8	25	20	190	9	25	12	171	.	.	.	.	51	25	8	900	2	16	12	28	1289	13	1	315	70	1604
Chekiang	11	25	22	272	1	.	.	25	2	18	8	26	75	25	12	1480	.	.	.	.	1803	10	1	374	89	2177
Kiangsi	13	20	20	260	2	22	12	34	2	8	8	16	74	20	8	1040	.	.	.	.	1350	15	1	670	91	2020
Fukien †	12	20	13	227	2	18	18	36	.	.	.	.	68	20	2	945	.	.	.	.	1208	12	1	347	82	1555
Honan	9	20	17	173	10	22	15	164	1	.	.	8	96	23	8	1272	2	8	8	16	1633	12	1	235	118	1868
Shantung	10	20	18	196	11	20	15	202	.	.	.	.	96	20	8	1382	3	20	15	50	1830	10	1	123	120	1953
Shansi	9	17	15	151	16	20	8	232	7	2	2	14	85	20	8	1105	4	12	8	40	1542	10	1	84	121	1626
Hupeh	10	20	8	185	8	20	12	119	.	.	.	.	61	20	5	803	.	.	.	.	1107	13	1	427	79	1534
Hunan	9	25	14	161	7	20	15	125	5	8	6	34	61	20	8	909	.	.	.	.	1229	13	1	418	82	1647
Shensi	7	20	15	122	10	20	8	126	6	9	4	36	68	25	6	849	.	.	.	.	1133	10	1	103	91	1236
Kansu	8	20	12	138	12	15	6	152	6	8	2	28	49	15	2	541	3	12	3	23	882	5	1	7	78	889
Szechwan	11	20	8	178	19	15	8	206	10	12	2	57	113	12	5	918	2	8	7	15	1374	10	1	544	155	1918
Kwangtung	9	42	9	220	11	32	8	163	2	15	8	23	77	22	10	933	.	.	.	.	1339	14	1	409	99	1748
Kwangsi	10	22	6	176	19	20	4	255	2	4	2	6	50	20	4	590	.	.	.	.	1027	12	1	105	81	1132
Yunnan	14	20	10	224	29	20	12	465	17	22	2	130	38	20	3	522	3	12	8	28	1369	.	.	3	101	1372
Kweichow	12	23	17	210	14	15	4	172	7	10	4	45	33	20	4	333	1	.	.	6	766	.	.	1	67	767
Merchant ‡	.	.	.	.	.	.	.	.	.	.	.	.	.	.	.	.	7	.	.	89	89	10	1	21	7	110
Totals	186	.	.	3527	214	.	.	3244	78	.	.	456	1294	.	.	17748	38	.	.	490	25465	.	.	4648	1810	30113

* Source: *Ch'in-ting ta-Ch'ing hui-tien shih-li*, *chüan* 370-381. The book was published in 1886, but the figures are representative of the whole post-Taiping period since the significant changes in quota as shown in the column "permanent increases in quota" occurred during the Taiping period.

† Including Taiwan.

‡ See Table 17.

§ Quotas of schools having highest and lowest quotas are given in columns headed "highest" and "lowest." The totals were arrived at by actual count.

// Including *ch'i*, *hsiang*, *wei*, *sha*, *ssu-shih*, and *ching* schools.

TABLE 17

A Comparison of Sheng-yüan, Ling-sheng, Tseng-sheng, and Sui-kung Quotas for Merchants Before and After the Taiping Period*

Provinces	Before the Taiping Period				After the Taiping Period			
	Sheng-yüan Quota	*Ling-sheng* Quota	*Tseng-sheng* Quota	*Sui-kung* Quota	*Sheng-yüan* Quota†	*Ling-sheng* Quota	*Tseng-sheng* Quota	*Sui-kung* Quota
Chihli	10	20	20	1/2	11	20	20	1/2
Chekiang	50	.	.	.	60	.	.	.
Shantung	4	5	5	1/5	4	5	5	1/5
Shansi	10	20	20	1/2	20	20	20	1/2
Kwangtung	7	3	3	1/4	7	3	3	1/4
Szechwan	.	.	.	.	8	10	10	2/5
Total	81	48	48	1 9/20	110	58	58	1 17/20

* Sources: For figures before the Taiping period, see *Ch'in-ting hsüeh-cheng ch'üan-shu, chüan* 85. For figures after the Taiping period, see *Ch'in-ting ta-Ch'ing hui-tien shih-li, chüan* 381.

† These figures include the special permanent increase in quota of 21, divided as follows: Chihli 1, Chekiang 10, Shansi 10.

TABLE 18

DIFFERENCE BETWEEN CIVIL AND MILITARY SHENG-YÜAN QUOTAS

Locality	Pre-Taiping Quota		Permanent Increases	Post-Taiping Quota		Source
	Civil	Military		Civil	Military	
Wu-hsi, Kiangsu ...	12	7	5	17	12	*Wu-hsi Chin-kuei hsien-chih*, 6/16a
Chin-kuei, Kiangsu ..	13	8	6	19	14	,, ,, ,, 6/16a
Huai-an, Kiangsu ...	25	20	.	25	20	*Huai-an fu-chih*, 21/5b ff.
Shan-yang, Kiangsu .	21	12	4	25	16	,, ,, 21/5b ff.
Hsien-ch'eng, Kiangsu	21	12	7	28	19	,, ,, 21/5b ff.
Fou-ning, Kiangsu ..	16	8	.	16	8	,, ,, 21/5b ff.
Ch'ing-ho, Kiangsu .	23	15	.	23	15	,, ,, 21/5b ff.
An-tung, Kiangsu ..	20	12	.	20	12	,, ,, 21/5b ff.
Tao-yüan, Kiangsu..	20	12	.	20	12	,, ,, 21/5b ff.
Lu-chou, Anhwei ...	22	18	.	22	18	*Lu-chou fu-chih*, 17/76b
Ho-fei, Anhwei	20	12	13	33	25	,, ,, 17/76b
Lu-chiang, Anhwei..	16	8	12	28	20	,, ,, 17/76b
Shu-ch'eng, Anhwei.	16	8	5	21	13	,, ,, 17/76b
Wu-wei-chou, Anhwei	20	12	10	30	22	,, ,, 17/76b
Ch'ao-hsien, Anhwei	16	12	3	19	15	,, ,, 17/76b
Meng-ch'eng, Anhwei	16	8	.	16	8	*Meng-ch'eng hsien-chih shu*, 5/5b
Ch'u-chou, Anhwei..	22	17	.	22	17	*Ch'u-chou chih*, 3/18a
Yen-chou, Chekiang	25	20	.	25	20	*Yen-chou fu-chih*, 6/4a
Nan-yang, Honan ...	16	16	.	16	16	*Nan-yang hsien-chih*, 6/4b-5a
Pa-ling, Hunan	15	15	10	25	25	*Pa-ling hsien-chih*, 17/20b
Yung-chou, Hunan..	20	20	.	20	20	*Yung-chou fu-chih*, 4A/46 ff; *Shih-li*, 376/8b
Lin-ling, Hunan	20	15	5	25	20	*Yung-chou fu-chih*, 4A/46 ff; *Shih-li*, 376/8b
Chi-yang, Hunan ...	20	15	10	30	25	*Yung-chou fu-chih*, 4A/46 ff; *Shih-li*, 376/8b
Tung-an, Hunan ...	15	12	.	15	12	*Yung-chou fu-chih*, 4A/46 ff; *Shih-li*. 376/8b
Tao-chou, Hunan ...	15	15	6 civil and 5 military	21	20	*Yung-chou fu-chih*, 4A/46 ff; *Shih-li*, 376/8b
Ning-yüan, Hunan ..	12	12	10	22	22	*Tao-chou chih*, 5/33a *Yung-chou, fu-chih*, 4A/46 ff; *Shih-li*, 376/8b;
Heng-chou, Hunan..	17	17	10	27	27	*Heng-chou fu-chih*, 16/24 ff; *Shih-li*, 376/8b
Heng-yang, Hunan..	10	8	10	20	18	*Heng-chou fu-chih*, 16/24 ff; *Shih-li*, 376/8b
Ch'ing-ch'üan, Hunan	10	8	10	20	18	*Heng-chou fu-chih*, 16/24 ff; *Shih-lih*, 376/8b
Heng-shan, Hunan ..	20	15	10	30	25	*Heng-chou fu-chih*, 16/24 ff; *Shih-li*, 376/8b
Lai-yang, Hunan ...	20	15	10	30	25	*Heng-chou fu-chih*, 16/24 ff; *Shih-li*, 376/8b
Ch'ang-ning, Hunan .	15	12	2	17	14	*Heng-chou fu-chih*, 16/24 ff; *Shih-li*, 376/8b
An-jen, Hunan	12	12	3	15	15	*Heng-chou fu-chih*, 16/24 ff; *Shih-li*, 376/8b
Lin-hsien, Hunan ...	8	8	2	10	10	*Heng-chou fu-chih*, 16/24 ff; *Shih-li*, 376/8b
Hsing-kuo, Hupeh ..	20	15	12	32	27	*Hsing-kuo chou-chih*, 8/6a; *Shih-li*, 376/3a

TABLE 18

DIFFERENCE BETWEEN CIVIL AND MILITARY SHENG-YÜAN QUOTAS—*Continued*

Locality	Pre-Taiping Quota		Permanent Increases	Post-Taiping Quota		Source
	Civil	Military		Civil	Military	
Nan-ch'ang, Kiangsi	20	15	13	33	28	*Nan-ch'ang hsien-chih,* 12/3a; *Shih-li,* 373/2b
Li-p'ing, Kweichow	23	19	.	23	19	*Li-p'ing fu-chih,* 4A/76 ff.
K'ai-t'ai, Kweichow	13	12	.	13	12	" " 4A/76 ff.
Chin-ping-hsiang, Kweichow	6	8	.	6	8	" " 4A/76 ff.
Ku-chou, Kweichow	6	2	.	6	2	" " 4A/76 ff.
Yung-tsung, Kweichow	8	4	.	8	4	" " 4A/76 ff.
Yung-ning, Kweichow	10	9	.	10	9	*Yung-ning chou hsü-chih,* 5/26a
San-t'ai, Szechwan	12	12	10	22	22	*Tung-ch'uan fu-chih,* 13/41 ff.
She-hung, Szechwan	12	12	4	16	16	" " 13/41 ff.
Hsien-ting, Szechwan	12	12	1	13	13	" " 13/41 ff.
Chung-chiang, Szechwan	8	8	12	20	20	" " 13/41 ff.
Sui-ning, Szechwan	10	10	12	22	22	" " 13/41 ff.
P'eng-ch'i, Szechwan	8	8	8	16	16	" " 13/41 ff.
An-yüen, Szechwan	8	8	8	16	16	" " 13/41 ff.
Lo-chih, Szechwan	8	8	3	11	11	" " 13/41 ff.
Lu-chou, Szechwan	15	15	10	25	25	*Chih-li Lu-chou chih,* 3/19b
Kuang-chou, Kwangtung	36	37	5	41	42	*Kuang-chou fu-chih,* 72/3a ff.
Nan-hai, Kwangtung	20	15	14	34	29	" " 72/3a ff.
P'an-yü, Kwangtung	20	15	10	30	25	" " 72/3a ff.
Tung-kuan, Kwangtung	20	15	10	30	25	" " 72/3a ff.
Shun-te, Kwangtung	20	15	11	31	26	" " 72/3a ff.
Hsiang-shan, Kwangtung	20	15	10	30	25	" " 72/3a ff; also *Hsiang-shan hsien-chih,* 7/41
Hsin-hui, Kwangtung	18	12	13	31	25	*Kuang-chou fu-chih,* 72/3a ff.
Tseng-ch'eng, Kwangtung	15	12	6	21	18	" " 72/3a ff.
San-shuai, Kwangtung	15	12	7	22	19	" " 72/3a ff.
Hsin-ning, Kwangtung	12	8	5	17	13	" " 72/3a ff.
Lung-men, Kwangtung	8	8	1	9	9	" " 72/3a ff.
Ts'ung-hua, Kwangtung	8	8	3	11	11	" " 72/3a ff.
Hsin-an, Kwangtung	8	8	2	10	10	" " 72/3a ff.
Ch'ing-yüan, Kwangtung	8	8	4	12	12	" " 72/3a ff; also *Ch'ing-yüan hsien-chih,* 6/14
Hua-hsien, Kwangtung	7	7	2	9	9	*Kuang-chou fu-chih,* 72/3a ff.
Hsin-i, Kwangtung	10	8	2	12	10	*Hsin-i hsien-chih,* 3/19b
Kuei-lin-fu, Kwangsi	20	20	3	23	23	*Kwangsi t'ung-chih chi-yao,* 3/2b ff.
Lin-kuei, Kwangsi	20	15	12	32	27	" " " 3/13b
Yang-su, Kwangsi	12	12	1	13	13	" " " 4/3b
Yung-ning, Kwangsi	12	12	.	12	12	" " " 4/8b
Yung-fu, Kwangsi	8	8	.	8	8	" " " 4/13b
Hsing-an, Kwangsi	15	12	1	16	13	" " " 3/45b
Lin-ch'uan, Kwangsi	15	12	2	17	14	" " " 3/51b

TABLE 18

DIFFERENCE BETWEEN CIVIL AND MILITARY SHENG-YÜAN QUOTAS—*Continued*

Locality	Pre-Taiping Quota		Permanent Increases	Post-Taiping Quota		Source
	Civil	Military		Civil	Military	
I-ning, Kwangsi	8	8	.	8	8	*Kwangsi t'ung-chih chi-yao*, 4/18b
Ch'üan-chou, Kwangsi	20	15	10	30	25	,, ,, ,, 4/25a
Kuan-yang, Kwangsi	15	12	3	18	15	,, ,, ,, 4/42b
Liu-chou-fu, Kwangsi	22	20	.	22	20	,, ,, ,, 5/2a
Ma-p'ing, Kwangsi	12	12	1	13	13	,, ,, ,, 5/10b
Lo-jung, Kwangsi	12	12	.	12	12	,, ,, ,, 5/19a
Lo-ch'eng, Kwangsi	10	8	.	10	8	,, ,, ,, 5/22b
Liu-ch'eng, Kwangsi	12	12	1	13	13	,, ,, ,, 5/25b
Huai-yüan, Kwangsi	10	8	.	10	8	,, ,, ,, 5/29b
Jung-hsien, Kwangsi	15	15	.	15	15	,, ,, ,, 5/33b
Hsiang-chou, Kwangsi	15	15	.	15	15	,, ,, ,, 5/40b
Lai-pin, Kwangsi	8	8	.	8	8	,, ,, ,, 5/40b
Ch'ing-yüan, Kwangsi	20	20	.	20	20	,, ,, ,, 6/2b
I-shan, Kwangsi	15	15	4	19	19	,, ,, ,, 6/9b
T'ien-ho, Kwangsi	8	8	1	9	9	,, ,, ,, 6/20b
Ho-chih, Kwangsi	15	15	3	18	18	,, ,, ,, 6/24b
Shih-en, Kwangsi	8	8	3	11	11	,, ,, ,, 6/27b
Tung-lai, Kwangsi	4	4	2	6	6	,, ,, ,, 6/30b
Shih-en-fu, Kwangsi	20	20	.	20	20	,, ,, ,, 7/30b
Wu-yüan, Kwangsi	20	12	.	20	12	,, ,, ,, 7/10b
Pin-chou, Kwangsi	20	18	3	23	21	,, ,, ,, 7/15a
Ch'ien-chiang, Kwangsi	8	8	.	8	8	,, ,, ,, 7/20b
Shang-lin, Kwangsi	20	16	.	20	16	,, ,, ,, 7/23b
Pai-se, Kwangsi	4	4	.	4	4	,, ,, ,, 7/44a
En-lung, Kwangsi	4	4	.	4	4	,, ,, ,, 7/45a
En-yang, Kwangsi	4	4	.	4	4	,, ,, ,, 7/45a
Szu-ch'eng, Kwangsi	10	12	.	10	12	,, ,, ,, 8/2a
Hsi-lung, Kwangsi	6	6	.	6	6	,, ,, ,, 8/9b
Hsi-lin, Kwangsi	4	6	.	4	6	,, ,, ,, 8/9b
P'ing-lo-fu, Kwangsi	22	20	.	22	20	,, ,, ,, 9/2a
P'ing-lo, Kwangsi	15	15	.	15	15	,, ,, ,, 9/10b
Kung-ch'eng, Kwangsi	12	12	2	14	14	,, ,, ,, 9/19b
Fu-ch'uan, Kwangsi	17	15	.	17	15	,, ,, ,, 9/25b
Ho-hsien, Kwangsi	15	15	1	16	16	,, ,, ,, 9/31a
Li-p'u, Kwangsi	8	8	.	8	8	,, ,, ,, 9/38b
Hsiu-jen, Kwangsi	8	8	.	8	8	,, ,, ,, 9/43a
Chao-p'ing, Kwangsi	12	12	1	13	13	,, ,, ,, 9/46b
Yung-an, Kwangsi	15	12	.	15	12	,, ,, ,, 9/52a
Wu-chou-fu, Kwangsi	18	17	.	18	17	,, ,, ,, 10/2a
Ts'ang-wu, Kwangsi	20	15	1	21	16	,, ,, ,, 10/10b
T'eng-hsien, Kwangsi	12	12	4	16	16	,, ,, ,, 10/24b; also *T'eng-hsien chih*, 8/26a ff.
Jung-hsien, Kwangsi	8	8	.	8	8	*Kwangsi t'ung-chih chi-yao*, 10/32a
Ts'en-ch'i, Kwangsi	8	8	.	8	8	,, ,, ,, 10/40a
Huai-chi, Kwangsi	20	15	6	26	21	,, ,, ,, 10/47a
Hsün-chou-fu, Kwangsi	20	20	.	20	20	,, ,, ,, 11/2a
Kuei-p'ing, Kwangsi	15	12	2	17	14	,, ,, ,, 11/8b

TABLE 18

DIFFERENCE BETWEEN CIVIL AND MILITARY SHENG-YÜAN QUOTAS—*Concluded*

Locality	Pre-Taiping Quota		Permanent Increases	Post-Taiping Quota		Source
	Civil	Military		Civil	Military	
P'ing-nan, Kwangsi	12	8	4	16	12	*Kwangsi t'ung-chih chi-yao,* 11/18 b
Kuei-hsien, Kwangsi	15	12	3	18	15	,, ,, ,, 11/25 b
Wu-hsüan, Kwangsi	8	8	.	8	8	,, ,, ,, 11/32 b
Nan-ning-fu, Kwangsi	20	20	.	20	20	,, ,, ,, 12/2 a
Hsuan-hua, Kwangsi	20	20	.	20	20	,, ,, ,, 12/10 b
Hsin-ning, Kwangsi	20	15	.	20	15	,, ,, ,, 12/19 b
Lung-an, Kwangsi	15	12	.	15	12	,, ,, ,, 12/24 a
Heng-chou, Kwangsi	20	15	1	21	16	,, ,, ,, 12/29 a
Yung-ch'un, Kwangsi	15	12	.	15	12	,, ,, ,, 12/38 a
Shang-shih, Kwangsi	15	15	.	15	15	,, ,, ,, 12/42 b
T'ai-p'ing, Kwangsi	20	20	.	20	20	,, ,, ,, 13/2 a
Ch'ung-shan, Kwangsi	8	4	.	8	4	,, ,, ,, 13/10 a
Tso-chou, Kwangsi	12	15	.	12	15	,, ,, ,, 13/15 a
Yang-li, Kwangsi	12	12	.	12	12	,, ,, ,, 13/17 b
Yung-kang, Kwangsi	15	15	.	15	15	,, ,, ,, 13/20 b
Ning-ming, Kwangsi	15	15	.	15	15	,, ,, ,, 13/23 a
T'ai-p'ing, Kwangsi (native *chou*)	4	4	.	4	4	,, ,, ,, 13/32 a
Chen-an-fu, Kwangsi	12	12	.	12	12	,, ,, ,, 14/2 a
T'ien-pai, Kwangsi	4	4	3	7	7	,, ,, ,, 14/6 a-b
Feng-i, Kwangsi	4	4	.	4	4	,, ,, ,, 14/10 b
Kuei-shun, Kwangsi	4	4	.	4	4	,, ,, ,, 14/1[illegible] a
Kuei-shun chih-li *chou,* Kwangsi	6	6	2	8	8	,, ,, ,, 14/26 b
Chen-pien, Kwangsi	2	2	.	2	2	,, ,, ,, 14/27 b
Yü-lin, Kwangsi	25	18	7	32	25	,, ,, ,, 15/5 a; also *Yü-lin chou-chih,* 6/1
Po-pai, Kwangsi	12	12	.	12	12	*Kwangsi t'ung-chih chi-yao* 15/20 a
Pei-liu, Kwangsi	12	12	4	16	16	,, ,, ,, 15/29 a
Lu-ch'uan, Kwangsi	12	8	4	16	12	,, ,, ,, 15/34 b
Hsing-yeh, Kwangsi	8	8	2	10	10	,, ,, ,, 15/40 a
Pai-se, Kwangsi	4	4	.	4	4	,, ,, ,, 16/2 b
En-lung, Kwangsi	4	4	.	4	4	,, ,, ,, 16/12 b
En-yang, Kwangsi	2	2	.	2	2	,, ,, ,, 16/15 b
Kuei-shun, Kwangsi	7	7	.	7	7	,, ,, ,, 17/2 a
Chen-pien, Kwangsi	2	2	.	2	2	,, ,, ,, 17/9 a
Total	2,095	1,787	458 civil 457 military	2,553	2,244	

TABLE 19

AGE OF DEATH OF MEN HAVING BIOGRAPHIES AND BORN BETWEEN 1731 AND 1880, ARRANGED IN FIVE-YEAR AGE GROUPS*

Period of Birth	1731–1780		1781–1830		1831–1880	
Age of Death	Number of men	Per cent	Number of men	Per cent	Number of men	Per cent
20 and below	1	0.2	3	0.7	2	0.6
21–25	4	0.8	.	.	4	1.2
26–30	10	1.8	5	1.0	7	2.1
31–35	7	1.3	16	3.3	11	3.3
36–40	11	2.0	16	3.3	13	3.8
41–45	24	4.4	34	7.1	25	7.3
46–50	22	4.0	37	7.7	28	8.2
51–55	42	7.6	50	10.4	50	14.6
56–60	59	10.7	49	10.2	54	15.8
61–65	83	15.1	64	13.3	45	13.1
66–70	85	15.5	72	15.0	44	12.8
71–75	75	13.6	69	14.4	26	7.6
76–80	63	11.5	36	7.5	20	5.8
81 and over	63	11.5	29	6.1	13	3.8
Total	549	100.0	480	100.0	342	100.0
	Average age of death: 63.6		Average age of death: 61.1		Average age of death: 57.8	

* Data collected from Chiang Liang-fu's *Li-tai ming-jen nien-li pei-chuan tsung-piao,* where ages, native places, and source of biographies are given. Based on information collected from various biographies, personal notes, official histories, unofficial histories, chronological biographies, newspapers, magazines, etc., this book lists more than 12,000 men distributed in all dynasties.

TABLE 20

NUMBER OF SHENG-YÜAN IN THE PRE-TAIPING PERIOD AND THEIR DISTRIBUTION OVER PROVINCES*

Provinces and Other Quota Divisions	Civil Quota	Civil *Sheng-yüan*	Military Quota	Military *Sheng-yüan*	Total *Sheng-yüan*	Per cent
8 Banners	109	2,289	93	930	3,219	0.4
Fengt'ien	71	1,491	60	600	2,091	0.3
Chihli	2,845	59,745	2,418	24,180	83,925	11.4
Kiangsu	1,402	29,442	1,192	11,920	41,362	5.6
Anhwei	1,289	27,069	1,096	10,960	38,029	5.1
Chekiang	1,800	37,800	1,530	15,300	53,100	7.2
Kiangsi	1,350	28,350	1,148	11,480	39,830	5.4
Fukien	1,187	24,927	1,009	10,090	35,017	4.8
Honan	1,631	34,251	1,386	13,860	48,111	6.5
Shantung	1,830	38,430	1,556	15,560	53,990	7.3
Shansi	1,536	32,256	1,306	13,060	45,316	6.1
Hupeh	1,087	22,827	924	9,240	32,067	4.3
Hunan	1,219	25,599	1,006	10,060	35,659	4.8
Shensi / Kansu	1,865	39,165	1,585	15,850	55,015	7.4
Szechwan	1,366	28,686	1,161	11,610	40,296	5.4
Kwangtung	1,326	27,846	1,127	11,270	39,116	6.3
Kwangsi	1,019	21,399	866	8,660	30,059	4.0
Yunnan	1,323	27,783	1,130	11,300	39,083	5.3
Kweichow	753	15,813	640	6,400	22,213	3.0
Merchant	81	1,701	.	.	1,701	0.3
Total	25,089	526,869	21,233	212,330	739,199	100.0

* *Sheng-yüan* figures here include those who later became *kung-sheng*, *chü-jen*, *chin-shih*, and officials, i.e., these figures represent the gentry members through the "regular" (examination) route.

TABLE 21

Increase of Number of Sheng-yüan in the Three Districts of Ch'ang, Yüan and Wu of Soochow Prefecture Before and After the Taiping Period*

Period	No. of examinations: No. of *sui* exam.	No. of examinations: No. of *k'o* exam.	Total	Total no. of *sheng-yüan* admitted	Note
1811–1820 . . .	4	3	7	431	
1821–1830 . . .	3	4	7	470	One *k'o* and 1 *sui* exam. had temporary quota increases by imperial favor.
1831–1840 . . .	3	3	6	374	
1841–1850 . . .	4	3	7	449	One *sui* examination had temporary quota increase by imperial favor.
Total for forty years before Taiping period	14	13	27	1,724	
1851–1860 . . .	3	4	7	591	One *sui* had temporary increase by imperial favor. One *sui* had temporary increase by contribution. One *sui* had temporary and permanent increases by contribution. One *k'o* had permanent increase by contribution. Actually, only 5 examinations took place (2 *sui* and 1 *k'o* combined once; 1 *sui* and 1 *k'o* combined once). One *k'o* had temporary and permanent quota increases. The rest had permanent increases by contribution.
1861–1870 . . .	4	4	8	764	All had permanent increases by contribution.
1871–1880 . . .	3	3	6	683	All had permanent increases by contribution.
1881–1890 . . .	3	4	7	752	All had permanent increases by contribution.
Total for forty years during and after the Taiping period	13	15	28	2,790	

* Source: *Kuo-ch'ao san-i chu-sheng p'u.*

TABLE 22

NUMBER OF SHENG-YÜAN IN THE POST-TAIPING PERIOD AND THEIR DISTRIBUTION OVER PROVINCES *

Provinces and Other Quota Divisions	Civil Quota	Temporary Increases	Total	Civil *Sheng-yüan*	Military Quota	Military *Sheng-yüan*	*Sheng-yüan* Total	Per cent
8 Banners ..	142	3	145	3,045	128	1,280	4,325	0.5
Fengt'ien ...	159	3	162	3,402	143	1,430	4,832	0.5
Chihli	2,888	4	2,892	60,732	2,545	25,450	86,182	9.4
Kiangsu	1,768	36	1,804	37,884	1,587	15,870	53,754	6.0
Anhwei	1,604	32	1,636	34,356	1,440	14,400	48,756	5.3
Chekiang ...	2,177	37	2,214	46,494	1,948	19,480	65,974	7.2
Kiangsi	2,020	67	2,087	43,827	1,837	18,370	62,197	6.8
Fukien	1,555	35	1,590	33,390	1,399	13,990	47,380	5.2
Honan	1,868	24	1,892	39,732	1,665	16,650	56,382	6.2
Shantung ...	1,953	12	1,965	41,265	1,730	17,300	58,565	6.5
Shansi	1,626	8	1,634	34,314	1,438	14,380	48,694	5.3
Hupeh	1,534	43	1,577	33,117	1,388	13,880	46,997	5.2
Hunan	1,647	42	1,689	35,469	1,486	14,860	50,329	5.5
Shensi	1,236	10	1,246	26,166	1,096	10,960	37,126	4.1
Kansu	889	1	890	18,690	783	7,830	26,520	2.9
Szechwan ...	1,918	54	1,972	41,412	1,735	17,350	58,762	6.5
Kwangtung .	1,748	41	1,789	37,569	1,574	15,740	53,309	5.9
Kwangsi	1,132	11	1,143	24,003	1,006	10,060	34,063	3.7
Yunnan	1,372		1,372	28,812	1,207	12,070	40,882	4.5
Kweichow ..	767		767	16,107	671	6,710	22,817	2.5
Merchant ...	110	21	131	2,751			2,751	0.3
Total	30,113	484	30,597	642,537	26,806	268,060	910,597	100.0

Sheng-yüan figures here include those who later became *kung-sheng*, *chü-jen*, *chin-shih*, and officials, i.e., these figures represent the gentry members through the "regular" (examination) route.

TABLE 23

NUMBER OF MEN PURCHASING CHIEN-SHENG TITLES DURING THE TAO-KUANG REIGN, THE AMOUNT OF MONEY COLLECTED, AND THE PROPORTION OF PURCHASERS TO POPULATION FROM TAO-KUANG 1 TO 30 (1821 TO 1850) IN FIVE-YEAR GROUPS*

Period	Tao-kuang 1–5		Tao-kuang 6–10		Tao-kuang 11–15		Tao-kuang 16–20		Tao-kuang 21–25		Tao-kuang 26–30		Grand Total		Popu-lation	Per cent
Province	Amount Collected (taels)	No. of Men	Amount Collected (taels)	No. of Men	Amount Collected (taels)	No. of Men	Amount Collected (taels)	No. of Men	Amount Collected (taels)	No. of Men	Amount Collected (taels)	No. of Men	Amount Collected (taels)	No. of Men		
Kiangsu †	1,015,580	10,169	980,220	8,674	552,946	5,113	386,636	3,593	440,088	4,088	347,640	2,832	3,723,110	34,469	29,600,000	0.12
Anhwei	305,020	3,054	264,850	2,365	304,812	2,822	249,306	3,057	247,938	2,299	225,024	2,087	1,596,950	15,684	36,600,000	0.04
Chekiang	687,550	6,878	772,850	6,858	619,858	5,738	588,150	5,449	518,506	5,628	358,200	3,318	3,545,114	33,869	30,400,000	0.11
Kiangsi	894,060	8,941	824,210	7,270	665,520	6,157	611,772	5,665	617,604	5,629	527,914	4,890	4,141,080	38,552	26,500,000	0.15
Fukien	435,240	4,353	305,700	2,849	459,642	4,248	344,472	3,190	328,700	3,025	266,760	2,470	2,140,514	20,135	25,800,000	0.08
Honan	547,730	5,488	371,480	3,314	413,200	3,827	440,592	4,080	434,418	4,123	208,548	1,931	2,415,968	22,763	29,100,000	0.08
Shantung	233,900	2,340	171,250	1,518	275,566	2,551	131,760	1,220	215,077	1,993	144,294	1,337	1,171,847	10,959	36,200,000	0.03
Shansi	192,067.2	1,847	137,818.8	1,347	145,908	1,351	82,296	762	48,276	447	32,274	296	638,640	6,050	10,300,000	0.60
Hupeh	616,220	6,163	470,110	4,128	315,660	2,929	319,182	2,960	214,836	1,990	193,272	1,790	2,129,280	19,960	28,600,000	0.07
Hunan	735,980	7,362	632,440	5,632	497,312	4,123	353,916	3,277	462,638	4,155	341,712	3,164	3,023,998	27,713	20,000,000	0.14
Shensi	384,540	3,846	356,740	3,159	199,696	1,845	140,274	1,299	90,378	837	85,410	791	1,257,038	11,777	10,300,000	0.11
Kansu	73,682	650	148,882	1,272	64,632	598	47,952	444	29,440	271	46,136	242	410,724	3,477	19,500,000	0.02
Szechwan	457,380	4,574	359,790	3,178	276,780	2,562	233,106	2,159	125,478	1,162	143,856	1,332	1,596,390	14,967	22,300,000	0.07
Kwangtung	1,036,343	10,366	954,395	8,317	676,323	6,267	422,502	3,922	534,288	4,951	479,292	4,441	4,103,143	38,264	21,100,000	0.18
Kwangsi	188,420	1,885	163,120	1,433	239,658	2,217	134,334	1,244	163,296	1,512	139,086	1,288	1,027,914	9,579	8,100,000	0.12
Yunnan	74,900	749	56,920	496	67,512	623	80,352	744	80,136	742	78,310	728	438,130	4,082	6,200,000	0.07
Kweichow	56,100	561	55,180	478	68,260	648	51,840	480	59,940	555	54,486	513	345,806	3,235	4,800,000	0.07
Total	7,934,712.2	79,226	7,025,955.8	62,288	5,843,285	53,619	4,618,442	43,545	4,611,037	43,407	3,672,214	33,450	33,705,646	315,535	365,400,000	0.08

* Source: Reworked from data collected by T'ang Hsiang-lung in "A Statistical Study of the *Chüan-chien* System in the Tao-kuang Period," pp. 432-444. The population figures are those of 1842 based on Popoff's collection from the Board of Revenue (data for Chihli are lacking).

† In the original, it was divided into Chiang-ning-tao and Soochow-tao.

TABLE 24

ESTIMATE OF SIZE OF GENTRY FAMILY
BASED ON A STUDY OF A GROUP OF CHIN-SHIH *

Size of family	No. of gentry members	Per cent
2	17	9.0
3	31	16.0
4	31	16.0
5	39	20.0
6	24	12.3
7	20	10.3
8	10	5.1
9	4	2.1
10	3	1.5
11	1	0.5
12	1	0.5
No information	13	6.7
Total	194	100.0

Average size of gentry family – 4.96

* Source: *Hui-shih t'ung-nien ch'ih-lu,* 1895.

TABLE 25

PROPORTIONS OF VARIOUS TYPES OF UPPER GENTRY

Types of gentry	*Chin-shih*	*Chü-jen*	Regular *kung-sheng*					Officials through purchase	Officials through recom-mendation	Mili-tary *chin-shih*	Mili-tary *chü-jen*	Military officers through			Here-ditary offices and titles	Source
			en	*pa*	*sui*	*fu*	*yu*					pur-chase	rank and file	mili-tary merit		
Locality																
Ch'ang-ning .	5	20	34	20	143	8		161*		3	53	3	30	6	8	*Ch'ang-ning hsien-chih*, *chüan* 11 (Hunan) †
Mien-chou ..	6	27	24	14	86	10	3	89	23	2	21	22	16	15	7	*Mien-chou chih*, 36/7 ff. (Szechwan)
Te-yang	2	45	25	12	36	8		19	3		13				3	*Mien-chou chih*, 36/7 ff. (Szechwan)
An-hsien	3	23	16	13	72	6		26		2	17				1	*Mien-chou chih*, 36/7 ff. (Szechwan)
Mien-chu	4	54	21	16	80	12	1	26		1	24		1			*Mien-chou chih*, 36/7 ff. (Szechwan)
Tzu-t'ung ...	1	19	21	12	83	3		9	4		2		1			*Mien-chou chih*, 36/7 ff. (Szechwan)
Lo-chiang ...	2	13	10	9	42	5		14	2		2					*Mien-chou chih*, 36/7 ff. (Szechwan)
Jen-huai	2	21	22	14	41	9	2		2		13					*Jen-huai t'ing-chih*, 3/5 b ff. (Kweichow)
Nan-ch'ang ..	157 ‡	765	53	59	288	138	50		45	23	239					*Nan-ch'ang hsien-chih*, *kung-chü* section (Kiangsi)
Mou-ming ...	5	91			344			64		1	42		91		28	*Kao-chou fu-chih*, *chüan* 30–36 (Kwangtung)
T'ien-pai	1	39			236			39		5	55		22		28	*Kao-chou fu-chih*, *chüan* 30–36 (Kwangtung)
Hsin-i	4	37			195			54			6		17		4	*Kao-chou fu-chih*, *chüan* 30–36 (Kwangtung)
Hua-chou	1	36			246			33			6		13		6	*Kao-chou fu-chih*, *chüan* 30–36 (Kwangtung)
Wu-ch'uan ..	6	69			294			85		1	15		58		15	*Kao-chou fu-chih*, *chüan* 30–36 (Kwangtung)
Shih-ch'eng ..	1	21			193			38			14		12		4	*Kao-chou fu-chih*, *chüan* 30–36 (Kwangtung)
Mien-yang ...	51	286			423 §			197		4	119		47		17	*Mien-yang chou-chih*, 8 (Hupeh)

* This figure includes purchase to official titles. A survey of the origin of these purchasers reveals the following: 116 *chien-sheng*, 4 *ling-kung*, 5 *fu-kung*, 1 *li-kung*, 1 *ling-sheng*, 3 *tseng-sheng*, 2 *fu-sheng*, 1 *yin-sheng* and others.

† This gazetteer gives recommendations to official posts since Han; *chin-shih* records since T'ang; *chü-jen* and also *en-kung*, *pa-kung*, and *sui-kung* records since Ming.

‡ This high figure of *chin-shih*, according to the editor, is already lower than the record set in Ming times. In Ming, Kiangsi had a total of 3,470 *chin-shih*, of which 250 came from Nan-ch'ang.

§ According to the editor of this gazetteer, some "irregular" *kung-sheng* may have been included in this figure.

TABLE 26

ORIGIN OF MILITARY OFFICERS, 1881*

Origin	Provincial commander in-chief	Brigade-gen.	Col.	Lt. col.	Major	First captain	Second captain	Lieutenant	Sub-lieutenant	Total
Examination: Military *chin-shih*	1	3		5	9	7	12	5	2	44
Examination: Military *chü-jen*		1	3	1	12	13	49	97	100	276
Examination: Military *sheng-yüan*		3	1	5	9	9	26	63	90	206
Examination: Military *t'ung-sheng* †	1	1	5	6	33	40	45	101	178	410
Imperial guard		2	6	9	16	44	23	1		101
Military merit	5	21	27	28	47	39	51	58	58	334
Militiamen			2	1	9	9	9	20	31	81
Rank and file	10	46	57	80	180	238	565	1,454	2,914	5,544
Hereditary ranks				1	9	19	35	16	4	84
Purchase	2			1	2	2	4	19	11	41
Bannermen ‡	1	3	13	28	22	41	20	4		132
Unknown		1	2		2	3	9	11	10	38
Total	20	81	116	165	350	464	848	1,849	3,398	7,291

* Source: *Ta-Ch'ing chin-shen ch'üan-shu*, 1881.

† Slightly more than half of the *t'ung-sheng* here recorded were Hunanese who served in the Chiang-nan water force.

‡ Refers to those of the eight banners not through examination or other routes.

TABLE 27

NUMBER OF CHIN-SHIH AND KUNG-SHIH DEGREES CONFERRED IN THE METROPOLITAN EXAMINATIONS DURING THE CH'ING DYNASTY*

Year	No. of *kung-shih*	Number of *chin-shih* First rank	Number of *chin-shih* Second rank	Number of *chin-shih* Third rank	Total	No. admitted to Han-lin Academy
Shun-chih 3rd (1646)	400	3	77	293	373	49
4th (1647)	300	3	57	238	298	23
6th (1649)	400	3	77	315	395	43
9th (1652)	450	3	77	317	397	46
12th (1655)	450	3	77	319	399	33
15th (1658)	351	3	80	260	343	35
16th (1659)	350	3	96	277	376	44
18th (1661)	400	3	77	303	383	13
Subtotal	3,101	24	618	2,322	2,964	286
K'ang-hsi 3rd (1664)	150	3	40	157	200	18
6th (1667)	150	3	40	112	155	15
9th (1670)	300	3	57	239	299	31
12th (1673)	150	3	40	123	166	35
15th (1676)	195	3	50	156	209	35
18th (1679)	150	3	40	108	151	35
21st (1682)	200	3	40	136	179	35
24th (1685)	150	3	40	121	164	38
27th (1688)	150	3	40	103	146	37
30th (1691)	150	3	40	114	157	36
33rd (1694)	150	3	40	125	168	43
36th (1697)	159	3	40	107	150	34
39th (1700)	300	3	60	242	305	46
42nd (1703)	162	3	50	113	166	52
45th (1706)	300	3	50	237	290	53
48th (1709)	300	3	50	239	292	67
51st (1712)	192	3	50	124	177	69
52nd (1713)†	186	3	50	143	196	56
54th (1715)	200	3	40	147	190	47
57th (1718)	174	3	40	122	165	58
60th (1721)	176	3	40	120	163	65
Subtotal	4,044	63	937	3,088	4,088	905
Yung-cheng 1st (1723)†	180	3	63	180	246	61
2nd (1724)	214	3	81	216	300	43
5th (1727)	210	3	50	173	226	40
8th (1730)	407	3	100	296	399	58
11th (1733)	347	3	92	233	328	73
Subtotal	1,358	15	386	1,098	1,499	275
Ch'ien-lung 1st (1736)	300	3	90	251	344	67
2nd (1737)†	313	3	80	241	324	62
4th (1739)	316	3	90	235	328	66
7th (1742)	316	3	90	230	323	57
10th (1745)	307	3	90	220	313	54
13th (1748)	259	3	72	189	264	54
16th (1751)	241	3	70	170	243	45
17th (1752)†	235	3	70	158	231	41
19th (1754)	241	3	70	168	241	38
22nd (1757)	235	3	70	169	242	37

TABLE 27 *(Continued)*

Year	No. of *kung-shih*	Number of *chin-shih*			Total	No. admitted to Han-lin Academy
		First rank	Second rank	Third rank		
Ch'ien-lung 25th (1760)	191	3	50	111	164	37
26th (1761)†	207	3	66	148	217	38
28th (1763)	187	3	55	130	188	32
31st (1766)	206	3	69	141	213	34
34th (1769)	143	3	50	98	151	29
36th (1771)†	161	3	55	103	161	35
37th (1772)	169	3	54	105	162	39
40th (1775)	153	3	52	103	158	46
43rd (1778)	158	3	51	103	157	38
45th (1780)†	158	3	51	101	155	29
46th (1781)	168	3	56	111	170	35
49th (1784)	110	3	40	69	112	25
52nd (1787)	137	3	45	89	137	32
54th (1789)	97	3	33	62	98	24
55th (1790)†	102	3	33	61	97	27
58th (1793)	102	3	29	49	81	23
60th (1795)†	114	3	18	90	111	18
Subtotal	5,426	81	1,599	3,705	5,385	1,062
Chia-ch'ing 1st (1796)	148	3	40	101	144	28
4th (1799)	210	3	74	143	220	73
6th (1801)†	271	3	98	174	275	79
7th (1802)	245	3	84	161	248	94
10th (1805)	233	2	96	144	243	84
13th (1808)	259	3	115	143	261	79
14th (1809)†	241	3	100	138	241	69
16th (1811)	237	3	92	142	237	72
19th (1814)	225	3	100	124	227	70
22nd (1817)	250	3	100	152	255	74
24th (1819)†	223	3	99	122	224	66
25th (1820)	241	3	100	143	246	79
Subtotal	2,783	36	1,098	1,687	2,821	867
Tao-kuang 2nd (1822)†	223	3	100	119	222	41
3rd (1823)	240	3	107	136	246	48
6th (1826)	258	3	110	152	265	51
9th (1829)	214	3	106	112	221	54
12th (1832)†	203	3	100	103	206	57
13th (1833)	222	3	100	117	220	62
15th (1835)	269	3	117	152	272	57
16th (1836)†	174	3	72	97	172	42
18th (1838)	182	3	82	109	194	53
20th (1840)	183	3	87	90	180	58
21st (1841)†	200	3	96	103	202	69
24th (1844)	230	3	106	100	209	47
25th (1845)†	212	3	98	116	217	54
27th (1847)	211	3	110	118	231	53
30th (1850)	207	3	104	105	212	54
Subtotal	3,228	45	1,495	1,729	3,269	807

† See footnotes at end of Table.

TABLE 27 *(Concluded)*

Year	No. of *kung-shih*	Number of *chin-shih*			Total	No. admitted to Han-lin Academy
		First rank	Second rank	Third rank		
Hsien-feng 2nd (1852)†	244	3	108	128	239	85
3rd (1853)	237	3	107	112	222	68
6th (1856)	192	3	100	113	216	63
9th (1859)	191	3	86	91	180	42
10th (1860)†	191	3	80	106	189	40
Subtotal	1,055	15	481	550	1,046	298
T'ung-chih 1st (1862)	196	3	72	118	193	53
2nd (1863)†	198	3	78	119	200	59
4th (1865)	252	3	100	162	265	80
7th (1868)	271	3	127	140	270	87
10th (1871)	326	3	120	200	323	93
13th (1874)	345	3	132	202	337	93
Subtotal	1,588	18	629	941	1,588	465
Kuang-hsü 2nd (1876)†	339	3	156	165	324	92
3rd (1877)	323	3	131	194	328	81
6th (1880)	323	3	133	193	329	93
9th (1883)	316	3	124	181	308	80
12th (1886)	316	3	130	186	319	90
15th (1889)	318	3	132	161	296	90
16th (1890)†	328	3	136	187	326	89
18th (1892)	317	3	132	182	317	98
20th (1894)†	320	3	132	179	314	82
21st (1895)	266	3	99	190	292	69
24th (1898)	337	3	150	193	346	95
29th (1903)	306	3	138	174	315	77
30th (1904)†	276	3	120	150	273	64
Subtotal	4,085	39	1,713	2,335	4,087	1,100
Grand Total	26,668	336	8,956	17,455	26,747	6,065

* Source: For *kung-shih* figures from 1646 to 1886, see *K'o-ch'ang* 22/5a-26a; also *Shih-li*, 350/9b-25b. The latter source has one mistake in addition: the total for 1784 is given as 115 instead of as the correct total 110. Hsieh Pao-chao, *op. cit.*, p. 184, also has a table on *kung-shih* figures from 1646 to 1886 but mistakenly calls them *chin-shih* figures. Hsieh states that the data are based on the *Ch'in-ting ta-Ch'ing hui-tien shih-li* and *Tung-hua-lu* but does not give *chüan* and page numbers. After careful checking, a number of mistakes have been found. For the year 1646, he says 1647; for 1647, he says 1648; for 1658, he says 1656; for 1661, when the number of *kung-shih* is 400, he says 540; for 1697, when the number is 159, he says 150; for 1784, he has also 115 instead of 110; he omitted 1793; for 1817, when the number is 250, he says 249; for 1819, the number is 223 — he says 224; for 1826, the number is 258—he says 257; for 1829, it should be 214—he says 215; for 1844, it should be 230—he says 229; for 1845, it should be 212—he says 213; and for 1859, it should be 191—he says 192.

For the *kung-shih* figure of 1889, see *Shih-lu*, Te-tsung, 268/14b; for 1890, *ibid.*, 283/12b; for 1892, *ibid.*, 309/9a-b; for 1894, *ibid.*, 337/9b–10a; for 1895, *ibid.*, 364/8a–b; for 1898, *ibid.*, 416/16 b; for 1903, *ibid.*, 513/14b; and for 1904, *ibid.*, 528/16b.

For *chin-shih* and *han-lin* figures, see *Tseng-chiao Ch'ing-ch'ao chin-shih t'i-ming pei-lu*, Fang Chao-ying and Tu Lien-che, esp. pp. xv–xvii.

† Referring to *en-k'o*, or special examinations held through imperial favor. Fang and Tu, *op. cit.*, pp. xvi, 191, calls 1862 also *en-k'o* which is incorrect. It is a regular examination year as can be verified in *Shih-li*, 350/6b.

TABLE 28

ANNUAL QUOTA FOR SUI-KUNG-SHENG BEFORE AND AFTER THE TAIPING PERIOD*

Provinces and other Quota Divisions	Before the Taiping Period	After the Taiping Period
8 Banners	3 8/15 †	3 8/15
Fengt'ien	4 11/15	7 4/15
Chihli	89 1/6	91 2/3
Kiangsu	36 23/60	36 23/60
Anhwei	39 2/3	40 1/6
Chekiang	50	50
Kiangsi	52 1/3	52 1/3
Fukien ‡	42 1/6	45 3/20
Honan	64 5/6	64 5/6
Shantung	75 1/6	75 1/6
Shansi	63 1/3	63 1/3
Hupeh	43 5/12	43 5/12
Hunan	43 7/12	43 11/12
Shensi and Kansu	88 1/15	91 8/15
Szechwan	77 5/12	77 11/15
Kwangtung	54 1/3	54 1/3
Kwangsi	39 5/12	39 2/3
Yunnan	48 1/12	48 1/3
Kweichow	37 5/12	38 1/4
Merchant	1 9/20	1 17/20
Total	954 1/2	968 13/15

* Figures for the pre-Taiping period are taken from *Ch'in-ting hsüeh-cheng ch'üan-shu*, *chüan* 66–86. Figures for the post-Taiping period are taken from *Ch'in-ting ta-Ch'ing hui-tien shih-li*, *chüan* 370–381.

† Annual quota for *sui-kung-sheng* for the various schools varies from 2 to 1/6, which means in the first case that 2 would be selected annually, and in the second case that one would be selected in six years.

‡ Includes Taiwan.

TABLE 29

A Comparison of the Five Kinds of Kung-sheng in the Prefectural and Hsien Schools in Sung-chiang Prefecture *

Period	Kinds of *kung-sheng*	Sung-chiang Prefectural School	Hua-t'ing *Hsien* School	Feng-hsien *Hsien* School	Lou-hsien *Hsien* School	Chin-shan *Hsien* School	Shanghai *Hsien* School	Nan-hui *Hsien* School	Ch'ing-p'u *Hsien* School	Total
Chia-ch'ing 21–25 (1816–1820)	*Sui-kung*	5	1	1	4	2	2	2	3	20
	En-kung	2	2	2	3	2	2	2	2	17
	Pa-kung	.	.	.	.	.	.	.	.	.
	Fu-kung	.	.	1	1	1	.	.	.	3
	Yu-kung	.	.	.	.	.	.	.	.	.
Tao-kuang 1–30 (1821–1850)	*Sui-kung*	30	7	9	8	7	7	7	15	90
	En-kung	4	4	7	4	4	4	4	4	35
	Pa-kung	6	1	2	2	1	2	2	3	19
	Fu-kung	3	1	.	1	.	2	.	6	13
	Yu-kung	2	3	2	1	.	.	3	.	11
Hsien-feng 1–11 (1851–1861)	*Sui-kung*	11	3	3	3	3	3	3	5	34
	En-kung	5	5	5	5	5	5	5	5	40
	Pa-kung	2	1	.	.	1	1	.	1	6
	Fu-kung	1	1	.	1	.	.	.	1	4
	Yu-kuug	.	.	.	.	.	.	.	.	.
T'ung-chih 1–13 (1862–1874)	*Sui-kung*	13	3	3	3	3	3	3	7	38
	En-kung	2	2	2	2	2	2	2	2	16
	Pa-kung	2	1	1	1	1	1	1	1	9
	Fu-kung	2	5	.	2	2	.	1	3	15
	Yu-kung	1	.	1	.	2	.	.	.	4
Kuang-hsü 1–8 (1875–1882)	*Sui-kung*	7	1	2	2	2	1	2	3	20
	En-kung	2	.	.	.	.	.	.	2	4
	Pa-kung	.	.	.	.	.	.	.	.	.
	Fu-kung	1	.	2	1	.	.	.	2	6
	Yu-kung	1	.	.	.	.	.	1	1	3

* Source: *Sung-chiang-fu hsü-chih, chüan* 22, pp. 19–34.

TABLE 30

Proportion of Regular to Irregular Kung-sheng *

District	No. of regular *kung-sheng*	Per cent	No. of irregular *kung-sheng*	Per cent	Total	Per cent	Source
Heng-yang, Hunan..	169	72	65	28	234	100	*Heng-chou fu-chih*, 23/46 ff.
Ch'ing-ch'uan, Hunan	13	33	26	67	39	100	,, ,, 23/46 ff.
Heng-shan, Hunan..	92	74	33	26	125	100	,, ,, 23/46 ff.
Lai-yang, Hunan....	91	92	7	8	98	100	,, ,, 23/46 ff.
Ch'ang-ning, Hunan.	79	83	16	17	95	100	,, ,, 23/46 ff.
An-jen, Hunan.....	74	84	14	16	88	100	,, ,, 23/46 ff.
Lin-hsien, Hunan...	40	65	22	35	62	100	,, ,, 23/46 ff.
Hsin-t'ien, Hunan...	113	97	4	3	117	100	*Yung-chou fu-chih*, 12 B/20 b-31 a; 34 b-36 a
Lin-ling, Hunan....	155	61	100†	39	255	100	*Yung-chou fu-ehih*, 12 B/20 b-31 a; 34 b-36 a
Tao-chou, Hunan...	196	73	73	27	269	100	*Tao-chou chih*, 8/14 a ff.
Jung-hsien, Kwangsi‡	188	83	39	17	227	100	*Jung-hsien chih*, 17/11 b-13a
Total	1,210	75	399	25	1,609	100	

* The records cover the Ch'ing dynasty up to the time of publication of the respective gazetteers: Heng-chou—to 1875; Yung-chou—to 1867; Tao-chou—to 1877; Jung-hsien—to 1908.

† Of the 100 irregular *kung-sheng*, 28 obtained official titles.

‡ 110 in this district purchased the title of *chien-sheng*.

TABLE 31

A Comparison of Number of Ling-sheng and Tseng-sheng Before and After the Taiping Rebellion*

Provinces and Other Quota Divisions	Before the Taiping Rebellion		After the Taiping Rebellion	
	Ling-sheng	*Tseng-sheng*	*Ling-sheng*	*Tseng-sheng*
8 Banners	99	99	99	99
Fengt'ien	68	68	122	122
Chihli	3,568	3,558	3,580	3,570
Kiangsu	1,392	1,392	1,396	1,396
Anhwei	1,590	1,590	1,590	1,590
Chekiang	1,988	1,988	1,998	1,998
Kiangsi	2,060	2,060	2,060	2,060
Fukien †	1,634	1,634	1,688	1,688
Honan	2,640	2,640	2,640	2,640
Shantung	2,750	2,750	2,750	2,750
Shansi	2,590	2,590	2,585	2,585
Hupeh	1,706	1,706	1,716	1,716
Hunan	1,622	1,622	1,628	1,628
Shensi and Kansu	3,509	3,509	3,526	3,526
Szechwan	2,962	2,962	2,952	2,952
Kwangtung	2,198	2,184	2,198	2,184
Kwangsi	1,141	1,141	1,140	1,140
Yunnan	2,106	2,106	2,114	2,114
Kweichow	1,506	1,506	1,521	1,521
Merchant	48	48	58	58
Total	37,177	37,153	37,361	37,337

* Source: Figures for pre-Taiping period are taken from *Ch'in-ting hsüeh-cheng ch'üan-shu, chüan* 66–86. Figures for post-Taiping period are taken from *Ch'in-ting ta-Ch'ing hui-tien shih-li, chüan* 370–381.

† Includes Taiwan.

TABLE 32

SIZE OF GENTRY IN VARIOUS PROVINCES AND ITS RELATIONSHIP TO SIZE OF POPULATION BEFORE AND AFTER THE TAIPING PERIOD *

Provinces and other quota divisions	Pre-Taiping Period						Post-Taiping Period					
	Regular gentry	Irregular gentry	Total	Total incl. family	Population	Per cent	Regular gentry	Irregular gentry	Total	Total incl. family	Population	Per cent
8 Banners	3,219	.	3,219	16,095	.	.	4,325	.	4,325	21,625	.	.
Fengt'ien	2,091	.	2,091	10,455	.	.	4,832	.	4,832	24,160	.	.
Chihli	83,925	40,000	123,925	619,625	36,900,000	1.7	86,182	60,000	146,182	730,910	17,900,000	4.1
Kiangsu	41,362	34,469	75,831	379,155	29,600,000	1.3	53,754	51,704	105,458	527,290	21,300,000	2.5
Anhwei	38,029	15,684	53,713	268,565	36,600,000	0.7	48,756	23,526	72,282	361,410	20,600,000	1.7
Chekiang	53,100	33,869	86,969	434,845	30,400,000	1.4	65,974	50,804	116,778	583,890	11,700,000	5.0
Kiangsi	39,830	38,552	78,382	391,910	26,500,000	1.5	62,197	57,828	120,025	600,125	24,500,000	2.4
Fukien	35,017	20,135	55,152	275,760	25,800,000	1.1	47,380	30,202	77,582	387,910	23,500,000	1.7
Honan	48,111	22,763	70,874	354,370	29,100,000	1.2	56,382	34,145	90,527	452,635	22,100,000	2.0
Shantung	53,990	10,959	64,949	324,745	36,200,000	0.9	58,565	16,438	75,003	375,015	36,500,000	1.0
Shansi	45,316	6,050	51,366	256,830	10,300,000	2.5	48,694	9,075	57,769	288,845	10,800,000	2.7
Hupeh	32,067	19,960	52,027	260,135	28,600,000	0.9	46,997	29,940	76,937	384,685	33,600,000	1.1
Hunan	35,659	27,713	63,372	316,860	20,000,000	1.6	50,329	41,570	91,899	459,495	21,000,000	2.2
Shensi, Kansu	55,015	15,254	70,269	351,345	29,800,000	1.2	63,646	22,881	86,527	432,635	8,700,000	5.0
Szechwan	40,296	14,967	55,263	276,315	22,300,000	1.2	58,762	22,450	81,212	406,060	71,100,000	0.6
Kwangtung	39,116	38,264	77,380	386,900	21,100,000	1.8	53,309	57,396	110,705	553,525	29,700,000	1.8
Kwangsi	30,059	9,579	39,638	198,190	8,100,000	2.4	34,063	14,369	48,432	242,160	5,100,000	4.7
Yunnan	39,083	4,082	43,165	215,825	6,200,000	3.5	40,882	6,123	47,005	235,025	11,700,000	2.0
Kweichow	22,213	3,235	25,448	127,240	4,800,000	2.7	22,817	4,852	27,669	138,345	7,700,000	1.8
Merchant	1,701	.	1,701	8,505	.	.	2,751	.	2,751	13,755	.	.
Total	739,199	355,535	1,094,734	5,473,670	402,300,000	1.3	910,597	533,303	1,443,900	7,219,500	377,500,000	1.9

* Source: Under the division, "Pre-Taiping Period," for figures on regular gentry, see Table 19, column on total *sheng-yüan*. For irregular gentry, see Table 23, column on grand total of number of men purchasing *chien-sheng* titles. An approximate estimated figure has been added for Chihli. For population figures, see Popoff's collection from the Board of Revenue (Wang Shih-ta, *op. cit.*, II, 1, pp. 58, 65).

Under the division, "Post-Taiping period," for figures on regular gentry, see Table 22, column on total *sheng-yüan*. The figures on irregular gentry are only approximate estimated figures. Population figures are taken from Raymond C. Tenney's collection from the Board of Revenue (Wang Shih-ta, *op. cit.*, pp. 85, 97, 104b).

PART THREE

The Examination Life of the Gentry Of Nineteenth-Century China

In Part One it has been pointed out that gentry status was formalized through the government-controlled examination system. Only those who held examination grades, titles, degrees, or their "irregular" equivalents were members of the gentry. Thus, through this system, the government had the final say as to who would be gentry. In Part Two we have seen that the examination quota was used to regulate and control the size of the gentry. This, together with the manipulation of the sale of academic titles, enabled the government to restrain the gentry's power. Part Three will deal with the examinations themselves.

PREPARATION FOR EXAMINATION—A MAJOR ACTIVITY OF THE GENTRY

Membership in the gentry (*shen-shih*), the privileged group in nineteenth-century Chinese society, was gained mainly through the examination system. This was the "regular" route to gentry status. The largest group of gentry consisted of *sheng-yüan* or students of the government district schools.[1] These students were those who had succeeded in the *t'ung-shih* or student selecting examinations. The participants in such examinations had spent many years in preparation[2] and often succeeded only after many attempts.[3]

[1] On the proportion of the number of *sheng-yüan* to the total number of gentry, see Part Two.

[2] To give some examples of what was studied and how long it took, in *Hsi-Chin yu-hsiang t'ung-jen tzu-shu hui-k'an, ts'e shang*, p. 1 b, Yang Chih-lien says that he finished the Four Books by the age of thirteen, completed the Five Classics, studied the histories and other works, and practiced for examination writing by the age of fifteen, and succeeded in the *t'ung-shih* in 1871 at the age of twenty. *Ibid.*, p. 13 b, Yang En-p'ei says that he first studied *The Great Learning*, *The Doctrine of the Mean*, and *The Analects*, and that beginning at the age of nine, he studied *Mencius*, *The Book of Odes*, *The Book of*

However, their "examination life" did not end when they became *sheng-yüan* and members of the gentry. Also many of those who had entered the gentry through the "irregular" route by purchasing the title of *chien-sheng*, or students of the Imperial College, thus becoming members of the gentry without passing any examination, were not satisfied to remain always in the lower layer of the privileged group [4] but endeavored to continue their climb up the social ladder toward the upper layer of the gentry or into officialdom.

Although *sheng-yüan* and *chien-sheng* already enjoyed certain influence and prestige denied the commoners, their influence and prestige could be greatly increased if they succeeded in the *k'o-shih*, or qualifying examination to the provincial examination, and the *hsiang-shih*, or provincial examination, and became provincial graduates, holders of the *chü-jen* degree.[5] Those

History, *The Book of Changes*, and *The Book of Rites*, and then *The Spring and Autumn Annals*, *The Tso Commentaries* and *The Collection of Ancient Essays*. After the age of fifteen, he learned to write examination papers, participated in the *t'ung-shih* for the first time at the age of sixteen and succeeded at the age of nineteen in 1880. *Ibid.*, p. 34 b, Ku Tsu-kao says that at the age of five he learned characters, completed *The Analects* at six, studied *Mencius* and *The Book of Odes* at seven, *The Book of History* and *The Book of Rites* at eight, *The Book of Changes* and *The Spring and Autumn Annals* at nine, *The Collection of Ancient Essays* at eleven, learned poetry writing at twelve, and began examination paper composition at thirteen, first participated in the *t'ung-shih* at fifteen, and succeeded at the age of twenty-one in 1886. In "Notes of Ling-hsiao and I-shih," *Kuo-wen chou-pao*, *chüan* 9, No. 28, July 18, 1932, p. 1, Chang Ch'ien, native of Nan-t'ung, Kiangsu, who later founded the big cotton mills, is described as beginning to study poem and eight-legged essay writing at twelve, becoming *sheng-yüan* at the early age of sixteen. Ling-hsiao and I-shih are brothers with the surname of Hsü who wrote a series of short articles on a number of episodes in the examination system and officialdom of the Ch'ing dynasty.

[3] E.g., in Wu Ching-tzu, *Ju-lin wai-shih*, 12/4, Chuan Fu-yung is described as never having been successful even in the *hsien* examination, the first of the series of three examinations of the *t'ung-shih*. He continued to attend the *hsien* examinations for more than thirty years in order to keep his teaching position. *Ibid.*, 3/5, Fan Chin of Kwangtung was described as having participated in the *t'ung-shih* from the age of twenty and having failed in more than twenty attempts. When he finally succeeded he was fifty-four but officially reported his age as thirty. (This indicates that the official age record of candidates was sometimes unreliable.) According to Hu Shih's "Wu Ching-tzu nien-p'u," in *Ju-ling wai-shih*, p. 31, Wu Ching-tzu (1701–1754), a native of Ch'üan-chiao, Anhwei, wrote this popular realistic novel between 1740 and 1750. Although it is dated earlier than the period studied here, several examples which seem pertinent will be brought into this paper. Many examples can be given for the nineteenth century. For instance, Tseng Kuo-fan's father was unsuccessful in seventeen attempts before he finally succeeded. See Tseng Kuo-fan, *Tseng Wen-cheng-kung ch'üan-chi*, nien-p'u, p. 1 b.

[4] In fact, some candidates purchased the title of *chien-sheng* solely for the purpose of skipping the *t'ung-shih* and directly qualifying for the provincial examinations. Wu Ching-tzu, *op. cit.*, chap. 2 and 3, especially chap. 3, pp. 3–4, relates how Chou Chin, who at the age of sixty had not yet succeeded in becoming *sheng-yüan*, was aided by friends to purchase the title of *chien-sheng* in order to participate in the provincial and metropolitan examinations without further delay.

[5] In Li Pao-chia, *Kuan-ch'ang hsien-hsing-chi*, chap. 1, it is related that when Chao Wen of Shensi succeeded in the provincial examination, his success was admired by others, the family celebrated the occasion, and the local gentry accepted the invitations to the celebration. Li Pao-chia (1867–1906) wrote this realistic novel between 1901 and 1905

in the position of *chü-jen* worked toward the *hui-shih*, or metropolitan examination, and the *tien-shih*, or palace examination, in order to secure immediate appointment to office, to gain a more influential position, to be admired and respected, and to bring glory to their ancestors.[6]

A considerable number of *sheng-yüan* and *chien-sheng* prepared for participation in the provincial examinations,[7] although some of the wealthy ones participated in the purchase system and entered officialdom through the "irregular" route.[8] In Chihli the examination hall was filled with candidates, including both *sheng-yüan* of Chihli and *chien-sheng* of the various provinces, while in other provinces the candidates were mainly *sheng-yüan*.[9] The total number of candidates in the provincial examinations has

and gives a good description of Ch'ing officialdom in the late nineteenth century. Also, in Wu Ching-tzu, *op. cit.*, chap. 3, a description is given of the treatment Fan Chin received after he was successful in the provincial examination. Local upper gentry came to visit him, gave him money and a new house, and poor people seeking protection offered themselves as servants.

[6] Cf. Li Pao-chia, *op. cit.*, 1/2, the words of Wang Jen. Also in Wu Ching-tzu, *op. cit.*, 15/13, Ma-erh hsien-sheng said, "Work in preparation for examination is the main task. Besides this, there is nothing that would make people outstanding. Fortune-telling is a lowly job, but teaching and being personal assistants to magistrates are also not good endings. Only by entering district schools, becoming *chü-jen* and *chin-shih*, then only can you immediately bring glory to your ancestors." In Pai Ching-wei, *op. cit.*, Pai, who was a *chü-jen* of Shensi and was in charge of the construction of fortresses in his locality to guard against Moslem rebels, wrote that he had to leave the unfinished work to other gentry members so that he could attend the metropolitan examination. To participate in the examination was the most important activity of all.

[7] Some *kung-sheng* also participated in the provincial examinations. The regular *kung-sheng* and the *kung-sheng* through purchase that had formerly been *ling-sheng* were already qualified for selection to officialdom. But to speed up entrance to officialdom and gain better prospects, some also worked for the examinations. Also, some *kung-sheng* through purchase that had not been *ling-sheng* wanted to try their luck. In Chang Chung-ju, *Ch'ing-tai k'ao-shih chih-tu*, pp. 14–16, in the description of the tour of the provincial director-of-studies to the prefectural and independent *chou* cities for the *k'o-shih*, it is pointed out that the seventh day of his stay in each city was set aside for the examination of *kung-sheng* who wanted to take the provincial examination. Their number was much smaller than the number of *sheng-yüan*, however.

[8] In *K'o-ch'ang*, 21/18 b, it is pointed out that the merchant quota for *sheng-yüan* in Shantung was four on each occasion of the *t'ung-shih* which occurred twice in three years. But during the interval between the triennial provincial examinations, four to five *sheng-yüan* might have participated in the purchase system. Very few of the *sheng-yüan* who were admitted on the merchant quota participated in the provincial examinations.

[9] *Kung-sheng* and *chien-sheng* who actually studied in the Imperial College were first examined by the College before being sent to participate in the *hsiang-shih*, held in the metropolitan prefecture. Those who did not study at the College could participate either at the metropolitan prefecture or in their own province. Those who wished to participate in the provinces were first examined by the provincial directors-of-studies, while those who wished to participate in the metropolitan prefecture were first examined by the Imperial College. The technical term for the qualifying examination to the *hsiang-shih* is *lu-k'o*. For details see *Shih-li, chüan* 337; also *K'o-ch'ang, chüan* 5. But in the metropolitan prefectural examination, there was a separate quota for the admission of *chien-sheng* to *chü-jen* degrees. It was to the advantage of those *chien-sheng* who could afford to go to the metropolitan prefecture to do so, since they did not have to participate on equal grounds with *sheng-yüan*. A review of the quota for *chü-jen* degrees conferred

been conservatively estimated at 89,600,[10] while another report shows that in Kwangtung province alone there were more than 9,000 candidates in

in one examination year, as shown in *K'o-ch'ang*, 20/1 a–3 a, and also in *Ch'ing-kuo hsin-cheng-fa fen-lun*, 3/132–33, reveals the following:

Provinces	*Quota*
Shun-t'ien (metropolitan prefecture) *hsiang-shih*:	
Man-tzu-hao, Manchu and Mongol bannermen	27
Ho-tzu-hao, Chinese bannermen	12
Chia-tzu-hao, *sheng-yüan* of Fengt'ien	8
Ch'eng-tzu-hao, *sheng-yüan* of Ch'eng-te prefecture	3
Tan-tzu-hao, *sheng-yüan* of Hsüan-hua prefecture	4
Pei-tzu-hao, *sheng-yüan* of Chihli	97
Nan-min, *kung-sheng* and *chien-sheng* of Chiang-nan, Chekiang, Kiangsi, Fukien, Hupeh, and Hunan	36
Pei-min, *kung-sheng* and *chien-sheng* of Fengt'ien, Chihli, Shantung, Shansi, Honan, Shensi, and Kansu	36
Chung-min, *kung-sheng* and *chien-sheng* of Szechwan, Kwangtung, Kwangsi, Yunnan, and Kweichow	1 out of each 20 candidates, not exceeding a total of 36
Shantung *hsiang-shih*	69
Shansi " "	60
Szechwan " "	60
Honan " "	71
Chiang-nan " "	114
Chekiang " "	94
Kiangsi " "	94
Fukien " "	87
Hupeh " "	47
Hunan " "	47
Shensi " "	41
Kansu " "	30
Kwangtung " "	72
Kwangsi " "	45
Yunnan " "	54
Kweichow " "	40

For a detailed study of the minor changes in *chü-jen* quota from time to time, see *Shih-li, chüan* 348, 349; see also *K'o-ch'ang, chüan* 20. An edict in 1744, *Shih-li*, 337/10 a, indicated that there were not many candidates in the *man-tzu-hao*, *ho-tzu-hao*, *chia-tzu-hao*, *tan-tzu-hao*, *nan-min*, *pei-min*, and *chung-min*. It was clearly provided that one out of twenty of the *chung-min* would be successful, which gave the candidates a much better chance of success than the ratio in the provinces. That *kung-sheng* and *chien-sheng* through purchase in various provinces preferred to participate in the Shun-t'ien *hsiang-shih* was also pointed out in Teng Ch'eng-hsiu, *Yü-ping-ko tsou-i*, 3/16 a–21 a, in a memorial dated Kuang-hsü 8/12–15 (1882), in which censor Teng said it was very difficult for these men to gain success in their native provinces.

10 From *Ch'ing-kuo t'ung-k'ao*, as quoted in *Ch'ing-kuo hsin-cheng-fa fen-lun*, 3/123, which also stated that the *chü-jen* quota was 1,439. This estimate of the number of candidates is conservative. It must have been based on the reasoning that the number of candidates admitted to participate in the provincial examinations was related to the quota according to the size of the province. The relation varied during the Ch'ing dynasty. Finally in 1744, according to *Shih-li*, 337/10 a, it was fixed that there would be 80 candidates for each degree conferred in the big provinces of Chihli, Chiang-nan, Kiangsi, Fukien, Chekiang, and Hu-kuang, 60 for the middle provinces of Shantung, Shansi, Honan, Shensi, Szechwan, and Kwangtung, and 50 for the small provinces of Kwangsi, Yunnan, and Kweichow. Also, in the provincial examinations, for every 5 *chü-jen* degrees conferred, 1 *fu-pang* would be conferred. And for each *fu-pang*, an additional 40 candidates could

1870.[11] In a third estimate, the number of candidates was put at 7,000 to 8,000 in some provinces.[12] Of course, the number varied from province to province. According to Feng Kuei-fen, chief examiner for the provincial examination in Kwangsi in 1844, there were approximately 2,400 candidates in that examination.[13] According to Lung Ch'i-jui, vice-examiner for the provincial examination in Kwangtung in the same year, there were more than 7,500 candidates.[14] According to *The Chinese Repository*, there were

be sent by the large provinces, 30 by middle provinces, and 20 by small provinces. Cf. *K'o-ch'ang* 3/1 a–2 b. However, in actual practice, the provincial directors-of-studies did not stick to these ratios and governors-general, governors, and other high officials would again send in many who had been disqualified by the provincial directors-of-studies. Thus, as early as 1742, as recorded in *Shih-li* 337/8 a–b, an edict pointed out the actual ratio was well over one to a hundred and requested the provincial directors-of-studies to restrain themselves and not seek to acquire the name of being lenient. Cf. *K'o-ch'ang* 3/8 a–9 b. Teng Ch'eng-hsiu, *loc. cit.*, also points out that in provincial examinations the ratio of candidates to quota was originally set at eighty to one, but that this regulation was ignored.

[11] F. H. Ewer, "The Triennial Examinations," *The Chinese Recorder*, pp. 330–32. "Another triennial examination has been held; once more have the rising minds of the Southern Provinces been collected together in the city of Canton, the chaff sifted from the wheat, and the choicest promises of intellectual power culled from amongst more than 9,000 candidates. . . ." If the regulation had been strictly complied with, the number of candidates would have been 4,740, since in Kwangtung there would be 72 *chü-jen* and 14 *fu-pang* conferred, and for each *chü-jen* there would be 60 candidates, and for each *fu-pang* 30 candidates. Ewer's record was based on actual experience and should therefore be reliable. The actual number of candidates in provincial examinations in Canton was therefore twice the theoretical number.

[12] T. L. Bullock, "Competitive Examinations in China," *Nineteenth Century*, p. 91.

[13] Feng Kuei-fen, *Hsien-chih-t'ang kao*, 1/23 b. Feng stated that of this number of candidates 45 were granted *chü-jen* degrees and 9 were granted *fu-pang*; fourteen of the best essays were presented for imperial perusal. Theoretically, for each of the 45 *chü-jen* conferred, there would be 50 candidates, and for each of the *fu-pang* there would be 20. The total of candidates theoretically should be 2,430. In Kwangsi at that time, therefore, the actual number of candidates coincided with the theoretical number. This might have been caused by the strictness of the provincial director-of-studies there, or there may have been a smaller number of candidates applying for the qualifying examinations to the *hsiang-shih*. The former reason is more likely since a review of the number of *sheng-yüan* in Kwangsi reveals a considerable number of potential candidates.

[14] Lung Ch'i-jui, *op. cit.*, *wen-chi*, 6/15 a–17 a. Lung says that from this number of candidates, 890 examination papers were recommended to the chief examiner. The quota for Kwangtung was 72 *chü-jen* and 14 *fu-pang*. The total of candidates theoretically should have been 4,740. (Cf. note 11.) The actual number of candidates was about 60 per cent more than theoretically provided. Additional information is available on the number of seats in the Kwangtung provincial examination hall in Canton. In *Kuang-chou fu-chih*, 65/11 a–b, a stone tablet inscription, composed by Governor-general Lao Ch'ung-kuang, in 1861, on the occasion of the reconstruction of the examination hall, says there were 8,154 compartments. A more detailed account is given on a stone tablet inscription composed by Governor Chiang I-li, in 1867, on the occasion of the enlargement of the examination hall. Here it is stated that in earlier times there were approximately 4,000 candidates to 71 admissions in the Kwangtung provincial examination. Since K'ang-hsi times there had been more than 5,000 compartments. The number was increased to over 7,600 in 1822. Another 500 were added in 1842, and 500 more were added in 1863. The total at that time was 8,654. In 1867, following an increase in quota through contribution to the military fund (more *sheng-yüan* were thereby admitted), space still fell short of demand. Gentry and commoners contributed funds to build another 3,000 compartments. In 1867 there was a total of 11,708 compartments, and 109 became *chü-jen* in that year. These figures correspond very well with the records on number of candidates mentioned above.

more than 8,000 candidates in Kwangtung in 1846.[15] According to Wang Hsien-ch'ien, chief examiner for the provincial examination in Chekiang, there were more than 10,000 candidates in each of the six provincial examinations held in Chekiang between 1865 and 1876.[16] In Shantung, according to the memorial of Ting Pao-chen, governor of Shantung, there were more than 12,900 candidates in late T'ung-chih times (*ca.* 1873), the quota being only 69.[17] In Chihli, approximately 13,000 candidates competed in 1874.[18] In Chiang-nan, in 1864, there were approximately 16,000 candidates.[19]

Thus thousands of candidates competed for the relatively small number of degrees to be granted under the quotas. Moreover, the number of lower gentry members preparing for advanced examinations was even larger than the number of actual participants. Some were disqualified from taking the provincial examinations because of literary deficiency, nonpayment of taxes,[20] involvement in offenses pending possible deprival of title, temporary suspension from participation in examination,[21] mourning period for the death of parents,[22] compliance with the regulation of "respectful withdrawal" because the candidate was a relative of the examiners or officials on duty in the examination hall,[23] or were unable to participate for other reasons.

[15] *Chinese Repository*, XV, No. 10, Oct., 1846, p. 527.

[16] Wang Hsien-ch'ien, *Hsü-shou-t'ang wen-chi*, 2/8 a. Wang says that Chekiang had always produced more talent than other places. During the Taiping period, Chekiang suffered from loss of talents, but in each of the six provincial examinations from 1865 to 1876, there were more than 10,000 candidates. Several hundred candidates were successful (in the total of six examinations).

[17] *K'o-ch'ang*, 21/7 a. This memorial was referred to in an edict issued in 1873.

[18] *K'o-ch'ang,* 3/3 b; an edict of 1748 pointed out that the 10,000 compartments in the examination hall were short of the actual need. *Ibid.*, pp. 5 b–7 a; in 1874 it was pointed out that there were 13,000 compartments and still more were needed.

[19] Tseng Kuo-fan, *Tseng Wen-cheng-kung tsou-kao*, 21/18 b, a memorial of T'ung-chih 3/8/13 (1864) reported that the 16,000 compartments in the examination hall at Nanking were not destroyed by the Taipings and that orders had been given for the examiner's offices to be repaired and boards lost from the compartments replaced. A memorial of Chang Fei, *op. cit.*, 3/10 b, dated *Hsien-feng* 9/6/4 (1859) stated that the Chekiang examination hall could hold more than 12,000 candidates. The writer pointed out that the Kiangsu and Anhwei provincial examinations had always been held together. Kiangsu had from 6,000 to 7,000 candidates and Anhwei had 5,000 to 6,000. According to these figures, the number of Chiang-nan (referring to Kiangsu and Anhwei jointly) candidates before and during the Taiping period was approximately 12,000 to 13,000. Therefore, Chang requested that Kiangsu and Anhwei provincial examinations be held jointly in Chekiang while the Chiang-nan examination hall was in the hands of the Taipings.

[20] *K'o-ch'ang*, 4/4 a–b, 7/3 a; *sheng-yüan* or *chü-jen* who had not cleared tax payments were not to be permitted to participate in the provincial or metropolitan examinations.

[21] *Ibid.*, 4/11 a, gives an example of several *sheng-yüan* who were suspended from participation in one provincial examination because they had used incorrect terminology in their examination papers (e.g., quoting the Emperor's name).

[22] Candidates sometimes withheld news of the death of parents. In Lung Ch'i-jui, *op. cit.*, *ts'e shang*, pp. 9 a–10 a, Lung says that, as provincial director-of-studies of Hupeh, he issued a notice pointing out that at Hsiang-yang two military *t'ung-sheng* and one military *sheng-yüan* did not report the death of their parents, and stressed that further happenings of this nature would be severely dealt with.

[23] In Chang Chung-ju, *Ch'ing-tai k'o-chü chih-tu*, p. 30, we find that in provincial and

To show how hard many worked and tried for the provincial examinations, some individual cases will be mentioned. One candidate tried and failed eight times before he gave up.[24] Another tried unsuccessfully seven times.[25] Another tried unsuccessfully fourteen times.[26] Still another succeeded only after five failures.[27] A popular realistic novel describes how in one clan, among the sixty to seventy brothers and cousins, only two welcomed guests, while the others closed their doors, lived on their estates, and devoted themselves to *chü-yeh*, the task of preparing for examinations.[28] In the same novel, a candidate succeeded only after remaining in the position of *sheng-yüan* for seventeen years.[29]

For men who held the degree of *chü-jen*, the work for the metropolitan examination was also time-consuming. In one case, the candidate failed four times before he succeeded.[30] In another case, the candidate repeatedly failed and finally gave up.[31] In the novel mentioned above, the candidate succeeded only after remaining in the position of *chü-jen* for ten years.[32]

metropolitan examinations, if the chief examiners, associate examiners, supervisors, proctors, inspectors, receivers and sealers of examination papers, transcribers and proofreaders, and officials in charge of the commissariat department of the chief examiner found among the candidates persons of their own clans, related to them as grandfather-in-law, brother, nephew, cousin, father-in-law, son of a cousin, uncle, son-in-law, grandson-in-law, etc., they should list their names and post them outside the examination hall and order the persons concerned to withdraw from the examination. For detailed regulation on this point, see *K'o-ch'ang*, *chüan* 26.

[24] *Hsi-Chin yu-hsiang t'ung-jen tzu-shu hui-k'an, ts'e shang*, p. 13 b, the autobiography of Yang En-p'ei. The provincial examination was held triennially. To participate eight times would take about twenty years.

[25] *Ibid.*, p. 15 b, the autobiography of Ku Ch'ien.

[26] *Hsü-chou fu-chih* (Szechwan), 36/96 b.

[27] "Notes of Ling-hsiao and I-shih," *Kuo-wen chou-pao*, *chüan* 9, No. 28, p. 1.

[28] Wu Ching-tzu, *op. cit.*, 31/5, referring to the Tu brothers. It is generally thought that Tu Shou-ch'ing in this book represents the writer himself.

[29] *Ibid.*, chap. 36, especially p. 7, on the description of the examination life of Yü Yü-te of Ch'ang-shu, Kiangsu. Yü's grandfather was a *hsiu-ts'ai* (*sheng-yüan*) for thirty years. Yü became *hsiu-ts'ai* at the age of twenty-four but succeeded in the provincial examination only at forty-one.

[30] "Notes of Ling-hsiao and I-shih," *loc. cit.* The metropolitan examination was also held triennially.

[31] Wang Hsien-ch'ien, *op. cit.*, 3/19 a–20 a. In the preface (1884) to the collected poems of his deceased friend, Ting Chu-yün, Wang points out that Ting was *chü-jen* at the age of little over twenty. He was talented and people all looked upon him as having a great future. But he failed successively in the metropolitan examination and had to contribute money to become a second-class secretary of the Board of Revenue. Wang comments that Ting had studied widely, was an expert in eight-legged essay writing, and excellent in calligraphy, and that it should have been easy for him to head the examinations. However, he was not successful and after repeated failures felt annoyed and expressed his feeling in poetry. Wang also says that, in 1864, twenty-four from the same place became *chü-jen* but only four (including himself and Ting) were able to gain office, at least up to 1884, and Ting had obtained his office through purchase.

[32] Wu Ching-tzu, *op. cit.*, 36/7. Yü became a *chin-shih* at fifty. Many *chin-shih* obtained their degrees at the age of fifty or sixty, according to Wu, but did not report their actual ages. As Yü reported his true age, the Emperor considered him old and appointed him a doctor of the Imperial College.

A review of the average ages of successful candidates in the various examinations shows that the title of *sheng-yüan* was obtained at approximately twenty-four, *chü-jen* at approximately thirty, and *chin-shih* at approximately thirty-five.[33] Thus, for the fortunate ones, it still took more than ten years of preparation on the average to rise from *sheng-yüan* to *chin-shih* while many others tried in vain throughout their lives to advance beyond the lower gentry group. Nevertheless, many persisted. As a novelist said ironically, "Talent is gained through preparation for examination. If Confucius were present, he would devote himself to preparation for examination. How else could one gain office?"[34]

A large number of the gentry were thus constantly occupied in preparing for advanced examinations. But what of those who did not wish to participate or gave up early their ambition for further advancement? Were they free from the necessity to prepare for examination? The *chien-sheng* could do as they pleased, but the *sheng-yüan*, the large group of "regular" gentry, were never free from examinations. They were supposed to be examined monthly and quarterly by the *hsien*, *chou*, or *fu* directors-of-studies, although in actual practice in the nineteenth century this was not always done.[35] The more important examination in which they had to participate, however, was the *sui* examination which was supervised by the provincial director-of-studies. Their promotion or demotion depended upon the results of this examination.[36] All absences were recorded except those of students who were in mourning. The regulation was that those absent from three *sui* examinations would be

[33] See Part Two.

[34] Wu Ching-tzu, *op. cit.*, 13/8, in the words of Ma-erh hsien-sheng. *Hsüeh-cheng*, 4/10 b–12 b, contains an essay on the Imperial Exhortation to students issued in 1740 in which this statement about Confucius was quoted and attributed to Chu Hsi, the founder of the Ch'eng-Chu school of Sung Neo-Confucianism.

[35] *Shih-li*, 382/1 a. In 1727 it was ordered that monthly and quarterly examinations should be strictly held. Except for those who were in mourning, suffering from illness, or studying in other places, those who were absent three times would be stripped of their titles. Educational officials who did not treat these examinations seriously would be dismissed. *Ibid.*, p. 1 b; in 1736 the regulation had become more lenient. Only those absent without reason for the whole year would be deprived of their titles. *Ibid.*, p. 2 a–b; in 1812 it was pointed out by Censor Hsin Ts'ung-i that monthly examinations had not been held for a long time. The teacher-student relationship between directors-of-studies and *sheng-yüan* existed in name only. According to Ling Sen-mei, "Stone Tablet Inscription on the Occasion of the Establishment of a Charity School at Yung-ch'un," *Nan-ning fu-chih*, 51/15 b, the quarterly examinations of *sheng-yüan* were supervised by magistrates, while monthly examinations were supervised by educational officials.

[36] Theoretically there would be six grades according to the result of the examination. Those ranked in the 1st or 2nd grade could be promoted, for instance, from *fu-sheng* to *tseng-sheng*. Those ranked in the 4th and 5th grade would be demoted. Those in the 6th grade might be deprived of their titles. For details see *Ch'in-ting ta-Ch'ing hui-tien*, 32/1 a. However, as pointed out by Chang Chung-ju, *Ch'ing-tai k'ao-shih chih-tu*, pp. 7–14, in his description of *sui-k'ao*, in the nineteenth century there were actually only three grades. The provincial directors-of-studies tried not to demote the *sheng-yüan*.

stripped of their titles.[37] They were exempt only if they were serving in military camps, had been granted official titles, or had been recommended to *hsiao-lien fang-cheng* with sixth-rank honors.[38] Those who had been enrolled in the government school for more than thirty years, were of the age of seventy or more, or were suffering from recurrent illness were also exempted.[39]

Indeed, whether they were seeking to advance or merely to maintain their position, the gentry spent a great share of their time in preparing for examinations. They truly led a life of examination.[40] Chang Ch'ien, a man who succeeded in climbing to the upper layer of the gentry, spent 35 years preparing for examinations and 160 days in the examination hall itself.[41] As he put it, the best years of his life had been exhausted in preparing himself to meet the examiners' standards.[42] Another gentry member, who never succeeded in advancing into the upper gentry but continued to take the examinations in order to maintain his position as *ling-sheng*, participated in the *sui* and *k'o* examinations until the last day of the examination system, an examination life of almost thirty years.[43]

[37] *Shih-li*, 382/3 a, shows that this rule was still emphasized in 1881. *Ibid.*, p. 2 b; several edicts pointed out that quite a number of *sheng-yüan* had failed to observe the regulation. For instance, in 1819, it was reported that 770 had been absent from *sui-k'ao* from three to eight times. Those absent more than five times were deprived of their titles and the rest were ordered to take make-up examinations. In 1821, in Anhwei, there were 120 civil and 80 military *sheng-yüan* who were absent three times. It was ordered that they be given one more chance. In 1862 over 1,000 *sheng-yüan* of the prefectures of Wu, Han, and Huang were deprived of their titles because they had been absent three times from *sui-k'ao*, but those who had fled before the approaching rebels were to have their titles restored when their accounts of their actions had been verified.

[38] *Ch'in-ting ta-Ch'ing hui-tien*, 32/1 a; see also in Wu Ching-tzu, *op. cit.*, 34/3; an example is given of one who, after being recommended to participate in the *po-hsüeh hung-ju* examination, did not actually participate but was exempt from *sui* and *k'o* examinations. See also "Wu Ching-tzu nien-p'u," pp. 18–19.

[39] *Ch'in-ting ta-Ch'ing hui-tien*, 32/1 a. *Shih-li*, 382/3 a, edict of 1882. That the *sui-k'ao* had to be attended by the *sheng-yüan* even in late Ch'ing times is shown in another example. *Hsi-Chin yu-hsiang t'ung-jen tzu-shu hui-k'an, ts'e hsia*, pp. 7 b–8 a; the autobiography of Ting Fu-pao states that he was invited in 1903 to teach mathematics and physiology at a new government college in Peking. The supervisor thought Ting taught well and it would be a pity to let him return south in order to participate in the *sui-k'ao*. The supervisor therefore officially wrote to the provincial director-of-studies of Kiangsu requesting Ting's exemption.

[40] In Liang Ch'i-ch'ao, *Yin-ping-shih ho-chi, wen-chi* 1, p. 26, Liang said that it took a month to attend the several parts of the *hsien* examination. After a month, one attended the *fu* examination which also took a month. After another month, one was examined by the provincial director-of-studies. When the three sets of *t'ung-shih* were over, half a year was gone. When one failed, one became discouraged and could not concentrate on study for several months. Not long after, however, the *hsien* examination was again due. Even after one became a *sheng-yüan*, it was as difficult to pass the provincial examination and then the metropolitan examination.

[41] *Nan-t'ung Chang Chi-chih hsien-sheng chuan-chi*, 3/25–29, contains a table listing the various examinations attended.

[42] "Notes of Ling-hsiao and I-shih," *loc. cit.*

[43] *Hsi-Chin yu-hsiang t'ung-jen tzu-shu hui-k'an, ts'e shang*, p. 13 b; Yang En-p'ei

CONTENT OF THE EXAMINATIONS AND ITS RELATION TO THE SELECTION OF OFFICIALS

Success in the examinations was then a major goal of the gentry. On this depended their advancement into higher gentry position and into officialdom. What did these examinations consist of and what were the studies with which the gentry were so constantly occupied? How effective were these examinations in selecting able officials?

The officially compiled *Ch'ing-ch'ao t'ung-chih* praised the system highly and claimed that it was the most efficient means of selecting officials. It stated:

> Examination as a means of selection to officialdom is truly a measure adapted to the need of the times. Our dynasty, in referring to ancient times to establish a system, gives equal importance to civil and military examinations. This way of treating the numerous scholars is truly most lenient and favorable. The devices to eliminate corruption and regulate fraudulence are also detailed and lucid. The ultimate aim is to obtain true talents for the use of the state. Our Emperor, succeeding and exalting the sages, treats the selection of talents as most important. In the literary arts, elegance and refinement is the aim. In military examination, familiarity with riding and shooting is important. From all these examinations the truly profound meaning of practical application is expected. How excellent. The abundance of talented officials and defenders of the state has surpassed that of the Three Dynasties.[44]

Obviously this was exaggerated praise and a theoretical justification of the system. The inaccuracy of the description can be revealed by studying the content of the examinations. The gulf between theory and practice is especially evident in the nineteenth century.

The Ch'ing examinations consisted always of three parts.[45] The examination subjects were mainly topics selected from the Confucian classics.[46]

said that at the age of 16 he began to participate in the *t'ung-shih*, became *sheng-yüan* at the age of 19 in 1880, became *ling-sheng* at the age of 32, and participated in the *sui* and *k'o* examinations until 1905 in order to keep his *ling-sheng* privilege of guaranteeing *t'ung-sheng*.

[44] *Ch'ing-ch'ao t'ung-chih*, 72/175. The book was compiled under imperial auspices, having been ordered in 1767. The period covered extends from the beginning of the Ch'ing dynasty to 1785.

[45] Wang Ch'ing-yün, *op. cit.*, 1/32 b–34 b. In 1663 eight-legged essay writing was discontinued and the examination contained only two parts. Immediately afterward, because of a memorial arguing that the sages' teachings were neglected because the students were not examined on the classics, the old way of examination was restored.

[46] Wang Hsien-ch'ien, *op. cit.*, 1/2 a, 6 a–b, 2/6 b. During K'ang-hsi times, examination questions on the classics were abolished and discussion questions were employed. But before long, the old system was restored. In the Ch'ien-lung period it was Shu Ho-te and Yang Shu-tseng and in Kuang-hsü 1 (1875) it was the grand secretary, Li, who suggested that examination questions on the classics be dropped in favor of discussion questions. Although the court did not adopt their suggestions, it did not reproach them. Ch'en K'ang-ch'i, *Lang-ch'ien erh-pi*, 15/6 a, points out that in Yung-cheng times, some suggested abolishing the essay writing on the Four Books. The Emperor asked Chang Wen-ho for his opinion; he replied that if it were abolished, nobody would read the

In the nineteenth century, the first part of the examinations required the writing of essays on questions based on the Four Books and the composing of poems. The second part consisted of questions on the Five Classics. The third part consisted of discussion questions.[47]

Before 1757, however, in addition to the writing of essays on the classics, the poetical composition and discussion questions, there had been the writing of memorials, verdicts, and essays on the court-supported Ch'eng-Chu school of Sung Neo-Confucianism. Although the emphasis in examinations was always on the Confucian classics, the mere existence of examination questions on memorials, verdicts, and Sung Neo-Confucianism at least displayed some practicality and toleration of ideological discussion. However, the writing of memorials and verdicts, subjects which were more related to the practical work of administration, was dropped from examinations in 1757. In 1793 the essays on Sung Neo-Confucianism were also dropped as if this subject needed no further discussion.[48]

Four Books and discuss the principles of righteousness and reason. The proposal was dropped. Ch'en commented that before and during the Sung and Yüan dynasties, there was no such essay examination, but many studied the Four Books and discussed the principles of righteousness and reason.

[47] E.g., Chang Chung-ju, *Ch'ing-tai k'o-chü chih-tu*, p. 21, says that in the provincial examination, the first part was traditionally held on the 9th day of the 8th month and consisted of one question on *The Analects*, one on *The Doctrine of the Mean*, one on *Mencius*, and lastly the composition of an original poem. The 12th day was given to the second part and included questions on the Five Classics, namely, *The Book of Changes*, *The Book of History*, *The Book of Odes*, *The Spring and Autumn Annals*, and *The Book of Rites*. On the 15th day, the last section included five discussion questions.

[48] The change in examination subjects is recorded in detail in Wang Ch'ing-yün, *op. cit.*, 1/32 b–34 b. At the beginning of the Ch'ing dynasty, following the Ming system, the first part of the examination consisted of three essays, the topics of which were quoted from the Four Books, and four essays on classical subjects. The second part consisted of one theme, one memorial, and five verdicts. The third part consisted of five discussion questions. In 1658 and thereafter the topics from the Four Books were personally selected by the Emperor for the metropolitan examination. From 1685 on, this practice was also applied to provincial examinations, and the subject for the memorial was also imperially decided. Beginning in 1756, interpretation of the classics became questions of the second part. In the metropolitan examinations, the second part still retained the problem of memorial composition. In provincial examinations, the memorial, the theme, and the verdicts were no longer required. Shortly afterwards, poetical composition superseded the drafting of a memorial, and to the first section was added an essay on Sung Neo-Confucianism. Several edicts of the time mentioned that the style should be refined and elegant. One edict states that questions on the Four Books would be considered the most important, because the best part of the classics was covered by the Four Books. In 1782 the examination on poetry writing was moved to the first part, and that on Neo-Confucianism to the second part. In 1787 court officials all agreed that the Five Classics should be added, one topic to be selected from each. In 1793 the examination question on Neo-Confucianism was dropped. This system, Wang says, continued until his time. Wang Hsien-ch'ien, *op. cit.*, 1/3 b, says that in early Ch'ing there were examination questions on Sung Neo-Confucianism, memorials, and verdicts. In 1757 questions on memorial and verdict composition were abolished, and examination on poetical ability was adopted. In late Ch'ien-lung the examination question on Neo-Confucianism was abolished. Cf. also Ch'eng K'ang-ch'i, *Lang-ch'ien chi-wen*, 6/1.

The part of the examinations consisting of discussion questions also underwent important changes over a period of time. In 1699, for instance, the discussion questions had still covered current problems on civil administration and river works.[49] This indicates that although the K'ang-hsi emperor intended to suppress opposition to the Manchu rule over China by promoting the study of Sung Neo-Confucianism and the examination writings on Confucian classics, and by ordering the compiling and editing of authorized books and the burning of "unworthy" books, he still permitted some discussion of current political and economic problems relating to the welfare of the country. But after the late eighteenth century the discussion questions turned toward philological issues[50] and the candidates were discouraged from discussing current affairs.[51]

The nineteenth century thus saw the complete domination of the Confucian classics in the examination questions. Furthermore, form rather than content was stressed in the writing of the examination papers. They were bound by many regulations and had to follow definite schemes of presentation.[52] Even the length of the essay was defined.[53] The candidates adhered strictly to these regulations since the examiners generally paid attention only to

[49] *Shih-lu,* Sheng-tsu, 198/18. The question reads: "Various measures have been carried out to let the people rest, but the favor probably has not been able to reach downward. Imperial inspection tours have been conducted often, but the suffering [of the people] may have been blocked from reaching the above. The incorrupt are rewarded and the avaricious punished, but the clerks in the yamens are still mostly wicked. Grain is highly valued and farmers are treated with importance, but the families have not yet been elevated to opulence. Is it that the traditional malpractices are difficult to get rid of, or is it that the officials have not effectively carried out the measures? Now, desiring that the high officials observe their status and that the low ones be incorrupt, that the people be peaceful and the products plentiful, so that a rule of sincerity and greatness shall be gradually attained, what is the appropriate method?

"As regards the two rivers of Huai and Huang, they are related with people's livelihood and transportation. I, the Emperor, have inspected them several times and given instructions, but the river-works officials are lazy and irresponsible, causing the delay of the work and the impossibility of expecting a minimum accomplishment. What way will make the high and low officials of the river works perform their duties wholeheartedly, dredging or dike-building appropriately, and send in an early report of accomplishment, so that the tribute rice boats will not be delayed and the people's dwellings will not be unsettled, thus relieving me of deep worry?"

[50] Wang Hsien-ch'ien, *op. cit.*, 1/3 b.

[51] There were regulations forbidding the criticism of high officials and policy-makers at any occasion other than in the examinations. Offenders were subject to execution, their family members became slaves, and their property was confiscated. See Wu Yung-kuang, *op. cit.*, 20/4 b. In *Shih-li,* 383/8 b, an edict of 1856 condemned the attempt of a *sheng-yüan* to present proposals on current affairs to the Emperor. Although there was no disagreeable word in his proposals, he was ordered to be punished severely.

[52] Cf. "Notes of Ling-hsiao and I-shih," *Kuo-wen chou-pao, chüan* 6, No. 43, Nov. 3, 1929, p. 1; also *chüan* 7, No. 24, June 23, 1930.

[53] Wang Ch'ing-yün, *loc. cit.*, points out that, in 1778, Grand Secretary Yü Min-chung memorialized that the practice of composing long essays was increasing. Therefore, the essay was limited to 700 words. In fact, an earlier regulation existed which set the limit at 550, and in K'ang-hsi times, regulations allowed 650 words.

form.[54] Other rigid rules were also imposed. Characters in imperial names could not be used. Many terms required the beginning of a new line in format to show respect. Offenders who broke these latter rules not only were failed but were not allowed to participate in the next two or three examinations.[55]

Prosody was also stressed. One provincial director-of-studies said that he would not consider examination papers in which rhyme patterns were neglected or improperly used. As he put it, such compositions bore the "smell of village mediocrity." [56] It has also been said that dexterity in poetical composition might not enable one to pass the provincial and metropolitan examinations, but the lack of skill might well hamper success.[57] Calligraphy was also very important, especially in the palace examinations, and could well affect a candidate's future official career.[58]

[54] Cf. "Notes of Ling-hsiao and I-shih," *loc. cit.*

[55] Wu Yung-kuang, *op. cit.*, 4/6 a, 8 a–b, says that when terms or references to the various sages, the state altar, the imperial clan temple, or the Emperor had to be used, the candidate had to follow a set form. If the candidate made a mistake in technique such as failing to begin a new line, or setting certain terms down and then crossing them out, or directly using the names of past and present emperors, or of Confucius, the candidate would be punished by being excluded from three examinations (i.e., for about a decade). If the whole essay was an exact copy of an essay written by former candidates, if the topic was mistakenly omitted, or if certain other rules were broken, the candidate would be denied the right to take the next two examinations.

[56] Lung Ch'i-jui, *op. cit.*, *wen-pi-chi*, *shang*, pp. 11 b–12 b. As provincial director-of-studies he issued a notification saying that the results of this [*yüan*] examination showed that bad syntax was frequent in examination papers, and some papers paid no attention to the rhyming of phrases. Such writing, even if it were good otherwise, would not be considered. He also said that some who did fairly well in essay composition but misused one or two words in poetical expression stood on the margin of admission to *sheng-yüan*. In the provincial examination and in the *k'o-shih*, which he was soon to supervise, if attention was still not paid to rhyme patterns, failure would be certain. For examples of various types of examination papers, see Chang Chung-ju, *Ch'ing-tai k'ao-shih chih-tu*.

[57] "Notes of Ling-hsiao and I-shih," *Kuo-wen chou-pao*, *chüan* 7, No. 9, March 10, 1930, pp. 1–2. Here we see that those who were preparing for examinations had to be skilful in poetic composition. In the provincial and metropolitan examinations, if the form and rhyming of the poem were faulty, even if the essay was good, the candidate was failed. *Ibid.*, *chüan* 7, No. 30, August 4, 1930, p. 2, points out that the first part of the provincial and metropolitan examinations, which was on the Four Books and poetical composition, was most important in the eyes of the examiners; if the candidates failed in the first part, they failed in the whole examination, no matter how well they did in the rest. This was also pointed out in early Ch'ing by Ku Yen-wu in *Jih-chih-lu*, 16/15 a. *Kuang-chou fu-chih*, 5/23 a, an edict of 1872, based on Censor Wu Feng-tsao's memorial, tried to warn that all three parts of the examination should be emphasized.

[58] Wang Ch'ing-yün, *op. cit.*, 1/40 a. Wang points out that success in the palace examination bore directly on appointment to office. The examiners on this occasion usually stressed the importance of good calligraphy. If the paper conformed with all restrictions and was in a good script, it was highly recommended. If the calligraphy was given the third grade, while the essay itself received the highest grade, the grades would be averaged and the paper considered medium. Ch'en K'ang-ch'i, *Lang-ch'ien erh-pi*, 11/12 b, says that, in the late nineteenth century, calligraphy was considered the most important point in the grading of palace examination papers while the content of the essay was neglected. Hsüeh Fu-ch'eng, *Yung-an-ch'üan-chi*, *wen-wai-pien*, 1/5 a–b,

Such emphasis in the examinations greatly affected the attitude of the people toward study. Thus it was said:

> Since the full flower of the institution of the examination system, people look forward to speedy success. If one reaches the age of fifteen and has not yet participated in the examinations, his father and elder brothers consider him unworthy. If one reaches the age of twenty and is still unable to join the government district school, the village people despise him. Without concluding the study of the classics, one has to work hard on the practice of examination compositions. When one is able to compose, the classics are then bound to the high shelf. The teachers will not teach them. The students will not learn them. At this time, not only are there no scholars who are profound in the study of the classics and enlightened in applying them to practical use, but it is even hard to find one who understands the commentaries and construction of the classics.[59]

This description was written in the early nineteenth century. In the latter part of the century, the tendency away from scholarship and toward examination writing as a technique became even more pronounced. As pointed out by one writer, from Tao-kuang and Hsien-feng onward, scholars took the acquiring of examination degrees as their sole aim. They tried to write in the manner that they thought the examiners would appreciate. They did not study the classics or the works of early scholars, but only the works of those who had passed in the recent examinations, so as to meet the standards of the examiners of the time.[60]

Indeed, as Wang Hsien-ch'ien also points out, the examination system, as it developed in the late nineteenth century, had utterly changed the nature of study among scholars. In his father's words, "When I was learning to write essays, the teachers still taught the sages' teachings. Your teachers only

states that if the candidate qualified in the content of his examination paper but failed to meet the standards for calligraphy, he would at most be appointed to a magistrateship. The positions considered very important, such as *han-lin*, censors, and secretaries of the Grand Secretariat and the Grand Council, were given to those with talent for calligraphy. In "Notes of Ling-hsiao and I-shih," *Kuo-wen chou-pao*, *chüan* 6, No. 37, September 22, 1929, p. 1, it is pointed out that in provincial and metropolitan examinations, calligraphy was not important since the papers were recopied before being sent to the examiner. After 1902 recopying was not required. Examples are given of those who then succeeded in the examinations because of good calligraphy.

[59] Ch'en Tung-yüan, *op. cit.*, 24/421, quoted from Tai Chün-heng, "T'ung-hsiang shu-yüan ssu-i" in *Ch'iu-shih-chai-wen-ts'un.* For information on Tai Chün-heng (1814–1855) see *Hsü-pei-chuan-chi*, *chüan* 79.

[60] Chang Chung-ju, *Ch'ing-tai k'ao-shih chih-tu*, p. 1 a–b, describes that at first the youths studied the thirteen classics before learning to write examination papers. Also they read the early writings as of T'ang and Sung, including Han, Liu, Ou-yang and Su's works. In preparing for poetical composition, one began with reading poems of T'ang and Sung, then those by famous Ch'ing poets, to build a good foundation before reading poems written by high officials of literary fame in the contemporary period. All these practices changed since Tao-kuang and Hsien-feng. Cf. examples given earlier which show that some still studied the classics in late Ch'ing. But the emphasis certainly had changed.

pay attention to examination paper writing. I am afraid of the change of worldly ways." [61]

Thus, the successful candidates had learned compliance with rigid form and restriction, rhyme and phraseology in composition, elegant poetical expression, and good calligraphy. How this training prepared men for the practical work of government is difficult to see.[62] How much did the study of books on ancient moral codes, to which much time and energy was devoted, contribute to the administration of state affairs? How could competent officials be selected through this system?

One critic, writing in the late nineteenth century, stated that the system merely "drove several hundred thousands to several millions of scholars to exhaust their physical and mental energy in the formalized writings, without studying the art of regulating the world or the cases in history." [63]

He went on to say that even if various types of malpractices in the examinations could be wiped out, only one-tenth of the successful candidates were really able to write, and among these only one-tenth really were virtuous and had a sound learning. In other words, this writer would say that, excluding the element of corruption and malpractices, only one out of a hundred successful candidates was possibly a good choice. He concluded by favoring a recommendation system rather than the examination system.

A review of some discussions by contemporary writers on the efficiency of officials selected through the examination system as compared with those who gained official position through purchase might throw further light on the effectiveness of the examination system. An influential *chü-jen*, writing during the late Taiping period, describes the two groups as follows:

[61] Wang Hsien-ch'ien, *op. cit.*, 3/25 a. This was written in early Kuang-hsü. Wang's father had said these words twenty years earlier, in the Hsien-feng period. Some examinees even copied whole essays written by previous candidates. However, if they then ranked too high, they were afraid of being detected and punished. "Notes of Ling-hsiao and I-shih," *Kuo-wen chou-pao, chüan* 7, No. 21, June 2, 1930, p. 1 a, relates that in the provincial examination of 1870 in Shun-t'ien, the first among the successful candidates, Li Huang-lun, had copied an old essay on classics in the second part of the examination. He was afraid of punishment and requested that his new *chü-jen* degree be taken away. It also points out that in Ch'en K'ang-ch'i, *Lang-ch'ien chi-wen*, it is recorded that in one year among the eighteen men who were listed at the top of the eighteen provincial examinations, four asked to be deprived of their degrees because they had copied old essays. This practice of copying old essays existed even in the T'ang dynasty. See memorial of Hsüeh Teng in *Chiu-T'ang-shu*, 101/2 b–3 a; *Hsin-T'ang-shu*, 112/7 a.

[62] The usefulness of questions on poetry in determining the ability of candidates was questioned in the T'ang dynasty. See the first of the ten weaknesses in the examination system as described by Chao K'uang in *T'ung-tien*, 17/97. In Sung times, Feng Cheng and Wang Tan discussed the examination system before the Emperor. Feng requested that more emphasis be given discussion questions and that poetical composition have less emphasis. The Emperor said, "That which can reveal talent is the discussion essay." See *Sung-shih*, 285/11 a.

[63] Hsüeh Fu-ch'eng, *Yung-an ch'üan-chi, wen-wai-pien*, 1/1 a and 3 b ff.

The uselessness of officials selected through examination is the same as those selected through other routes. But they are even more inefficient since they do not understand the world situation while they are more arrogant and proud. For example, in the contribution bureau of Hsi-hsien, Anhwei, there are forty to fifty commissioners, each receiving administrative expenses of thirty to forty dollars monthly. They need eight dishes for their meals. When they go to collect from a contributor, they demand travelling expenses of thirty dollars and take along twenty militiamen who require another thirty dollars, all simply to raise the prestige of such men as Chang Fei.[64] They do not bring much to the contribution bureau; they spend extravagantly and thus burden the people, bringing no fruitful results by their actions.[65]

An official, himself a product of the examination system, made this comment:

The poor administration of *chou* and *hsien* is not all the fault of the magistrate. Inappropriate selection, insufficient emphasis on the importance of the post, and unfair treatment are all causes. There are four routes of origin [of magistrates], namely: *chin-shih*; *chü-jen* and *kung-sheng*; through purchase; and from assistants. The first two are engrossed in their studies, concerned with memorization and aiming at examination. Once in the post, the pedants merely lower their heads and listen to personal assistants and clerks. Even the clever and talented need long training to become acquainted with their work. But when one is finally able to employ acquired experience, the order of transfer has arrived. As for those selected through purchase, the reason they purchase office is to get more money. Among the assistants, many come from purchase and from clerks who have no sense of shame but who flatter their superiors and oppress the people.[66]

These arguments cast doubt on the effectiveness of the examination system in selecting able administrators for civil posts. The effectiveness of the military examinations in selecting competent officers is even more doubtful. The military examinations were tests of the archer's skill on horse and afoot, skill with the sword, the ability to pull the heavy bow, lifting of stones, and written reproduction from memory of part of the Military Classic.[67] Certainly

[64] Chang Fei began his career in the Han-lin Academy. In his *Chang Wen-i-kung tsou-kao*, 1/28 b ff., 2/27 ff., 7/27 ff., 8/28 ff., memorials presented in 1858, 1859, and 1860 show that he collected more than a million taels through contributions between 1855 and 1860. The charges made by Wang should probably be treated with some reservations.

[65] Wang Shih-to, *Wang Hui-weng i-ping jih-chi*, 3/10 b.

[66] Sun Ting-ch'en, "On Administration," in *Huang-ch'ao chin-shih-wen-hsü-pien*, compiled by Sheng K'ang, 10/3 b–4 b. Also Sun's "Pen-t'ang ch'u-lun" in *Ts'ang-lang ch'u-chi*, 1/12 a–14 b. Sun also points out that five or six officials were assigned to supervise the magistrates and thus restrain their actions. Once one began his official career as a magistrate, he was left in the provinces; very few ever rose to ministership. Allowances for magistrates were in some cases over 1,000 taels, but they had to take care of public funds overappropriated by former magistrates and unreportable expenditures.

[67] Chang Chung-ju, *Ch'ing-tai k'o-chü chih-tu*, p. 25, also relates that the chief examiners for the Shun-t'ien *hsiang-shih*, according to regulations, would be two members of the Han-lin Academy and four other court officials. In the provinces, the governors-general and governors were the supervising chief examiners, assisted by provincial officials

this type of examination could not reveal talents for military strategy or effective leadership. When the Western weapons were introduced, these examinations were even more useless.[68]

That the court itself did not give serious consideration to the candidates in the military examination and that the subjects in these examinations were not related to practicality is shown in the following memorial:

> In civil administration, those selected by examination are considered as those who come through the regular route. But in considering promotions in the military administration, those selected by examination are to be put after those who began their career in the rank and file or have risen because of military merit. ... The knowledge of military affairs among the former group can not at all be compared with those from among the rank and file. Their spirit of bravery and ability to bear hardship can not at all be compared with those who rise because of military merit. The reason is that what they learn is not of practical use.[69]

The ineffectiveness of the whole examination system in selecting able men is well summarized in the words of Lung Ch'i-jui, who was a member of the upper gentry and had on several occasions served as examiner:

> Fishermen in spreading nets in the rivers and lakes aim to catch fish; they catch fish because of the nets. ... If the nets are thrown away and the fishermen ordered to procure fish... even the most stupid would know it impossible. However, if one, relying on the nets, thinks he catches all the fish, this again is absurd. ... There are many talents in the world. If I devise various means of seeking them, they cannot escape from me. Today many such men are missed. Some would say that men

who were *chin-shih* or *chü-jen*. In the field examinations, the provincial commanders-in-chief and brigade-generals assisted them. The two chief examiners of the military metropolitan examinations were appointed from among the heads of the Grand Secretariat, the Board, the Censorate, the Han-lin Academy, and the Imperial Supervisorate of Instruction. Four other examiners were from the members of the Grand Secretariat, the Censorate, and the Boards. The control of military examinations was thus in the hands of civil officials. This is another expression of the greater importance of civil officials, despite entries in official documents stating that the civil and military examinations were of equal importance. *Ch'ing-ch'ao t'ung-chih*, 72/7175. "Notes of Ling-hsiao and I-shih," *Kuo-wen chou-pao*, *chüan* 6, No. 41, Oct. 20, 1929, pp. 1 and 2, also points out that from the lowest examinations to the highest, the civil officials were in charge of military examinations.

68 There were firearms of native manufacture, but they were not used in examinations.

69 Shen Pao-chen, "A Note Requesting the Abolition of the Military Examinations," *Huang-ch'ao chin-shih-wen-hsü-pien*, compiled by Ke Shih-chün, 54/4 b, written in 1878, when Shen was governor-general of Liang-Chiang. Shen also said of those selected by military examination, that the ones who stayed in the camps usually conducted themselves satisfactorily but those residing at home frequently relied upon their military dress and insignia to oppress the villagers. In name they were *shih*; in reality they were loafers. According to Shen, it was mostly the military rather than the civil *sheng-yüan* who violated the regulations on the horizontal stone tablet and were marked as bad. Hummel, *op. cit.*, II, p. 644, also mentions that Shen presented such a memorial and that it was not approved. "Notes of Ling-hsiao and I-shih," *loc. cit.*, also points out that those selected by military examination were not nobler than those who came up from the rank and file. More of those who held high posts such as provincial commanders-in-chief and brigade-generals were from the rank and file. No such term as "through the regular route" existed in the military administration.

today are different from those of ancient times. Talking again of public recommendation,[70] cheating would prevail. If we resume the system of *chung-cheng chiu-p'in*,[71] personal affection would operate. If we sought everywhere, there would be those with false reputation. Out of necessity, therefore, we examine them on poetry, the classics, and so on. The number of scholars and that of farmers, artisans, and merchants [is made] a ratio. However worldly affairs decline, there are always scholars. However poor in quality are the scholars, there are always examinations. It becomes as regular as the coming and going of winter and summer, the high and low of hill and marsh, the rich or the poor, and the long lives or the short lives of men. Everything is so definite, and the scholars' entry into officialdom becomes so ordinary that people regard them only lightly. They also treat themselves lightly. Gather the men in the market and pick an outstanding one; get hold of a man on the street and give him office; his quality of loyalty and trustworthiness, his ability to observe and discern would probably equal the scholars' and even surpass them. What he lacks is the unimportant training in literature, rhyming, and ceremonial observation. But literature, rhyming, and ceremonial observation do not help one in administration, and the administrators probably are not good at it either. What is the difference between such an administrator and a man in the market or a man on the street? Some still say that some outstanding and extraordinary talents have grown out of the system. *However, it is not that the examination system can uncover extraordinary talent, but that extraordinary talent sometimes emerges out of the examination system.*[72]

THE SO-CALLED "SPIRIT OF EQUALITY" IN THE EXAMINATION SYSTEM

It has been said that the examination system lasted for more than a thousand years because of its "spirit of equality." [73] In theory, the way was open for any commoner to rise to gentry status and official position. The examination system did indeed make possible a certain "equality of

[70] This refers to the Three Dynasties and the Han system of selecting officials, termed *ch'a-chü, kung-chü,* or *p'i-chü.* This paper cannot take up the history of the examination system; for details see Ma Tuan-lin, *Wen-hsien t'ung-k'ao, chüan* 13, also *T'ung-tien, chüan* 13. The examination system, as such, was begun in the T'ang dynasty, according to Teng Ssu-yu, "A Study Into the Origin of the Chinese Examination System," *Shih-hsüeh nien-pao, chüan* 2, No. 1, Sept., 1934, pp. 275–281, although examinations were held as early as the reign of Emperor Wu of the Han dynasty. Cf. also Chu Hsieh, "The Chinese Examination System," *Tung-fang tsa-chih, chüan* 24, No. 20, Oct. 25, 1927.

[71] This was the method of selecting officials during the Six Dynasties. It was initiated by Ch'en Ch'ün of the Wei dynasty. According to this method, certain "talented and virtuous" ministers and other high officials were designated as *chung-cheng.* To the *chung-cheng* was delegated the power to select officials from the various provinces, prefectures, and districts and to differentiate these officials into nine ranks. See *Wen-hsien t'ung-k'ao,* 2/266–67. However, it developed that the *chung-cheng* considered only the family background rather than the actual ability of a person. Thus the saying that "In the upper ranks, there were none from poor families and in the lower ranks there were none from the influential families." See also Yang Yün-ju, *Chiu-p'in chung-cheng yü liu-ch'ao men-fa.*

[72] Lung Ch'i-jui, *op. cit.,* 1/2 a–3 b. Lung concluded that in his time the method of the Three Dynasties could not be used, nor that of Wei and Chin. The examination system could not be abolished, but selection should be strict.

[73] E.g., Jen Shih-hsien, *Chung-kuo chiao-yü szu-hsiang-shih, ts'e shang,* p. 160.

opportunity," but the advantages were heavily in favor of those who had wealth and influence.

One social group was entirely excluded. Members of families of slaves, servants, prostitutes, entertainers, lictors, and others classified among the "mean people" [74] were forbidden to participate in the examinations.

Many exceptions to the principle of equality can also be seen within the examination system. For instance, *chü-jen* degrees or official positions were sometimes granted to sons or grandsons of high officials, to those who detected and reported rebellious activities, or to those who contributed to the military fund or were active in relief work.[75] Some could thus obtain degree or office through imperial favor without having to compete in the examinations.

The rich had a special advantage in entering the gentry. They could purchase the title of *li-chien-sheng* or *li-kung-sheng* [76] and thus skip the *t'ung-shih*, the examination for admitting *sheng-yüan*. They could then

[74] Wu Yung-kuang, *op. cit.*, 2/1 a, 2 a–3 a, says that the "four people" (literati, farmers, artisans, and merchants) were of good descent, and that slaves, servants, prostitutes, entertainers, and lictors were of mean origin. The *yüeh-hu*, or "entertainer families" of Shansi and Shensi, the *kai-hu*, "beggar families" of Chiang-nan, the *to-min*, or "degenerated people" of Chekiang were all, one after another, exempted from the permanent classification of "mean people" in 1723, 1729, and 1730. If it was reported officially that they had changed the nature of their employment, and if after four generations none of their relatives were employed in "mean" jobs, they would be permitted to participate in examinations and become officials. The *tan-hu* or "boat people" of Kwangtung and the *yü-hu* or "fishermen families" of Chekiang were also thus treated. Those serving in the yamen as treasury keepers, granary keepers and irregular police were listed among the commoners. The lictors, cavalry police, jailers, gatekeepers, coroners, grain collectors, police, and runners were all classified as "mean people." Bond servants were treated the same as slaves. Slaves freed by their masters were expected to report to local officials, who would in turn report to the Board of Revenue. There a record was made, and after three generations their heirs could participate in examinations along with commoners; but if they became court officials, they could not become department heads; as provincial officials they could not reach the 3rd rank. In *Yin-hsien-chih*, 2/9 a–b, a quotation from the *To-min wei-pien* and *Pi-chou-hsi sheng-yü* is used to describe the *to-min*. Cf. *Kuang-chou fu-chih*, 2/24 b–25 a for a description of the *tan-hu*.

[75] Chang Chung-ju, *Ch'ing tai k'o-chü chih-tu*, pp. 58–61. Also in Wu Yung-kuang, *op. cit.*, 5/10 a–16 b, there are many examples of imperially bestowed *chü-jen* and *chin-shih* degrees, granted to heirs of meritorious officials and to those who rendered services to the empire between 1729 and 1812. Wang Ch'ing-yün, *op. cit.*, 1/36 a, says that the son of Grand Secretary Chiang T'ing-hsi and twelve others were granted *chü-jen* degrees in 1729. Ch'en K'ang-ch'i, *Lang-ch'ien erh-pi*, 7/18 a-b says, however, that before the metropolitan examination of 1730 the Emperor ordered that, among the sons of high officials who participated but failed in the provincial examinations of 1727, twelve should be permitted to participate in the metropolitan examination. In the nineteenth century the practice continued. For instance, Ch'ien Ting-ming, *op. cit.*, pp. 1–2, describes that upon the death of the Honan governor, Ch'ien Ting-ming, the Emperor promoted one son, who was already an official, and granted to another son, a *sheng-yüan*, the degree of *chü-jen*.

[76] There were six kinds of *kung-sheng*. The *li-kung-sheng* had obtained their titles through purchase—the "irregular" route, and the other five were "regular" *kung-sheng*. There were four kinds of *chien-sheng*; the *li-chien-sheng* had purchased their titles. For details see Part One.

directly participate in the provincial examinations leading to the *chü-jen* degree.

Special favor was shown to the salt merchants by the separate merchant quotas in both the *t'ung-shih* and the provincial examinations. An edict stated that the government's purpose in establishing such separate quotas was to enable merchants and their heirs, who did business in places away from their native provinces, to participate in the examinations without having to return home.[77] However, the quota was set so that one out of ten succeeded in the *t'ung-shih*[78] and one out of fifty in the provincial examinations.[79] They therefore had a much better chance to succeed than other commoners had.[80]

The provincial examinations also gave distinct advantage to the sons and brothers of high officials. Their papers were separated from the rest and marked as "official examination papers," and a separate quota was assigned to them.[81] This gave them a very good chance to succeed.[82] This procedure

[77] *Hsüeh-cheng*, 85/4 b–6 b; *Shih-li*, 381/3 b–4 b, edict of 1778.

[78] *Hsüeh-cheng*, 85/4 a, edicts of 1776; pp. 7 b–8 a, edicts of 1778; pp. 10 a–15 b, edicts of 1779.

[79] *Ibid.*, 85/5 b; *K'o-ch'ang*, 21/17 b–18 b.

[80] *Ibid.*, a memorial of 1863 by Ting Pao-chen, governor of Shantung, requesting that the merchant quota be revised and changed from its traditional ratio of 1 successful candidate out of 50 to a ratio of 1 out of 30 or 35, was rejected. It was pointed out that in that province the total participants in the *hsiang-shih* had been shortly before reported as 12,900. The quota of *chü-jen* for that province was only 69, a ratio of 1 successful candidate out of 180 to 190. It was therefore considered that (salt) merchants were already treated leniently.

[81] *Ibid.*, 25/1 a. The regulation designated the officials whose relatives were to receive such special consideration. They were: at the court, among Manchu and Chinese civil officials, those who were heads of departments and above, members of the Han-lin Academy, the Imperial Supervisorate of Instruction, the Censorate; among the military officers, deputy lieutenant-generals and above; in the provinces, those who were financial and judicial commissioners and above among the civil officials, and those who were lieutenant-generals, brigade-generals, and above among the military officers. Persons related to the above-mentioned officials as their sons, grandsons, great-grandsons, elder and younger brothers of the same parents, and sons of their elder and younger brothers of the same parents, were to have their examination papers classified as "official examination papers," *kuan-chüan*. One point of interest is that those in the Han-lin Academy, whether high or low in rank, had this privilege. Cf. Sun Ting-ch'eng, *loc. cit.*, which points out that in the classification into *kuan-chüan* in the provincial examinations, sons and relatives of those as low as *shu-chi-shih* or *han-lin* bachelors (ranked 7 b) were classified together with sons and relatives of the other high officials. For example, see *K'o-ch'ang*, 25/7 b–8 b.

[82] *K'o-ch'ang*, 21/1 a–b, stated that the quota for "official examination papers" in late Ch'ing was as follows: Manchu and Mongol bannermen, 6; Chinese bannermen, 1; *pei-tzu*, 4; *nan-min*, 2; *pei-min*, 1; *chung-min*, 1; Kiangsu, 4; Anhwei, 2; Chekiang, 6; Kiangsi, 5; Fukien, 4; Shantung, 3; Shansi, 3; Honan, 3; Hunan, 2; Hupeh, 2; Kwangtung, 2; Szechwan, 2; Yunnan, 2; Shensi, 1; Kansu, 1; Kwangsi, 1; Kweichow, 1. For Manchu, Mongol, and Chinese banner "official examination papers," 1 shall be successful out of 10; for *nan-pei* and *chung-min*, 1 out of 15; for *pei-tzu* (*sheng-yüan* of Chihli), Kiangsu, Anhwei, Chekiang, Kiangsi, Hunan, Hupeh, Fukien, 1 out of 20; for Shantung, Shansi, Honan, Kwangtung, Shensi, Kansu, and Szechwan, 1 out of 15; for Kwangsi, Yunnan, and Kweichow, 1 out of 10. The maximum to be admitted to *chü-jen* was the quota set in the above. Actually, however, the regulations were not held to. The gover-

of handling "official examination papers" separately was introduced in 1700. The original purpose was to give poor scholars a better chance, since the results of several earlier examinations had shown that the successful candidates were mostly sons and brothers of high officials.[83] But the practice furthered discrimination instead of correcting it. In setting the quotas, the ministers favored their sons and relatives and assigned them a higher quota.[84] The total quota for each province was fixed. Therefore, the more places that were assigned to the sons of officials, the fewer were the openings available to other candidates. Thus the original intention of helping the poorer scholars became a means for officials' sons and brothers to gain easy admission.[85]

When the papers were first checked, the coexaminers almost always recommended all the "official examination papers" to the chief examiners,[86] while a large proportion of the other papers were eliminated in the first round. Then, as the quota for these "official examination papers" was comparatively high, the participants who qualified under this category had very good chance of success.[87] Many of them could first

nors and examiners would request increases in quota if there were a large number of participants. But when there were few participants, they still filled the quota without reference to the ratio. In 1858 the Chekiang governor, Hu Hsing-jen, was aggressive enough to request that because the quota for "official examination papers" was not sufficient, one of the five places recently added to the quota in consideration of contributions to the military fund be assigned to the "official examination papers." When the Emperor ordered the Board of Rites to investigate, it was revealed that there were only 25 participants under this category. According to regulation, only one could be admitted, but the chief examiner, Pao-yün, had already filled the quota (of 6 according to the above). In this example approximately 1 out of 4 candidates succeeded, as compared with the ratios of 1 out of 50 among the salt merchants and 1 out of over 100 among others. This is why some who were already in the salt merchant category still wanted to be shifted to the official quota. *K'o-ch'ang*, 25/7 b–8 b, relates that Hsü Yü-pei, nephew of *han-lin* compiler Hsü Wen-kuang, a native of Anhwei, and Wang Shao-hsien, nephew of *han-lin* bachelor Wang Ying-yü, also a native of Anhwei, followed their fathers to the salt-selling district of Chekiang and became *sheng-yüan* under the merchant quota. They requested the Emperor to permit them to return to Anhwei and be classified under the "official examination papers," but their request was refused.

[83] *Ibid.*, 25/4 a.

[84] *Ibid.*, 21/4 b–6 b.

[85] *Ibid.* There were other categories in provincial examinations. For instance in Shantung, there was the *erh-tzu-hao*, a special quota for descendants of Confucius, Mencius, Tsengtzu, and Yentzu. *Ibid.*, 25/17 b–18 a, in 1831 the son of Kung Chao-ch'ien, financial commissioner of Kweichow, participated in the provincial examination at Shantung. The Emperor was asked whether Kung's son should be classified *erh-tzu-hao* or *kuan-chüan.* He was classified as *erh-tzu-hao.*

[86] Ch'en K'ang-ch'i, *Lang-ch'ien erh-pi*, 6/1 a–b; the example is from late Ch'ing. This was done despite imperial instructions against it. *K'o-ch'ang*, 25/10 b–11 a; in 1767 it was stressed that only good *kuan-chüan* should be recommended. If there were no good papers, the category should be left vacant. The practice had been to recommend all *kuan-chüan* without reference to the quality of their papers.

[87] *K'o-ch'ang*, 25/11 b, shows that in 1741 the quota for the "official examination papers" was set up in Kwangsi following the example in Kweichow. Of the total quota of 50 for the province, 5 were to be reserved for "official examination papers"; the number of participants under that category was only 10. In this extreme case, one out of two candidates in this category would succeed.

purchase *kung-sheng* or *chien-sheng* and then easily pass the provincial examination.[88]

With all these advantages leading sons and brothers of high officials to the degree of *chü-jen*, the high officials could still exert influence and pressure in the metropolitan examinations. After all, the examiners were their colleagues. Such meddling in examinations was especially common in the nineteenth century. It was said that "since Chia-ch'ing and Tao-kuang, the heirs of high officials looked upon the examinations as their personal property."[89]

In addition, the bribery and corruption that had always existed in the examinations increased during the nineteenth century. All these factors made for inequality within the examination system.

However, the greatest inequality of all was in the preparation for examinations. The poor simply could not afford to spend many years studying for examinations. There was no public education system. Students preparing for *sheng-yüan* examinations were educated by private tutors or teachers conducting small schools.[90] There were, of course, the *i-hsüeh*, charity schools maintained by the local gentry. In some localities, these schools were quite numerous.[91] However, there is no evidence to show that such schools produced many scholars who participated in and passed the examinations.[92] Most of the poor families needed their sons' help on the

[88] For instance, in *K'o-ch'ang*, 25/28 a, in 1727, the Kwangtung governor, Ch'ang Lai, memorialized that among the "official examination papers," half were from the *kung-sheng* and *chien-sheng* who had all purchased the titles and received the *chü-jen* degree quite easily. He requested that "official examination papers" should include only those who were originally *ling-sheng*, *tseng-sheng*, *fu-sheng*. If they had participated in the purchase system as commoners, they should be classified with the *min-chüan*. The Emperor rejected this suggestion on the ground that such candidates would further occupy the quota of *min-chüan* and such a procedure would be contrary to the original purpose of "sympathizing with the poor." In Chang Chung-ju, *Ch'ing-tai k'ao-shih chih-tu*, p. 28, and also in Ch'en Tung-yüan, *op. cit.*, 23/389–90, there is a quotation from "A Poem on the Chekiang Provincial Examination," written by Miu Ken of Jen-ho, Chekiang, in 1816, collected in *Wen-chang yu-hsi*, Vol. 2, in which he contrasts the candidates who were sons and brothers of high officials to the educational officials. He says that, "The servants and followers of these candidates [*kuan-sheng*] were as fierce as tigers, and the clothing and headgear of the educational officials were as old as cattle."

[89] Ch'en K'ang-ch'i, *Lang-ch'ien chi-wen*, 1/5 b–6 b.

[90] For a description of private schools in the Ch'ing dynasty, see Ch'en Tung-yüan, *op. cit.*, 25/425–43.

[91] In *P'u-an chih-li-t'ing chih*, 7/1 a-2 a, it is described that there were six such charity schools in the city and towns in P'u-an and thirty-four in the various villages. Some of these schools were established by officials and supported by means of the granary, and some were established and maintained by the local gentry.

[92] There are occasional mentions of successful candidates who had been educated in this way. For instance, in *Lu-lung hsien-chih*, 21/2 b, it is said that the *i-hsüeh* there produced more than 20 *sheng-yüan*. In *Kansu hsin-t'ung-chih*, 66/73 b, in the biography of Chu Kuang-ch'ien, it is said that he, as a *sheng-yüan*, was a teacher of a charity school having a large number of students, many of whom were "successfully cultivated," implying that many of them passed the examinations.

farms and could not let them spend long years in study. The preparation for military examinations required expensive equipment, and the poor were therefore especially handicapped in these examinations.[93]

Candidates had to pay fees to participate in the examinations. Students had to pay for each set of examination papers they were to write. For instance, in Jen-huai, the examination papers for the first part of the examination cost 1,050 cash. The papers for the military examination cost 2,100 cash. When the candidates succeeded, they had to pay the customary fees to the educational officials (their new superiors) and to the *ling-sheng* who had guaranteed them so that they could participate in the examinations. The rich *sheng-yüan* paid 70 to 80 taels on these items. The poorer ones paid some 20 to 30 taels. The rich military *sheng-yüan* paid more than 100 taels and the less wealthy paid 60 to 70 taels.[94]

Thus the examination system did not actually afford equal opportunities to all. Wealth, influence, and family background were powerful factors operating for the advantage of special groups. Nevertheless, some opportunity did exist for men without these advantages to rise through their own ability and diligence, and many men did indeed rise in this way. If there was not equality in the examination system, there was a general belief in the "spirit of equality," and this belief together with the fact that some social mobility did exist helped to stabilize the society and maintain the status quo.

However, in the latter half of the nineteenth century, after 1853, the government encouraged people to contribute to the public fund not only by granting the contributors personal rewards, but also by increasing the *sheng-yüan* quota of their native localities and the *chü-jen* quota of their

[93] "Notes of Ling-hsiao and I-shih," *loc. cit.*; the writer describes the military *t'ung-sheng* he saw in the examinations supervised by his father, a *hsien* magistrate of Ch'ang-shan, Shantung, as mostly handsome young men of luxurious dress, some of whom used rouge and powder. They were entirely different from the civil *t'ung-sheng*, many of whom were poor and wore ragged clothing. When he questioned someone about this, he was told that the poor could still manage to study literature, but only the rich could afford to practice the military art since the costs of bows and arrows, stones, swords, horses, instructors, and fields for practice were heavy. *The Chinese Repository*, IV, No. 3, July, 1835, pp. 125 ff., gives the following excerpt from the *Canton Register*, Dec. 3, 1832. "At ten o'clock at night (of November 27, 1832), nine guns or petards announced the moment of decision on the forty-nine fortunate candidates out of several thousands for the military honor of *chü-jen*. All the successful candidates hit the target on foot six times successively; on horseback six times; once with the arrow they hit a ball lying on the ground as they passed it at a gallop; and they were of the first class in wielding the iron-handled battle-axe and in lifting the stone-loaded beam. . . . Since they all performed the same feats, we inquired on what principle the order of one, two, three, etc., from first to last, was made; we were told in reply that the preference was given to the best looking men or to gentlemen; for the candidates are all persons of property, who find their own horses, dresses, arms, etc., but their arrows they never get back again, they being the perquisites of the target watchers."

[94] *Jen-huai t'ing-chih*, 3/14 ff.

native provinces.[95] Wealthy localities were able to boost their quotas while the quotas of poorer localities remained unchanged.

Finally, as the purchase system was applied on an increasingly wide basis throughout the nineteenth century, many more entered officialdom through the "irregular" route.[96] Formerly, the candidates who had passed the higher examinations were promptly assigned to actual offices. Now, not only had the total number of officials increased but the proportion of "irregulars" had become larger. Many of those who had purchased office were able to obtain appointments to actual posts, while many who had obtained official rank through the "regular" route had to wait a long time for such assignments.[97] As the stream of officials emerging from the purchase system increased, the traditional principle of equality of opportunity through examinations disappeared.

CORRUPTION IN THE EXAMINATION SYSTEM

Regulations were provided to guard against corruption in the examination system. For example, the following regulation stated:

> In examinations presided over by the provincial directors-of-studies, those habitual offenders who tour the examination places to take examinations for others, when detected and identified, shall wear the cangue, be displayed for three months, and then exiled to malaria-infested areas to serve in military camps. Those who hire these offenders or act as agents shall be similarly punished. The *ling-sheng* who know the actual situation but still sign the guarantees shall be lashed one hundred strokes. In *sheng-yüan* and *t'ung-sheng* examinations, those habitual villains who falsely claim connections with examiners and give out hints in order to swindle, regardless of whether the agreement is written, money is paid, or the agreement is only verbal, shall be cangued and displayed for three months and exiled to malaria-

[95] See *supra*, Part Two.

[96] Feng Kuei-Fen, *Chiao-pin-lu k'ang-i, chüan shang*, p. 20 b; see also Feng Kuei-fen, *Hsien-chih-t'ang kao*, 11/1 b, and Fukien governor Wang K'ai-t'ai's memorial in *Huang-ch'ao ching-shih-wen-hsü-pien*, compiled by Ke Shih-chün, 10/12 a–15 a. All relate that following the reduction in the purchase price of offices, with about 100 taels one could become an assistant magistrate; with about 1,000 taels one could become a magistrate; for intendants and prefects, the original sum was over 10,000 but was reduced to 3,000 to 4,000 taels. Those who were not rich borrowed from relatives and friends or from merchants. This money was treated as capital invested.

[97] *Ch'ing-ch'ao hsü wen-hsien t'ung-k'ao*, 135/8952–53. An edict was issued in 1835, based on a censor's report, that many assistant officials had been appointed as acting *hsien* magistrates and acted in that capacity for a long period. They did not come up through the regular route, and when entrusted with heavy responsibilities often became corrupt. On the other hand, when *hsien* magistrates selected by the Board of Civil Office arrived at the provinces, the governors instructed them to become acquainted with official duties before appointment to actual office. The Emperor commented that this implied favoritism without regard to qualification and greatly affected the efficiency of civil administration. This shows that the central government might send to the provinces a number of magistrates, but appointment to actual offices was controlled by governors or governors-general, and the Emperor had to step in when the situation became serious.

infested areas to serve in military camps. The *sheng-yüan* or *t'ung-sheng* who have been swindled shall receive one hundred lashes and be imprisoned for three years.[98]

Chü-jen, *chien-sheng*, *sheng-yüan*, and *t'ung-sheng* who participate in the examinations, and the officials, clerks and others [on duty], who bring with them pieces of literature or money, when searched out on the spot, shall be cangued and displayed for one month and receive one hundred lashes and be deprived of their positions. Those who go to others' compartments to write for others or exchange their examination papers, who spend money to hire others to bring in or pass pieces of literature, and those lictors and service men who accept money to bring in or pass pieces of literature, or who know such cases and do not report them, shall all be exiled to the nearest border territories to serve in military camps. The larger the bribes received, the heavier shall be the punishment. If the examiners are completely without corruption, but the unsuccessful candidates are unsatisfied and start disturbances, such candidates shall be exiled to near-by places to serve in military camps.[99]

In actual practice, severe punishments were sometimes imposed during various periods of the dynasty. In 1645, 1652, 1654, and 1657, several officials involved in corruption in metropolitan and provincial examinations were executed and several were deprived of office.[100] In 1858 it was discovered that, through the influence of certain officials, candidates of poor literary caliber had succeeded in obtaining the *chü-jen* degree in the metropolitan prefectural examination. The chief examiner, who was a Grand Secretary, and several others were executed and many others involved were severely punished.[101] In 1893 three cases of corruption in examinations were investigated by the Emperor, all resulting in appropriate punishments.[102]

Despite these severe penalties, however, corruption seems to have been

[98] Wu Yung-kuang, *op. cit.*, 22/16 a–17 a.

[99] *Ibid.*, 20/4 a–b.

[100] Ch'en K'ang-ch'i, *Lang-ch'ien chi-wen*, 12/15 a–16 b.

[101] Wang Sung-ju, *Chang-ku ling-shih*, 3/20–22; Ch'en K'ang-ch'i, *op. cit.*, 1/5 b–6 b; Hsüeh Fu-ch'eng, "Yung-an pi-chi," *Ch'ing-tai pi-chi ts'ung-k'an*, 3/14 b–16 a; *Shih-li*, 340/8 a–9 b. According to Ch'en K'ang-ch'i, *op. cit.*, 1/5 b–6 b, the inside story of this famous and unusual case was that the Emperor did not intend to punish Po-chün and the others so severely, but Su-shun, president of the Board of Punishment, who had gained his position through purchase, disliked Po-chün and officials who came up through the examination route, and insisted on the punishments. When the T'ung-chih emperor ascended the throne, Su-shun became more uncontrollable and the Emperor finally executed him. This examination case was raised by Censor Meng Ch'uan-chin, and all remarked that he talked too much.

[102] "Notes of Ling-hsiao and I-shih," *Kuo-wen chou-pao*, *chüan* 6, No. 50, Dec. 22, 1929, p. 1, describes these three cases: (1) The first case involved the Shensi chief examiner, Ting Wei-t'i, who before his appointment to Shensi tried to get the post of Szechwan chief examiner by bribing the eunuchs. The go-between was *han-lin* compiler Jao Shih-teng. He was detected and impeached by Censor Lin Shao-nien. Jao committed suicide and Ting died from illness before the case was concluded. (2) While the Chekiang chief examiner, Yin Ju-chang, was on his way to Chekiang, Chou Fu-ch'ing, a native of Chekiang and secretary of the Grand Secretariat, visited him and requested his cooperation in misdealings. This was reported by Yin. (3) In Peking a censor charged that the examination papers of several new *chü-jen* were written by others. After re-examination, only one of those charged was retained as *chü-jen* while the rest were deprived of their titles and punished.

ever present in the Ch'ing examination system, although it varied in degree during different periods. Early in the K'ang-hsi reign, ten traditional malpractices were discussed, most of which continued on into the nineteenth century.[103] In late Ch'ing times, Feng Kuei-fen stated:

> Malpractices in examination are practiced by seven or eight out of ten men. Only one case in several years has been punished according to law. The sages in ruling the world emphasize justice. To have different punishments for the same crime is unjust. What would one say of punishing one out of a thousand guilty of the same crime? Everyone knows it except the Emperor.[104]

Foreign observers also have reported on the matter as follows:

> Of late the censors have made a succession of charges against the manner in which the examinations are conducted. One man states that it is not at all unusual for a candidate to throw a copy of the theme, as soon as it is announced, over the wall to a confederate on the other side, who sends back the required essay by the same means. The servants in attendance on the candidates are often professional essay-writers... Substitutes are often introduced to impersonate the real candidates. It is true that little consideration is extended to any culprit found guilty of these malpractices; but when the stake to be won is so high, and the chances of discovery are so slight, the temptation is too great to be checked.[105]

Since the names of the candidates did not appear on the examination

[103] *Hsüeh-cheng*, 16/2 a–3 a, edict of 1679. It was directed mainly at the *t'ung-shih*, *sui-shih*, and *k'o-shih*. First, *t'ung-sheng* who had not participated in the prefectural examinations were admitted to *sheng-yüan* by direct contact with the provincial directors-of-studies. Second, in examinations in certain localities, more were admitted to *sheng-yüan* than provided by the quota. These extra ones were assigned to other district government schools, occupying the vacancies of other localities. Third, although names of candidates did not appear on examination paper, the records of the numbers of the papers were available for check so that the paper of any examinee could still be identified. Fourth, after the examination was over, the announcement of the result was purposely delayed in order to make changes. Fifth, clerks and lictors were sent out as agents for receiving bribes and detecting the wealthy *sheng-yüan* and threatening that they would be graded in the lowest rank [for which they could be deprived of their titles]. Sixth, as civil *t'ung-sheng* were numerous compared to the quota, while military *t'ung-sheng* were few, civil *t'ung-sheng* were permitted to take the military examinations and after being admitted to military *sheng-yüan* status, managed to change back to civil *sheng-yüan*. The "mean people" were also admitted while those who were actually skilful in riding horses and shooting arrows were not considered. Seventh, examination sheds were established in all prefectures, but some provincial directors-of-studies would not go to certain localities. Instead, *sheng-yüan* and *t'ung-sheng* had to go to certain places. Those *sheng-yüan* who were reported as sick were also ordered to be carried to their offices for verification. Eighth, the district educational officials were encouraged to be agents of corruption and divide the spoils with the provincial directors-of-studies. Ninth, the examiners took into consideration their personal affection toward superior officials or colleagues, or private letters from court officials, or retired officials. They allowed relatives and friends to follow them and arrange for illegal income. The poor scholars were naturally barred from success. Tenth, in sending records to the Board of Rites, names which should have been taken off the *sheng-yüan* list were retained, and others, using these names of *sheng-yüan* who were deceased or had been removed from the list for other reasons, illegally became *sheng-yüan*.

[104] Feng Kuei-fen, "Proposal to Permit Poem Writing to Convey Public Opinion," *Huang-ch'ao chin-shih-wen-hsü-pien*, compiled by Ke Shih-chün, 10/7 a–8 b.

[105] "The Peking Tripos," *The Saturday Review*, Vol. 62, Oct. 30, 1886, pp. 582–83.

papers, various subterfuges were employed to identify the papers. In the metropolitan and palace examinations, some candidates often met in a group before the examinations to practice composition and asked the prospective examiners to be critics. The examiners could then recognize their style and calligraphy and would be able to practice favoritism.[106]

The candidates also used other devices to identify their papers when they were sent up for grading.[107] The commonest method was to send the readers slips containing hints on how the papers were written. Needless to say, the readers were rewarded when these candidates succeeded.[108]

A censor reported that in the southeast provinces the copyists who were employed to copy the papers before they were sent up for reading were *chü-jen*, *kung-sheng*, or *sheng-yüan*. The candidates often bribed these copyists to change sentences or even rewrite the whole papers for them.[109]

Substitutes sometimes came in to take examinations for the examinees,[110] and in one memorial it was reported that even court officials went to take examinations for others.[111] Also, it was not uncommon for a candidate in an examination to write several essays for others in addition to his own paper. In one example, the candidate who did this failed, but the paper he wrote

[106] Teng Ch'eng-hsiu, *op. cit.*, 3/16 a–21 a, memorial of Censor Teng written in 1882. In 1678 an edict had been issued prohibiting such practices. Either the imperial instruction was not very effective or the practice had revived in the nineteenth century. See *Shih-li*, 340/1 b.

[107] Teng Ch'eng-hsiu, *loc. cit.*

[108] Hsüeh Fu-ch'eng, "Yung-an pi-chi," *loc. cit.*, says that on the slips certain sentences used in certain parts of the prose and poems written would be explained. These were given to examiners whom the candidates knew. When the examiners began to read the papers, they could trace the papers which they wanted to pass by referring to these slips. By this means, the purpose of sealing the names and recopying the examination papers was completely circumvented. Hsüeh says that this practice was at its height in the early Hsien-feng period. The slips were passed around even in public. Some shameless candidates would mark three or five circles on the slips indicating that if they should succeed they would pay three hundred or five hundred taels.

[109] Teng Ch'eng-hsiu, *loc. cit.* The practice of having copyists to copy the examination papers in the provincial and metropolitan examinations was not abolished until 1902 according to "Notes of Ling-hsiao and I-shih," *Kuo-wen chou-pao*, *chüan* 6, No. 37.

[110] Teng Ch'eng-hsiu, *loc. cit.*, says that this refers mainly to the *kung-sheng* and *chien-sheng* through purchase who participated in the qualifying examination to the *hsiang-shih* at the Imperial College in the capital because it was very difficult for them to succeed in their native provinces. Also Wu Ching-tzu, *op. cit.*, 19/8–10, describes how a man who pretended to be a clerk in the financial commissioner's office acted as a middleman and managed to send a substitute (who was already a *sheng-yüan*) to participate in the *t'ung-shih* for a person who was almost illiterate. He and the substitute together received 500 taels as a reward. Kuo Sung-tao, *Kuo Shih-lang tsou-su*, 4/51 a–52 a, memorial of 1874, reports the discovery of a *chien-sheng* taking part in the provincial examination for another *chien-sheng*. *Kuang-chou fu-chih*, 5/22 a–b, an edict of 1872, based on the report of Censor Yüan-Ch'eng-i, pointed out that in the examination to select instructors for banner schools and in other examinations there were many cases of substitutes taking examinations. Various malpractices in provincial, metropolitan, and palace examinations also existed.

[111] Teng Ch'eng-hsiu, *loc. cit.*

for another won success for that candidate.[112] It has even been said that Li Hung-chang's papers in the metropolitan examination were written by his friend, and both of them succeeded.[113] In a third example, brothers cooperated in the examination hall. Both succeeded in becoming *chü-jen* but were suspected, investigated, and finally deprived of their degrees and punished.[114]

According to regulations, candidates were to be searched before they entered the examination hall, to make sure that they did not bring in books. Later, this regulation existed only in name, and it was said that all candidates brought in books.[115] Discipline was lacking. There was no order when the candidates were entering the examination hall. They were permitted to leave their compartments and were therefore able to communicate with each other.[116]

[112] *Hsi-Chin yu-hsiang t'ung-jen tzu-shu hui-k'an*, p. 15 b. Ku Ch'ien in his autobiography says that he failed in seven attempts in the provincial examinations. On one occasion, one of his relatives also participated in the examination. The relative was suffering from dysentery, and Ku wrote the examination papers for him. Returning home, he repeated the compositions to his father. His father said that he had given a *chü-jen* degree to somebody else. It happened to be true.

[113] Chin Liang, *Szu-ch'ao i-wen*, p. 19 a, relates that Li Hung-chang, when participating in the metropolitan examination of 1847, was sick in the examination hall. He was in the same group of compartments as Yang Yen-chün, and Yang completed the examination papers for him. Chin's book brought out historical materials not embodied in the *Ch'ing-shih kao* of which Chin was one of the compilers. Also in *Shih-li*, 341/5 b, it is said that the examination papers of a successful *chü-jen* candidate were found to differ in calligraphy in parts. After investigation, it was found that the candidate concerned was sick and could not complete the writing and that another candidate had therefore finished it for him.

[114] Tso Tsung-t'ang, *Tso Wen-hsiang-kung ch'üan-chi*, 19/93 a–95 b, memorial of T'ung-chih 5/10/15 (1866). Tso, in compliance with an imperial edict, reported on the result of investigation of the two sons of the brigade general of Taiwan, Tseng Yü-ming, in connection with charges of cheating during a provincial examination. It was revealed that both had studied under the same teacher and that they sat in the same group of compartments in the examination hall, so that it was possible for them to copy from each other. It was also revealed that they had obtained their *sheng-yüan* titles in different places. The two were deprived of their degrees and punished according to regulation, and the father was dismissed from office.

[115] Teng Ch'eng-hsiu, *loc. cit.*, and Chang Chung-ju, *Ch'ing-tai k'ao-shih chih-tu*, pp. 23 and 24, both of which refer to the nineteenth century. This malpractice was also a problem of earlier times. *Shih-li*, 341/2 a–3 b, says that in 1744 in the Shun-t'ien *hsiang-shih*, when the Emperor personally appointed several high officials to supervise the search, twenty-one were found guilty of smuggling books in the first part of the examination. Another twenty were involved in the second part. About four hundred candidates handed in blank papers and about two thousand gave up their attempt to participate in the examination when they saw the situation. However, the edicts of later years show that the practice of smuggling books into examination halls never ceased to be a serious problem. *Shih-li*, 340/5 ff., an edict of 1789, points out that pocket-size books of classics and annotations were brought into examination halls. The publishers were ordered to burn such books. The same problem was raised again in 1792 and 1793, in 1822, and in 1831. In *ibid.*, 341/6 a, in 1893, it is pointed out that in provincial and metropolitan examinations, there were regulations designed to prevent the smuggling of books which limited the things candidates could bring into the examination halls. However, the regulation was ignored, and candidates brought in cushions and heavy bedding in which books could easily be hidden.

[116] Teng Ch'eng-hsiu, *loc. cit.,* Wu Ching-tzu, *op. cit.*, 26/2–3, gives a description of a *fu* examination where the *t'ung-sheng* wrote for others, passed or threw papers to each

After the examinations were over, revision examinations were held to make sure that the successful candidates were really the persons who had participated in the examinations, but these tests do not seem to have been effective. It was reported, for instance, that one person who was still in Shanghai succeeded in the examination held in the capital.[117]

Regulations forbade the "mean people" to participate in examinations. This rule, too, was broken. In the latter part of the nineteenth century, several cases were raised concerning the participation in examinations by sons of gatekeepers and servants of magistrates.[118] Since these were mostly cases of offenders who had succeeded in the examinations, it is likely that the breaking of this regulation was not uncommon.

Despite the fraud and cheating in examinations on the part of the candidates, the situation would have been less serious if the examiners had all been honest.[119] It is true that one of the reasons that members of the Han-lin Academy and the Supervisorate of Imperial Instructions desired to be examiners was that the position was an honored one. Even Li Hung-chang is supposed to have regretted that he had never been an examiner.[120] However, profit was also a very strong motive, as the following quotations show:

other, made signs, and so on. One even went to the earthen wall, dug a hole, and tried to get information from outside. *Shih-li,* 342/4 b–5 b, describes disorderly behavior of candidates. They went to and fro in the examination hall making loud noises. The opium smokers even smuggled opium-smoking equipment into the examination hall.

117 Teng Ch'eng-hsiu, *loc. cit.*

118 Wu Ching-tzu, *op. cit.*, 32/8–10, describes how one son of a member of the "mean people" pretended to be of good origin and participated in the *t'ung-shih* with the support of an influential *sheng-yüan.* In 1872, a supervising censor, Lu Shih-chieh, memorialized that Li T'ien-hsi, an assistant *chou* magistrate through purchase, was formerly the servant of the magistrate of Shang-ch'eng, Honan. Li's son had purchased a *chien-sheng* title and participated in the provincial examination. The father and son were both deprived of their positions and titles and punished. See Wang K'ai-t'ai's memorial in *Huang-ch'ao ching-shih wen-hsü-pien,* 10/12 a–15 a. Teng Ch'eng-hsiu, *op. cit.,* 1/5 a–6 a, records that in 1874 Censor Teng memorialized that an expectant *chou* magistrate with the title of prefect had formerly been a gatekeeper to the former governor-general of Liang-Kwang, Yeh Ming-ch'en. The son had become *yu-kung-sheng* through examination. Teng said, "The latter title is what the scholars hope to obtain and is the stepping-stone to officialdom." Teng recommended deprival of titles; this was approved. *Shih-li,* 340/9 b, records the memorial of Censor Liu Tseng, written in 1877, regarding a gatekeeper's son who had taken the examinations and had become a *chü-jen.* The offender was deprived of his degree. In the same year, Censor Teng Hua-hsi memorialized that the son of a gatekeeper who served in several *hsien* yamens in Kwangtung had become a *sheng-yüan* and had later purchased the post of second-class assistant secretary of a Board, and that another son had changed his name and succeeded in the provincial examination held at Shun-t'ien-fu. The sons were deprived of their titles and both the father and sons were punished.

119 *Shih-li,* 340/2 a; an edict of 1722 discusses this matter. It points out that individual candidates trying to smuggle books into the examination hall or send in substitutes were trying to further their own interests. Such malpractices, the edict says, were not so serious as the corruption of the examiners who delayed the announcement of the list of successful candidates, meanwhile changing examination papers, changing the order of success, and so forth. The censors knew of these practices but kept silent because they were bound by personal ties or were afraid of incurring the enmity of their colleagues.

120 "Notes of Ling-hsiao and I-shih," *Kuo-wen chou-pao, chüan* 7, No. 40, Oct., 13,

The capital, which is supposed to be the model of virtue, is a place which spoils talents. As the country is more and more in a haphazard situation, the worse are the customs and habits. The post of *han-lin* is supposed to be a reservoir of talents but several hundred of them are trying to get assignments as examiners. By becoming such, they will receive supplies from the localities they pass by and presents from various officials.[121]

When a *han-lin* obtains an assignment to supervise examinations, the districts he passes by pay his supplies and the officials send many gifts. When the duty is finished and he goes back to report to the Emperor, when asked about the good and bad practices of the provinces he passes by, he will then not speak the truth.[122]

A friend of mine who holds office in the Han-lin Academy already has white hair and beard. But he still practices examination essays, poetical composition and calligraphy. He sets up timetables to keep himself working as hard as possible. His whole life is as if he were a young student standing beside a strict master. In his

1930, p. 1 b, says that when a friend of Li Hung-chang scolded him for not being able to acquire an assignment as an examiner during his official career, Li became annoyed and tried to beat him with a stick. The writer comments that this incident shows that even though Li rose to the honor of having a title of nobility, he still regretted never having been an examiner. One could infer that Li never succeeded in the examinations through which examiners were selected, although he was a member of the Han-lin Academy.

[121] Pai Ching-wei, *op. cit.*, 3/25 b–27 b. Chang Chung-ju, *op. cit.*, pp. 43 and 44, says that in earlier times no qualification was necessary for examiners. Beginning in 1725, only *chin-shih* could serve. *Shih-li*, 333/2 b–3 a, memorial of Censor Li Ch'ing-fang, written in 1744, says that among the 49 chief examiners recommended by high officials, only 4 were Manchus, 16 were from various provinces, and the remaining 29 were Kiangsu and Chekiang men. Li indicated that those recommended were rich and had powerful men to rely on. Beginning in 1761, examinations were held to select examiners. All officials of the Han-lin, the Grand Secretariat, and the Boards could participate. However, according to *Shih-li*, 333/8 a, the examination papers were not recopied, and the readers, who were the Grand Secretaries, presidents or vice-presidents of Boards, knew well which papers were written by whom. Hence, it could be easily imagined that the ones they recommended were the ones they liked. However, the Emperor rejected a censor's suggestion for reform in this examination on the ground that he did not want to show that he suspected these high officials of favoritism or malpractices.

[122] Pai Ching-wei, *op. cit.*, 3/29 a–b. Trips to some of the provinces took a long time. Lung Ch'i-jui, *op. cit.*, *wen-chi*, 6/15 a–17 a, describes his journey as vice-examiner of the Kwangtung provincial examination. He left from the capital with five servants in 1844—Tao-kuang 24th year, 5th month. During the sixth month, he passed Shantung, Kiangsu, Anhwei, Hupeh, and Kiangsi. In the 7th month, he arrived at Kwangtung. He visited the historical places en route. In the 8th month, the examination was held, and in the 9th month he left Canton. He was back at the capital in the 12th month. The journey took seven months of which more than five months were spent on the way. The actual work of reading papers was only a month. He remarks that he passed seven provinces and travelled a distance of 5,600 *li* but still had not visited many scenic places. In "Diary of Shen Wen-ting's Trip to Supervise the Kwangtung Provincial Examination," *Chung-ho yüeh-k'an*, *chüan* 1, No. 4, April 1, 1940, pp. 95–103; No. 5, May 1, 1940, pp. 79–84; No. 6, June 1, 1940, pp. 92–98, it is said that Shen was appointed as chief examiner of Kwangtung in 1861. In that year only Chihli, Kansu, Shensi, Shansi, Kwangtung, and Kwangsi were able to have provincial examinations. The other provincial examinations were not given because of the war. He started the journey on the 5th day of the 7th month and arrived at Canton on the 29th day of the 9th month. He spent a month in Canton, but the examination work was actually done within a fortnight. The editor of the monthly mentions that there were also published diaries of Hua Hsüeh-lan, Lu Pei-fen, and Yen Hsiu, describing their trips to provincial examinations. However, their accounts are of late Kuang-hsü times.

words, "If I depart from these practices for one day, I would not be able to obtain assignments to supervise examinations. As *han-lin* but without any assignment as examiner, this is the road to starvation." Later on he actually succeeds in becoming chief examiner for a provincial examination and provincial director-of-studies of one province.[123]

Regulations provided that the provinces should pay a sum of money to the examiners to cover their travelling expenses. The amount was supposedly fixed in 1738, varying according to the distance from the capital.[124] Actually, they usually obtained much larger sums. For instance, in 1802 a chief examiner received large amounts of money from the provincial officials in addition to presents such as fur coats and other valuables. In addition to these bribes from officials who wanted them to hide malpractices in provincial administration, examiners and provincial directors-of-studies were also able to profit from the conducting of examinations.[125]

Of course there were upright examiners and provincial directors-of-studies. One provincial director-of-studies of the late Tao-kuang period wrote to relatives requesting them not to come to the place where he was holding the examination as he wished to avoid criticism.[126] He issued notifications

[123] Hsüeh Fu-ch'eng, *Yung-an ch'üan-chi*, 1/5 b. The insufficiency of the salaries of the court officials was a problem of which high officials were fully aware. For instance, Wang K'ai-t'ai, *loc. cit.*, proposed in late T'ung-chih that the salaries of court officials should be doubled. The insufficiency of salaries did lead some who were not able to obtain assignments as examiners to use their influence in examinations. An edict of 1721 says, "The country in cultivating talents puts first importance on the Han-lin Academy and the Supervisorate of Imperial Instruction. After having studied many books, they should be of perfect conduct and prudent intention, thus not ashamed to face the officials' maxims. I have heard that there are some opportunists who form cliques at ordinary times, and in years of examinations they cooperate in sending out requests for favoritism in examinations. Some straightforward officials who are afraid of the punishments and do not want to cooperate will then be slandered and falsely accused. This tendency should not remain and such men should be sorted out and forced to retire. . . ." *Shih-li*, 340/2 b.

[124] *Shih-li*, 333/2 b. For Yunnan, 800 taels; Kweichow, 700 taels; Szechwan, Kwangtung, Kwangsi, Fukien, and Hunan, 600 taels; Chiang-nan, Chekiang, Kiangsi, Hupeh, and Shensi, 500 taels; Honan, Shantung, Shansi, 400 taels. The governors-general or governors were not to give more and the examiners were not to accept more than the stipulated amount.

[125] *Ibid.*, p. 4 b. See also Ch'en K'ang-ch'i, *Lang-ch'ien chi-wen*, 3/18 b, where it is described that in the beginning of the dynasty, provincial directors-of-studies, following Ming practices, permitted favoritism and received bribes. The Emperor hated this. At this time, the Chekiang governor, Chang Peng-ho was known for his honesty, and Chiang-nan was known for its corruption. Hence, Chang was sent there. People who received letters of recommendation from the court officials then did not use them. For late Ch'ing, see Li Pao-chia, *op. cit.*, 2/13, which describes the arrival at the capital of Chao Wen, a new *chü-jen*, who was going to take the metropolitan examination. Chao went to see the examiner, Wu Tsai-shan, who had admitted him to *chü-jen*. Wu expected a present of two to three hundred taels since he had made inquiries and found that Chao's family was wealthy. If Chao had complied with his wishes, Wu might have helped him to succeed in the metropolitan examination. The writer says that such practices were common at the time. That examiners demanded customary fees can also be seen in an edict of 1872 as recorded in *Kuang-chou fu-chih*, 5/5 b–6 b.

[126] Lung Ch'i-jui, *op. cit.*, *wen-pi-chi*, *ts'e hsia*, pp. 7 a–8 b. He went on to say that there were no jobs available except for scholars who were very good in literature, some

to candidates pointing out the traditional malpractices and stated that neither he nor his assistants and servants would accept bribes.[127]

On the other hand, a censor described how one corrupt provincial director-of-studies in early Kuang-hsü openly accepted bribes. One *t'ung-sheng* bribed him and asked to be the third on the list of successful candidates; his request was complied with. He deprived more than ten *ling-sheng* of their titles and restored them only after each paid three hundred dollars. There were also many other cases of bribery, so openly carried out that the censor concluded it was like trading between merchants.[128]

One Western writer mentioned that "Literary chancellors [provincial directors-of-studies] also sell bachelor's degrees [*sheng-yüan*] to the exclusion of deserving poor scholars; the office of the *hiohching* [*hsüeh-cheng*, provincial director-of-studies] of Kiangsi was searched in 1828 by a special commission and four lacs of taels found in it; he hung himself to avoid further punishment, as did also the same dignitary in Canton in 1833, as was supposed, for a similar cause." [129]

A survey of the conduct of provincial directors-of-studies in Kwangtung in the twenty-year period between early T'ung-chih and early Kuang-hsü, as given by a censor who was a native of that province, shows that half of them could be considered as incorrupt while the other half were notorious for corruption, greediness, and inefficiency.[130]

of whom could be employed as readers of examination papers. He said that after two more years, when his term of office expired, he would have several thousand taels accumulated and promised that some of the money would be set aside for the welfare of the clan.

[127] *Ibid., wen-pi-chi, ts'e shang,* pp. 3 b–5 b–6 b, points out the traditional practices of sneaking notes into the examination hall, writing essays for others, changing information on examination questions, bribing examiners, etc. Since none of his staff would accept bribes, he warned candidates to be careful of villains who would try to extort money from them by pretending to have connections with him. Lung (1814–1858, *Pei-chuan-chi* 41) became provincial director-of-studies of Hupeh in 1847 and stayed there for two terms, i.e., six years. He also issued notices warning military *t'ung-sheng* against cheating by such methods as secretly tying leather strips on their arms, waist, and feet, so that they would have extra strength for opening the heavy bows.

[128] Teng Ch'eng-hsiu, *op. cit.*, 1/12 a–b. Teng, as censor of Yunnan circuit but native of Kwangtung, memorialized in Kuang-hsü 5/7/29 (1879) that Wu Pao-shu, provincial director-of-studies in Kwangtung acted corruptly, smoked opium, daily gambled with his assistants, and did not care about examination matters. In Teng's native place, Kuei-shan, there were 3,000 candidates. They handed in their examination papers late in the evening, and the results were made known the next morning. Teng thought the papers were not actually read. He said that some *ling-sheng* paid money to have their titles restored. *Sheng-yüan* of another locality who were deprived of their titles found out that Wu's father had been an official there and petitioned to list the deceased father of Wu in the famous officials' shrine; their titles were later restored. When the governor-general was asked to investigate, he denied these charges. However, there must have been some truth in them, as Teng in other writings repeatedly listed Wu as corrupt.

[129] S. W. Williams, *The Middle Kingdom*, p. 569.

[130] Teng Ch'eng-hsiu, *op. cit.*, 3/22 a–23 a, memorial of 1882. Teng concludes that the present provincial director-of-studies should be ordered to correct the situation.

One can conclude, therefore, that corruption was rife in the examination system despite the strong regulations to prevent it and the severe punishments imposed on some offenders. Many examiners and candidates were corrupt although there were also some honest ones. For the examiners, this was their opportunity to profit. For the examinees, the risk of being caught and punished for cheating and bribery was outweighed by the greater chance of success in the examinations. The rewards made the risk worth while. Thus the words of the early Ch'ing scholar, Ku Yen-wu, remained true in the nineteenth century:

> Many people desire to be *sheng-yüan*, not necessarily for the honor of the title, but for the protection of their persons and their families. ... This is contradictory to the original purpose of the establishment of the examination system and is not beneficial to the country. But as for human feelings, whose are not directed towards themselves and their families? Therefore, day and night they seek it. Or even in carrying out bribery, they come in conflict with the law and suffer punishments, and yet they do not stop; circumstances have forced them to do so.[131]

THE PURPOSE OF THE EXAMINATION LIFE OF THE GENTRY

Previous sections have shown that the gentry had to be constantly occupied with preparing for and taking examinations, devoting themselves to an "examination life." This practice, developed to its utmost refinement by the Ch'ing dynasty, was obviously not accidental.

Although the avowed purpose of the examination system was to select able men for offices, this purpose could have been accomplished with fewer examinations. Moreover, the content of the examinations had no relation to this theoretical aim. In the early part of the Ch'ing dynasty, there were still some questions dealing with administrative matters and with political philosophy. These parts of the examinations were eliminated in the second half of the dynastic period and the examinations became completely formal in content. Yet the gentry worked hard for these examinations since this was the only way to gain and keep their privileged positions. It has also been shown that the examination system did not provide an equal opportunity for everyone. Still for those who took the examinations, there was a worthwhile chance.

The question still remains as to what purpose was served by the constant occupation of a whole social group with formalized studies. What the examination system meant to the imperial government has been best expressed by an emperor of the T'ang dynasty who at the sight of his new successful examination candidates jubilantly exclaimed, "The heroes of the

[131] Ku Yen-wu, "T'ing-ling wen-chi," 1/17 b–18 a.

world have fallen within the range of my arrow shot!"[132] He knew well that through the examination system he had brought under control the free-ranging thought of the leading social group. The Ch'ing dynasty went further. The constant drilling in traditional Confucian moral principles and the writing of formalized essays kept the minds of the gentry so occupied that they had little time for independent thought and study. Ch'in Shih-huang-ti had tried to control the scholars by forbidding them to read the classics, but the Ch'ing government tried to control them by making them read the classics. Their thought was channelled into the lines of official ideology in which the aspects of authority and discipline in the Confucian tradition were emphasized. The principles of loyalty and service, which were fundamental parts of this doctrine, were stressed not only in the examinations themselves but also in the schools, which were related to the examination system.

At the beginning of the dynasty the Emperor drew up eight principles for the *sheng-yüan* to observe.[133] On imperial orders, these were carved on stone tablets which were placed in the main halls of all government schools. The eight principles were:

(1) In the family of a *sheng-yüan*, if the parents are worthy and wise, the son should obey their teachings. Should the parents be ignorant and stupid or not abiding by the law, since the son has read books and understands what is right, he should repeatedly persuade and implore them so as to prevent his parents from falling into perilous positions.

(2) A *sheng-yüan*, in making his resolutions, should aim at being a loyal minister and incorrupt official. All loyal and incorrupt deeds recorded in the books and histories should be carefully studied, and all matters relating to the welfare of the country and the people should be given special attention.

[132] "Notes of Ling-hsiao and I-shih," *Kuo-wen chou-pao*, *chüan* 6, No. 2, July 21, 1929, pp. 1–2, attributed the first use of this phrase to Emperor T'ang T'ai-tsung who was pleased at the sight of new *chü-jen*.

[133] *Yung-cheng ta-Ch'ing hui-tien*, 76/7 a–8 b; *Shih-li*, 389/1 a–2 a; *Hsüeh-cheng*, 4/1 a–2 b; *Kuang-hsü ta-Ch'ing hui-tien*, 32/10 b–11 a; *Hsü-hsiu Lu-chou fu-chih*, 17/25 b–26 b; *Po-pai hsien-chih*, 6/2 a. These eight principles were proclaimed by the Shun-chih emperor in the 9th year of his reign (1652). (*Shih-lu*, Sheng-tsu, 63/3 a; *Hsüeh-cheng*, 9/1 a.) *Hsüeh-cheng*, 4/10 b, gives an imperial edict of 1739 which states: "The schools in the provinces have all erected the horizontal tablet [with the eight principles] in the Hall of Understanding Human Relationships. The metropolitan prefectural school, which is situated in the first city, still lacks such a tablet. It should be permitted, for uniformity, to erect the horizontal tablet in the Hall of Understanding Human Relationships to pass down eternally so that all students will know how to obey reverently." The placing of the horizontal tablets in the halls of many local schools can be verified from records in various local gazetteers. See *Hsü-hsiu Lu-chou fu-chih*, 17/25 b–26 b. *Ibid.*, p. 52 b, relates that the Hall was of five-room frontage. In the right side of the middle three-room space, the horizontal tablet was erected. The two side rooms were the school storehouses for storing musical instruments, sacrificial articles, etc. *Kuang-chou fu-chih*, 97/1 a–2 a, 66/12 b. See also *Pa-ling hsien-chih*, 17/1 ff.; *Hsing-kuo chou-chih*, introductory *chüan*; *Ch'ing-yüan hsien-chih*, introductory *chüan*, pp. 3 ff.; *Yung-chou fu-chih*, 4 A/3 ff.; *P'u-an chih-li-t'ing chih*, 5/2 a.

(3) A *sheng-yüan* should be sincere and upright in his intentions. Only then will what he has studied in books have practical use, and only then, when he obtains an official post, can he definitely become a good official. If his intentions are erroneous and vicious, his study will definitely amount to nothing and he will come to a disastrous end when becoming an official. Anyone who injures others usually injures himself. This should be noted and kept in mind.

(4) A *sheng-yüan* should not seek advancement through entreating officials or superiors or by making friends with powerful personages. If he has truly a good heart and flawless virtue, Heaven will recognize him and reward him with blessing.

(5) A *sheng-yüan* should guard his personal integrity and be persevering. He should not enter the offices of the local authorities lightly. Even if there be something personal involved, he should ask his family members to bring the lawsuit for him. He should not meddle with other peoples' lawsuits, and others should not bring in *sheng-yüan* as witnesses.

(6) In learning, one's teacher should be revered. Lectures should be listened to wholeheartedly. When a point is not thoroughly understood, one should ask unhurriedly. He should not resort ruthlessly to rebuttal. The teacher should also devote his whole heart to teaching and not be idle and indolent.

(7) A *sheng-yüan* should not present written discourses on the welfare or ills of military or civil affairs. Should he do so, he would be judged as offending the regulations and his grade would be taken away and he would be punished.

(8) *Sheng-yüan* should not collect groups of people to establish alliances or form societies, or to control the local authorites, or to settle matters by force in their localities. Their compositions and essays should not be printed and published at will. Anyone who disobeys will be punished by the authorities.

Thus, the first three principles stressed the gentry's duties of loyalty and service to the government and its laws. The rest of the principles warned them against overextending their power.

The same purpose of indoctrination was served by the Sixteen Maxims of the "Sacred Edict," which were issued in 1670 and further amplified in 1724.[134] Among the maxims were these: "Keep the school in high regard in order to direct the scholar's conduct." "Denounce heretical sayings in order to exalt the orthodox doctrines." The Han-lin Academy was ordered to write a rhymed essay on the maxim of denouncing heretical sayings; this essay was to be distributed to all schools for recitation so that "good custom would be formed and the people's hearts rectified."[135] The whole tenor of the Sixteen Maxims stresses obedience and submissiveness. Semimonthly meetings were held in the schools at which these maxims were expounded.[136] In the nineteenth century when these meetings were not always held

[134] See Part One, note 285, for complete text of the Sixteen Maxims. These maxims were first issued by the K'ang-hsi emperor in 1670 (*Hsüeh-cheng* 9/2 a–b) and were amplified by the Yung-cheng emperor in 1724 (*Hsüeh-cheng* 9/4 a).

[135] *Shih-lu*, Hsüan-tsung, 327/6 a–b; also 38 b, in 1839.

[136] *Hsü-hsiu Lu-chou fu-chih*, 5/8 a–b.

regularly, imperial edicts urged the observance of this ceremony.[137] One edict ordered that the educational officials, in addition to examining the students, should expound the principles of Confucius and Mencius to the students so as to "polish their minds." Even the provincial director-of-studies, on arriving in a locality to give an examination, was first to expound the orthodox teachings to the students so that they would know "which direction to follow." [138] So indoctrinated, the students could then be used to preach these maxims to the population at large.[139]

In addition to these principles and maxims, there were the imperial "Exhortations to Students," one issued in K'ang-hsi 41 (1702) and the other in Ch'ien-lung 5 (1740). An imperial edict of 1729 ordered that the K'ang-hsi essay be distributed to all schools, stored in the Hall of Honoring the Classics, and read on the arrival of new officials and the provincial directors-of-studies and on Confucius' birthday.[140] An edict was issued in 1745 regarding the Ch'ien-lung essay. This edict stated that the educational officials of all schools should on the first and fifteenth day of each month expound this exhortation together with the Sixteen Imperial Maxims of K'ang-hsi and the Treatise on Cliques issued by the Yung-cheng emperor.[141]

Both of these imperial exhortations stressed the importance of studying for the examinations and the connection between good conduct and the Confucian tradition as related to the examination system. The K'ang-hsi essay stated, "Good conduct counts first, and literary attainment comes next. ... Students with real talent and solid learning should have no fear that they will not be successful sooner or later. ... Through these triennial examinations held by the government are accorded the distinctions of 'rolls of silk' and 'bows and flags,' by which not only you yourselves are honored, but also your grandfathers and fathers share the glory." [142]

The Ch'ien-lung essay stated:

...the habit of working for the degrees for the sake of name and profit is deeply entrenched in the people's minds and cannot be easily reformed. This alone is what the students earnestly pursue. They do not work on the principles of the sages. ... Chu-tzu [Chu-hsi] in his office at T'ung-an instructed the students saying, "Learning is for oneself. In the present world, what the fathers order their sons, what the elder

[137] *Kuang-chou fu-chih*, 5/5 b–6 b, edict of 1862, which also says that the Emperor, like the Emperor before him, wanted the students to study Sung Neo-Confucianism.

[138] *Ibid.*, pp. 8 b–9 b, edict of 1865, in which the Emperor expressed his regret that the practice had been neglected despite his warning at the time he ascended the throne.

[139] See Part One, p. 65.

[140] *Hsüeh-cheng*, 4/9 b. The record of the *Kuang-chou fu-chih*, 66/10 a, 97/2 a–3 a, showed, for instance, that the essay had been carved on stone and kept in a special pavilion.

[141] *Ibid.*, 4/12 b–13 a.

[142] *Hsüeh-cheng*, 4/2 b–4 b; *Shih-lu, Sheng-tsu*, 208/10 a–12 a; *Shih-li*, 389/2 b–3 a, *Kuang-chou fu-chih*, 97/1 a–2 a; *Po-pai hsien-chih*, 6/3 b–4 b.

brothers urge the younger brothers, what the teachers instruct their students, and what the students learn is only examinations and nothing else. ... They think that if they can meet the demands of the authorities there is nothing else to worry about. Thus they indulge in idleness, and throughout their whole lives do not pursue learning. ..." Chu-tzu's words indeed refer to common ills of former and present times. The two words "for oneself" are the gate to enter among the sages. Chu-tzu said, "It is not that examinations burden men but that men burden the examinations. If a far-sighted student reads the books of the sages and participates in examinations, according to my thinking, he will disregard success or failure. Even if he should participate in examinations daily, he is not burdened. Even if Confucius were reborn and living in the present world, he could not help but participate in examinations. But would this burden Confucius?"[143]

Study for examinations was thus meant as a thorough training in the traditional learnings. The effort to indoctrinate the gentry was further seen in the physical set-up of the schools. The government school and the Confucian temple of each district were contained in the same group of buildings. The names of the different buildings indicate the constant emphasis on Confucian principles. In Ch'u-chou, Anhwei, for instance, the district school was situated next to the office of the educational officials and the Palace of the God of Literature. The main hall of the temple and the school was called the Palace of Great Achievement in honor of Confucius. In front of it was the Golden Gate on either side of which were two shrines, the Shrine of Famous Officials and the Shrine of the Local Virtuous. In front of this was the School Pond, the Arch, and the tablet with the inscription, "Model of Teachers of Ten Thousand Generations." To the rear of the Palace of Great Achievement was the Hall of Understanding Human Relationships. To the east was the Shrine for Revering Sages. The Hall of Honoring the Classics was to the left of the Palace of the God of Literature.[144] The *Nan-ning fu-chih* states that this design was to be uniformly complied with by all schools.[145] Other examples showing the same basic design can be cited for Shanghai[146] and Po-pai, Kwangsi.[147]

In the Palace of Great Achievement, ceremonies were held to honor

[143] *Hsüeh-cheng*, 4/10 b–12 b.

[144] *Ch'u-chou chih*, introductory *chüan*, pp. 6 b–7 a; *chüan* 3, part 3, p. 16 a; a map is shown.

[145] *Nan-ning fu-chih*, 51/7 a–b.

[146] *Shanghai hsien-chih*, introductory *chüan*, p. 13 b–14 a; the school is shown as the Confucian temple in the map. *Ibid.*, p. 21 b, indicates that the Hall of Understanding Classics and the Hall of Honoring Classics were considered as parts of the school, while the Hall of Great Achievements and others were considered as the Confucian temple. *Ibid.*, 9/7 b; the whole group of buildings is here referred to as the school.

[147] *Po-pai hsien-chih*, 4/1 a. The compiler traced back the connection between Confucian temple and school to Cheng-kuan, 4th year of the T'ang dynasty, when it was imperially ordered that all districts should establish a Confucian temple or *wen-miao*, where the school would also be located.

Confucius. The Hall of Understanding Human Relationships was for lectures and study. One gazetteer compiler described its purpose as "to make possible the expounding of the sages' principles, the promulgation of imperial edicts, and the examining of students."[148] A stone inscription in one school strongly emphasizes the importance of the Hall of Understanding Human Relationships in the examination and school system. It emphasizes the value of the schools in promoting harmonious "human relationships," by which was meant an orderly society with the Emperor at the top. The inscription reads as follows:

> Schools are established for the understanding of human relationships. When human relationships are understood in the upper level, the people are harmonious in the lower level. Therefore, [as stated] in the regulation governing school building, besides the palace, shrines and others, there is the Hall of Understanding Human Relationships. ... [Here] the principle of emperor-official, father-son, husband-wife, elder-younger brothers, and friends' relationship is expounded. Here those who comply with the teachings are praised and those who do not comply are remonstrated with. The administrator of the locality will examine the degree of diligence of the students here. This hall is indeed very important.[149]

The Hall of Honoring the Classics was the place where the imperially compiled or authorized books were stored. Its purpose was to set up certain books as orthodox. These books were the classics, commentaries on the classics, histories, imperial instructions and edicts, and other imperially compiled or authorized books. They were either bought by the provincial director-of-studies or given by the Emperor.[150] The importance placed on these books is further shown in Tso Tsung-t'ang's memorials. After certain cities were recaptured from the Moslem rebels, he immediately requested the speedy reissuance of the books missing from the schools of these cities.[151]

Thus the schools and the whole examination system aimed at forcing the gentry and those who were striving to become gentry into an "examination life" and channeling their thoughts into the lines of official ideology which emphasized the principles of loyalty and service. The indoctrinated gentry were then to inculcate these principles upon the masses. The goal was a peaceful world satisfied with the Manchu rule and the existing social structure.

[148] *Nan-ning fu-chih*, 51/7 a–b.

[149] Ling Sen-mei, "Stone Inscription on the Newly-Constructed Hall of Understanding Human Relationships in Yung-ch'un," *Nan-ning fu-chih*, 51/13 a–b.

[150] *Hsü-hsiu Lu-chou fu-chih*, 17/73 b. *Ibid.*, pp. 95 a–98 a, contains the list of books kept there. Also *Shanghai hsien-chih*, 9/27 a–b; *Chung-hsiu Meng-ch'eng hsien-chih-shu*, 5/4 b. See also *Hsüeh-cheng*, *chüan* 12, the issuance of books.

[151] Tso Tsung-t'ang, *Tso Wen-hsiang-kung ch'üan-chi*, 52/67 ff., a memorial of Kuang-hsü 4/2/22 (1878).

COLLAPSE OF THE CH'ING EXAMINATION SYSTEM

The examination system described above had its roots deep in the past. Dynasty after dynasty used it as a means of controlling society and maintaining a despotic rule. It constantly developed in detail up until Ch'ing times when we find the gentry and would-be gentry devoting their lives to the preparation for examinations. Through this scheme the court aimed at channeling the thought of the members of the upper group, indoctrinating them with the official line of Confucianism, and securing their loyalty and service. This system operated well in the early part of the Ch'ing dynasty, but in the nineteenth century it began to break down. The overformalization of essay writing and the overemphasis on calligraphy and poetical composition led the students to neglect the study of the Confucian classics. The trend was more and more toward empty forms without content or meaning. This change in the examination system affected the nature of the gentry. The ideological basis of the system was neglected, and the original aim of indoctrination in Confucian principles was no longer being well served. The government was losing its qualitative control over the gentry, just as it was losing its quantitative control through the breakdown of quota and purchase regulation.

By the close of the Ch'ing dynasty, the examination system was doomed to end. The changing international situation after 1840, and the changing economic conditions and social structure revealed the inadaptability of the old examination system to a new life. The ignorance of the people and the weakness of the state were fully exposed by the series of uprisings within the country and the contacts with the West.

Wang Hsien-ch'ien discussed the failure of the examination system to justify its existence in late Ch'ing as follows:

> Scholars of a unified world can be created by examination on formalized writings; scholars of a world of many countries cannot be created by examination on formalized writings. The present world, if looked at within the seas, is unified, but if looked at as the whole earth, it is of many countries. However, the examination system was established for competing talents in classics in accordance with traditional practice, and scholars were selected through eight-legged essay writing without knowing change and adaptation. ... The method of examination and the scheme of prohibitions were amplified in comparison with the T'ang dynasty so that the scholars would concentrate their minds and devote their aspirations toward seeking acceptance by the examiners. Their aim of favor and glory was satisfied so that wild ambition would not grow. The outstanding would lower their heads and fall within the range of arrow-shot and the stupid would know their own incapability. The Emperor could rest deep in the palace while always holding the power of whipping the 10,000 *li*. However, in later years, a situation of accumulated weakness has formed. As foreign invaders arrive, all watch without a plan. Although the people have the spirit of

loyalty and righteousness, their hands and feet are as if chained and they can only angrily die as martyrs. These are obvious facts. The reason is that the advantage of restraining the people is understood, but the disadvantage of the uselessness of the people has been neglected.[152]

Liang Ch'i-ch'ao also gave the analogy of a master who worried that his servants would steal his treasures and so bound them and locked them up. When strong invaders came, they were met with no resistance and stole all that they found. The men who were bound realized the catastrophe but could give no help.[153]

Although the examination system was not actually abolished until close to the end of the dynasty, its weakness was gradually felt since the opening of the five ports in 1842 and the establishment of a new type of school by Western missionaries. The first government move toward Western learning, however, came after the Tientsin Treaty in 1860 when the need of translators arose. In 1860 we find the first edict accepting the principle of the study of foreign language.[154] In 1862 the first foreign language school was established in the capital, and early in 1863 another was established in Shanghai through the request of Li Hung-chang who reasoned as follows:

In China, those who understand foreign language are only some [private] translators. All matters relating to negotiations [with foreigners] in bureaus and troops are handled by locating these translators to transmit the message, and they then do great harm to the foreign affairs aspect [of the government]. ... The key to this important governmental function is thus entrusted to their hands, causing misunderstanding between the parties and inability to discern truth or falsity.[155]

The leading statesmen, Tseng Kuo-fan, Hu Lin-i, Li Hung-chang, and Tso Tsung-t'ang in the provinces, and Prince Kung and Grand Councillor Wen-hsiang in the capital, were among the first to see the importance of Western learning. They promoted the arsenal, translation bureaus, language schools, and the sending of students abroad, and endeavored to adopt various Western technological achievements. But before 1884, the year in which the battle against the French at Ma-chiang, Fukien, occurred, the majority of the officials still opposed the study of Western learning.[156] Ch'en K'ang-ch'i wrote in that year that the language school had foreign instructors to teach

[152] Wang Hsien-ch'ien, *Hsü-shou-t'ang wen-chi*, 1/1 a–b.

[153] Liang Ch'i-ch'ao, "Wu-hsü cheng-pien chi," *Yin-ping-shih ho-chi, wen-chi* 1, p. 15.

[154] *Shih-i-ch'ao tung-hua lu*, Hsien-feng, 97/72 b, which says, "Prince Kung, I-hsin, and others memorialize to request the dispatch of two men who understand foreign language from each of the two places of Shanghai and Canton to the capital. ... Also approved to select men from the eight banners to learn foreign language."

[155] Li Hung-chang, *Li Wen-chung-kung ch'üan-chi, tsou-kao*, 3/11 ff., memorial of T'ung-chih 2/1/22 (1863).

[156] Liang Ch'i-ch'ao, *op. cit.*, p. 21, also marked this year as a dividing line in the development of the reform movement. His four periods begin respectively at 1840, 1862, 1884, and 1895.

astronomy, shipbuilding, machine-making, and so forth. According to Ch'en, the Grand Secretariat at first proposed that officials below 5th and 6th rank from the Grand Secretariat, the various boards, and the Han-lin Academy be selected to study there. But Censor Chang Sheng-tsao memorialized that astronomy should be studied by *t'ien-wen-sheng,* students of astronomy, and engineering by those in the Board of Works, and said that officials and scholars should not learn such skills under barbarians. The subordinates of the various departments and the Academy also considered such a shift as shameful. Up to the time of Ch'en's writing, no officials had joined.[157]

Even in the T'ung-chih period (1862–1874), a few far-sighted statesmen had expressed ideas on modernization, but no one had yet dared to make open proposals on changing the examination system. Such a drastic proposal was made, however, in Kuang-hsü 1 (1875), but it was received with very little sympathy even among the progressive officials.[158] Thus Wang Hsien-ch'ien, later a critic of the examination system, wrote that as Kiangsi provincial examiner he also had shown his disapproval of such a change at that time. He defended his earlier position by saying that, at that time, trade and the navy seemed to him the most important things to be considered.[159]

The unpopularity of Western learning was also shown by the lack of interest in the publications of the translation bureau attached to the Chiang-nan Arsenal. In the thirty years preceding the Sino-Japanese War, only about 13,000 copies of books on Western technology, translated by the bureau, were sold, an average of only about 400 copies sold each year.[160]

[157] Ch'en K'ang-ch'i, *Lang-ch'ien chi-wen*, 1/3 a–b. *T'ung-chih chung-hsing ching-wai tsou-i yüeh-pien*, 5/35–39, contains the memorial by Prince Kung which recommended that officials of 5th rank and below who were from the regular route should be selected to study in *tung-wen-kuan*. *Ibid.*, pp. 40 and 41, contains the memorial by Censor Chang Sheng-tsao who objected to the proposal.

[158] Wang Hsien-ch'ien, *op. cit.*, 1/3 b–4 a. In an essay on the examination system, Wang pointed out that in 1875 Li of Ho-fei submitted a memorial suggesting abolishment of formalized writing in the examination system. The memorial collection of Li Hung-chang does not contain this important memorial. However, in the collection of letters, *Li Wen-chung-kung ch'üan-chi, p'eng-liao han-kao*, 15/4 a–b, in Li's letter dated Kuang-hsü 1/1/8 to Liu Ping-chang, governor of Kiangsi, who was a native of a district neighboring Li's district, Li discussed and criticized formalized writing and calligraphy as having no relation to current affairs. He pointed out that contemporary men had proposed changes, all of which had been opposed by the Board of Rites. He argued with Liu and mentioned that great men did not necessarily come from examinations. He said that he had sent a memorial proposing changes. For information on Liu (1826–1905) see *Hsü pei-chuan-chi*, 31/10 a; *Ch'ing-shih kao*, 453/5 b; *Ch'ing-shih lieh-chuan*, 61/35 b.

[159] Wang Hsien-ch'ien, *loc. cit.* See also 2/6 a–9 a, his preface to the record of the Kiangsi provincial examination. *Ibid.*, 1/1 b–2 a; Wang states that during Tao-kuang and Hsien-feng, the foreign countries were known, but their situation was not well known. Since T'ung-chih and Kuang-hsü, the reason for the other countries being stronger began to be known, but the situation was not critical. The court promoted trade and the governors-general and governors trained the navy. Financial resources did not flow outward, and the situation was self-stimulating. It was not harmful to retain the old examination system.

[160] Liang Ch'i-ch'ao, *op. cit.*, p. 22.

As described also by Liang Ch'i-ch'ao and others, after 1884 the attitude toward foreign studies changed a little, but opposition was still strong. It was the Sino-Japanese War of 1895 that greatly stimulated the acceptance of Western learning.

Wang Hsien-ch'ien said, "Between Kuang-hsü *ting-yu* [1897] and *wu-hsü* [1898], the decline of eight-legged essay writing has reached its utmost. Many have discussed changing the examination system. I also do not favor [the examination system] and write this essay."[161] Wang's essay reflects a general change in the attitude of men of the time. They no longer held the opinion that China could adapt herself to the new situation merely by acquiring Western-style battleships and weapons and machines. The defeat of 1895 demonstrated to these men the administrative weakness of the system, a weakness which resulted from the use of the old examination system to select personnel. Indeed, the old examination system merely drove the literate population to useless and endless efforts and could not survive in a changed situation.

The first real attempt to change the old examination system came in 1898 when an imperial edict ordered the abolishment of the part of the examination on formalized essay writing on the Four Books.[162] In the same year an edict, based on a memorial written by Chang Chih-tung and Ch'en Pao-chen, ordered the abolishment of the section on poetry writing as well as the emphasis on calligraphy.[163] However, the old system was restored shortly afterwards upon the failure of the reform movement led by K'ang Yu-wei, and the content of the examinations was not changed again until after the Boxer Rebellion of 1900.

Thus, the government's first response to the growing demand for a change in the examination system was to shift the traditional emphasis on formalized essay writing, poetry writing, and calligraphy to discussions of current national and international affairs. The edict of Kuang-hsü 24/6/1 (1898) rearranged the three parts of the provincial and metropolitan examination so that the first part dealt with Chinese history and current political issues, and the second part with foreign political and technological knowledge. The third

[161] Wang Hsien-ch'ien, *op. cit.*, 1/1 a. On pp. 1 b–2 a, Wang said, "Since the Sino-Japanese war, the prestige of the country is lost and the other countries are robbing us. Our financial energy is exhausted and the situation is critical. What the country is hoping for is talented men. However, the way of creating them is not different from restraining the people's activity. If one wants to save the situation and give life to the country, needless to say, he will decide that [the old examination system] should not exist."

[162] Liang Ch'i-ch'ao, *op. cit.*, p. 25, edict of 1898. Attached to the edict are Liang's comments and description of earlier attempts by K'ang Yu-wei and others to bring about such a move.

[163] *Ibid.*, p. 34; also see Chang Chih-tung, *Chang Wen-hsiang-kung ssu-kao*, 30/2 a, memorial of Kuang-hsü 24/5/16 (1898).

part still dealt with the classics. This subject which had formerly had sole importance was reduced to the least important position.[164]

Schools which gave new courses on Western learning but still retained Chinese classics as the main subject were promoted, beginning in 1901.[165] However, their progress was slow because of the continuing existence of the examination system, even though it was modified in content. The incompatibility of the existence of the examination system with the process of promoting schools was discussed by several leading statesmen after the Boxer Rebellion. Several memorials requested the gradual reduction of the examination quota with the aim of eventually abolishing the examination system. One joint memorial of 1903 by Chang Po-hsi, Yung-ch'ing, and Chang Chih-tung stated:

> Since the issuance of the edict to promote new schools, it has already been more than two years. But up to the present time there are not many new schools in the various provinces. The cause is the difficulty in obtaining funds. Public funds are limited. Therefore, contribution from among the people is completely relied upon. ... But with the examination system not changed and the quota not reduced, people will hesitate. ... Those who enter the new schools can rely on the examination system and would not only not devote themselves to study but also would not obey discipline.[166]

The regulation governing schools, *Tsou-ting hsüeh-t'ang chang-ch'eng*, was issued on Kuang-hsü 29/11/26 (1903). It marked the beginning of a new era in the Chinese educational system by establishing for the first time a complete school system. The policy of the government was now firmly set that schools were to be emphasized while the examination system was eventually to be concluded. For the time being, the suggestion of gradual reduction of examination quotas was adopted.[167] The demand for new schools was greatly increased by the Russo-Japanese War of 1904, since many Chinese attributed the victory of Japan to the development of new schools.[168] Finally, Yüan Shih-k'ai and others memorialized and argued strongly on the inappropriateness of the continued existence of the old examination system and requested its immediate abolition to facilitate the establishing of new schools. The memorial contains the following statement:

164 Liang Ch'i-ch'ao, *loc. cit.*

165 Yüan Shih-k'ai, *Yang-shou-yüan tsou-i chi-yao*, 10/4–7, memorial of Kuang-hsü 27/9/14. Yüan Shih-k'ai proposed tentative regulations on establishment of schools in response to an imperial edict of Kuang-hsü 27/8/2 on promotion of schools.

166 *Tsou-ting hsüeh-t'ang chang-ch'eng*, *ts'e* 1, p. 12, memorial of 1903. It also referred to another memorial written jointly by Chang Chih-tung and Yüan Shih-k'ai on the bad effects of the examination system in blocking the development of new schools.

167 *Ibid.*, p. 1.

168 Yüan Shih-k'ai, *op. cit.*, 35/3 a–b.

The reduction of examination quotas, with the expectation that they will be abolished after three examination years, so that after ten years the selection of scholars will all be done in the schools, has truly been proclaimed to the world. ... Your officials, in observing the worldly situation and watching the progressing trend, feel that the present critical condition is even more serious than it was formerly. Immediate wholehearted effort is imperative. But with the old examination system not discontinued for one day, the scholars all have the thought of success through luck, thus reducing their aspirations toward industrious and fruitful studies. The people are all watching, and schools established through private efforts have been very few. ... Even if the examination system were immediately discontinued, for wide establishment of schools [throughout the country], more than ten years will be needed before talent can thrive. If a delay of ten years is permitted for the discontinuance of the examination system, ... it will be more than twenty years before the use of talents is available. With strong neighbors surrounding and waiting, how could they wait for us? [169]

Finally, on Kuang-hsü 31/8/4 (1905), an historic edict was issued marking the end of the old examination system:

Instructions to Grand Secretariat: Regarding the memorial of Yüan Shih-k'ai and others requesting the discontinuance of the examination system in order to promote schools and reporting on the plans concerning it, in the period of the Three Dynasties and earlier, the selection of scholars was all through schools and talented men were thriving, which is really the honored way of China in promoting the virtuous and cultivating talents. Also the results of the richness and strength of Eastern and Western countries are all based on schools. At present the situation is critical and the storing of talent is urgent. The court, in considering that recent examinations often fall into empty subjects, has on various occasions issued edicts ordering governors-general and governors of various provinces to establish schools widely in the hope that the people of the country will all approach toward concrete learning to be ready for service. The intention is indeed deep and profound. Formerly, upon the memorial of the educational minister, the provincial and metropolitan examination quotas were permitted to be gradually reduced and abolished within three examination periods. Now according to memorials of the governor-general and others, if the examination system is allowed to continue, the people will hesitate, and in order to promote the establishment of schools, the examination system must be first discontinued. What is presented is not without foresight. It is hereby ordered that beginning from the *ping-yu* examination year (1906), all provincial and metropolitan examinations will be discontinued. The *sui* and *k'o* examinations [to admit *sheng-yüan*] in the various provinces will also be then discontinued. The former *chü-jen*, *kung-sheng*, and *sheng-yüan* will be given an appropriate outlet and other items shall all be dealt with as requested. In essence the [modern] school system is the same as the system of schools in ancient times. In its encouragement of talent, it is also not different from the examination system. Regulations on various occasions have considered the refining of conduct and reading of classics as the base, while the various branches of natural sciences are all of practical use. The officials and gentry should thus make known these aims and rise, after hearing this, to establish more schools and popularize education. The state will

[169] *Ibid.*, pp. 2 a–7 a, memorial of 1905.

then obtain the benefit in cultivating talent and the localities will also share the honor. After the issuance of this edict, the educational minister should speedily publish and distribute various textbooks to ascertain the direction and broaden the cultivation of talent. The respective governors-general and governors are also held responsible for devoting their full attention to the making of over-all plans and for giving strict instructions to the *fu*, *t'ing*, *chou*, and *hsien* magistrates to establish grade schools speedily all over the cities and countryside and to select instructors carefully and broaden the people's knowledge. Each should seriously engage in the work and constantly keep watch. Shun slovenly attitudes that will lead to malpractices. It is definitely expected that virtue will be advanced and knowledge improved and that *t'i* [body] and *yung* [use] [170] will both be provided. Let all meet the utmost intention of the court in promoting learning and cultivating talent.[171]

Thus, the Manchu court, even though reluctantly, had to yield to the trend of the time and make this historic move. The actual development of the school system was yet to come, but the way was now cleared with the abolition of the examination system.

In short, the examination system had operated well when it fulfilled its basic purpose of channeling thought. But in the nineteenth century it suffered an inner breakdown and proved inadaptable to the new needs brought about by the impact of the West. The Ch'ing examination system could no longer serve as a prop to a changed society.

[170] The terms *t'i* and *yung* were of Buddhist origin, later borrowed by Chinese philosophers to express the relation between substance and attribute or reality and appearance. In the late nineteenth century, they were embodied in the popular slogan, "Chinese learning is the body and Western learning is the use." Sometimes it is known as, "Chinese learning is the principle and Western learning is the support." This is elaborated by Chang Chih-tung in his memorials and especially in his *Ch'üan-hsüeh-p'ien* or Exhortation to Learning. *T'i* was considered as the substance, the foundation or base, and the spiritual core. *Yung* was considered as the attribute, the activity and technological application. This was an effort at a compromise between the traditional ideology and the new thought tide advocated by Chang and others, a phenomenon of a transitional period.

[171] *Shih-lu*, Te-tsung, 548/4 a–5 a.

PART FOUR

A Quantitative Analysis of Biographies Of Nineteenth-Century Chinese Gentry

The three studies presented above are intended to describe the gentry's position in Chinese society. They are by no means exhaustive, and a great number of additional studies will have to be made to answer the many questions which pose themselves. To expand the scope of our studies, we have attempted to apply a quantitative method of approach to certain material with the intention of obtaining more information about gentry functions and also of exploring some of the questions concerning the social mobility of the gentry as well as the economic basis of the gentry group. In this way, additional information has been found which has been useful in strengthening some of the points brought out in the preceding studies, and interesting questions have been raised which may point the way toward productive lines of inquiry.

It may be useful to say a few words on the use of quantitative methods in the study of Chinese society. In the social sciences, quantitative methods have been employed mainly in the study of contemporary societies where reliable statistical material exists and field studies can be undertaken. Only few attempts have been made to use historical material not already in statistical form for a quantitative analysis. Least of all have such methods been applied to the rich and complicated Chinese material.

The data used in these studies were taken from gentry biographies collected in the voluminous biographical sections of the local histories—the gazetteers of the provinces, prefectures, and districts. Many such compilations were made as late as the nineteenth century, and almost all of them have biographical sections.[1] Here then is a mass of relatively unexploited mate-

[1] Compilation of these different kinds of local histories generally followed certain patterns. See Li Yüan-tu's correspondence on regulations governing form in the compiling of provincial gazetteers as collected in *Huang-ch'ao chin-shih-wen hsü-pien*, compiled by Ke Shih-chün, 4/5 b–7 b. Li stated that provincial gazetteers were official

rial—thousands of accounts of gentry members, giving specific information on their degrees and titles, their family background, their contributions to community affairs, their economic status. Needless to say, many biographies do not give complete information on all these points. The accounts vary a great deal in emphasis and reliability.[2] These are some of the obvious limitations of the data. However, it was felt that these difficulties could be overcome to some extent by a cautious use of the data. The method of selection employed was to collect a large number of cases from the most reliable sources[3] with a view to obtaining a representative group from each

documents which had to observe regulations and were presented for imperial perusal. According to Li, in K'ang-hsi times, *Honan t'ung-chih* was set by imperial order as a model for other provincial gazetteers. Li stated further that in Yung-cheng 7 (1729) an edict was issued encouraging the compilation of provincial gazetteers, and that regulations on form were also issued. Chu Shih-chia in "Lin-an san-chih k'ao," *Yenching Journal*, No. 20, Dec. 1936, points out that *Lin-an Chih*, which was compiled in the Sung dynasty and is the oldest existing gazetteer, has often been referred to for form and style in gazetteer compilation. Provincial and district gazetteers are quite similar in general outline and kinds of data collected. As the compiler of a Kweichow district gazetteer stated, "A district having gazetteers follows the same principle as a province. There should be definite categories and sections in order to comply with regulations in form and style. Hence the form and style of the *Kweichow t'ung-chih* is followed and eight main categories are made to embody the various sections. . . ." (*Hsü-hsiu Mei-t'an hsien-chih*, introductory *chüan*)

[2] Decisions on which gentry members should be included in the biographical sections could be affected by the personal bias of the gazetteer compilers. However, gazetteers were compiled by regular gentry, and most of them tried to follow some acceptable criterion of selection. One compiler described his standards as follows: "Local virtuous men are naturally models for scholars and are the first to be recorded in the gazetteers. Loyal, filial, chaste, and righteous examples are useful in the maintenance of moral principles and in encouraging others to follow suit. But only those already officially commended or those who have received insignia are to be included in the gazetteers. Others, if unanimously claimed to be worthy and proof can be definitely traced, are also included." (*P'ing-yüan chou hsü-chih*, introductory *chüan*) In another district, the gentry compilers posted notices to the effect that they wanted to include only "worthy" men and requested local inhabitants to let them know if any "unworthy" men had been included in the intended biographical sections. (*Hsü-hsiu Mei-t'an hsien-chih*, 15/6 b) On the other hand, in two district gazetteers where contributors to the compilation and publication fund of these gazetteers are given, many who are listed as "chaste women" are also listed as contributors. (*Po-pai hsien-chih-yü pei-lan, ts'e hsia*; *Ch'ing-yüan hsien-chih*, 16/5 a–24 b) It might well be that contribution to the publication fund was one factor in having one's biography included.

[3] The following list gives the number of cases for each province and the sources from which they were taken:

Province	*No. of Cases*	*Sources*
Kiangsu	366	*Sung-chiang-fu hsü-chih*; *Hsü-chou fu-chih*; *Soochow fu-chih*; *Hsü-tsuan Yang-chou fu-chih*; *T'ung-chou chih*; *Huai-an fu-chih*; *Hsü-tsuan Chiang-ning fu-chih.*
Chekiang	303	*Hangchow fu-chih*; *Ch'u-chou fu-chih*; *Hu-chou fu-chih*; *Chia-hsing fu-chih*; *Kan-shuai hsin-chih.*
Anhwei	156	*Anhwei t'ung-chih.*
Kiangsi	167	*Kiangsi t'ung-chih*; *T'ai-ho hsien-chih.*
Hupeh	239	*Hupeh t'ung-chih*; *Mien-yang hsien-chih.*
Hunan	194	*Hunan t'ung-chih.*

province during each of the reign periods[4] in the nineteenth century. Provincial gazetteers were used if they covered the right period and showed a fair amount of notable data on gentry members of all levels. Some provincial gazetteers could not be used because they had their last edition in the late eighteenth or early nineteenth century. Others also were of no help because their biographical sections were devoted mainly to gentry who held official positions. For provinces whose gazetteers were unsatisfactory for these reasons, examples were taken from the prefectural and district gazetteers. Altogether, 5,473 cases were examined and classified according to certain categories.

First the gentry were grouped according to their functions (Table 33). As we saw in Part One, these functions cover a wide field, comprising in the main eight categories: raising funds for charitable and civic organizations; arbitration; organizing and commanding local defense corps; supervising the financing, construction, and operation of public works; acting as intermediaries between the government and the people; raising funds for government expenses; maintaining Confucian institutions; and giving alms to the poor. Most of the gentry members under observation appear to have been

Province	*No. of Cases*	*Sources*
Szechwan	264	*Hsü-chou fu-chih*; *Chih-li Mien-chou chih*; *Lu-chou chih-li-chou chih*; *T'ung-ch'uan fu-chih*; *K'uei-chou fu-chih*.
Chihli	215	*Chi-fu t'ung-chih*; *Pao-ting fu-chih*; *Tientsin fu-chih*; *T'ung-chou chih*; *Yung-p'ing fu-chih*; *Ting-chou chih*; *Shun-t'ien fu-chih*; *Luan-chou chih*; *Ting-chou hsü-chih*; *Lu-lung hsien-chih*; *Ch'ang-p'ing chou-chih*.
Shantung	601	*Shantung t'ung-chih*; *Chi-nan fu-chih*.
Honan	118	*Nan-yang hsien-chih*; *Sui-chou chih*; *Lu-i hsien-chih*; *Hsiang-fu hsien-chih*.
Shansi	279	*Shansi t'ung-chih*.
Shensi	516	*Shensi t'ung-chih kao*.
Kansu	658	*Kansu hsin t'ung-chih*.
Fukien	163	*Fukien t'ung-chih*; *Ming-hou hsien-chih*.
Kwangtung	396	*Kuang-chou fu-chih*; *P'an-yü hsien hsü-chih*; *Fu-shan chung-i-hsiang chih*; *Wei-chou fu-chih*; *Hsiang-shan hsien-chih*; *Nan-hai hsien-chih*; *Hsiang-shan hsien-chih hsü-pien*; *Kao-chou fu-chih*.
Kwangsi	268	*Ho-hsien chih*; *Hsün-chou fu-chih*; *Jung-hsien chih*; *P'ing-nan hsien-chih*.
Yunnan	444	*Yunnan t'ung-chih*.
Kweichow	126	*Kweichow t'ung-chih kao*; *T'ung-jen fu-chih*; *Li-p'ing fu-chih*.

[4] The distribution of cases over reign periods is as follows:

Reign Period	*No. of Cases*
Chia-ch'ing (1796–1820)	1,171
Tao-kuang (1821–1850)	1,293
Hsien-feng and T'ung-chih (1851–1861–1874)	2,776
Kuang-hsü (1875–1908)	233
Total	5,473

engaged in one or more of these activities; only 32 per cent were classified as "inactive." The term "inactive" is used in a relative sense; that is, these gentry members are not recorded for merit in any of the special functions listed above but received mention for some other reason. For example, some were mentioned as being "filial" or in some other way meritorious. It is true that the mere presence of such gentry members, representing a cultural tradition and commanding the respect of the commoners, was in itself a factor in maintaining the traditional Confucian society. However, compared to those who took an active part in community affairs these men were relatively "inactive" and have therefore been so classified. We find a higher percentage of inactive members among the upper gentry (41 per cent) than among the lower (19 per cent). But we should not forget that inactive lower gentry would be more likely to escape the recorder's attention than would upper gentry.

The activities were, of course, very uneven in their importance. Almsgiving was the easiest way for a gentry member to acquit himself of the obligations imposed by his standing. Under this less significant function, there is listed a larger proportion of lower gentry (24 per cent) than of upper gentry (16 per cent). In both cases we have to allow, however, for the factor of "adjustment" which is shown in the tables and which indicates the duplication of activities. In the much more important activities, as for instance the development of local defense corps, actual command of the units was mostly handled by the lower gentry (30 per cent of their activities) while organization was left largely to the upper gentry (20 per cent of their activities). This confirms our contention that in this field also the upper gentry held the more powerful position. In educational and religious matters, the upper gentry were more active than the lower, while in public works the percentages are almost the same for both groups.

When we study the differentiation by periods (Table 34), we are not surprised to find the proportion of local defense corps activities to be highest in the Tao-kuang (1821–1850) and Hsien-feng and T'ung-chih (1851–61–74) periods, the years of the great rebellions. It could be expected that the all absorbing work for defense was to the detriment of other activities except those connected with the war, such as the collection of funds for government expenses (which moreover was stimulated by premiums; cf. Part Two) and the gentry's intercession with officials in the interest of the local areas.

We have now observed the functions of the gentry as regards scope and time. As we turn to the stress laid upon certain functions in the different provinces (Table 35), the gazetteers give exactly the results that could be expected. In the province of Anhwei it appears that both upper and lower gentry took a remarkable interest in public works. Nowhere would public works be more important than in the vast area of the Huai River. The province of Hunan presents a picture of an extremely low number of inactive gentry together with high activity in "maintenance of Confucian institutions." This is what one would expect from the home province of Tseng Kuo-fan. Other areas affected by the great rebellions, as Shensi-Kansu (Moslem Rebellion), Shantung (Nien Rebellion), Yunnan (Moslem Rebellion), also show a high number of gentry engaged in defense leadership.

These findings are hardly surprising. Interesting results are seen, however, when we introduce the factor of social mobility into our tabulations. Entrance to the status of gentry was theoretically open to anyone except those belonging to the "mean people." However, it was naturally easier for the sons of gentry to acquire gentry status than it was for the sons of commoners. A study of the mobility of the gentry has then to determine what percentage of the gentry came from gentry families and what percentage came from commoner families. These two groups we have termed respectively "established" gentry and "newcomers." For our purpose it seemed sufficient to establish whether a person's father or grandfather possessed gentry status in order to classify him as "established" gentry. The others are considered "newcomers."

The study of social mobility in nineteenth-century China gains a special importance when it is kept in mind that an increasing part of the newcomers came to their gentry status through purchase, the so-called "irregular" way. The regular gentry had to undergo the rigid classical training, though it may be said that with the increase in examination quotas in the middle of the century, the standards of education and discipline were somewhat relaxed. However, the newcomers of the irregular group, who had neither the family background nor the training of the examinations could not be expected to take up the traditional gentry functions in the same spirit as the regulars had.

A study of the increase of the group of newcomers among the gentry may thus help to explain the deterioration of the gentry ideal in the nineteenth century. Whether or not the gentry were "active" and the ways in which they were "active" may indicate to what extent the gentry were still fulfilling their traditional functions or to what extent gentry status had become a mere prerequisite for greater wealth and a means of promoting personal interests.

Some 5,473 cases were studied. Of these it was possible to classify 2,146 as either newcomers or established gentry. Of the cases classified we find that for the whole nineteenth century 35 per cent belong to the group of newcomers (Table 36). This is quite a high percentage. It might be argued that the compilers of the gazetteers from which these data were taken would have shown a natural predilection toward listing more members of established gentry families than newcomers. We may therefore surmise that the proportion of newcomers was even higher than the cases would indicate.

As far as we can follow the cases in the gazetteers throughout the nineteenth century, the percentage of newcomers increases from 32 per cent during the first half of the century to 37 per cent during the Hsien-feng period and afterwards (Table 36). Again the increase shown may be somewhat less than the actual increase because of the subjective element mentioned above.

If we group the cases according to province (Table 37), we find the highest percentage (65 per cent) of newcomers in Hunan, the home province of Tseng Kuo-fan. Obviously this had some relation to the growth of local gentry power connected with the Hunan militia during the middle of the century. Similar conditions may have existed in Kweichow and Yunnan where also within the known cases the percentages of newcomers (55 and 54 per cent respectively) still exceeded that of the established gentry. In the capital province of Chihli, the newcomers also formed a majority (56 per cent). High percentages of newcomers are also shown in the province of Anhwei (47 per cent) and Kwangtung (40 per cent) where the commercial wealth may have accounted for many of the newcomers who mostly entered through purchase.

When we examine the influx of newcomers into the lower and upper strata of the gentry (Table 36), we note a different development during the various periods. In the Chia-ch'ing period (1796–1820), the proportion of newcomers was 34 per cent among the lower gentry and 32 per cent among the upper gentry, a fairly even distribution of about a third of newcomers in both the upper and the lower group. In the Tao-kuang period (1821–1850), however, a great increase of newcomers is found in the lower gentry (48 per cent), while in the upper gentry the newcomers have dropped to 26 per cent. The total of newcomers in the group as a whole is still about one third, but the percentages indicate the large inroad which the newcomers have made in the lower gentry during this period of deterioration without as yet being able to penetrate into the upper gentry, the core of officials and holders of higher academic degrees. In the Hsien-feng and T'ung-chih periods (1851–61–74) the total percentage of newcomers increases to 37 per cent, but more important still seems to be the shift in distribution of the newcomers among the upper and lower groups. The low percentage in the lower group (24 per cent) and the high one in the upper group (42 per cent) seem to indicate that the newcomers rushed directly into positions of control and influence during the years of civil war. In the last period, Kuang-hsü (1875–1908), the percentage of newcomers in both groups combined remains high (37 per cent), but it becomes somewhat more evenly distributed with 32 per cent in the lower and 38 per cent in the upper gentry group. When at the end of the rebellions the situation had become settled again, a slightly more conservative trend in the proportion can thus be observed, though it may be safely assumed that the total increase of newcomers influenced the quality of the gentry.

Having applied a quantitative analysis to gentry functions and social mobility, we may attempt a combination of the two, in other words, try to analyze the participation of the newcomers in gentry functions. For this purpose we have made a separate table for the various reign periods (Table 38). In the first half of the nineteenth century we find an almost equal percentage of inactive members among the established gentry and the newcomers (52 and 50 per cent in Chia-ch'ing and 43 and 42 per cent in Tao-kuang). During the next period, however, in which entry through purchase into gentry status was greatly facilitated, the percentage of inactive members among the newcomers rises to 65 per cent, while that among the established gentry remains almost stationary with even a slight decrease.

This may indicate that of the increased number of newcomers a somewhat higher percentage was either unwilling or as yet unable to assume the traditional gentry responsibilities. The proportional decline in the newcomers' activities is, as would be expected, in such activities as "fund-raising for and supervision of public works" and "maintenance of Confucian institutions" as well as almsgiving, these activities being of lesser concern at a time of civil war. The strongest increase in newcomer activities is, as is also to be expected, in the organization and command of local defense corps (15 per cent for both combined). But it should be added that this increase is still much below the corresponding increase of such activities among the established gentry (39 per cent of the activities of this group).

In the last period, Kuang-hsü (1875–1908), the percentages go up in all the fund-raising activities. This could be interpreted as an indication of the greater commercialization of the period, especially since this applies to both the newcomers and established gentry. When we keep in mind that the established gentry of one period include the newcomers of the preceding period, it can be understood why the changes in emphasis are gradual rather than abrupt.

Last, we have attempted a preliminary survey of the economic situation of these gentry members. The data have been arranged (Table 39) for the various reign periods to facilitate comparison. In many cases it was impossible to find any data at all, and these cases had to be listed as unknown. Especially in the period of civil wars (1851–74) the percentage of these cases is very high (61 per cent); for the other periods it varies from 28 to

36 per cent. Where information is given, the largest number of cases has to be classified under the category, "No record other than indication of wealth." The biographies of these gentry show that they possessed some wealth but do not indicate where this wealth came from. They are mentioned merely as having made financial contributions—often amounting to considerable sums—for local purposes. The percentage for this group is quite high, varying from 17 to 28 per cent. This indicates the significant fact that a high proportion of the gentry had large sums of ready cash at their disposal. Although nothing is said about the origin of such liquid wealth—sometimes from several thousand to several hundred thousand taels—the quantity and kind of this wealth indicates strongly a source of income other than rent from land or even regular business enterprise. Further study will be given to this question. This will lead to a study of income which this group might have had from gentry status itself as opposed to the private income which gentry members could have had from their land or from business or other private activities.

Of a somewhat mixed character is the income from teaching, which is as much a social function as a private activity. In this category the upper gentry almost monopolize the lecturer positions in the *shu-yüan*.[5] In the first half of the century they also dominate the field of so-called private teaching which they share more evenly with the lower gentry in the latter half of the century (Table 40). However, it can be assumed that lower gentry teachers are more frequently omitted from the gazetteers or appear as "unknown." Throughout the whole century a sizable proportion of gentry were deriving an income from their work in the teaching profession. During the period 1851–1874, the period of civil wars, there is a proportional decline in this field; but a great increase is observed again among the much smaller number of cases listed in the last period. (Table 39.)

That gentry status did not necessarily come from wealth or lead to wealth is shown by the category, "no record other than indication of poverty." Such "poverty" is, of course, relative. The so-called poor gentry were in straitened circumstances but probably better off than poor commoners. Besides, the number of cases which could be classified in this way amounted to only 2 to 3 per cent.

Among the categories of what we call private income—with due regard to the benefits of gentry privilege—the percentage of landowners is in steady decline. In the first period it is 12, but it drops to 11 in the next, and to 4 in the period of the great rebellions, rising again to 8 in the Kuang-hsü period. The percentage of merchants seems more stable, varying between

[5] See *supra*, pp. 63, 64.

2 and 3 per cent, a relative increase as compared with the landowners.

The tables also show that certain income patterns are carried over from father to son. In the smaller categories of private income from land and from merchant activities, this is already clearly apparent. In practically all periods (Table 39), the largest number of the gentry who have been identified as landowners had fathers or grandfathers who were also identified as landowners. Among the gentry who were merchants, again the largest number had merchant fathers or grandfathers. Even in the much smaller number of gentry who tilled their own land, this tendency of following their father's economic activities is clearly indicated. In our table, which marks the sons' economic activities vertically and the fathers' economic activities horizontally in the same numerical order, this trend is shown in the diagonal line which is formed by the intersections of lines 1 and 1, 2 and 2, 3 and 3, and so on.

This trend becomes more interesting still if we follow the diagonal line into the category, "indication of wealth," (lines 6 and 6), which we are interpreting as a factor indicating the economic opportunities of gentry status. In this category also, the largest known group had fathers in the same category. Indeed, the most outstanding figures of the diagonal line are those at the intersection of lines 6 and 6. This holds true for all periods. The fact that in the great majority of known cases considerable wealth without any indication of a private source of income can be observed in more than one generation strengthens our thesis that this wealth had a special origin—namely, gentry status. It may also be significant that the largest figures of "unknown" both in the gentry and in the column of the parents are concentrated in both lines 6 (intersection 6 and 10, and intersection 10 and 6). In other words, of the largest number of gentry of which we know only that they were wealthy, the economic status of the parents is unknown. Of the largest number of gentry whose economic status is unknown, we know only that their parents were wealthy. This again holds true for all periods. As to the wealthy gentry whose parents' economic status is unknown, we may assume that they included a number of newcomers. But whether newcomers or not, it is important that the unknown figure is also so overwhelmingly much larger than the number of such gentry of wealth whose parents were known to have been landowners, merchants, or of any other especially mentioned economic background. It also may be significant that of the large number of gentry whose economic status is not given and who are therefore listed as "unknown" in the vertical column, by far the largest number had parents with "indication of wealth." This again is true of all periods.

The emphasis of the diagonal line which carries over into the teaching category (7 a–b and 7 a–b) is too slight to develop here.

Table 41 shows economic data on gentry members according to province and period. In all cases a high percentage appears under the category, "no record other than indication of wealth." Interesting, for instance, are the high percentages in this category for Kiangsu and Anhwei. There are also other percentages worth mentioning. Hunan stands out as having had the highest proportion of landowning gentry before the Taiping Rebellion. This phenomenon could be connected with the active part that the Hunan gentry took in the fight against the Taipings. The percentage declines somewhat in later periods. Chihli is among the other provinces with a comparatively high percentage of landowners. The percentages in the merchant category are much smaller. Anhwei and Kwangtung have the highest proportions of merchants, with Shansi following. Inland provinces like Yunnan, Honan, and Kansu have a high proportion of teachers and of gentry with "no record other than indication of poverty," as compared with coastal provinces or with richer inland provinces.

We should like to stress again that these results of our first attempt to make a quantitative analysis of gentry biographies have to be regarded as very tentative. As far as they go, however, they lend support to some of the hypotheses set forth in the previous sections. The tables listing the gentry's actions under the various categories of functions bear out and describe in more detail the gentry's functional role in Chinese society. In all provinces and in all periods of the nineteenth century, a large part of the gentry are shown to be active in all the more important functions with the emphasis shifting according to the needs of place and time. The data on "newcomers" show a high and increasing social mobility. All through the economic tables, the high percentages of gentry with wealth in the form of ready cash point to the economic advantages which gentry status itself provided. It is interesting to note the great disproportion between this figure and the small number of cases in which there is information on private sources of income such as land or merchant enterprises. Among these latter small percentages, there can be seen a minor trend of declining landownership and increasing business activities which reflects the changing economy. The far more outstanding figure of general wealth has been an unexpected result of our tabulations. It has greatly strengthened our hypothesis that gentry status itself provided the possibility of income. We are well aware, however, that this figure, like a number of the others, raises new questions which cannot immediately be answered. These questions will lead us to further study of the economic basis of the Chinese gentry.

TABLE 33

GENTRY PARTICIPATION IN FUNCTIONS (ALL PROVINCES AND ALL PERIODS)

Type of Gentry		Fund raising for and trusteeship of charitable and civic organizations	Arbitration (Settling disputes)	Local defense leadership: Organizing	Local defense leadership: Commanding	Fund raising for and supervision of public works*	Maintenance of Confucian institutions†	Spokesmanship (Intermediaries between officials and people)	Fund raising for government expenses (esp. military)	Almsgiving and other private charity	Inactive gentry members	Total	Adjustment	Cases Studied
Upper	No.	238	96	680	176	280	470	172	118	521	1364	4115	836	3279
	P.c.	8	3	20	5	9	15	5	4	16	41	126	26	100
Lower	No.	133	99	303	670	216	246	59	64	525	402	2717	523	2194
	P.c.	6	5	13	30	10	11	3	3	24	19	124	24	100
Total	No.	371	195	983	846	496	716	231	182	1046	1766	6832	1359	5473
	P.c.	7	4	18	15	9	13	4	3	20	32	125	25	100

See footnotes at bottom of Table 34.

TABLE 34

GENTRY PARTICIPATION IN FUNCTIONS—BY PERIOD (ALL PROVINCES)

Period	Type of Gentry		Fund raising for and trusteeship of charitable and civic organizations	Arbitration (Settling disputes)	Local defense leadership: Organizing	Local defense leadership: Commanding	Fund raising for and supervision of public works*	Maintenance of Confucian institutions†	Spokesmanship (Intermediaries between officials and people)	Fund raising for government expenses (esp. military)	Almsgiving and other private charity	Inactive gentry members	Total	Adjustment	Cases Studied
Chia-ch'ing	Upper	No.	60	25	33	16	75	140	45	5	173	381	953	179	774
		P.c.	7	3	4	2	10	18	6	1	22	50	123	23	100
	Lower	No.	42	26	19	51	58	81	11	4	132	105	529	132	397
		P.c.	10	6	5	13	15	20	3	1	33	27	133	33	100
Tao-kuang	Upper	No.	83	31	65	9	110	158	43	21	193	365	1078	252	826
		P.c.	10	4	8	1	13	19	5	3	23	44	130	30	100
	Lower	No.	46	38	11	8	84	87	20	14	215	99	622	155	467
		P.c.	10	8	2	2	18	19	4	3	46	21	133	33	100
Hsien-feng and T'ung-chih	Upper	No.	60	34	569	150	76	138	72	81	128	557	1865	346	1519
		P.c.	4	2	38	10	5	9	4	5	9	37	123	23	100
	Lower	No.	31	31	267	611	69	66	27	40	146	180	1468	211	1257
		P.c.	2	2	21	49	6	5	2	3	12	14	116	16	100
Kuang-hsü	Upper	No.	35	6	13	1	19	34	12	11	27	61	219	59	160
		P.c.	22	4	8	.	11	21	7	7	17	38	137	37	100
	Lower	No.	14	4	6	.	5	12	1	6	32	18	98	25	73
		P.c.	19	6	8	.	7	16	1	8	44	25	134	34	100

* Including dikes, dams, bridges, roads, irrigation projects, city walls, ferries, etc.

† Including establishment and repair of schools, shrines, etc., publication of books, as well as moral exhortation, etc.

TABLE 35

Gentry Participation in Functions—By Province (All Periods)

Province	Type of Gentry	Fund raising for and trusteeship of charitable and civic organizations	Arbitration (Settling disputes)	Local defense leadership		Fund raising for and supervision of public works*	Maintenance of Confucian institutions†	Spokesmanship (Intermediaries between officials and people)	Fund raising for government expenses (esp. military)	Almsgiving and other private charity	Inactive gentry members	Total	Adjustment	Cases Studied
				Organizing	Commanding									
Kiangsu . . .	Upper	34	3	51	5	22	23	26	3	47	59	273	61	212
	Lower	33	6	18	22	12	18	7	4	36	36	192	38	154
Chekiang . .	Upper	15	7	17	4	15	16	7	2	24	102	209	26	183
	Lower	20	4	11	14	15	8	2	.	28	35	137	17	120
Anhwei	Upper	4	3	15	4	18	20	1	12	40	17	134	59	75
	Lower	11	2	12	14	23	15	3	6	43	5	134	53	81
Kiangsi	Upper	7	3	16	9	16	33	4	1	22	35	146	35	111
	Lower	7	1	4	10	11	19	1	4	11	10	78	22	56
Hupeh	Upper	8	7	16	3	19	15	8	7	18	58	159	43	116
	Lower	4	11	11	26	24	13	7	3	45	19	163	40	123
Hunan	Upper	13	7	8	7	33	40	4	4	38	57	211	80	131
	Lower	11	11	4	1	29	24	4	1	32	3	120	57	63
Szechwan . .	Upper	9	4	15	10	8	22	6	.	21	55	150	20	130
	Lower	6	8	7	46	16	13	7	3	29	39	174	40	134
Chihli	Upper	9	2	18	3	8	25	6	9	41	56	177	42	135
	Lower	4	10	5	12	6	18	4	2	42	6	109	29	80
Shantung . .	Upper	12	6	210	5	10	16	8	10	12	31	320	32	288
	Lower	2	2	79	217	2	6	2	2	4	3	319	6	313
Honan	Upper	7	2	17	1	4	7	2	2	11	38	91	16	75
	Lower	2	3	7	6	1	7	.	1	22	6	55	12	43
Shansi	Upper	5	4	10	6	16	23	3	4	44	77	192	34	158
	Lower	1	2	4	1	12	14	.	1	75	35	145	24	121
Shensi	Upper	36	5	51	30	28	59	17	27	52	58	363	109	254
	Lower	15	9	28	145	18	25	1	13	31	20	305	43	262
Kansu	Upper	2	6	62	25	11	23	10	11	43	227	420	33	387
	Lower	6	7	72	43	16	20	9	14	56	84	327	56	271
Fukien	Upper	26	4	16	.	15	23	17	2	16	76	195	51	144
	Lower	.	1	.	.	1	2	.	.	7	11	22	3	19
Kwangtung	Upper	33	17	53	7	25	59	28	7	45	152	426	100	326
	Lower	6	9	11	4	8	17	4	2	18	26	105	35	70
Kwangsi . . .	Upper	6	9	69	17	19	28	12	10	14	43	227	54	173
	Lower	2	3	22	43	8	8	4	3	13	11	117	22	95
Yunnan . . .	Upper	11	3	21	37	11	30	10	5	27	173	328	30	298
	Lower	.	7	4	54	9	14	4	4	24	41	161	15	146
Kweichow .	Upper	1	4	15	3	2	8	3	2	6	50	94	11	83
	Lower	3	3	4	12	5	5	.	1	9	12	54	11	43
Total	Upper	238	96	680	176	280	470	172	118	521	1364	4115	836	3279
	Lower	133	99	303	670	216	246	59	64	525	402	2717	523	2194
Grand Total		371	195	983	846	496	716	231	182	1046	1766	6832	1359	5473

* Including dikes, dams, bridges, roads, irrigation projects, city walls, ferries, etc.

† Including establishment and repair of schools, shrines, etc., publication of books, as well as moral exhortation, etc.

TABLE 36

"NEWCOMER" AND "ESTABLISHED" GENTRY — BY PERIOD (ALL PROVINCES)

Period	Type of Gentry	"Newcomer" No.	"Newcomer" Per cent	"Established" No.	"Established" Per cent	Total	Per cent
Chia-ch'ing	Upper	138	32	298	68	436	100
	Lower	49	34	96	66	145	100
		187	32	394	68	581	100
Tao-kuang	Upper	108	26	307	74	415	100
	Lower	88	48	94	52	182	100
		196	33	401	67	597	100
Hsien-feng and T'ung-chih	Upper	262	42	357	58	619	100
	Lower	57	24	178	76	235	100
		319	37	535	63	854	100
Kuang-hsü	Upper	33	38	53	62	86	100
	Lower	9	32	19	68	28	100
		42	37	72	63	114	100
Total		744	35	1402	65	2146	100

TABLE 37

"NEWCOMER" AND "ESTABLISHED" GENTRY — BY PROVINCE (ALL PERIODS)

Province	"Newcomer" No.	"Newcomer" Per cent	"Established" No.	"Established" Per cent	Total	Per cent
Kiangsu	29	18	134	82	163	100
Chekiang	9	9	91	91	100	100
Anhwei	27	47	30	53	57	100
Kiangsi	32	41	46	59	78	100
Hupeh	35	31	78	69	113	100
Hunan	57	65	30	35	87	100
Szechwan	23	20	92	80	115	100
Chihli	55	56	43	44	98	100
Shantung	15	19	65	81	80	100
Honan	10	17	48	83	58	100
Shansi	34	32	70	68	104	100
Shensi	75	42	104	58	179	100
Kansu	92	35	174	65	266	100
Fukien	36	28	91	72	127	100
Kwangtung	84	40	127	60	211	100
Kwangsi	17	17	83	83	100	100
Yunnan	77	54	66	46	143	100
Kweichow	37	55	30	45	67	100
Total	744	35	1402	65	2146	100

TABLE 38

"NEWCOMER" AND "ESTABLISHED" GENTRY—PARTICIPATION IN FUNCTIONS, BY PERIOD (ALL PROVINCES)

Period	Type of Gentry		Fund raising for and trusteeship of charitable and civic organizations	Arbitration (Settling disputes)	Local defense leadership		Fund raising for and supervision of public works *	Maintenance of Confucian institutions †	Spokesmanship (Intermediaries between officials and people)	Fund raising for gov't. expenses (esp. military)	Almsgiving and other private charity	Inactive gentry members	Total	Adjustment	Cases Studied
					Organizing	Commanding									
Chia-ch'ing	Established	No.	38	18	8	2	29	70	21	5	101	202	494	100	394
		Per cent	9	4	2	.	7	18	5	2	26	52	125	25	100
	Newcomer	No.	11	5	3	6	17	29	6	1	48	94	220	33	187
		Per cent	6	3	2	3	9	15	3	.	26	50	117	17	100
Tao-kuang	Established	No.	37	16	31	1	47	59	24	6	105	173	499	98	401
		Per cent	9	4	8	.	11	17	6	2	26	43	127	27	100
	Newcomer	No.	12	10	11	1	30	36	6	10	67	81	264	68	196
		Per cent	6	5	6	.	15	18	3	5	35	42	135	35	100
Hsien-feng and T'ung-chih	Established	No.	30	23	145	61	39	68	29	37	58	213	703	168	535
		Per cent	6	4	28	11	8	13	6	7	11	41	131	31	100
	Newcomer	No.	14	9	29	18	14	23	13	13	46	210	389	70	319
		Per cent	5	3	9	6	5	7	4	4	14	65	122	22	100
Kuang-hsü	Established	No.	22	2	8	1	12	16	6	8	12	24	111	39	72
		Per cent	31	3	11	1	17	22	9	11	16	33	154	54	100
	Newcomer	No.	11	3	1	.	7	9	.	1	10	16	58	16	42
		Per cent	26	7	2	.	16	22	.	2	24	39	138	38	100

* Including dikes, dams, bridges, roads, irrigation projects, city walls, ferries, etc.

† Including establishment and repair of schools, shrines, etc., publication of books, as well as moral exhortation, etc.

TABLE 39

ECONOMIC DATA ON GENTRY MEMBERS AND THEIR PROGENITORS *
(ALL PROVINCES)

Gentry Members	Fathers and/or Grandfathers												
	Chia-ch'ing Period, 1796–1820												
	1	2	3	4	5	6	7 a	7 b	8	9	10	Total	Per cent
1. Big and small landowners	13	1	.	.	1	8	.	.	.	3	100	126	12
2. Farmers cultivating own land; tenants, laborers	.	.	.	.	.	1	.	.	.	3	7	11	1
3. Usurers	2	.	1	.	1	2	.	.	.	.	15	21	2
4. Rich merchants	.	1	.	1	1	1	.	.	.	1	7	12	1
5. Small merchants	.	.	.	.	.	.	.	.	.	2	5	7	1
6. No information other than indication of wealth	7	2	4	6	4	45	2	2	.	9	222	303	24
7. Teachers (a) *Shu-yüan*	.	.	.	.	.	1	3	4	1	10	52	71	5
7. Teachers (b) Private	2	7	.	.	1	5	2	7	2	9	130	165	13
8. Medical doctors and professors of geomancy, and personal assistants	.	.	.	1	.	5	.	2	.	.	18	26	2
9. No information other than indication of poverty	.	.	.	.	.	2	.	1	.	5	35	43	3
10. Unknown	22	7	3	9	6	55	15	26	8	15	280	446	36
Total	46	18	8	17	14	125	22	42	11	57	871	1231†	100
Per cent	4	1	1	1	1	10	2	3	1	5	71	100	.
	Tao-kuang Period, 1821–1850												
	1	2	3	4	5	6	7 a	7 b	8	9	10	Total	Per cent
1. Big and small landowners	8	1	.	1	.	9	.	.	2	4	123	148	11
2. Farmers cultivating own land; tenants, laborers	.	2	.	.	.	.	.	.	.	.	7	9	1
3. Usurers	3	.	.	1	.	.	.	.	.	.	27	31	2
4. Rich merchants	.	.	.	3	.	.	.	.	.	3	18	24	2
5. Small merchants	.	.	.	.	.	.	.	1	.	2	6	9	1
6. No information other than indication of wealth	8	5	4	6	4	51	2	4	1	6	248	339	25
7. Teachers (a) *Shu-yüan*	1	1	.	2	.	4	1	1	.	2	74	86	6
7. Teachers (b) Private	2	5	.	1	.	3	2	4	2	10	148	177	13
8. Medical doctors and professors of geomancy, and personal assistants	2	.	.	1	.	1	.	1	5	3	38	51	3
9. No information other than indication of poverty	.	1	.	1	1	1	.	1	.	2	32	39	3
10. Unknown	27	4	7	8	8	70	17	33	6	28	231	439	33
Total	51	19	11	24	13	139	22	45	16	60	952	1352	100
Per cent	4	2	1	2	1	10	1	3	1	4	71	100	.

* Horizontal numbers correspond to items enumerated under vertical listing.
Actual cases studied—1,171. . Actual cases studied—1,293.

TABLE 39 *(concluded)*

Gentry Members	Hsien-feng and T'ung-chih Periods, 1851–1861–1875												
	1	2	3	4	5	6	7		8	9	10	Total	Per cent
							a	b					
1. Big and small landowners	8	.	2	2	.	7	.	.	.	.	100	119	4
2. Farmers cultivating own land; tenants, laborers	.	7	.	.	.	.	.	.	.	5	10	22	1
3. Usurers	.	.	.	.	.	5	.	.	.	.	11	16	1
4. Rich merchants	.	1	.	4	.	1	.	.	.	6	17	29	1
5. Small merchants	.	.	.	.	.	.	.	.	.	5	10	15	1
6. No information other than indication of wealth	5	3	.	9	1	61	.	1	1	8	402	491	17
7. Teachers (a) *Shu-yüan*	.	1	.	.	.	6	1	1	.	2	91	102	3
7. Teachers (b) Private	.	3	.	3	1	1	.	.	1	9	182	200	7
8. Medical doctors and professors of geomancy, and personal assistants	.	1	.	.	.	2	.	.	1	2	43	49	2
9. No information other than indication of poverty	.	.	.	.	2	.	.	1	.	4	45	52	2
10. Unknown	18	13	4	9	11	75	19	36	18	17	1518	1738	61
Total	31	29	6	27	15	158	20	39	21	58	2429	2833*	100
Per cent	1	1	.	1	1	6	1	1	1	2	85	100	.
	Kuang-hsü Period, 1875–1908												
	1	2	3	4	5	6	7		8	9	10	Total	Per cent
							a	b					
1. Big and small landowners	.	.	.	1	.	2	.	.	.	.	15	18	8
2. Farmers cultivating own land; tenants, laborers	.	1	.	.	.	.	.	.	.	.	1	2	1
3. Usurers	.	.	.	.	.	1	.	.	.	.	2	3	1
4. Rich merchants	.	.	.	2	.	.	.	.	.	1	3	6	2
5. Small merchants	.	.	.	.	.	.	.	.	1	.	.	1	1
6. No information other than indication of wealth	2	.	.	4	.	8	.	.	.	4	48	66	26
7. Teachers (a) *Shu-yüan*	.	.	.	1	.	.	1	1	.	3	25	31	13
7. Teachers (b) Private	.	1	.	1	.	.	.	.	.	1	24	27	11
8. Medical doctors and professors of geomancy, and personal assistants	.	.	.	1	.	.	.	.	1	3	11	16	6
9. No information other than indication of poverty	.	.	.	.	.	.	.	.	1	.	5	6	3
10. Unknown	6	.	2	9	1	9	2	5	1	2	33	70	28
Total	8	2	2	19	1	20	3	6	4	14	167	246†	100
Per cent	3	1	1	7	1	8	1	2	1	6	69	100	.

* Actual cases studied—2,776. † Actual cases studied—233.

TABLE 40

ECONOMIC DATA ON UPPER AND LOWER GENTRY

	Chia-ch'ing						Tao-kuang						Hsien-feng T'ung-chih						Kuang-hsü					
	Upper		Lower		Total	Per cent	Upper		Lower		Total	Per cent	Upper		Lower		Total	Per cent	Upper		Lower		Total	Per cent
	No.	Per cent	No.	Per cent			No.	Per cent	No.	Per cent			No.	Per cent	No.	Per cent			No.	Per cent	No.	Per cent		
1. Big and small landowners	54	11	72	23	126	16	47	9	101	27	148	16	48	8	71	15	119	11	6	5	12	20	18	11
2. Farmers cultivating own land; tenants, laborers	8	2	3	1	11	1	5	1	4	1	9	1	14	2	8	2	22	2	.	.	2	3	2	1
3. Usurers	6	1	15	5	21	3	8	1	23	6	31	3	4	1	12	3	16	1	.	.	3	5	3	2
4. Rich merchants	4	1	8	3	12	1	10	2	14	4	24	3	17	3	12	3	29	3	3	1	3	5	6	3
5. Small merchants	5	1	2	1	7	1	3	1	6	2	9	1	10	2	5	1	15	1	1	1	.	.	1	.
6. No information other than indication of wealth	179	37	124	40	303	40	195	37	144	38	339	38	284	45	207	45	491	45	47	42	19	33	66	38
7. Teachers (a) *Shu-yüan*	68	14	3	1	71	9	85	16	1	.	86	9	96	15	6	1	102	9	31	26	.	.	31	17
(b) Private	114	24	51	17	165	21	124	23	53	14	177	19	101	15	99	21	200	19	15	13	12	20	27	16
8. Medical doctors and professors of geomancy, and personal assistants	7	2	19	6	26	3	28	5	23	6	51	6	25	4	24	5	49	4	11	9	5	9	16	9
9. No information other than indication of poverty	33	7	10	3	43	5	29	5	10	2	39	4	32	5	20	4	52	5	3	3	3	5	6	3
Subtotal	478	100	307	100	785	100	534	100	379	100	913	100	631	100	464	100	1095	100	117	100	59	100	176	100
10. Unknown	320	.	126	.	446	.	342	.	97	.	439	.	915	.	823	.	1738	.	56	.	14	.	70	.
Total	798	.	433	.	1231	.	876	.	476	.	1352	.	1546	.	1287	.	2833	.	173	.	73	.	246	.

TABLE 41

ECONOMIC DATA ON GENTRY MEMBERS—BY PROVINCE

Economic Data on Gentry Members	Chia-ch'ing Period																																				
	Kiangsu		Chekiang		Anhwei		Kiangsi		Hupeh		Hunan		Szechwan		Chihli		Shantung		Honan		Shansi		Shensi		Kansu		Fukien		Kwangtung		Kwangsi		Yunnan		Kweichow		
	No.	P. c.	No.	P. c.	No.	P. c.	No.	P. c.	No.	P. c.	No.	P. c.	No.	P. c.	No.	P. c.	No.	P. c.	No.	P. c.	No.	P. c.	No.	P. c.	No.	P. c.	No.	P. c.	No.	P. c.	No.	P. c.	No.	P. c.	No.	P. c.	Totals
1. Big and small landowners .	5	5	6	8	1	9	20	34	2	10	14	48	7	11	12	36	1	5	4	31	21	35	12	23	2	6	.	.	10	10	.	.	6	10	3	30	126
2. Farmers cultivating own land; tenants, laborers	1	1	.	.	1	9	2	3	.	.	.	.	.	.	1	3	.	.	.	.	1	1	.	.	2	6	.	.	.	.	1	65	2	3	.	.	11
3. Usurers	4	4	2	3	.	.	.	.	.	.	5	18	1	1	1	3	.	.	.	.	8	13	.	.	.	.	.	.	.	.	.	.	.	.	.	.	21
4. Rich merchants...........	.	.	2	3	.	.	2	3	.	.	1	3	1	1	1	3	.	.	.	.	2	3	.	.	.	.	.	.	3	3	.	.	.	.	.	.	12
5. Small merchants	.	.	1	1	.	.	3	5	.	.	.	.	1	1	.	.	.	.	.	.	1	1	.	.	.	.	.	.	.	.	.	.	1	2	.	.	7
6. No information other than indication of wealth	59	59	30	41	8	73	30	50	10	50	8	28	25	39	9	26	11	50	1	8	13	21	25	49	8	24	11	46	37	36	6	40	11	18	1	10	303
7. Teachers (a) *Shu-yüan*	7	7	10	13	.	.	.	.	2	10	.	.	8	13	.	.	1	5	.	.	3	5	5	10	7	22	7	29	10	10	.	.	9	14	2	20	71
(b) Private	16	16	13	18	1	9	3	5	5	25	1	3	18	29	9	26	5	22	7	53	5	8	6	12	8	24	5	21	31	30	4	27	26	42	2	20	165
8. Medical doctors and professors of geomancy, and personal assistants	4	4	4	5	.	.	.	.	.	.	.	.	3	5	1	3	3	13	.	.	3	5	2	4	1	3	1	4	2	2	1	65	.	.	1	10	26
9. No information other than indication of poverty......	4	4	6	8	.	.	.	.	1	5	.	.	.	.	.	.	1	5	1	8	4	7	1	2	5	15	.	.	9	9	3	20	7	11	1	10	43
Subtotals	100	100	74	100	11	100	60	100	20	100	29	100	64	100	34	100	22	100	13	100	61	100	51	100	33	100	24	100	102	100	15	100	62	100	10	100	.
10. Unknown	41	.	33	.	2	.	24	.	22	.	11	.	47	.	15	.	15	.	12	.	18	.	39	.	32	.	21	.	58	.	7	.	38	.	11	.	446
Totals	141	.	107	.	13	.	84	.	42	.	40	.	111	.	49	.	37	.	25	.	79	.	90	.	65	.	46	.	160	.	22	.	100	.	21	.	1231

TABLE 41 *(continued)*

Ecomomic Data on Gentry Members	Tao-kuang Period																																				
	Kiangsu		Chekiang		Anhwei		Kiangsi		Hupeh		Hunan		Szechwan		Chihli		Shantung		Honan		Shansi		Shensi		Kansu		Fukien		Kwangtung		Kwangsi		Yunnan		Kweichow		
	No.	P. c.	No.	P. c.	No.	P. c.	No.	P. c.	No.	P. c.	No.	P. c.	No.	P. c.	No.	P. c.	No.	P. c.	No.	P. c.	No.	P. c.	No.	P. c.	No.	P. c.	No.	P. c.	No.	P. c.	No.	P. c.	No.	P. c.	No.	P. c.	Totals
1. Big and small landowners	14	17	6	8	12	27	4	17	14	23	31	50	1	3	16	24	3	18	2	6	17	14	12	21	7	18	.	.	2	3	5	13	.	.	2	14	148
2. Farmers cultivating own land; tenants, laborers	.	.	.	.	.	.	1	4	.	.	2	3	.	.	1	1	.	.	.	.	2	2	.	.	1	3	.	.	.	.	2	5	.	.	.	.	9
3. Usurers	2	3	1	1	4	9	1	4	5	8	1	2	.	.	4	6	.	.	.	.	9	7	2	4	1	3	.	.	.	.	1	2	.	.	.	.	31
4. Rich merchants	1	1	1	1	4	9	2	8	.	.	2	3	.	.	4	6	.	.	.	.	5	4	.	.	1	3	2	12	2	3	.	.	.	.	.	.	24
5. Small merchants	1	1	2	3	2	4	.	.	.	.	1	2	.	.	1	1	.	.	.	.	1	1	.	.	.	.	.	.	.	.	1	2	.	.	.	.	9
6. No information other than indication of wealth	39	47	30	37	20	45	12	50	25	42	18	30	10	32	32	47	5	29	10	33	46	39	18	32	6	15	5	29	27	39	14	35	18	31	4	29	339
7. Teachers (a) *Shu-yüan*	4	5	7	9	.	.	.	.	1	2	2	3	4	13	.	.	3	18	1	3	8	7	12	22	5	12	5	29	17	24	5	13	8	14	4	29	86
(b) Private	12	14	14	17	.	.	4	17	10	17	3	5	13	42	7	10	5	29	11	36	14	12	9	17	17	43	2	12	17	24	9	23	28	47	2	14	177
8. Medical doctors and professors of geomancy, and personal assistants	5	6	12	15	1	2	.	.	3	5	1	2	2	7	2	4	.	.	2	6	14	12	2	4	1	3	2	12	.	.	1	2	3	5	.	.	51
9. No information other than indication of poverty	5	6	7	9	2	4	.	.	2	3	.	.	1	3	1	1	1	6	5	16	3	2	.	.	.	.	1	6	5	7	2	5	2	3	2	14	39
Subtotals	83	100	80	100	45	100	24	100	60	100	61	100	31	100	68	100	17	100	31	100	119	100	55	100	39	100	17	100	70	100	40	100	59	100	14	100	.
10. Unknown	22	.	36	.	10	.	17	.	27	.	19	.	30	.	42	.	11	.	13	.	27	.	14	.	32	.	21	.	53	.	13	.	46	.	6	.	439
Totals	105	.	116	.	55	.	41	.	87	.	80	.	61	.	110	.	28	.	44	.	146	.	69	.	71	.	38	.	123	.	53	.	105	.	20	.	1352

TABLE 41 *(continued)*

Economic Data on Gentry Members	Hsien-feng and T'ung-chih Periods																																				
	Kiangsu		Chekiang		Anhwei		Kiangsi		Hupeh		Hunan		Szechwan		Chihli		Shantung		Honan		Shansi		Shensi		Kansu		Fukien		Kwangtung		Kwangsi		Yunnan		Kweichow		
	No.	P. c.	No.	P. c.	No.	P. c.	No.	P. c.	No.	P. c.	No.	P. c.	No.	P. c.	No.	P. c.	No.	P. c.	No.	P. c.	No.	P. c.	No.	P. c.	No.	P. c.	No.	P. c.	No.	P. c.	No.	P. c.	No.	P. c.	No.	P. c.	Totals
1. Big and small landowners..	4	4	1	2	16	23	3	13	6	11	12	23	6	16	10	30	1	4	4	15	6	15	6	7	21	11	.	.	4	8	12	12	4	6	3	7	119
2. Farmers cultivating own land; tenants, laborers	.	.	.	.	.	.	.	.	.	.	7	13	.	.	.	.	.	.	.	.	.	.	.	.	12	6	.	.	1	2	.	.	1	2	1	2	22
3. Usurers	.	.	.	.	4	6	1	5	1	2	.	.	.	.	.	.	.	.	.	.	.	.	3	3	2	1	.	.	.	.	.	.	3	5	2	5	16
4. Rich merchants	1	1	.	.	8	11	2	9	.	.	1	2	1	3	.	.	.	.	.	.	.	.	.	.	2	1	2	6	9	16	.	.	.	.	3	7	29
5. Small merchants	1	1	2	4	1	1	.	.	.	.	2	4	.	.	1	3	.	.	.	.	.	.	1	1	4	2	2	6	.	.	.	.	1	2	.	.	15
6. No information other than indication of wealth.......	68	70	26	48	36	51	12	55	29	55	22	41	9	24	18	55	21	81	15	58	17	44	38	41	49	26	19	52	19	34	59	60	14	21	20	47	491
7. Teachers (a) *Shu-yüan*	2	2	5	9	2	3	3	13	7	13	1	2	5	13	1	3	3	11	.	.	7	18	19	20	22	11	8	22	6	11	6	6	2	3	3	7	102
(b) Private.......	13	13	15	28	3	4	1	5	5	9	5	9	12	33	2	6	1	4	5	19	4	10	13	14	61	32	3	8	9	16	17	17	29	44	2	5	200
8. Medical doctors and professors of geomancy, and personal assistants	6	6	4	7	1	1	.	.	4	8	3	6	3	8	.	.	.	.	.	.	.	.	9	10	5	3	2	6	3	5	.	.	5	7	4	9	49
9. No information other than indication of poverty	3	3	1	2	.	.	.	.	1	2	.	.	1	3	1	3	.	.	–	8	5	13	4	4	13	7	.	.	4	8	5	5	7	10	5	11	52
Subtotals	98	100	54	100	71	100	22	100	53	100	53	100	37	100	33	100	26	100	26	100	39	100	93	100	191	100	36	100	55	100	99	100	66	100	43	100	.
10. Unknown	41	.	34	.	21	.	26	.	67	.	34	.	65	.	30	.	503	.	19	.	24	.	207	.	266	.	22	.	55	.	98	.	180	.	46	.	1738
Totals	139	.	88	.	92	.	48	.	120	.	87	.	102	.	63	.	529	.	45	.	63	.	300	.	457	.	58	.	110	.	197	.	246	.	89	.	2833

TABLE 41 (*concluded*)

Economic Data on Gentry Members	Kuang-hsü Period																																				
	Kiangsu		Chekiang		Anhwei		Kiangsi		Hupeh		Hunan		Szechwan		Chihli		Shantung		Honan		Shansi		Shensi		Kansu		Fukien		Kwangtung		Kwangsi		Yunnan		Kweichow		Totals
	No.	P. c.	No.	P. c.	No.	P. c.	No.	P. c.	No.	P. c.	No.	P. c.	No.	P. c.	No.	P. c.	No.	P. c.	No.	P. c.	No.	P. c.	No.	P. c.	No.	P. c.	No.	P. c.	No.	P. c.	No.	P. c.	No.	P. c.	No.	P. c.	
1. Big and small landowners	.	.	.	.	.	.	.	.	.	.	.	.	.	.	.	.	.	.	2	20	1	8	12	18	3	7	.	.	.	.	.	.	.	.	.	.	18
2. Farmers cultivating own land; tenants, laborers	.	.	.	.	.	.	.	.	.	.	.	.	.	.	.	.	.	.	.	.	.	.	.	.	2	4	.	.	.	.	.	.	.	.	.	.	2
3. Usurers	.	.	.	.	.	.	.	.	.	.	.	.	.	.	.	.	.	.	.	.	1	8	2	3	.	.	.	.	.	.	.	.	.	.	.	.	3
4. Rich merchants	.	.	.	.	.	.	.	.	.	.	.	.	.	.	.	.	.	.	.	.	1	8	.	.	1	2	2	9	2	33	.	.	.	.	.	.	6
5. Small merchants	.	.	.	.	.	.	.	.	.	.	.	.	.	.	.	.	.	.	.	.	.	.	.	.	.	.	.	.	1	17	.	.	.	.	.	.	1
6. No information other than indication of wealth	.	.	.	.	.	.	.	.	.	.	.	.	.	.	.	.	5	50	4	40	6	46	26	38	14	30	11	50	.	.	.	.	.	.	.	.	66
7. Teachers (a) *Shu-yüan*	.	.	.	.	.	.	.	.	.	.	.	.	.	.	.	.	3	30	.	.	.	.	16	23	10	21	.	.	2	33	.	.	.	.	.	.	31
(b) Private	.	.	.	.	.	.	.	.	.	.	.	.	.	.	.	.	1	10	2	20	4	30	6	9	11	24	3	14	.	.	.	.	.	.	.	.	27
8. Medical doctors and professors of geomancy, and personal assistants	.	.	.	.	.	.	.	.	.	.	.	.	.	.	.	.	.	.	.	.	.	.	5	7	4	8	6	27	1	17	.	.	.	.	.	.	16
9. No information other than indication of poverty	.	.	.	.	.	.	.	.	.	.	.	.	.	.	.	.	1	10	2	20	.	.	1	2	2	4	.	.	.	.	.	.	.	.	.	.	6
Subtotals	.	.	.	.	.	.	.	.	.	.	.	.	.	.	.	.	10	100	10	100	13	100	68	100	47	100	22	100	6	100	.	.	.	.	.	.	.
10. Unknown	.	.	.	.	.	.	.	.	.	.	.	.	.	.	.	.	1	.	1	.	1	.	21	.	23	.	10	.	13	.	.	.	.	.	.	.	70
Totals	.	.	.	.	.	.	.	.	.	.	.	.	.	.	.	.	11	.	11	.	14	.	89	.	70	.	32	.	19	.	.	.	.	.	.	.	246

Reign Periods of the Ch'ing Dynasty

Shun-chih	1644–1661
K'ang-hsi	1662–1722
Yung-cheng	1723–1735
Ch'ien-lung	1736–1795
Chia-ch'ing	1796–1820
Tao-kuang	1821–1850
Hsien-feng	1851–1861
T'ung-chih	1862–1874
Kuang-hsü	1875–1908
Hsüan-t'ung	1909–1911

Bibliography

(The Wade-Giles system has been employed in transcribing Chinese words, with the exception of names of provinces and a few well-known places.)

CHINESE SOURCES

Official Publications

Chekiang chung-i-lu 浙江忠義錄, compiled by Chekiang ts'ai-fang chung-i tsung-chü, 1875.

Ch'in-ting hsüeh-cheng ch'üan-shu 欽定學政全書, compiled by Kung-a-lu 恭阿祿, 1812.

Ch'in-ting hu-pu tse-li 欽定戶部則例, Ho-shen 和珅, and others, 1791.

Ch'in-ting k'o-ch'ang t'iao-li 欽定科場條例, Tu Shou-t'ien 杜受田, 1887.

Ch'in-ting ta-Ch'ing hui-tien 欽定大淸會典, K'un-kang 崑岡, and others, Shanghai, Commercial Press, 1908.

Ch'in-ting ta-Ch'ing hui-tien shih-li 欽定大淸會典事例, Li Hung-chang 李鴻章, and others, Commercial Press, 1908.

Ch'ing-ch'ao hsü wen-hsien t'ung-k'ao 淸朝續文獻通考, also known as *Huang-ch'ao hsü wen-hsien t'ung-k'ao* 皇朝續文獻通考, compiled by Liu Chin-tsao 劉錦藻, Commercial Press, 1936.

Ch'ing-ch'ao t'ung-chih 淸朝通志, Ch'ing Kao-tsung 淸高宗, Commercial Press, 1935.

Ch'ing-ch'ao wen-hsien t'ung-k'ao 淸朝文獻通考, also known as *Huang-ch'ao wen-hsien t'ung-k'ao* 皇朝文獻通考, Ch'ing Kao-tsung 淸高宗, Commercial Press, 1936.

Ch'ing-shih kao 淸史稿, Chao Erh-sun 趙爾巽, and others, Mukden, 1937.

Ch'ing-shih-lu 淸實錄, or *Ta-Ch'ing li-ch'ao shih-lu* 大淸曆朝實錄, compiled by Man-chou ti-kuo kuo-wu-yüan 滿洲帝國國務院, Tokyo, Okura shuppan kabushiki kaisha, 1937.

Ch'ing Shih-tsung Hsien-huang-ti sheng-hsün 淸世宗憲皇帝聖訓, Ch'ing Kao-tsung, prefaced 1740.

Hsü-wen-hsien t'ung-k'ao 續文獻通考, Ch'ing Kao-tsung, Commercial Press, 1936.

Hsüeh-cheng. See *Ch'in-ting hsüeh-cheng ch'üan-shu.*

K'o-ch'ang. See *Ch'in-ting k'o-ch'ang t'iao-li.*

Shan-sheng ko-fu-chou chüan-chien liang-shu t'iao-li 陝省各府州捐監糧數條例, n. p., n. d.

Shih-i-ch'ao tung-hua-lu 十一朝東華錄, compiled by Wang Hsien-ch'ien 王先謙, 1899.

Shih-li. See *Ch'in-ting ta-Ch'ing hui-tien shih-li.*

Shih-lu. See *Ch'ing-shih-lu.*

Ta-Ch'ing lü-li hui-chi pien-lan 大清律例彙輯便覽, compiled and published by the Board of Punishment, 1876.

Ta-Ch'ing t'ung-li 大清通禮, Heng-t'ai 恒泰, and others, 1824.

Tsou-ting hsüeh-t'ang chang-ch'eng 奏定學堂章程, Chang Po-hsi 張伯熙, Yung-ch'ing 榮慶, and Chang Chih-tung 張之洞, 1903.

Tung-hua hsü-lu 東華續錄, Chu Shou-p'eng 朱壽朋, Shanghai, Tu-shu chi-ch'eng, 1909.

CONTEMPORARY WRITINGS

Chang Chih-tung 張之洞, *Chang Wen-hsiang-kung ssu-kao* 張文襄公四稿, preface by Hsü T'ung-hsin 許同莘, 1920.

Chang Fei 張芾, *Chang Wen-i-kung tsou-kao* 張文毅公奏稿, T'ung-chih period.

Chang Shou-yung 張壽鏞, *Huang-ch'ao chang-ku hui-pien* 皇朝掌固彙編, Nei-pien 內編, Chiu-shih shu-she 求實書社, 1902.

Ch'en Ch'ing-yung 陳慶鏞, *Chou-ching-t'ang chi* 籀經堂集, 1874.

Ch'en K'ang-ch'i 陳康祺, *Lang-ch'ien chi-wen* 郎潛紀聞, n. p., 1884.

Ch'en K'ang-ch'i, *Lang-ch'ien erh-pi* 郎潛二筆, n. p., 1884.

Ch'ien Ting-ming 錢鼎銘, *Ch'ien Ming-su-kung tsou-su* 錢敏肅公奏疏, 1878.

Feng Kuei-fen 馮桂芬, *Chiao-pin-lu k'ang-i* 校邠廬抗議, 1898.

Feng Kuei-fen, *Hsien-chih t'ang kao* 顯志堂稿, 1877.

Hsüeh Fu-ch'eng 薛福成, *Yung-an ch'üan-chi* 庸庵全集, 1901.

Hsüeh Fu-ch'eng, "Yung-an pi-chi" 庸庵筆記, *Ch'ing-tai pi-chi ts'ung k'an* 清代筆記叢刊, Shanghai, Wen-min shu-chü 文明書局, n. d.

Hu Lin-i 胡林翼, *Hu Wen-chung-kung ch'üan-chi* 胡文忠公全集, World Book Co., 1936.

Huan-hai chih-nan wu-chung 宦海指南五種, compiled by Hsü Nai-p'u 許乃普, 1859.

Huang Liu-hung 黃六鴻, *Fu-hui ch'üan-shu* 福惠全書, 1893.

Huang-ch'ao ching-shih-wen-pien 皇朝經世文編, compiled by Ho Ch'ang-ling 賀長齡, 1826.

Huang-ch'ao ching-shih-wen-hsü-pien 皇朝經世文續編, compiled by Ke Shih-chün 葛士濬, 1888.

Huang-ch'ao ching-shih-wen-hsü-pien 皇朝經世文續編, compiled by Sheng K'ang 盛康, 1897.

Ju-mu hsü-chih wu-chung 入幕須知五種, compiled by Chang Han-po 張翰伯, 1887.

Ku Yen-wu 顧炎武, *Jih-chih-lu* 日知錄, 1795.

Ku Yen-wu, "T'ing-ling wen-chi" 亭林文集, *T'ing-ling i-shu shih-chung* 亭林遺書十種, published by P'eng-ying-ko 蓬瀛閣, n. d.

Kuo Sung-tao 郭嵩燾, *Kuo-shih-lang tsou-su* 郭侍郎奏疏, in *Yang-chih shu-wu ch'üan-chi* 養知書屋全集, 1892.

Li Huan 李桓, *Pao-wei-chai lei-kao* 寶韋齋類稿, 1880.

Li Hung-chang 李鴻章, *Li Wen-chung-kung ch'üan-chi* 李文忠公全集, compiled by Wu Ju-lün 吳汝綸, Nanking, 1908.

Li Pao-chia 李寶嘉, also known as Nan-t'ing t'ing-chang 南亭亭長, *Kuan-ch'ang hsien-hsing-chi* 官場現形記, Shanghai, World Book Co., 1936.

Liang Ch'i-ch'ao 梁啟超, *Ying-ping-shih ho-chi* 飲冰室合集, Shanghai, Chung-hua Book Co., 1926.

Liu Kuang-fen 劉光蕡, *Yen-hsia ts'ao t'ang i-shu hsü-k'o* 煙霞草堂遺書續刻, 1923–1925.

Lung Ch'i-jui 龍啟瑞, *Ching-te-t'ang chi* 經德堂集, 1878.

Mu-ling-shu 牧令書, compiled by Hsü Chih-ch'u 徐致初, 1848.

Pai Ching-wei 柏景偉, *Feng-hsi ts'ao-t'ang-chi* 灃西草堂集, Nanking, 1924.

Shantung chün-hsing chi-lüeh 山東軍興紀略, n. p., n. d.

Shen Chao-lin 沈兆霖. *Shen Wen-chung-kung chi* 沈文忠公集, 1869.

Sun Ting-ch'en 孫鼎臣, *Ts'ang-lang ch'u-chi* 蒼莨初集, 1859.

Teng Ch'eng-hsiu 鄧承修, *Yü-ping-ko tsou-i* 語冰閣奏議, 1918.

Ting Jih-ch'ang 丁日昌, *Fu-wu kung-tu* 撫吳公牘, 1877.

Tseng Kuo-fan 曾國藩, *Tseng Wen-cheng-kung ch'üan-chi* 曾文正公全集, 1876.

Tso Tsung-t'ang 左宗棠, *Tso Wen-hsiang-kung ch'üan-chi* 左文襄公全集, 1888—1897.

T'ung-chih chung-hsing ching-wai tsou-i yüeh-pien 同治中興京外奏議約編, compiled by Ch'en T'ao 陳弢, 1874.

Wang Ch'ing-yün 王慶雲, *Hsi-ch'ao chi-cheng* 熙朝紀政, also known as *Shih-ch'ü yü-chi* 石渠餘記, n. p., 1898.

Wang Hsien-ch'ien 王先謙, *Hsü-shou-t'ang wen-chi* 虛受堂文集, 1900.

Wang Shih-to 汪士鐸, *Wang Hui-weng i-ping jih-chi* 汪悔翁乙丙日記, compiled by Teng Chih-ch'eng 鄧之誠, Peiping, 1936.

Wang Shih-to, *Wang Mei-ts'un hsien-sheng chi* 汪梅村先生集, 1881.

Wang Sung-ju 王嵩儒, *Chang-ku ling-shih* 掌固零拾, 1936.

Wu Ching-tzu 吳敬梓, *Ju-lin wai-shih* 儒林外史, Shanghai, Ya-tung tu-shu-kuan 亞東圖書館, 1931.

Wu Yung-kuang 吳榮光, *Wu-hsüeh-lu ch'u-pien* 吾學錄初編, 1870.

Yüan Shih-k'ai 袁世凱, *Yang-shou-yüan tsou-i chi-yao* 養壽園奏議輯要, 1937.

Gentry Biographies and Records

Chia-shan ju-p'an t'i-ming-lu 嘉善入泮題名錄, compiled by Ch'ien Shao-cheng 錢紹楨, 1918.

Chia-wu chih-sheng t'ung-nien ch'üan-lu 甲午直省同年全錄, 1834.

Hsi-Chin yu-hsiang t'ung-jen tzu-shu hui-k'an 錫金游庠同人自述彙刊, Ting Fu-pao 丁福保, and others, 1931.

Hsin-hai chih-sheng t'ung-nien ch'üan-lu 辛亥直省同年全錄, 1851.

Hsin-mao-k'o hsiang-shih shih-pa-sheng t'ung-nien ch'üan-lu 辛卯科鄉試十八省同年全錄, 1891.

Hui-shih t'ung-nien ch'ih-lu 會試同年齒錄, for the years 1835, 1868, 1894, and 1895.

Kuo-ch'ao san-i (Soochow fu Ch'ang Yüan Wu san-i) chu-sheng-p'u 國朝三邑(蘇州府長元吳三邑)諸生譜, Ch'ien Kuo-hsiang 錢國祥, and others, 1904.

Kwangtung kuei-yu-k'o pa-kung yu-kung ch'ih-lu 廣東癸酉科拔貢優貢齒錄, Canton, 1873.

Nan-t'ung Chang Chi-chih hsien-sheng chuan-chi 南通張季直先生傳記, Chang Hsiao-jo 張孝若, 1930.

Ta-Ch'ing chin-shen ch'üan-shu 大清搢紳全書, for the year 1881, Peking.

Tseng-chiao Ch'ing-ch'ao chin-shih t'i-ming pei-lu 增校清朝進士題名碑錄, Harvard-Yenching Institute, Sinological Index Series, supplement no. 19, ed. by Fang Chao-ying and Tu Lien-che, June 1941.

LOCAL GAZETTEERS

Anhwei t'ung-chih 安徽通志, Wu K'un-hsiu 吳坤修, 1877.

Chang-chou fu-chih 漳州府志, Wu Lien-hsün 吳聯薰, 1887.

Ch'ang-hsing hsien-chih 長興縣志, Chao Ting-pang 趙定邦, 1875.

Ch'ang-ning hsien-chih 長寧縣志, Chin Fu-pao 金福保, 1899.

Ch'ang-p'ing chou-chih 昌平州志, Miao Ch'üan-sun 繆荃孫, 1878.

Chen-an fu-chih 鎮安府志, Yang Fu-li 羊復禮, 1892.

Ch'eng-hsien chih 嵊縣志, Yen Shih-chung 嚴世忠, 1870.

Chi-an ho-hsi fang-kuo hsiang-chih 吉安河西坊廓鄉志, Hsiao Keng-shao 蕭賡韶, 1937.

Chi-fu t'ung-chih 畿輔通志, Huang P'eng-nien 黄彭年, Commercial Press, 1885.

Chi-nan fu-chih 濟南府志, Wang Tseng-fang 王贈芳, 1839.

Chia-hsing fu-chih 嘉興府志, Hsü Yao-kuang 許瑤光, 1878.

Hsü-tsuan Chiang-ning fu-chih 續纂江甯府志, Wang Shih-to 汪士鐸, 1880.

Chien-ch'ang hsien hsiang-tu-chih 建昌縣鄉土志, T'an Hung-chi 譚鴻基, 1907.

Ching-chou hsiang-t'u-chih 靖州鄉土志, Chin Jung-ching 金蓉鏡, 1908.

Ch'ing-yüan hsien-chih 清苑縣志, Yao Shou-ch'ang 姚壽昌, 1934.

Chiu-chiang fu-chih 九江府志, Ta-ch'un-pu 達春布, 1874.

Chiu-chiang ju-lin-hsiang chih 九江儒林鄉志, Chu Tz'u-ch'i 朱次琦, 1883.

Cho-hsien chih 涿縣志, Chou Ts'un-p'ei 周存培, 1936.

Ch'u-chou chih 滁州志, Hsiung Tsu-i 熊祖詒, 1897.

Ch'u-chou fu-chih 處州府志, Chou Yung-ch'un 周榮椿, 1877.

Ch'üan-chou fu-chih 泉州府志, Huai-yin-pu 懷蔭布, 1927.

Ch'üeh-shan hsien-chih 確山縣志, Li Ching-t'ang 李景堂, 1931.

Feng-hua hsien-chih 奉化縣志, Li Ch'ien-p'an 李前泮, 1908.

Fu-shan chung-i-hsiang chih 佛山忠義鄉志, Hsien Pao-kan 洗寶榦, 1923.

Fukien t'ung-chih 福建通志, Ch'en Yen 陳衍, 1922.

Hangchow fu-chih 杭州府志, Wu Ch'ing-ti 吳慶坻, 1923.

Heng-chou fu-chih 衡州府志, Jao Ch'üan 饒佺, 1875.

Ho-hsien chih 賀縣志, Wei Kuan-ying 韋冠英, 1934.

Hsiang-fu hsien-chih 祥符縣志, Huang Shu-ping 黃舒昺, 1898.

Hsiang-shan hsien-chih 香山縣志, T'ien Ming-yao 田明耀, 1879.

Hsiang-shan hsien-chih hsü-pien 香山縣志續編, Li Shih-chin 厲式金, 1911.

Hsin-i hsien-chih 信宜縣志, Liang An-tien 梁安甸, 1889.

Hsin-ning hsien-chih 新甯縣志, Liu Ch'ang-yu 劉長佑, 1893.

Hsing-kuo chou-chih 興國州志, Ch'en Kuang-heng 陳光亨, 1889.

Hsü-chou fu-chih 叙州府志 (Szechwan), Wang Lin-hsiang 王麟祥, 1895.

Hsü-chou fu-chih 徐州府志 (Kiangsu), Wu Shih-yung 吳世榮, 1874.

Hsün-chou fu-chih 潯州府志, Hsia Chin-i 夏敬頤, 1896.

Hu-chou fu-chih 湖州府志, Tsung Yüan-han 宗源翰, 1874.

Huai-an fu-chih 淮安府志, Wu K'un-t'ien 吳昆田, 1884.

Hui-chou fu-chih 惠州府志, Teng Lun-pin 鄧掄斌, 1881.

Hunan t'ung-chih 湖南通志, Pien Pao-ti 卞寶第, 1887.

Hupeh t'ung-chih 湖北通志, Yang Ch'eng-hsi 楊承禧, 1934.

Jen-huai t'ing-chih 仁懷廳志, Chang Cheng-k'uei 張正炷, 1896.

Jung-hsien chih 容縣志, Feng Chu-t'ang 封祝唐, 1908.

Kan-shuai hsin-chih 澉水新志, Fang Yung 方溶, 1935.

Kansu hsin t'ung-chih 甘肅新通志, An Wei-chün 安維峻, 1909.

Kao-chou fu-chih 高州府志, Yang Chi 楊霽, 1889.

Kiangsi t'ung-chih 江西通志, Liu K'un-i 劉坤一, 1881.

Kuang-chou fu-chih 廣州府志, Tai Chao-ch'en 戴肇辰, 1879.

Kuei-chou chih 歸州志, Huang Shih-ch'ung 黃世崇, 1901.

K'uei-chou fu-chih 夔州府志, Liu Te-ch'üan 劉德銓, 1891.

Kwangsi t'ung-chih chi-yao 廣西通志輯要, Yang Fu-li 羊復禮, 1889.

Kweichow t'ung-chih kao 貴州通志稿, Huang Chia-k'un 黃家琨, 1909–1911.

Lan-ch'i hsien-chih 蘭谿縣志, Ch'en Wen-lu 陳文騄, 1887.

Li-p'ing fu-chih 黎平府志, Yü Wei 俞渭, 1892.

Lien-chou chih 連州志, Yüan Yung-hsi 袁泳錫, 1870.

Lin-chang hsien-chih 臨漳縣志, Chou Ping-i 周秉彝, 1904.

Liu-yang hsien-chih 瀏陽縣志, Lo Ch'ing-hsiang 羅慶薌, 1873.

Lo-ch'uan hsien-chih 洛川縣志, Liu Yü-hsiu 劉毓秀, 1944.

Chih-li Lu-chou chih 直隸瀘州志, T'ien Hsiu-li 田秀栗, 1882.

Hsü-hsiu Lu-chou fu-chih 續修廬州府志, Huang Yün 黃雲, 1885.

Luan-chou chih 灤州志, Yang Wen-ting 楊文鼎, 1896.

Kuang-hsü Lu-i hsien-chih 光緒鹿邑縣志, Yü-ch'ing 餘慶, 1896.

Lu-lung hsien-chih 盧龍縣志, Tung T'ien-hua 董天華, 1931.

Lung-an fu-chih 龍安府志, Teng Ts'un-yung 鄧存詠, 1858.

Hsü-hsiu Mei-t'an hsien-chih 續修湄潭縣志, Wu Tsung-chou 吳宗周, 1899.

Ch'ung-hsiu Meng-ch'eng hsien-chih shu 重修蒙城縣志書, Wang Ch'ih 汪篪, 1915.

Chih-li Mien-chou chih 直隸緜州志, Wen ch'i 文棨, 1871.

Mien-yang chou-chih 沔陽州志, Ke Cheng-yüan 葛振元, 1894.

Ming-hou hsien-chih 閩侯縣志, Ou-yang Ying 歐陽英, 1933.

Nan-ch'ang hsien-chih 南昌縣志, Wei Yüan-k'uang 魏元曠, 1919.

Nan-hai hsien-chih 南海縣志, Ho Ping-k'un 何炳堃, 1910.

Nan-ning fu-chih 南甯府志, Chi K'an-chin 紀堪謹, 1909.

Hsin-hsiu Nan-yang hsien-chih 新修南陽縣志, P'an Shou-lien 潘守濂, 1904.

Pa-ling hsien-chih 巴陵縣志, Yao Shih-te 姚詩德, 1891.

P'an-yü hsien hsü-chih 番禺縣續志, Wang Chao-yung 汪兆鏞, 1931.

Pao-ting fu-chih 保定府志, Li P'ei-hu 李培祜, 1881.

P'ing-nan hsien-chih 平南縣志, Chou Shou-ch'i 周壽祺, 1883.

P'ing-yüan chou hsü-chih 平遠州續志, Shao Chi-ch'eng 邵積誠, 1890.

Po-pai hsien-chih 博白縣志, Ch'ien Fu-ch'ang 錢福昌, 1832.

Po-pai hsien-chih-yü pei-lan 博白縣志餘備覽, Ch'ien Fu-ch'ang 錢福昌, 1832.

P'u-an chih-li-t'ing chih 普安直隸廳志, Ts'ao Ch'ang-ch'i 曹昌祺, 1889.

Shang-yü hsien-chih 上虞縣志, T'ang Hsü-ch'un 唐煦春, 1891.

Shanghai hsien-chih 上海縣志, Yü Yüeh 俞樾, 1872.

Shansi t'ung-chih 山西通志, Tseng Kuo-ch'üan 曾國荃, 1892.

Shantung t'ung-chih 山東通志, Yang Shih-hsiang 楊士驤, Commercial Press, 1934.

Shensi t'ung-chih kao 陝西通志稿, Sung Po-lu 宋伯魯, 1934.

Shun-t'ien fu-chih 順天府志, Chou Chia-mei 周家楣, 1884.

Shuo-fang tao-chih 朔方道志, Wang Chih-ch'en 王之臣, 1926.

Soochow fu-chih 蘇州府志, Feng Kuei-fen 馮桂芬, 1877.

Hsü-hsiu Sui-chou chih 續修睢州志, Yü-ch'ing 餘慶, 1892.

Sung-chiang-fu hsu-chih 松江府續志, Yao Kuang-fa 姚光發, 1884.

T'ai-ho hsien-chih 泰和縣志, Sung Ying 宋瑛, 1878.

Tao-chou chih 道州志, Li Ching-jung 李鏡蓉, 1877.

T'eng-hsien chih 藤縣志, Ch'en Chung-pin 陳仲賓, 1908.

Tientsin fu-chih 天津府志, Shen Chia-pen 沈家本, 1899.

Chih-li Ting-chou chih 直隸定州志, Pao-lin 寶琳, 1850.

Chih-li Ting-chou hsü-chih 直隸定州續志, Wang Jung-chi 王榕吉, 1860.

Tung-kuan hsien-chih 東莞縣志, Ch'en Po-t'ao 陳伯陶, 1911.

T'ung-chou chih 通州志, Kao Chien-hsün 高建勳, 1879.

T'ung-chou chih-li-chou chih 通州直隸州志, Liang Yüeh-hsin 梁悅馨, 1875.

T'ung-ch'uan fu-chih 潼川府志, Wang Lung-hsün 王龍勳, 1899.

T'ung-jen fu-chih 銅仁府志, Yü-hsün 喻勳, 1890.

Wu-hsi Chin-kuei hsien-chih 無錫金匱縣志, P'ei Ta-chung 裴大中, 1881.

Hsü-tsuan Yangchow fu-chih 續纂揚州府志, Yen Tuan-shu 晏端書, 1874.

Yen-chou fu-chih 嚴州府志, Wu Shih-yung 吳世榮, 1882.

Yen-yüan hsiang-chih 剡源鄉志, Chao P'ei-t'ao 趙霈濤, 1916.

Yin-hsien chih 鄞縣志, Tai Mei 戴枚, 1877.

Yü-lin chou-chih 鬱林州志, Feng Te-ts'ai 馮德材, 1894.

Yü-yao hsien-chih 餘姚縣志, Chou Ping-ling 周炳麟, 1899.

Yung-chou fu-chih 永州府志, Lü En-chan 呂恩湛, 1867.

Yung-ning chou hsü-chih 永甯州續志, Shen Yü-lan 沈毓蘭, 1894.

Yung-p'ing fu-chih 永平府志, Yu Chih-k'ai 游智開, 1876.

Yunnan t'ung-chih 雲南通志, Wang Wen-shao 王文韶, 1894.

SECONDARY SOURCES

Chang Chung-ju 章中如, *Ch'ing-tai k'ao-shih chih-tu* 清代考試制度, Shanghai, 1932.

Chang Chung-ju, *Ch'ing-tai k'o-chü chih-tu* 清代科舉制度, Shanghai, 1932.

Ch'en Ch'ing-chih 陳青之, *Chung-hua chiao-yü shih* 中華教育史, Commercial Press, 1936.

Ch'en Tung-yüan 陳東原, *Chung-kuo chiao-yü shih* 中國教育史, Commercial Press, 1937.

Chien Yu-wen 簡又文, *T'ai-p'ing chün Kwangsi shou-i shih* 太平軍廣西首義史, Commercial Press, 1946.

Ch'ing-kuo hsin-cheng-fa fen-lun 清國行政法分論, compiled by Taiwan tsung-tu-fu, Tokyo, Toyo insatsu kabushiki kaisha, 1915—1918.

Ch'ü T'ung-tsu 瞿同祖, *Chung-kuo fa-lü yü chung-kuo she-hui* 中國法律與中國社會, Commercial Press, 1947.

Fu Tseng-hsiang 傅增湘, *Ch'ing-tai tien-shih k'ao-lüeh* 清代殿試考略, Ta-kung-pao-shuai, Tientsin, 1933.

Hsü Ta-ling 許大齡, *Ch'ing-tai chüan-na chih-tu* 清代捐納制度, Peking, 1950.

Jen Shih-hsien 任時先, *Chung-kuo chiao-yü ssu-hsiang-shih* 中國教育思想史, Commercial Press, 1937.

Lo Erh-kang 羅爾綱, *Chung-wang Li Hsiu-ch'eng tzu-chuan yüan-kao ch'ien-cheng* 忠王李秀成自傳原稿箋證, Peking, 1951.

Lo Yü-tung 羅玉東, *Chung-kuo likin shih* 中國釐金史, Commercial Press, 1936.

Yang Yün-ju 楊筠如, *Chiu-p'in chung-cheng yü liu-ch'ao men-fa* 九品中正與六朝門閥, Commercial Press, 1930.

ARTICLES AND PERIODICALS

Chu Hsieh 朱偰, "The Chinese Examination System," *Tung-fang tsa-chih* 東方雜誌, *chüan* 24, No. 20, October 25, 1927.

Chu Shih-chia 朱士嘉, "Lin-an san-chih k'ao" 臨安三志考, *Yenching Journal,* No. 20, December 1936.

Chung-ho yüeh-k'an 中和月刊, Peking, 1940.

Hsia Nan 夏鼐, "Land Tax Problems in Yangtse Provinces Before and After the Taiping Period," *Ch'ing-hua hsüeh-pao* 清華學報, *chüan* 10, No. 2, April 1935.

Huang Yen-p'ei 黄炎培, "Ch'ing-tai ko-sheng jen-wen t'ung-chi chih i-pan" 清代各省人文統計之一斑, *Jen-wen yüeh-k'an* 人文月刊, *chüan* 2, No. 6, August 15, 1931.

I-ching 逸經, Shanghai, 1936.

Kuo-wen chou-pao 國聞周報, Shanghai, 1929.

Shen Shou-chih 沈守之, "Chieh-ch'ao pi-chi" 借巢筆記, *Jen-wen yüeh-k'an, chüan* 7, No. 3, April 15, 1936.

T'ang Hsiang-lung 湯象龍, "A Statistical Study of the Chüan-chien System in the Tao-kuang Period," *She-hui k'o-hsüeh tsa-chih* 社會科學雜誌, II, No. 4, Peking, December 1931.

Teng Ssu-yü 鄧嗣禹, "A Study into the Origin of the Chinese Examination System," *Shih-hsüeh nien-pao* 史學年報, *chüan* 2, No. 1, Peiping, September 1934.

Wang Shih-ta 王士達, "Estimates on Recent Chinese Population," *She-hui k'o-hsüeh tsa-chih,* I, No. 3, Peking, 1930.

Wen-hsien ts'ung-pien 文獻叢編, Palace Museum, Peking, 1934.

REFERENCE AND OTHER WORKS

A Catalogue of Chinese Local Histories in the Library of Congress, Chu Shih-chia 朱士嘉, Washington, 1942.

Ch'ing-shih Lieh-chuan 清史列傳, Ch'ing-shih-kuan compiled, Shanghai, 1928.

Chiu-T'ang-shu 舊唐書, Liu Hsü 劉昫, and others, Commercial Press, 1937.

Hsin-T'ang-shu 新唐書, Ou-yang Hsiu 歐陽修, and others, Commercial Press, 1937.

Hsü-pei-chuan-chi 續碑傳集, Miao Ch'üan-sun 繆荃孫, Chiang-ch'u pien-i shu-chü, 1910.

Li-tai ming-jen nien-li pei-chuan tsung-piao 歷代名人年里碑傳總表, Chiang Liang-fu 姜亮夫, Commercial Press, 1937.

Pei-chuan-chi 碑傳集, Ch'ien I-chi 錢儀吉, Chiang-su shu-chü, 1893.

Sung-shih 宋史, T'o-t'o 脫脫, and others, Commercial Press, 1936.

T'ai-p'ing t'ien-kuo shih-liao 太平天國史料, compiled by T'ien Yü-ch'ing 田餘慶, and others, Peking, 1950.

T'ung-tien 通典, Tu Yu 杜佑, Commercial Press, 1935.

Wen-hsien t'ung-k'ao 文獻通考, Ma Tuan-lin 馬端臨, Commercial Press, 1936.

BOOKS AND ARTICLES IN WESTERN LANGUAGES

Books

Bard, Emile, *Chinese Life in Town and Country,* adapted by H. Twitchell, New York, 1905.

Chen Ta, *Population in Modern China,* Chicago, 1946.

Cordier, Henri, *Dictionnaire Bibliographique des Ouvrages Relatifs à l'Empire Chinois,* Bibliotheca Sinica, Paris, 1906.

Douglas, Robert K., *Society in China,* London, 1894.

Holcombe, Chester, *The Real Chinaman,* New York, 1895.

Holcombe, Chester, *The Real Chinese Question,* New York, 1900.

Hsieh Pao-chao, *The Government of China (1644—1911),* John Hopkins, Baltimore, 1925.

Hu Hsien-chin, *The Common Descent Group in China and Its Functions,* New York, 1948.

Hummel, Arthur W., *Eminent Chinese of the Ch'ing Period,* Library of Congress, 1944.

Latourette, K. S., *The Chinese, Their History and Culture,* New York, 1934.

Legge, James, *The Chinese Classics,* 1893.

Li Chow Chung-cheng, *L'Examen Provincial en Chine (Hsiang Che) sous la Dynastie des Ts'ing (de 1644 à 1911),* thèse pour le doctorat, Paris, 1935.

Lin Yu-tang, *My Country and My People,* New York, 1939.

Martin, William A. P., *The Chinese; Their Education, Philosophy and Letters,* New York, 1893.

Mayers, William Frederick, *The Chinese Government* (3rd ed.), Shanghai, 1896.

Soothill, William Edward, *The Analects of Confucius,* 1910.

Voltaire, *The Age of Louis XIV,* tr. by R. Griffith, Fielding and Walker, London, 1779—1781.

Weber, Max, *The Religion of China,* tr. by H. H. Gerth, Glencoe, Ill., 1951.

Williams, S. W., *The Middle Kingdom,* New York, 1883.

Wittfogel, Karl A., and Feng Chia-sheng, *History of Chinese Society—Liao (907—1125),* Philadelphia, 1949.

Wylie, Alexander, *Chinese Researches,* Shanghai, 1897.

Yu Yuan Chang, *Civil Service Examination System in China, 1644—1905,* doctoral thesis, Columbia University, 1934.

Articles and Periodicals

Bridgman, E. C., "The Emperor Taokwang: his succession to the throne of his father, coronation, with notices of his character and government," *Chinese Repository,* Vol. X, No. 2, Canton, February 1841, pp. 87—98.

Bullock, T. L., "Competitive Examinations in China," *Nineteenth Century,* ed. by James Knowles, Vol. 36, London, July 1894.

The Chinese Repository, Vol. I, No. 11, Canton, March 1833, *et passim.*

"Competitive Examinations in China," *Blackwood's Edinburgh Magazine,* October 1885.

Ewer, F. H., "The Triennial Examinations," *The Chinese Recorder,* Vol. III, No. 11, Foochow, April 1871.

Martin, William A. P., "On the Competitive Examination System in China," *American Oriental Society Journal,* Proceedings at Boston, May 1869.

North China Herald, No. 140, Shanghai, April 2, 1853, *et passim.*

Oxenham, E. L., "Ages of Candidates at Chinese Examinations," *Journal of the China Branch of the Royal Asiatic Society for the Year 1888,* new series, Vol. XXIII, Shanghai, 1889, pp. 286—287.

Rockhill, W. W., "An Inquiry into the Population of China," *Report of the Smithsonian Institution for 1904,* Washington, 1905.

Seifert, H. E., "Life Tables for Chinese Farmers," *Milbank Memorial Fund Quarterly,* Vol. XI, No. 4, New York, October 1933; Vol. XII, Nos. 1, 2, 3, January, April, July, 1934.

Teng Ssu-yü, "Chinese Influence on the Western Examination System," *Harvard Journal of Asiatic Studies,* Vol. VII, No. 4, September 1943.

Willcox, Walter F., "A Westerner's Effort to Estimate the Population of China and Its Increases Since 1650," *Journal of the American Statistical Association,* Vol. XXV, No. 171, September 1930, pp. 255—268.

Wittfogel, Karl A., "Public Office in the Liao Dynasty and the Chinese Examination System," *Harvard Journal of Asiatic Studies,* Vol. 10, No. 1, June 1947.

Yuan, J. C., "Life Table for a Southern Chinese Family from 1365 to 1849," *Human Biology,* Baltimore, May 1931.

Zi, Etienne, "Pratique des Examens Litteraires en Chine," *Varieties Sinologiques,* No. 5, Shanghai, 1894.

Zi, Etienne, "Pratique des Examens Militaires en Chine," *Varieties Sinologiques,* No. 9, Shanghai, 1896.

Index and Glossary

THE CHINESE GENTRY

STUDIES ON THEIR ROLE IN NINETEENTH-CENTURY CHINESE SOCIETY

By Chung-li Chang

Introduction by Franz Michael

"Professor Chang has inaugurated a great service to those concerned with the study of Chinese society. He has also made a considerable contribution to those interested in more general problems such as those concerning elite groups, bureaucracy, and so forth. His and similar contributions will make many analytical ventures possible that might otherwise never get beyond the speculative level. Far Eastern specialists will also bless the publishers for a bibliography and glossary that give the Chinese characters for the titles and terms used in the text."—*Annals of the American Academy of Political and Social Science*

"Although its main purpose is to demonstrate the power exercised by the educated class—here designated 'gentry'—on nineteenth-century Chinese society, the principal contribution of this book lies in its detailed analysis of the workings of the civil service examination system which determined who should enter the group. No other existing work in English sets forth with such particularity the merits and abuses of this system, nor is there another book that defines so clearly the terminology created by the Chinese to describe the system in all its aspects. To support his conclusions, the author has made wise use of many hitherto little-used Chinese documents."—*United Service Quarterly*

"Chang's study is an important contribution to the institutional history of recent China. Its conscientious research goes far to establish the China of yesterday as a root of modern pre-Communist and Communist China."—Karl A. Wittfogel in *American Historical Review*

"A fine piece of research, punctiliously documented and exhibiting an immense range of learning."—Arthur Waley in *Journal of the Royal Asiatic Society*

CHUNG-LI CHANG wrote this study and its companion volume, *The Income of the Chinese Gentry,* during his years as a member of the Modern Chinese History Project of the Far Eastern and Russian Institute and assistant professor of economics at the University of Washington.

First paperback edition, 1967

UNIVERSITY OF WASHINGTON PRESS
Seattle and London